Basic Principles of CIVIL LAW in China

中
CHINESE
STUDIES
▪ ON ▪
CHINA

THE CHINESE COMMUNIST PARTY'S NOMENKLATURA SYSTEM
Edited by John P. Burns

THE ASIATIC MODE OF PRODUCTION IN CHINA
Edited by Timothy Brook

BASIC PRINCIPLES OF CIVIL LAW IN CHINA
Edited by William C. Jones

Basic Principles of CIVIL LAW in China

Edited by WILLIAM C. JONES

Routledge
Taylor & Francis Group
LONDON AND NEW YORK

First published 1989 by M.E. Sharpe

Published 2015 by Routledge
2 Park Square, Milton Park, Abingdon, Oxon OX14 4RN
52 Vanderbilt Avenue, New York, NY 10017, USA

Routledge is an imprint of the Taylor & Francis Group, an informa business

Library of Congress Cataloging-in-Publication Data

Min fa yüan li. English. Selections.
Basic principles of civil law in China.

Selected translation of : Min fa yüan li.
1. Civil law—China. I. Jones, William C.
II. Title.
LAW 346.51 89-10667
345.106

ISBN 13: 9780873325745 (hbk)

CONTENTS

Editor's Introduction
William C. Jones xv

PART I: GENERAL DISCUSSION OF CIVIL LAW

1. Introduction 3

2. The General Concept of Civil Law of the People's Republic of China 14

I
The Objects of Adjustment of Our Country's Civil Law 14
II
The Differences Between Civil Law and Other Types of Law 17
III
The Basic Principles of the Civil Law of the People's Republic of China 19
IV
The Sources of Our Country's Civil Law 23
V
The Interpretation of Civil Law Norms 25
VI
The Scope and Application of Civil Law 27

3. Civil Law Relationships 31

I
General Discussion of Civil Law Relationships 31

II
Legal Facts 33
III
The Essential Elements of Civil Law Relations 34
IV
The Types of Civil Law Rights 36
V
Prohibition of the Abuse of Rights 38
VI
The Protection of Civil Law Rights 40
VII
Civil Responsibility 42

4. Citizens 50

I
The Legal Position of Citizens 50
II
The Capacity of Our Country's Citizens to Have Civil Law Rights [Rechtsfähigkeit] 52
III
The Capacity of Citizens to Act [Handlungsfähigkeit] 55
IV
Guardianship 57
V
Names, Household Registration, and Domicile 59

5. Juristic Persons 61

I
The General Nature and Characteristics of Juristic Persons 61
II
The Appearance, Development, and Use of the Institution of the Juristic Person 62
III
Types of Juristic Persons 66
IV
The Establishment of Juristic Persons and Their Conditions 67
V
The Juristic Person's Capacity to Hold Rights and Capacity to Act 71
VI
The Alteration or Dissolution of a Juristic Person 73

VII
The Name, Domicile, and Production Mark 75
VIII
State Supervision of Juristic Persons 76

6. Partnerships and Joint Ventures 79

I
The General Concept and Special Characteristics of Partnerships and Joint Ventures 79
II
The Formation of Partnerships and Joint Ventures 82
III
The Management and Control of the Property of Partnerships and Joint Ventures 83
IV
Alteration or Termination of a Partnership or Joint Venture 84

7. Property [*Sachen*] 86

I
*The General Concept of Property [Things—*Sachen*]* 86
II
Different Types of Property 86
III
Money and Negotiable Instruments 93
IV
Foreign Exchange 94

8. Juristic Acts 96

I
The General Concept of Juristic Acts 96
II
Types of Juristic Acts 97
III
Forms of Juristic Acts 100
IV
Conditions for the Effectiveness of Juristic Acts 102
V
Conditional Juristic Acts and Juristic Acts With a Time Limit 104

VI
Ineffective Civil Law Acts and Their Consequences 107

9. Representation 113

I
The General Concept of Representation 113
II
The Basis for the Creation of Representation and the Types of Representation 116
III
Certificate of Representation 118
IV
The End of a Representation Relationship 120
V
Representation Without Authority 122

10. Prescription 124

I
General Discussion of the System of Prescription 124
II
Procedural Prescription 127
III
Suspending, Cutting Off, or Prolonging Prescription 129

PART II: PROPERTY
[*Chapters 11–17 Omitted*]

PART III: OBLIGATIONS

18. The General Statements of Obligations 135

I
The Concept and Meaning of Obligations 135
II
Types of Obligations 141
III
The Bases for Obligations Coming into Existence 145

IV
Performance of Obligations 149
V
Nonperformance of an Obligation 154
VI
Changes in Obligations 161
VII
Termination of an Obligation 165
VIII
Guaranty of Obligations 168

19. Obligations Arising from Acts that Infringe on Rights [Delicts] 174

I
The Concept and Characteristics of Obligations Arising from Acts that Infringe on Rights 174
II
The Essential Conditions for Civil Responsibility for Acts in Infringement of Rights 177
III
Several Specific Types of Civil Responsibility for Acts in Infringement of Rights 182
IV
The Scope and Methods of Compensation for Injuries Caused by the Infringement of Rights 186

20. Unjust Enrichment and Management of Affairs Without Mandate [*Negotiorum Gestio*] 189

I
Obligations that Arise Out of Unjustified Enrichment 189
II
Obligations that Arise Out of Management of Affairs Without Mandate [Negotiorum Gestio] 192

21. Obligations Arising Out of Contract 196

I
The General Concept of Contract 196

II
The Evolution of the System of Contracts 197
III
The Nature and Function of Our Country's System of Contracts 200
IV
The Types of Contracts 203
V
The Forms of Contracts 208
VI
The Formation of Contracts 211
VII
Essential Provisions of Contracts 215

22. Contracts of Sale, Exchange, and Gift 218

I
The General Concept of the Contract of Sale 218
II
The Object and Price of the Contract of Sale 222
III
The Rights and Duties of Parties to a Contract of Sale 223
IV
Transfer of the Ownership (or Management Right) of the Object and Liability for Unintentional Loss 225
V
Contracts for the Purchase and Sale of Industrial and Mineral Products 226
VI
Contracts for the Purchase and Sale of Agricultural Sideline Products 233
VII
The Contract of Exchange 237
VIII
The Contract of Gift 238

23. Contract of Hire 240

I
An Introduction to the Contract of Hire 240
II
The Rights and Obligations of the Parties to a Contract of Hire 243

III
Capital Construction Contracts 246

24. The Contract of Lease 256

I
General Discussion of Contracts of Lease 256
II
Contracts of Lease for Ordinary Property 259
III
The Lease of Buildings 261

25. Loans for Consumption and Loans for Use 269

I
General Discussion of the Loan for Consumption 269
II
The Contract of Debt 272
III
The Legal Relation of Settling Accounts 278
IV
Other Loans for Consumption 281
V
Loans for Use 283

26. Transport Contracts 286

I
A Brief Introduction to Transport Contracts 286
II
The Major Rights and Obligations of the Parties to a Contract of Transportation Involving Goods 289
III
The Contract for the Transport of Goods by Rail 291
IV
Other Contracts for the Transport of Goods 293
V
[Contracts for] the Carriage of Passengers, Their Baggage, and Bundles 295
VI
The Coordinated Contract of Transport 297

27. Contracts of Deposit 299

I
Contracts of Deposit 299
II
The Most Important Rights and Duties of Parties to a Contract of Deposit 302

28. Partnership Contracts 306

I
General Discussion of Partnership Contracts 306
II
The Principal Rights and Duties of Parties to a Partnership Contract 309
III
The Formation and Termination of a Partnership Contract 311

29. Mandate, Commission Agency, and Brokerage Contracts 313

I
The Contract of Mandate 313
II
The Contract of Commission Agency 317
III
The Brokerage Contract 321

30. Technology Contracts 324

I
A General Discussion of Technology Contracts 324
II
Technology Development Contracts 327
III
Contracts for the Transfer of Technology 336
IV
Technology Service Contracts 341

31. The Contract of Insurance 345

I
A General Discussion of the Contract of Insurance 345

II
The Classification of Insurance and the Meaning of the Basic Terms of the Legal Relationship of Insurance 348
III
The Formation of Insurance Contracts, Principal Rights, and Duties of the Parties 352
IV
The Procedure for Demanding that the Insurer Perform His Obligations 354

32. Foreign Economic Contracts 355

I
Foreign Economic Contracts and Our Country's Foreign Economic Contract Law 355
II
Formation of Foreign Economic Contracts 358
III
Performance of the Contract and the Guaranty of the Performance of the Contract 363
IV
Liability for Breach of Contract 365
V
The Assignment, Amendment, Cancellation, and Termination of Foreign Economic Contracts 369
VI
The Settlement of Disputes 373
VII
The Question of the Applicable Law of the Contract 375

1 Editor's Introduction

William C. Jones

China's new civil law—the General Provisions of Civil Law, promulgated in 1986—has been the subject of an enormous amount of discussion. Books on civil law flood from the presses in what are, by non-Chinese standards, enormous runs (300,000 or more is common). Clearly something of importance is perceived to have happened. And yet the General Provisions is a rather strange and incomplete statute. In essence, it is the General Part of a German-style civil code for which all the other parts are missing.

The Chinese are perfectly aware of this. The chairman of the committee that is said to have drafted the General Provisions stated, when he presented it to the National People's Congress, that it would have to be supplemented by other statutes such as the Economic Contracts Law, and he implied that there would be gaps.

What it is really supplemented by is treatises such as the one translated here. To be sure, all civil codes, however complete, are supplemented by treatises. Whatever the theory may be, no one really tries to understand a new system of law like a civil code without a treatise. But of course a treatise in China plays a very special role. It has to provide very basic rules that are not provided in the code. For example, it differentiates between negligence and intentional fault in discussing delictual liability, and between movables and immovables in discussing property. It tells when the offer is regarded as being accepted, etc. Obviously all law students, including the judges who are being introduced to the formal study of law in short courses taken after they have been on the bench, are taught from a treatise such as this. This is the role of treatises in general and this one in particular. This is one of a series of texts in many areas of law that are designed to be the basic texts for use in Chinese law schools. At least during the academic year 1987–88 (and previously) it was used in most, if not all of them. It seems to be the most authoritative treatise on Chinese civil law that is available to the general public. It furnishes the basis of the legal formation of Chinese jurists and is the logical first place to look for answers to questions regarding Chinese law.

It is, in other words, an indispensable reference work on Chinese civil law. But it is considerably more than that. It is also a policy statement about the role of law in Chinese society issued with the evident approval of the highest levels of the Chinese government. This statement has two aspects: ideological and doctrinal.

The ideology is pervasive in a work which is also quite technical. It takes two forms: In the first place, there is evidently a very active opposition to what is perceived as bourgeois law. No doubt this is connected with the opposition to the current economic policies. Consequently, there is a good deal of space devoted to proving the ideological correctness of providing a system of civil law to deal with the commodity economy which is correct for the current stage of China's development. Almost every chapter has a ritual quotation from Marx and occasionally one from Lenin. Mao Zedong thought is passed over quietly.

But the ideological statements are not merely defensive. They are also offensive. The Chinese civil law of the General Provisions and this treatise is, in effect, German civil law. The conceptual heart of the very conceptual system that is German civil law is the juristic act and its basis, the declaration of intention. One of the foremost modern German jurists describes the essence of this system as being private autonomy. This is also, of course, the heart of classical economics: The individual intelligence making decisions as to economic activity—buying, selling, saving, manufacturing, etc.—all with the aim of maximizing his own interest. Or as one of its earlier apologists (Mandeville) described it—behaving selfishly and thus benefitting society.

While the *Basic Principles of Civil Law* has a reference to the primacy of socialist ownership of the means of production on almost every page, there is very clear support for the notion that China's industrialization will be achieved by permitting individuals to make contracts on their own and to organize collective entities—juristic persons or corporations—that will act independently and in accordance with the market. The function of civil law is to further and protect this development.

Whether this aim will be achieved is anyone's guess. That is, the success of China's economic plans is scarcely assured, nor is it certain that the current program will continue after the death of its author. What does seem clear is that unless the legal system that was established after the Third Plenum in 1978 is abolished (a possibility of course), China has now joined the world of western law, specifically the world of German law.

This has been clear enough from the structure of the various codes that have been enacted since 1979, beginning with the Criminal Code. But it is made very clear in the text translated here. The organization is that of the German Code (except that property law and obligation law are transposed). At the time the book was published, the General Provisions had not been promulgated, but in the analysis of every rule from conditions precedent to the computation of damages for loss of work it is assumed that there is Chinese "law," whatever it is and wherever it may be found, which recognizes and deals with these problems. There is also recognition of a worldwide community of law and legal ideas all of which are related and of which China is a member.

There are many references to the laws of specific countries, both communist and non-communist. It seems clear that Chinese legal scholars are quite willing to look outside Chinese legal sources for the answers to problems for which there are no Chinese answers. In theory, Germany would be the logical place to look, but it seems probable that the place they are most likely to look is Taiwan. The "Guomindang" codes are scarcely mentioned in the text, but they, and the treatises that interpret them, are widely available in Chinese libraries. They are, of course, solidly German in origin.

In other words, in dealing with Chinese jurists, it would seem to be completely acceptable to make arguments based not only on Chinese sources, including treatises and other secondary sources, but also on those of other countries which can be cited explicitly and regarded as making general statements of law. Taiwan sources can also be referred to though perhaps not explicitly. Instead, one could make an argument based in fact on a Taiwan source but stated as if it were some sort of basic principle of civil law. Of course everyone would know the real source. It seems unlikely that the civil law of the Soviet Union or its various republics will be used as anything except a ritual gesture to Marxist orthodoxy. Once one has "opened to the outside" in the field of law, Soviet legal scholarship will not loom large.

There is nothing peculiar to China in this practice. Anglo-American lawyers tend to think of "civil law" systems as systems of codified law as opposed to their own systems of case law. Of course, at present almost all legal systems derived from Roman law are codified. But this is a relatively recent development. Continental law was developed primarily by scholars. Treatises formed the basis of the codes: Domat and Pothier in France, Windscheid and Dernberg in Germany for example. Even now, after codification, continental lawyers expect to use codes as, in effect, sources of law (not in theory to be sure). While cases are very important in European law at present, the treatise is still the place where most jurists would begin to investigate a problem. In other words, the treatise is required not only by the peculiarly incomplete nature of the Chinese statute; the use of treatises is commonplace in the legal system that China is becoming a part of. It is interesting to note that in discussing sources of law, the authors of this text indicate (Chapter 2.5.2) that the interpretations of statutes by courts are not to be cited in other cases. In other words, there is to be no law of precedent. The work of scholars is, however (Chapter 2.5.3), to be considered by courts. Of course it has no binding force.

In some ways, the most interesting aspect of this treatise is that the principles of German law are not only applied to the traditional fact situations in which they arose, they are made the dominant principles for considering all activities that could conceivably be classified as civil law. Thus, any activity that involves the distribution of goods is regarded as a "sale," which is a type of "contract," which is an "obligation" created by declarations of intention subject to the general principles of civil law. In consequence, contracts for the sale of agricultural sideline products and contracts for the sale of industrial and mineral products are classified as civil law sales and discussed in the chapter on sales, though each is governed by special regulations which could just as well be classified as administrative law. In other words, Chinese scholars of civil law are making the assumption that society is composed of discrete entities called persons (natural and juristic) that make decisions and that control their actions. Within broad limits, they are free to regulate their own affairs. The law enforces their individual decisions and holds them responsible for their individual acts. This analytical scheme is a commonplace for western jurists, but it is radically different from the Marxist view of man and society. In other words, even in its most technical discussions, this treatise is making a powerful ideological statement. There is every reason to suppose that Chinese jurists are perfectly conscious of what they are doing.

In any event, this treatise represents what the Chinese have to say about civil law. It seems safe to say that this treatise, or a similar one, is essential for anyone who is trying to understand that law.

NOTE ON THE TRANSLATION

The work that is translated here is the revised edition of *Basic Principles of Civil Law* published as one of the series of "Legal Materials for High Level Schools." The particular copies that I used were from the second printing in June 1987. Approximately two-thirds of the Chinese text is translated. The parts that have been omitted are property, intellectual property, and succession. The parts that have been translated are complete. Material in brackets [] is supplied by the translator. Everything else, including material in parentheses, is in the original. Footnotes have been omitted. They are almost all citations to the collected works of Marx and Engels in the Chinese edition and hence did not seem to be very useful.

The translation could unquestionably be improved. No doubt it contains many errors, including, I fear, some howlers. In many respects it could have been improved by consultation and additional advice, but in some respects it simply shares the problems of any translation of a Chinese legal text: there are a number of terms for which there are no generally accepted equivalents, or none that seem accurate. I have tried to use the translations employed in Taiwan where I am aware of them. These tend to be English equivalents of Roman law terms rather than common law terms (hire, mandate, succession, etc.).

ACKNOWLEDGMENTS

Mr. Jianbin Wei prepared draft translations of a number of chapters from the special part of obligations (Part II) in the first (1983) edition of the book. Mr. Yibing Dong read the first half of my translation of the revised (1985) edition and I am grateful for their help. The ultimate responsibility is, however, mine. I am very grateful to Mr. Wei and Mr. Mark Sidel of the Ford Foundation for obtaining copies of the revised edition for me. My secretary, Mrs. Beverly Jarboe, has been of immense help in getting out a very difficult text under trying circumstances.

Basic Principles of CIVIL LAW in China

I GENERAL DISCUSSION OF CIVIL LAW

1 Introduction

I

Like other parts of the law, civil law is a super-structure constructed on a certain economic base. Moreover, it exists to serve its economic base. Engels wrote, "Civil law norms are only the expression of the conditions of society's economic life in the form of law." Even more clearly, he said that civil law was that which "takes the direct reflection of economic relations as the principle of law" because civil law has an especially close relationship with an economic foundation that depends on and is constructed by a certain society. Consequently, if we look at the matter historically and from the point of view of the present circumstances of every country of the present day, civil law occupies an important position in the legal system and our country is no exception.

What are the objects that are adjusted by civil law? The objects adjusted by civil law are property relations and personal relations that are connected with property within a certain range. But how does one determine this "certain range"? At present there is no single point of view. Civil law is a general law. In every country the social relations adjusted by civil law are jumbled. Apart from economic relations, there are also a great number of personal relations. If the civil code to be promulgated by our country contains some legal rules that are very close to [those in other codes] or rules that do not fit within other codes, this is very common. However, since our country's civil law is an independent body [of law], its heart or leading aspect must be determined by the social relations it adjusts. We believe that the object of our country's civil law is our country's socialist commodity relations. Or, in other words, the heart or leading aspect of the social relations adjusted by our country's civil law is our country's socialist commodity relations.

In essence, civil law serves a certain society's commodity relationships. The phrase "civil law" comes from the ancient Roman "law of the people of the city [citizens]." At that time, the law of the people of the city was seen as collecting all rules necessary for defending the social life of the city-state. However, in the great jumble of Roman law, the essence lay in the so-called "private law" that adjusts every sort of dissimilar relationship among private persons. According to the earliest scholar of Roman law, Gaius, Roman private law was divided into the law of persons and things. This is the earliest scientific classification of Roman law. When the Emperor Justinian edited the legal treatises and formed the theoretical structure of the Corpus Juris, he took procedure out of property [thing] law and formed a new part. The Corpus Juris, promulgated in the sixth century A.D., divided Roman law into the three parts of the law of persons, things, and actions. This division had significance for the separation of public and private law. Roman private law earliest and most clearly recognized individual property rights and established the concept of property rights; it earliest and most clearly recognized personal rights, that is, the legal concept of the subject of rights; it earliest and most completely provided for the right freely to execute contracts. These three rights are precisely the legal reflection of the needs of commodity relations. As Engels, in writing about the nature of Roman law, stated, "Roman law is simply the perfect legislation for simple commodity production, that is to say, pre-capitalist commodity production."

The French Civil Code of 1804 absorbed the spirit of Roman law. It was constructed according to the system of the Corpus Juris. It is divided into three parts: (1) persons, including persons acting as subjects of rights, and also including persons who are members of the marriage household. (2) Property-ownership–rights. These include movable and immovable property (immovable property includes land). (3) Every method of obtaining property, including obligations, contracts, succession. The reason this code has been praised is that it was the earliest and most complete to provide clear and penetrating rules for the forms of capitalist production. As Engels pointed out, in talking about the nature of the French Code: "They took the first commodity producers' law of worldwide significance, i.e., Roman law with its incomparably clear rules regarding the legal relations of simple commodity owners (such as purchasers or sellers, obligees and obligors, contracts, obligations, etc., etc.) and produced these model bourgeois codes like the French civil code."

The civil code of Soviet Russia which was promulgated in 1922, and went into effect in 1923, was published by the Soviet authorities as the first civil code which took public ownership of the means of production as its basis. This civil code appeared with the background of what Lenin called "the economy governed in accordance with commercial principles." Moreover, it was drafted under his leadership. After Lenin died, the economic theory that occupied the dominant position in the Soviet Union would not recognize the existence of commodity relations in the production and circulation of the means of production. But looking at the content of the code, and the principles and methods of regulation specified by the said code, it actually takes the regulating of commodity relations in a socialist society as its central responsibility.

It is undeniable that the economic bases of civil law are different at different times. The class structures are exceptionally dissimilar. Their content and systems are of many sorts and kinds. But they all, in the end, maintain one thing in common—that is, that the basic content of the social relations regulated by civil law is composed of certain commodity relationships. Mankind has already gone through the two stages of the natural economy and the commodity economy. Civil law is also adapted to the development of the commodity economy and has gone through a very long stage of evolution. Beginning with the class society, in different historical periods, civil law norms were always the essential condition for the stabilization and development of commodity relations. In Roman times, the nature of the social economy was the natural economy. Consequently, Roman private law only adjusted the simple commodity exchange relations required for the consumption of the producers. Its application was limited by the natural economy. In the time of the Napoleonic Code, the highly developed commodity economy required a civil law that confirmed the position of the free and equal producers of commodities and that was freed from feudal, regional, and aristocratic ties. It advocated individuals, in a state of freedom and equality, exercising their own will to adjust their own mutual relations, and regularize the ordinary production and consumption relations between individuals and all the relations dependent on them. It ensured that labor was a commodity and that workers would form an object for capitalists to possess and exploit (and, moreover, that [capitalists would] take possession of the surplus value produced by the workers). It then used the civil law process to impel the development to a high level of the capitalist commodity economy.

The difference between socialist civil law and capitalist civil law does not lie principally in its reflection of ordinary commodity relations and the law of value in civil law techniques, [based on] equality and equal value. Rather, it lies in the special characteristics of the socialist system of public ownership which is realized in the civil law norms themselves and the new forms of commodity relations that reflect socialism. Socialist commodity relations are commodity relations that are based on public ownership and eliminate class conflict and class exploitation. They are commodity exchange relations that are carried on on the principle of exchange of truly equal labor. They are commodity relations that are under the leadership of the state plan and have as their aim the fulfillment of the people's needs. The brand new and special characteristics of our country's civil law rest on this basis.

In the course of historical development, civil law not only had to follow the specially designated commodity relations that were determined by the forms of production of the time, but, owing to the fact that commodity relations grew more complicated every day, in the system of legislation there was a gradual process of [development from a situation in which] the law was united to one in which all the law was divided. In this stage, the basic part of the social relations adjusted by civil law (commodity relations) also gradually appeared clearly from the midst of the confused mass of legal norms that reflected the many types of social relations. For example, in Roman law, there was no division between civil and criminal matters. Substantive law and procedural law were not separated. This [condition] no longer exists in the French Civil Code. But the French Civil Code, like all capitalist civil codes, calls labor relations, land relations, marriage and family relations, and commodity relations, private legal relations, and places them together within the area to which the civil law applies. The Soviet Russian Civil Code of 1923, according to Lenin's teaching, discarded the bourgeois theory regarding the "private law," "public law" distinction. It followed the principle of placing different types of social relations in different categories for adjustment. As to social labor relationships, or land relationships, and marriage and family relationships, separate bodies of law were established to adjust these matters. They were not again put in the category of objects to be adjusted by civil law. This sort of division of the areas of law was consistent with historical materialism, and was a great step forward in the legal history of mankind.

It may be seen from the above discussion that the three [categories of] the rights of the independent personality and property ownership, and the necessary corollary of these two rights—freedom of contract—which appear at different stages in different societies, are the necessary requirements for commodity economic relations to be expressed in legislation. Although the content of these rights was early reflected in Roman law, they were lost in the mist of the jumble of rules. [After] several thousand years passed with purification in the crucible of many kinds of social history, the leading position of commodity relations and civil law became ever clearer, not only in theory, but also in legislative practice. This sort of phenomenon shows us that all societies with commodity production and circulation require the promulgation of legislation that harmonizes with the essential special nature of the commodity relations particular to the said societies. This is civil law.

II

A developed commodity economy is a stage of human development that cannot be avoided, and the development to a high degree of the new style of socialist commodity relations is the way to realize our country's socialist modernization. If it is desired to have the commodity economy develop along normal lines, then it is necessary to construct the normal order of the commodity economy by means of civil law norms. Making use of the methods of civil law by giving full play to the active use of the law of value, and thus satisfying the development of the commodity economy—this is the urgent requirement of our country's reform of the economic system.

Beginning with the Third Plenum of the Thirteenth Party Congress, the Party, based on the requirement that production relations must harmonize with the level of production development, established the policy of opening to the outside, and, internally, activating the economy. At the same time, it put forward the task of carrying out the reform of our country's economic system. In recent years, the reform of the economic system has strongly impelled the development of a socialist commodity economy. The reform of agriculture, on the basis of stabilizing and perfecting the system of production responsibility, put forward many types of management, and agriculture proceeded from self-sufficiency and half self-sufficiency to a commodity economy. Urban reform also had a successful beginning.

In the midst of simplification and relaxation of government control and division of government enterprises, state managed enterprises greatly expanded their self-government. Many state managed small-scale enterprises began to use collective contracts or individual contracts or [contracts of] hire, or the payment of taxes to the state, using the methods of collective enterprises. The second step of carrying out of the change from the [the payment of] profits [into the payment of] taxes progressively strengthened the position of the state enterprises as commodity producers. Many levels of secondary economic structure development began to invigorate our country's economy. The reform of the system of circulation of our country's markets began to flourish. The opening of the special economic zones and the coastal cities promoted the development of the forces of civil law activity. In sum, the speeded development of the socialist commodity economy is an important change brought to our country's economy by the reform of the economic system.

The Third Plenum of the Twelfth Congress, in adapting to the necessary requirements of historical development, and the urgent desires of the people, put forth a strategic plan to speed up the reform of the entire economic system on the basis of the cities as the strong point. It put forth to the entire Party and the whole people the tremendous task of progressively opening up reform in every sector. The report of the Third Plenum of the Twelfth Congress stated, "A socialist planned economy must, on the basis of the Party, and using the laws of value, be a planned commodity economy that is based on a system of public ownership." Moreover, it put forward the task of developing the socialist commodity economy. Closely connected with this, the speedy improvement of a legal system for the activity of a commodity economy was an essential requirement for the development of a commodity economy in the reform of the economic system. Consequently, along with the carrying out of reform for the economic system in our country, it is necessary that the civil law develop and improve along with it. At the same time, civil law constitutes the essential law for adjusting economic relations. Its position in economic activity became more prominent every day.

Our country's civil law has the adjustment of commodity relations as its principal responsibility. Thus, the range of commodity relations determines the range of utilization of civil law. Owing to the fact that our recognition of how essential it is to the objective existence of a socialist commodity economy was insufficient, even to the point of regarding several measures for the development of socialist economy as constituting capitalism, the result was that, not only was there no solution of the problem of excessive collectivization of the economic control system established at the time of the formation of the country, but instead, a very rigid system of control was gradually formed, unsuitable for the development of the economic power of society. Under this kind of system, economic policy making was highly concentrated in the central [government]. Enterprises were subordinate objects of administrative organs. In the field of circulation, allocation and distribution in kind were the most important [methods used]. The forms of ownership of the means of production were ever more unified. This caused the commodity economy not to develop as needed. Consequently, it was difficult to make the best use of civil law in relation to economic life.

Following the carrying out of a profound reform in our country's economy which actively pressed the development of our country's economic socialist development, the position and use of civil law in economic life have become progressively more prominent. The documents of the Third Plenum of the Twelfth Party Congress clearly provide that the essential link in the reform of our country's economy is enterprises with increased vigor. Moreover, it points out: "Socialism with Chinese characteristics must first of all be a socialism with enterprises that are full of vigor." In the present reform of the economic structure, civil law is immensely useful in giving enterprises more autonomy and developing the commodity economy.

(1) The system of the juristic person of civil law

This is a legal form for dealing externally with the relations between the enterprises and government, and with internal enterprise relations. It bestows on enterprises the status of juristic persons. It can cause enterprises to be under legal protection and independently to carry on production and business. It can cause enterprises to have the property required to carry on their commodity-economy activities. It can make their rights and duties clear. Moreover, it establishes a system of scientific economic management and makes the enterprises under state control carry out economic activity. Moreover, when the capital does not amount to the obligations and this leads to bankruptcy, according to the principle of limited liability it settles the obligation with its own property. Consequently, clarifying the position of the enterprise as a juristic person is requisite for the enterprise to constitute a relatively independent economic entity. It forms a self-managed, independent accounting unit, a producer of commodities and manager that assumes sole responsibility for its profits and losses. This requires a simplification and decentralization [of government control]. The government and the enterprise are separated and the relationship between the government and enterprise is established. At the same time, the position of the enterprise as a juristic person is made clear and requires the individual interests of all staff and workers to be connected with the opposing interests of the enterprise. It brings together the stipends of the staff and workers of the enterprise to be linked up with the results of management. It establishes a clear relationship between the enterprise and the staff and workers and encourages the staff and workers to care for economic results of the enterprise and work hard to raise the economic benefits.

(2) The ownership system of civil law

This is the legal form for handling the mutual relationships between enterprises and the state. The state's ownership rights and the management rights of the enterprise can be appropriately separated. The improvement of enterprises must change the previous method of direct administrative control of enterprises by the state through legal recognition and protection of the management rights of enterprises. Consequently, our country's civil law, in addition to using its special methods of protection of property rights, as well as methods for protecting obligation rights, prescription and damages, and conscientiously protecting the state's property, must also recognize and protect management rights. These rights include the right to dispose of its reserve funds, the right to dispose of products that are in excess of the government plan, the right to dispose of surplus idle fixed assets, etc. The enterprise's management rights are in the nature of property rights. The exercise of these rights is not to receive any interference apart from the law. At the same time, the civil law, in its clarification of the rights of the enterprise, must also clarify the duty of the enterprise in respect to the state property which it manages and controls. In this way, the leadership of the state plan can be guaranteed, and it is also possible to give full play to the energy and creativity of the enterprise in order to arrive at an integration of macro and micro effects, and establish a proper relation between the state and the enterprise.

(3) The civil law system of obligation law and contracts is the legal means for regulating the relations between enterprises

Enterprises, by signing a contract, voluntarily select those who will be associated with them and obtain a contract with provisions that have been arrived at through agreement and negotiation. Moreover, they voluntarily receive the restraints and control of these provisions, and exchange their goods and labor according to the laws of value. Thus the previous method of controlling economic phenomena solely by administrative means can be changed. [This system] fully respects the initiative and mutual interests of the enterprise, promotes the point of view of production and marketing, frees the flow of goods. It can change [the former system] in which the division into geographical blocks and ministerial blocks hindered the development of horizontal relations and [can] greatly develop horizontal relations. It can alter the previous underestimated costs and undiscussed benefits and promote the enterprise's improvement and technology and reduce consumption and produce goods that are both of good quality and of lower cost. Consequently, [it] establishes a system of obligation [law] and contracts and confirms a certain degree of the right to independence of enterprises in signing contracts. Moreover, [it protects] them in their lawful interests in exchange. In connection with establishing and developing horizontal relationships, it is extremely important to make full use of the enterprises' energy.

(4) Civil law is the legal means for ensuring the realization of a policy of opening to the outside

In regard to the opening to the outside and developing foreign civil law relations, civil law is the essential standard for economic activity. We wish to encourage foreign investment, the opening of harbors on the sea coast, and the development of foreign trade—all of these [activities] are inevitably connected with the use of law. We cannot accept the unjust international customs which imperialist nations in former times imposed forcibly on colonial nations. We wish to uphold our lawful rights, and thus we want to have our own civil law. Our country's civil law must protect the state and economy and the lawful rights and interests of citizens. It can also protect the lawful interests of the foreign investors. This can effectively attract foreign investment and foreign civil law activities.

Above, we have discussed the use of civil law in the reform of the economic system. At the same time, we have explained the importance, in the process of reforming the economic system, of enacting as quickly as possible the civil code for the improvement of our civil law legislation. Since our own civil code has not been published up until now, many problems in economic life lack a basis in law. The lawful interests of the parties do not receive effective protection. At the same time this causes the people's courts to experience many difficulties in handling civil law matters. Since our civil law legislation is very incomplete, this means that our civil law has not yet been made use of to the extent it should have been. Thus, it is necessary at present, in the reform of the economy, to draft and promulgate a civil code as soon as possible and perfect our country's civil law legislation.

It is also necessary to observe that in the case of goods that circulate, the [nature] of the social basis of production does not change the nature [of these goods] as commodities. Consequently, all the general conditions of a civil law system that have existed historically or in foreign countries—the subject of law, ownership rights, contracts, etc.—are all matters that we consider and make use of in preparing our civil law and in studying civil law. They are all of value whether considered as positive or negative. However, law belongs to the superstructure, consequently, we certainly cannot get to know the essential nature of our own country's civil law system of organization and all the types of civil law systems from the contents of some other country's civil law. The existence and development of our country's civil law are determined by the social and economic system of our country and its stage of development. They are determined by the intention and demand of the people of our country to build socialism on the basis of the leadership of the working class. When working on and studying our country's civil law, we must consider the special characteristics and requirements of our country's socialist commodity production and circulation. Our country's commodity relations are planned commodity relations produced on the basis of a system of public ownership of the means of production. The purpose of commodity production is not to realize surplus value for capitalists, but to fulfill the needs of the people and society for material and cultural life. In order to use the laws of value consciously, and to insure that the national economy will proceed smoothly along the track of the state plan, we must still consider how our country's civil law can best take advantage of the active use of commodity monetary relationships, and at the same time prevent selfish departmentalism, decentralism and other anarchistic tendencies from appearing. This constitutes a very great responsibility. Moreover, to bring out the essential measures for the realization of this task in every aspect [of this law] poses many new problems for us to resolve in preparing and studying our country's civil law.

III

If we take that which is determined by our country's socialist commodity relationships as the basic content and dominant aspect of the social relations adjusted by our country's civil law, then the study of civil law in our country must be research into the special characteristics and general conditions of the legal norms that reflect our country's socialist commodity relations, the rules for the production and development of the legal system, as well as the science of their internal relations. Its essential content must be:

First, the subject of civil law rights. This is covered in chapters 4, 5, and 6 of this book. Our country's citizens and socialist organizations which are considered to be juristic persons and partnership organizations are [entities] that participate in the activities of society in many ways. When they act as the producers of commodities or transferors of commodities, then, in law, they appear as the subjects of civil law rights. "Commodities are things. They are not persons. They cannot go to market by themselves and exchange [themselves]. One must look for their custodians" [*Capital*]. Our country's civil law must reflect our country's commodity relations. It must establish a social order that affirms and protects socialist social commodity production and circulation. To be sure, we must give the guardians of the commodities—that is, the owners of the commodities (citizens, collective organizations, and the State and enterprises that represent the State in managing property owned by the whole people, etc.)—the necessary legal position to participate in these actions. That is, we must specify what sort of civil law rights they may enjoy, and what obligations they must assume.

Second, ownership rights. These are covered in this book in chapters 11–17. Ownership rights are the system of ownership expressed in the law. [This system of ownership rights] occupies an important position in our country's socialist legal system. In a country with the system of private property, ownership rights are manifested as private property rights, they are the basic content of civil—private—law. In our country, the protection of property and the strengthening and developing of the system of socialist ownership is the common responsibility of all parts of our country's legal system (criminal law, administrative law, financial law, labor law, civil law, etc.). Since the question of the ownership of property can be reflected in every sort or kind of social relationship, and since, moreover, there are also many sorts and kinds of infringements of property rights, these must be reflected in the different branches of the law by using different procedures to give protection. Our country's civil law lays particular emphasis on commodity relations. Since the ownership right (including the right to manage property) is the premise of the right to produce and circulate commodities, it is also the consequence and purpose of commodity production and circulation. The civil law provides in its system of ownership that the property rights obtained by the State, collectives, and individuals in a lawful manner are protected in respect to the right to possess, use, obtain benefits [from] and dispose [of property], and against infringement of rights, by means of restoration of possession, elimination of impediments, restoration of original conditions, damages, and other civil law remedies. Since these methods of protection belong to the civil law, they do not violate the principle of commodity relations based on the equality of compensation for equal value. Apart from this, the relations between the common subjects of property rights to the same property—common ownership as well as the relationships between different owners of adjoining property—the relations of neighbors—all must be looked into.

Third, obligations and contracts. This is the subject of chapters 18–32. The content of this part emphasizes the legal rights and duties of the parties that reflect the process of the exchange of commodities (the circulation of property). Among these, apart from studying the general theoretical legal questions of the process of commodity exchange—the general principles of contracts and obligations—we also study the separate elements in this process, and their theories ([such] as, the contract relations of sales, procurement and supply, hire [work], loans, transport, deposit, insurance, etc.). If one can say that the system of ownership is concerned with protecting property rights in the domain of production and consumption, then the system of obligation and contracts protects property rights in the field of exchange and circulation. To put it another way, the former is a method of adjusting property rights in the condition of stasis, while the latter is a method of adjusting property in a state of movement. In speaking of civil law property rights-duty relations, the contract and obligation relations are much richer and more complicated than the ownership relations.

The three systems of the subject of rights, ownership, and obligation and contract, together constitute the most basic content of our country's civil law.

In addition, reflecting the content of the system of obligations, the subject of the infringement of rights [delict] is treated in chapter 19. This considers the rights-duty relationships arising out of an unlawful infringement of a personal or property right. The infringement of rights is not within the field of commodity relations. Moreover this sort of action can, at the same time, give rise to several kinds of legal relationships (criminal law, administrative law, etc.) But the responsibility to pay for economic damages that arises out of this act is handled according to civil law principles of equality and equal value. Therefore the infringement of rights must also be included in civil law.

The first three chapters of this book are a summary of the theory of the general nature of the entire body of civil law. The seventh chapter, things [property], especially studies the material objects of civil law relationships. The eighth chapter concerns the juristic act. In it are studied the criteria for the actions of parties in civil law activities. Chapter 9 deals with representation. In it is studied the situation where one person carries on civil law actions on behalf of another, and creates a rights-duty relationship. Chapter 10 deals with prescription. In it are studied the effects of the element of time on civil law relations.

Intellectual property is [the subject of] Part IV of this book. The rights of intellectual production such as the rights of authorship and the rights of discovery are a sort of spiritual wealth. They are not commodities. But the right of publication which is formed and based on creative activity, the patent right which is based on and formed by discovery, as well as intellectual service may serve as commodities and enter circulation. The general rules of commodity relations may be applied [to these rights] and they may come within the scope of civil law adjustment.

What is discussed above is the entire body of civil law. Speaking generally, it is the expression in law of our country's commodity relationships.

The succession to property is covered in the last part of this book. Although the content of this part is not concerned with commodity relations, it affects the ownership of property after a person's death. It is an important element of civil law, and therefore it is included in this book.

At present, our country's civil code has not yet been promulgated, and the General Provisions of Civil Law are still being drafted, but among the laws executed since the founding of the country, many regulations dealing with civil law matters are included. The practice of economic construction and the experience of the work of deciding cases in civil law matters is very rich. These teaching materials are still in the stage of investigating the matters mentioned above. They have been written and revised on the basis of the original *Basic Principles of Civil Law* in the series "Trial Materials for Use in High Level Schools."

2 The General Concept of Civil Law of the People's Republic of China

I
THE OBJECTS OF ADJUSTMENT OF OUR COUNTRY'S CIVIL LAW

The civil law of the People's Republic of China is an important basic law of the country. It is an independent body of law within the totality of our country's law.

Since the founding of the People's Republic of China, the sovereign organs of the state at every level, and the administrative organizations, under the name and according to the line pointed out by the Party, with the practical experience of the united masses of the people in the class struggle and the struggle for production, according to the requirements of the revolutionary situation, and the unceasing development of the establishment of production, have successively published laws, regulations, rules and separate provisions. All are the superstructure built on our country's socialist economic foundation. All are the realization of the will of the great mass of the people under the leadership of the working class. They are all the tools of the state in realizing the socialist revolution and the work of construction. Together they form our country's socialist unified legal system.

In our country's unified legal system the different parts can be arranged according to the different objects for adjustment. Civil law is one of the important parts of our country's law. It has its own objects for adjustment. It adjusts particular social relations. The principles of civil law legislation, the methods of adjustment, its content and system are, in the last analysis, determined by the nature and content of the social relations it adjusts. Consequently, determining the objects of our country's civil law is the chief responsibility of our country's science of civil law.

There is still some dispute about the objects of adjustment of our country's civil law. According to the opinion of many, the object of adjustment of our country's civil law is a specified area of property relations and personal relations. These relations may arise among citizens, and they may also arise among state organizations, among economic organizations, among institutions and social collectives, as well as between [these various groups]. The present discussion is divided as follows:

(1) Property relations

"Property relations" refers to economic relations that are formed by persons in the production, allocation, transfer, and consumption of material goods. The content of property relations is very extensive. Civil law only adjusts specified portions, to wit, ownership relations and exchange relations. The former refers to relations that arise between the subjects [of rights arising] out of the occupation, use, or disposition of the means of production or the means of consumption. They are reflected in law as ownership relations. The latter refers to relations that arise between the subjects [of rights] that arise out of the exchange of the fruits of labor. They are reflected in law as obligation and contract relations. The mutual relations between the two reflect the fact that the important feature of our country's socialist civil law is to regulate commodity relations.

In the regulation by civil law of property relations, the position of the parties in relation to each other is one of mutuality and not subordination. Each is the subject of his own property rights. In economic contacts, they honor the principle of compensation for equal value. The use by the civil law, when it regulates property relations, of the principle of equality and equal value is determined by the nature of the social relations that are being adjusted. It is one of the important features that differentiates civil law from other branches of law.

(2) Personal relations

Personal relations are social relations that do not have a property-relations content but are of a personal nature. In law, they are incorporated in the rights of life, health, name, honor, etc. The rights of authorship, invention, and discovery, as well as publication rights, patent rights, and trademark rights are not the same. They all have a direct relation with the rights of a person's name and honor which cannot be transferred. Therefore they are personal rights. Although what these rights reflect are the products of men's minds, these products cannot be measured directly by the use of their price in money. Therefore they are not property. Even though personal rights do not have a property content, they often have a close connection with the property rights regulated by civil law and form prerequisites to property relations as [in the case of] those who have rights of authorship, invention, and discovery. They can obtain high fees, prizes, and royalties for the use of patents. Because of this, the violation of personal rights is often, at the same time, a violation of property rights. In view of the above discussion, those personal rights that have a relation with property rights are often treated as the objects of civil law regulation.

The law's object of adjustment determines the law's method of adjustment. The most important objects for adjustment by civil law are commodity relationships, in particular, the commodity relations in which those who are participating are equal and not subordinate to one another. In the field of occupation, use, and disposition of property they must not be mutually dependent. At the same time, those who are exchanging commodities must, while they are acquiring or transferring them, reward each other's labor in accordance with the principle of exchange for equal value. Consequently, the methods of civil law that reflect the special characteristics of civil law must have their own special characteristics.

First, the legal status of parties to civil law relations must be equal. Economically, there must be equality of value. These are the basic methods of civil law. They also reflect the laws of value in civil law. The civil law recognizes the independence of each subject of civil law and his right to administer property, and insists that each subject must occupy a position of equality. It does not permit one party to limit the rights of the other, nor does it permit any party to issue orders to the other because of his economic superiority [to that party]. The rights recognized by civil law are for the most part reciprocal. One party's right is thus the other party's duty. Each subject must exchange property according to the principle of equal value. He may not, without compensation, appropriate and occupy the other party's property. Any subject who unlawfully causes material loss to the other must compensate with the same amount of property. The methods of equality and equal value are basic characteristics of the civil law treatment of commodity relations.

Second, [there must be] a specified degree of arbitrariness. Marx pointed out: "In order to have these things serve as commodities and to have relations arise between them, the guardian of the commodity must have its own will realized in relations arising between persons out of these things. One party need only comply with the intention of the other. Then it is said that each side has engaged in the act that was mutually agreed upon. Only then can he transfer his own commodity and acquire that of the other party." The subjects of civil law are naturally equal and dependent. They must also have a definite degree of independence and self-determination. Civil law recognizes the independent position of subjects and their right to occupy, use, and dispose of property. They have the right, within the area specified by law, to create, change, and annul their mutual legal relations by means of agreement of their wills. However, under the conditions of our country's socialism, the state has the function of organizing and administering the economy. Consequently, in the domain of civil law the state plan and state administrative intervention have to be dominant. Within our country's civil law, many areas of law, such as the registration of juristic persons, land use control, restrictions on the circulation of property, the subjection of contracts to the plan, the enforcement of patents, etc., bring out state intervention in the domain of civil law. The intervention is to protect our country's unified leadership and to avoid the necessary measures that have to be used when there is blind adherence to the law of value. Consequently, the free exercise of will in our country's civil law is employed within the state's economic macro-planning. It is not unrestricted.

In sum, the means of adjustment of civil law are determined by the special characteristics of the commodity relations adjusted by civil law. Verifying the methods of civil law adjustment is significant for the understanding of the special characteristics of the civil law, and the correct use of civil law rules.

II
THE DIFFERENCES BETWEEN CIVIL LAW AND OTHER TYPES OF LAW

When we have determined the objects that are adjusted by civil law and its methods, we can begin to differentiate civil law from other branches of law (even though they also adjust certain areas of property relations). The object adjusted by the civil law also serves as a boundary between civil law and other branches of law.

1. The Difference Between Civil Law and Administrative Law

Administrative law is the legal device by which the state, through its own organizations, brings into play the functions of organization, direction, supervision, and control. In the field of administration, the state occupies a position of leadership and direction. Moreover, by means of its own will it determines the basic acts of the other party. Therefore administrative relations are subordinate relations that are formed according to the principle of leadership and obedience. But the commodity relations adjusted by civil law are relations of compensation for equal value [on the basis of] mutual equality. Since the state participates in circulation activity by means of state property, issuing public obligations [and] treasury certificates, carrying on international trade, and so forth, in these areas the state does not act as a subject of governmental rights, but appears as one independently engaged in commodity exchange. In the economic field certain administrative relations have to do with property. For example, relations arising from the allocation by the supervisory organization, according to administrative procedures, of the fixed capital of enterprise units. They realize macro-interests. There is no mutual interest between the parties. But the commodity relations regulated by the civil law arise for the most part out of the will of the parties based on their personal interests. The parties often perform and exchange for a return consideration. Therefore, they realize micro-interests.

2. The Differences Between Civil Law and Fiscal Law

Fiscal law is law which, in a monetary form, using state organizations, directs the allocation and sub-allocation of the national economy. It is what adjusts fiscal relations by means of a state budget, final accounts, the receipt of taxes, allocations, and other procedures. Fiscal law is a device for realizing the state's administrative functions. Fiscal relations are not commodity relations. Rather, they are a kind of administrative subordinate relation that has a fiscal content. For example, the relations of levying capital funds and transmitting key construction capital, levying bonus taxes, and construction taxes, and so forth, express the state's compulsory uncompensated obtaining of fiscal income. The methods of fiscal law, like those of administrative law, are a method of direction and submission, and thus are different from the methods of civil law.

3. Civil Law and Labor Law

Labor law's object of adjustment is the social labor relation. It determines the discipline relations of labor, the protection of labor, the procedures of labor, vacations, and wages, as well as the allocation of labor and similar problems. The wage for labor looks externally like a kind of circulation of property but it is received and paid according to the principle of from each, according to his ability, to each, according to his work. In our country, labor is not a commodity. Wages are not the price for labor. What is being practiced here is an allocation of labor, not a relation of exchange for equal value. Therefore, labor relations are not objects of adjustment by civil law.

Finally, we will talk about the difference between civil law and economic law.

At present, in our country, in academic circles the relationship between civil law and economic law has been much discussed and many opinions have been expressed. Speaking generally, there are five lines of opinion: one regards economic law as a general term for the legal norms for adjusting economic relations. All legal norms which affect economic matters are part of economic law. Thus economic law is a general area. Civil law is only a field within it. The second regards economic law as a general term for the legal norms that adjust relations of economic administration and economic agreement. It regards all vertical and horizontal relations between socialist organizations [as matters that are] to be adjusted by economic law. Civil law essentially regulates relations between citizens. The third regards economic law as a general term for the legal norms that adjust economic control relations. It only regulates vertical economic relations; horizontal relations are regulated by civil law. The fourth regards economic law as economic administrative law. It is the general term for the legal norms [governing the action of] the state relying on its administrative rights, intervening in the economy. It is the legal means for the state to engage in planning, organization, supervision, regulation, and other types of administrative control over economic activity. The fifth regards economic law as the body of law that adjusts every type of relation that is within the socialist planned economy. The heart of economic law is planning law and after that enterprise law. Goods and materials supply law (including the distribution and the allotment of goods and materials, not including the contracts themselves), capital construction law, etc.

We believe that, if economic law is regarded as administrative law, then economic law may constitute an independent body of law, regardless of whether it is an essential part of administrative law. If it is believed that economic law is law that adjusts every kind of economic relation or vertical and horizontal economic relation, then economic law cannot have particular objects and methods of adjustment since it is not a field of law. To be sure, the question still requires scholarly research.

From the point of view of the practice of our country's economic construction, and the development and requirements of our country's legislation, we believe that our country's economic law is the term for the laws, rules, and provisions of legal norms that are directed towards the actual economic activities carried on among socialist organizations, or the state's carrying out of management functions. But civil law takes the general provisions of certain types of social relations (commodity relations) that arise out of the great mass of actual economic activities to serve as its object of adjustment. Its objects are unified, its principle and methods of adjustment are also unified. It has a complete system. Scientifically it may be regarded as an independent body of law. But every legal norm within economic law makes certain actual economic phenomena and processes its own particular objects of adjustment. There are often included among these economic processes and phenomena many dissimilar economic relations. To take the economic process of capital construction as an example, this includes basic plans, fiscal allocations, land use, supply of materials, engineering contracts, as well as land surveys, engineering plans, and construction, etc. It must separately make use of the principle of adjustment and of legal methods from every branch of the law, for example, civil law, administrative law, fiscal law, labor law, land law, as well as criminal law, etc., to carry out its adjustment, since economic law does not have unified principles of adjustment and legal methods. Consequently, regardless of whether it is a single legal rule of economic law or all such rules, they do not constitute an independent branch of law. The inclusion of some civil law norms within economic law, (that is, norms that are related to commodity relations) may be regarded as the [use of] the civil law to supplement and develop the adjustment of economic activities by the said economic law norms. If [the norms] include administrative law, then this may be regarded as the [use of] administrative law to supplement and develop the adjustment of economic activities by the said economic law norms.

The work of scientific research into our country's civil law is far from being adequate for the needs of our country's economic construction. Many theoretical questions of civil law must await the reform of our economic system and judicial practice for profound research. The problem of the objects of adjustment of our country's civil law is even more a question that will be disputed for a long time. At present there is still no unified point of view. The above discussion of the objects of adjustment of civil law and the differences between civil law and economic law still requires profound theoretical enquiry. It also must be clearly provided for in the General Provisions of Civil Law which is in the course of being promulgated.

III
THE BASIC PRINCIPLES OF THE CIVIL LAW OF THE PEOPLE'S REPUBLIC OF CHINA

The basic principles of our country's civil law are the basic points of departure and bases for formulating, explaining, carrying out, and studying our country's civil law. They are the collective embodiment of the socialist nature of our country's civil law. They are also the basic standard for separating it from the civil law of the exploiting classes. These basic principles appear under the following headings:

1. The Principle that the Sanctity of Socialist Public Property Cannot Be Infringed

Socialist public property—that is, property owned by the whole people and the collective property of the laboring masses—is the foundation of the political and economic system of our country, and is our country's material guaranty for the ending of the oppression of man by man and the bringing about of the socialist Four Modernizations and the uninterrupted raising of the people's material cultural level and the level of communist morality. Because of this, our country's constitution clearly provides that "the sanctity of socialist public property may not be infringed." This rule regarding civil law which takes the regulation of property relations as its chief object is naturally a basic principle that must be implemented. Our country's civil law carries out this principle not only because it is a method for establishing and strengthening the socialist economy, and a key for the development for the national economy, but also because the collective embodiment of the welfare of the whole people as rulers of the country is embodied in socialist commonly owned property.

That private property is sacred and cannot be infringed on is a basic principle of all capitalist civil law. This principle bestows on private persons in regard to their property a right that is absolute, exclusive, and that can be freely exercised. The civil law of capitalist classes proceeds generally from the concept of ownership. It only provides for abstract ownership rights. In a capitalist society these rights are naturally only the rights of those who have property. That is, the capitalist class freely exploits the special rights of surplus labor of those who have no property. In consequence, the class contradictions intensify day by day. The capitalist countries cannot fail to put certain limits on absolute independent property rights. In the latter part of the 19th, and early part of the 20th century, there appeared the so-called tendency of "the socialization of property." This was merely a method for easing class conflicts. Moreover, it did not shake the principle that private property was sacred and might not be infringed. This principle is the basic theoretical principle of the theory on which capitalistic society relies for its existence. There cannot be any basic change in it in a capitalist society.

2. The Principle of Submission to the National Economic Plan

The establishment of our country's system of socialist public ownership has been an essential condition for the planned development of the national economy. The nation, by means of an economic plan, has consciously assured social production and the necessary balance. It has avoided the waste created by production without government [intervention]. In consequence, we have obtained much better economic results. This is another very important advantage of a socialist system over a capitalist. Civil law which takes our country's socialist property relations as the important object for regulation must completely carry out the principle that economic activity must follow the guidance of the nation's economic plan. This is particularly the case for its system of contracts. It may not conflict with this principle since it is only by following the leadership and guidance of the nation's economic plan that we are able to cause complicated cooperative relationships in the area of economic circulation to be coordinated. [This] causes the entire society's production, supply, transportation, and consumption to harmonize with the requirements of the rules for the country's economic development and consciously maintains every part of the whole in equilibrium and accelerates the rate of economic construction.

The principle of freedom of contract is the embodiment, in the field of economic circulation, of the principle in capitalist countries that private property is sacred and may not be infringed. In a capitalist society where labor has been made into a commodity, the principle of freedom of contract is a legal tool of the wage-labor system used in capitalist countries to carry out the exploitation of the workers. Under the conditions of the sharpened contradiction between the socialization of production [on the one hand] and private ownership [on the other], freedom of contract is the only method possible whereby a capitalist society, under the control of the law of value, [can] spontaneously regulate production by means of free competition. However, free competition leads inevitably to monopoly and economic crisis. Even though, in the 20th century, the civil law legislation of developed capitalist countries has adopted measures limiting the principle of freedom of contract, in an attempt to prevent economic crisis, since capitalist societies could not cast off the contradiction between socialization of production and private ownership, gradually they exerted limited state intervention over the freedom to contract. Basically, [however], they could not get rid of the continued appearance of economic crises. In capitalist countries, generally, there is clear evidence of increase in the rate of unemployment, stagnation of production, and inflation.

3. The Principle that the Lawful Rights and Interests of Citizens Are Protected

In our socialist nation the people are the governors. All power belongs to the people. Our country's constitution bestows on the citizens all the indispensable political and economic rights and the right to a cultural life, and assures to them the right of mankind to dignity and individual development. These rights have reliable material protection. This is our country's uninterruptedly developing and growing system of socialist public ownership. But the final aim of socialist production is to fulfill, in the largest measure, and to the greatest extent, the material and cultural needs of the citizens. In our country the protection of the citizen's rights and interests, and the assurance that they are not violated, is the common responsibility of all parts of the law. The protection that our country's civil law gives to the property and personal rights of citizens is also a principle that it must carry out in every system.

Capitalist countries raise the slogan "protection of human rights," but since they even uphold private ownership of the means of production, the human rights they protect cannot have any general significance, and are only the special rights of the bourgeoisie. The bourgeoisie flaunts its so-called heaven-bestowed rights on the basis of "freedom of ownership" and "freedom of contract." In fact, however, after they overthrew feudalism, and obtained these rights by their own struggle, they relied on these rights to seize surplus value from the great mass of working people. In a society of private ownership, rights are constituted for the benefit of those who have property. Anyone who cannot lay hands on the means of production is, in the economic sense, in a situation where he disposes of no rights. Thus, all the rights established by law have no meaning for him. In the 20th century the civil law legislation in capitalist countries gradually changed from the "principle of individualism" to the "principle of the general social good." This was not only to calm class contradictions. It was a necessity for the attempt to adjust the terrible economic conflicts inside the bourgeoisie. But in this [movement] there was not, and could not be, any decisive change, because the bourgeoisie, whether in the field of morals or [that of] legislation, has no way of abandoning selfishness. Consequently, the law always favors the bourgeoisie and upholds all the rights of the bourgeoisie.

4. The Principle of Equality and Exchange for Equal Value

Carrying out the principles of the parties' equality in the field of law and of [exchange for] equal value in the field of economic interests in civil law relationships is the necessary reflection of commodity relations serving as the essential object of adjustment of our country's civil law. It is also the essential requirement for carrying out economic accounting and the principle of allocation according to work. So far as economic organizations are concerned, our country's civil law clearly recognizes the equality of their legal positions. This is advantageous in developing a spirit of democratic consultation in their economic cooperation. It is the most reasonable method for selecting measures together to carry out their mutual responsibilities. Affirming equal value in economic benefits is of positive use in assuring our country's utilization of the law of prices. It is an effective procedure for supplementing economic planning in adjusting production. As regards the great mass of the people, equality and exchange for equal value are the standards for their independent exchange of the fruits of labor on the basis of fulfilling their own needs among themselves (by means of commercial organizations). It can be seen that our country's civil law carries out the principles of equality and exchange for equal value in developing our country's socialist commodity production [and] fulfilling commodity exchange. It upholds the economic order, it raises the economic benefits of enterprises, and protects the people's livelihood.

The general principle of equality and exchange for equal value in bourgeois civil law is an extension of their so-called theory of "private law autonomy." Since, in capitalist society, money may constitute capital, labor is a commodity. Therefore the bourgeois civil law principles of equality and exchange for equal value are a reflection of the bourgeoisie forcing the proletariat to carry out exchange for unequal value and [these principles] serve as the basis in law for surplus value. In the 20th century, after monopolistic organizations emerged in large number, there was, in capitalist countries, a wide-spread use of "compulsory contracts." These were contracts in which the monopolistic organizations, relying on their controlling economic power, forced the opposite parties (small or medium-sized enterprises) to accept [certain] conditions. In the dominant area of commodity circulation, the general principles of equality and equivalent price were in fact denied. Although the capitalist countries intervened in these actions by means of "anti-monopoly laws," in all societies under the control of money, the weak are meat for the strong to eat, the large take advantage of the small—these are phenomena that cannot be avoided. Consequently, the principles of equality and the equivalence of price cannot be realized in a capitalist society.

IV
THE SOURCES OF OUR COUNTRY'S CIVIL LAW

The concept of sources of law has many meanings. Here it is used to refer to the forms that are used to express legal norms. Only when the rules for actions are expressed as legal norms do they become effective by [being enforced by] state power. Consequently the sources of law are also a way of determining whether legal rules have compulsory force.

Our country's civil law, like the other branches of law, is the embodiment of the will of the great mass of the people on the basis of the leadership of the working class. The content of this will is ultimately determined by the conditions of our country's socialist material life. The forms used by the state express these conditions and cause them to form norms that must be honored by state organizations, state enterprises, collective enterprises and social groups, and other forms of juristic persons and the whole body of citizens.

Thus the sources of the civil law of the People's Republic of China are forms that express the legal norms for adjusting our socialist society's production relations and personal relations within a specified field.

The most important sources of our country's civil law are the written norms for civil activities issued by state organizations at every level within the limits of their authority. Since the issuing organizations are not the same, the position and effect of the written normative civil law provisions within the civil law are also not the same. Apart from this, the customs formed by the masses of the people in their daily life over many years are not written normative provisions, but they have a definite significance. We shall discuss below, one by one, each of the sources for our civil law.

(1) The Constitution

The Constitution is the country's basic law enacted by the National People's Congress. It is the highest legal authority. No civil law statute, regulation, rule, decision, order, or specific regulation may conflict with the provisions of the Constitution. All of the socialist principles defined in the Constitution are the basis of all civil law legislation. Because of this, the Constitution is the essential source of our country's civil law. The aim of establishing socialism [declared in] the Constitution, the rules for the line [to be taken], the rules regarding the system of ownership, the rules regarding the basic rights and duties of citizens, all have an especially great significance for civil law.

(2) Laws [statutes] and regulations

Laws and regulations (the "decisions" and "resolutions" of the National People's Congress, and the Standing Committee of the National People's Congress, have the same effect as laws) are promulgated by the National People's Congress and its permanent organ, the Standing Committee of the National People's Congress. The portions of laws and regulations devoted to civil law are the most important source of civil law.

The civil code has an especially great significance in civil law legislation. It takes the norms of each important system of our country's civil law and systematically edits them into legislation. At present the civil code of the People's Republic of China has still not been promulgated.

(3) The rules, resolutions, and orders of the State Council

The State Council is the executive organization of the highest sovereign organization of the state. The legal rules, resolutions, and orders of the State Council, promulgated and authorized in accordance with the Constitution, laws and regulations, which relate to civil law, are sources of our country's law. Our country's civil code has not yet been promulgated. Therefore, the rules, resolutions, and orders promulgated and authorized by the State Council are, in practice, of particular importance.

(4) Orders, directives, and ministerial rules issued by ministries and committees of the State Council

All of the orders, directives, and ministerial rules of every ministry or committee within the State Council, issued in accordance with the laws, regulations, rules, resolutions, and orders of the State Council, which are issued within the limits of their authority, supplement and develop the law. Moreover, they cause the general rules of the laws to be made more concrete and to be integrated with the ministry's functions. Such of these rules as are related to civil law rules are sources of civil law. They are of great utility to civil law.

(5) Resolutions, orders, and legal rules of a local nature; independent provisions; and particular provisions issued by local people's congresses and the people's governments at every level and self-governing organs of [minority] nationalities and autonomous areas

Resolutions, orders, and rules of a local nature; independent provisions and particular provisions decided upon and promulgated by the people's congresses at every level; and every level of the local people's government, self-governing organs of [minority] people's autonomous regions are, within the limits of their authority, sources of civil law. The above mentioned rules all have a territorial nature. They only have effect within the area in which they are promulgated. They are not enforced throughout the country.

(6) Guiding directives of the Supreme People's Court

The Supreme People's Court is our country's highest organ for deciding cases. It has the authority to supervise the work, in deciding cases, of the local people's courts of every level, and of the specialized people's courts. Its published directives, based on bringing together the practice of deciding cases, determine principles that are derived from interpreting the laws even though the laws have no clear provisions. They are used to explain the questions on the application of the legal norms raised by the people's courts at all levels. At the same time, they also lay down certain principles that must be followed in deciding cases. These directives have binding force on the people's courts of every level. At present, when our country's legislation is not complete, these directives which fill out the incomplete legislation, and unify the standards of cases with different standards, have especially great importance. Because of this, directives of a guiding nature of the Supreme People's Court have significance as sources of civil law.

(7) Custom

In our country, custom is limited as a source of civil law. Only customs that do not conflict with the rules of law and regulations, other written provisions of a normative nature, or that have been recognized by the state, have significance as sources of civil law. Our country is one with a vast territory and many races. In the areas which minority peoples inhabit, custom is clearly a source of civil law.

According to the "Resolution on the Question of the Effectiveness of Laws and Regulations Enacted Since the Founding of the People's Republic of China" enacted at the Twelfth Session of the Standing Committee of the Fifth National People's Congress, all laws and regulations enacted since the founding of the country continue to be in effect, except those which conflict with the present constitution, laws, or regulations. The great mass of civil law norms which are in harmony with the conditions for effectiveness, that are within the written provisions of a normative nature promulgated in the over 30 years since the founding of the nation by state organs at every level, are sources of our country's civil law.

V

THE INTERPRETATION OF CIVIL LAW NORMS

The purpose of formulating legal norms is to carry them out in the actual life of society. In regard to the study of the question of the interpretation of civil law norms, it is necessary to explain how to ensure that civil law norms, as they are realized in daily life, are correctly used and fully carried out.

Civil law norms are all directed towards the characteristics of the great majority of relations of the same type that arise out of civil law relationships. That is to say, legal norms must abandon the concrete characteristics of concrete civil law relationships and provide their basic characteristics and methods of dealing with them. Because of this, in order actually to apply civil norms in concrete civil law relations, it is necessary to explain their content and actual meaning, and then to interpret them.

Legal norms are standards for men's actions. Everyone who uses the legal norm can interpret the norm he is using. Thus, state organizations, people's courts, and citizens all may interpret the law, but since the subjects of interpretation are not the same, the results are also not the same and may be discussed separately as follows.

1. Legislative Interpretation

[''Legislative interpretation''] refers to interpretation of laws and regulations by the organs that have the authority to enact laws and regulations. The National People's Congress is the highest legislative organ. Because of this, it is the highest interpretative authority as to all laws and regulations included in the constitution. This authority is exercised by its standing committee. All other organs that have the power to enact and approve the carrying out of legal norms also have the power, within the limits of their authority, to interpret the legal norms they have enacted and whose enforcement they have approved. This kind of interpretation is binding on the application of the law.

2. Interpretation by Courts

According to the rule of our country's Organic Law for People's Courts, the Supreme People's Court, in the process of deciding a case, has, if there is any question as to the concrete use of laws and regulations, the power of interpretation. (See section 33 of the Organic Law of the People's Courts of the People's Republic of China of 1st January 1980.) The said power is exercised by the adjudicatory committees of the Supreme People's Court. (See the decision of 23d June 1955 of the 17th meeting of the first session of the Standing Committee of the National People's Congress.) The interpretations of the laws by the Supreme People's Court, made during the course of deciding cases, are binding on people's courts of every level.

Whenever a people's court of any level decides a concrete case, it interprets legal norms. The reasons given in the written decision collectively reflect this fact. However in the same case, the higher level people's court has the power to change the lower level court's interpretation. This is the basis for the ruling of the higher level court in changing the decision of the lower court. However, the interpretation of the people's court (including the Supreme People's Court) in its written opinion in a concrete case of a legal norm is only effective in that case. Whenever a people's court at any level disposes of a case, it may not quote cases as a basis for its decision.

3. Scholarly Interpretation

Scholarly interpretation refers chiefly to the interpretation by jurists in scientific works or in school texts, as well as [to] the explanation of civil law rules given by lawyers in their practice in representing people. It also includes the interpretation of any citizen in any form, with a scientific basis, in regard to legal norms. These have great significance for expounding the meaning of civil law norms and developing the science of civil law. In the work of the courts, these explanatory opinions are often referred to, but such interpretations have no binding effect on anyone.

There are many methods of interpreting legal norms. For example: on the basis of the words of the legal rules—analyzing in accordance with the words or expressions used and the grammar of the rules. This is called the literal meaning method of interpretation. [Another is] bringing together the social phenomena related to the content of the legal norm and reasoning about them logically. This is called logical interpretation, or comparing the position [of the legal norms] in the entire body of the legal system. [Another way is by] comparing them to related legal rules. This is called systemic interpretation. To carry on research into the historical conditions at the time the laws were promulgated, and the process for formulating them, or conducting a comparison of the new and old according to the course of development relating to the rules of law, is called historical interpretation, etc. In order to expound the precise meaning of legal rules, one cannot limit oneself to one method of legal interpretation. When necessary, one can select many methods or all methods.

Sometimes, in order to arrive correctly at the content and nature of legal norms, it is not possible to limit oneself to interpretation of the words of a given norm. When the verbal expression of a rule of law is not the same as its aim and scope, then it is necessary to interpret it in a narrow or broad way in accordance with the spirit of the legislation. The purpose is to bring to light the real meaning of the norm in order to arrive at the correct interpretation and utilization of the legal norms. Any use of a narrow or broad interpretation to change or evade the effect of the law does harm to the legal system. Apart from this, it is necessary to differentiate between the use of analogy and broad interpretation. Broad interpretation is simply extending the scope of the meaning of a legal norm. But analogy means taking questions that are not directly dealt with in the civil law and using the most similar civil law rule to deal with them. The use of analogy actually extends the scope of certain civil law legislation. Consequently it is necessary strictly to control the use of analogy so that the socialist legal system will not be injured.

VI
THE SCOPE AND APPLICATION OF CIVIL LAW

In order to use civil law rules, it is not enough merely to understand the precise meaning, one must also understand the scope of their application because the effectiveness of the individual concrete legal rules is not the same in regard to time, space or persons.

1. The Scope of Application of Civil Law Rules in Respect to Time

That is, the effectiveness of civil law norms in terms of time. Generally speaking, a civil law norm is effective from the day it goes into effect until the day it is repealed. The time when a legal norm takes effect can be determined from the norm itself as provided by law. It can also be set by an order or a decision of the organization that promulgates the rule. Sometimes the legal norm provides "this takes effect from the day of promulgation." Under these circumstances, the day of promulgation of the rule of law is its effective date. Sometimes, although the legal norm has been promulgated, a different effective date has been provided. In these circumstances, it is necessary for the day provided for to arrive, and then [the norm] becomes effective. The terminal date of the legal norm is often not provided by the legislation. Under these circumstances it is effective until the day the law clearly abolishes or amends it. There are also a small number of legal norms which provide, at the time of promulgation, the day at which they will cease to be effective. If, in formulating the law, it is provided that it will be effective during a certain period, then it will take effect when the effective date arrives, and at the time provided for its coming to an end it will cease to be of effect.

Since the state should not require the citizens or juristic persons to observe rules for behavior that do not exist, therefore the legal norm, in terms of time, generally does not have a retroactive effect. Consequently, if civil law relations are created prior to the coming into effect of a new legal norm, in handling the said civil law relations, after the new law has come into effect, the legal norm that was in effect at the time a civil law relation came into being is still applied. Sometimes civil law rules [or] norms can be retroactive, but their retroactivity must be clearly provided. For example, the October 1950 "Methods for Dealing with Disputes Regarding Peasants' Obligations in the Newly Liberated Areas" enacted by the Government Administration Council, provided that "the obligations of peasants and other workers to landlords [that arose] prior to Liberation are hereby entirely abolished." This was a legal rule that was made retroactive to cause the workers to get rid of the shackles of feudal obligations.

2. Scope of Application of Civil Law in Space

That is, the effectiveness of a civil law norm in space. Our civil law norms are all promulgated by the central organs. They are applied in the sovereign land, sea, and air of the People's Republic of China, as well as in the territory subject to our sovereignty according to the principles of international law and international custom. This is the necessary consequence of the principle of national sovereignty.

All laws of a local nature within our national territory can only be effective in the area administered by that locality's people's government. Areas outside can only take notice of them. They cannot be directly used as the legal basis for handling questions. Civil cases that cross several areas that come to the people's courts to be decided, must, in principle, be decided according to the law of the place where the legal relation came into existence.

Our country is one that has many races. According to the Constitution, the people's congresses of minority people's autonomous regions may, according to the special conditions of that area's political, economic, and cultural situation, formulate their own autonomous regulations and separate regulations that become effective after approval by the National People's Congress. The autonomous and separate provisions of autonomous prefectures and counties become effective upon approval of the standing committee of the people's congress of the province or autonomous region. The autonomous legal norms approved by the people's congresses of the said areas have a special legal nature. They must be used in handling relevant cases in those districts.

3. The Scope of Civil Law as to Persons

That is to say, civil law norms are effective in regard to which persons? According to the principle of the equality of rights and duties of our country's civil law, our country's civil law has the same effect towards all those who are registered as citizens of the People's Republic of China regardless of sex, age, occupation, origin, religion, race, or situation as to property. That is, they must all honor the rules of our country's civil law. They may all then receive protection from our country's civil law.

According to the private international law principle of the territoriality of law, when foreign citizens are living in our country, or citizens of our country are living in foreign countries, they must, in principle, use the civil law of the country in which they reside. But, according to our country's law and regulations, and according to treaties and agreements we have signed with other countries, as well as the rules of international custom recognized by our country, under certain circumstances, even citizens of our country who are living in foreign countries still use our country's law. Contrariwise, foreign citizens residing in our country can also use their own country's law. For example, diplomats who have legal immunity are in this category. These persons, except in cases where they wish to use the law of the country in which they reside, are not subject to the jurisdiction of the country in which they reside. Apart from this, there are certain legal questions regarding the capacity to hold rights, the capacity to act, as well as certain personal relations of natural persons, such as the conditions of support, guardianship, marriage, etc., in which, unless there is a clear conflict with the principles of our country's socialist legislation or rules of morality, the natural person will use his own law. This is the private international law principle of matters belonging to the person. According to the principle that persons without nationality use the law of the country where they reside, persons who do not have nationality [stateless persons] who reside in our country must use our law.

Our country's juristic persons (that is juristic persons organized according to our country's rules and permitted to be formed by our government), and our country's citizens, all use our country's laws. They must observe special rules provided in our country for every sort of juristic person. Apart from this, civil law rules on rights and duties that apply to citizens can, in general, be used for juristic persons, except for those which, by their nature, cannot apply to juristic persons.

Foreign juristic persons (that is, juristic persons that are not formed according to our law) which carry on activities in our country in the character of juristic persons, must, pursuant to the provisions of our country's laws, obtain permission from our country's government. The problem of what country's law to apply when there is a dispute relating to the external or internal affairs of a foreign juristic person can be handled on the basis of the concrete circumstances. If our country has a special agreement with the country of the foreign juristic person on the methods of the handling of disputes, then of course this will be used. Otherwise, in principle, we use our country's law. But in circumstances where there is no injury to the interests of our country's sovereignty or citizens and juristic persons, the use of international custom is not excluded. This is advantageous for upholding our country's sovereignty, assuring the security of our country's internal trade, and for protecting the foreign juristic person's necessary rights and interests.

3 Civil Law Relationships

I
GENERAL DISCUSSION OF CIVIL LAW RELATIONSHIPS

Civil law relationships are the concrete social relationships containing rights and duties which are affirmed by the civil law. They are the expression in law of certain property and personal relationships. For example, ownership relationships between subjects, obligation relationships, relationships arising out of the rights of authorship, etc., are all civil law relationships. Engels wrote, "Since economic facts must be legally recognized, they must, in each different situation, take legally provided forms." To cause, by means of forms that are recognized by the law, certain concrete social relationships of daily life to constitute civil law relationships, and to protect their realization by the force of the government, are essential measures [in order] for the state to organize social production and stabilize the social order.

The objects for study of our country's civil law are every type of civil law relationship that arises in our country's socialist society. To study their nature and special characteristics, consider their differences and connections, and master their internal rules, is helpful in explaining the aim of civil law legislation and [in] summing up civil law experience in adjudication. Because of this, in beginning the study of the principles of civil law, it is necessary first that there be a consideration of the general nature of civil law relationships.

Civil law relationships are social relationships. They embody the relationships between persons. There are some capitalist scholars who often speak of certain civil law relations as relations between persons and things. For example, they simply sum up the property relation as one that arranges the relationship between man and things. Actually, property relations originally were relations between persons that arose out of the possession of material objects. In a society of a system of private ownership, this sort of relation embodies, under many circumstances, the relationship of oppressor and oppressed, between a governing class and the class that is governed. It can be seen that they [capitalist scholars] characterize certain civil law relations as control relations between persons and things in order to cover up this sort of relationship of oppression.

A civil law relation is an ideological social relation. It belongs to the superstructure. Its content and origin are determined by a certain social and economic base. Since economic bases are not the same, in different social systems the content and principles of civil law relations are, of necessity, very different. For example, in a society [based on] public ownership of the means of production, the state fulfills, to the fullest extent, the needs of the citizens and society in production and daily life by realizing the national people's economic plan, with the result that in the field of such civil law relations as obligations, our country's civil law legislation particularly emphasizes the principle of actual [specific] performance. Moreover, it absolutely forbids, in all civil law actions, injury to the state economic plan, profiteering, or speculation. In a capitalist society the purpose of production is to obtain a profit, and thus, in civil law relations, there is no emphasis on the principle of actual [specific] performance. It only requires a penalty or damages to satisfy the need to make a profit. The parties would prefer to recover a penalty for breach or damages from the party who does not perform the contract. As for profiteering and speculation, they are simply the usual form of trade activity in capitalist countries.

Civil law relations are social relations whose realization is assured by the force of the state. They are civil law rights-duties relationships which are confirmed by the state and formed by parties. If the obligor does not perform his required obligation, thereby causing the other party to receive an injury, the obligee may bring suit in court and request the court to force the obligor to perform his duty in order to protect the realization of his lawful rights. This special characteristic of civil law relations causes them to be different from the moral relations which are upheld by relying on public opinion.

Civil law relations express the equal, nongratuitous relations between the parties. Moreover they are, in this respect, differentiated from administrative, fiscal, criminal, as well as marriage or family law relations. What must still be pointed out here is that the equal and nongratuitous nature of civil law relations causes them in many situations to have the characteristic of "arbitrariness"; that is, whether or not this sort of relation is formed, and how it is formed, [are matters] that the parties can freely decide on. They can negotiate them fully among themselves. It is abundantly clear that this is not merely something that is essential [in order] for citizens to satisfy their needs of daily life through civil law actions, it is also an essential condition for the measures which must be taken by social organizations to bring into play their initiative, energy, and creativity in fulfilling their obligations for production and construction under the plan.

II
LEGAL FACTS

1. General Concept of Legal Facts

"Legal Facts" refers to objective phenomena which can create, alter, or dissolve civil law relations, among the parties [to these relations]. If there were only legal norms, the civil law rights-duty relationships could not arise between the parties. The rights-duty relationship provided by the legal norm only expresses the possibility that the subject of civil law rights may have rights or assume duties. At the same time it is not every objective phenomenon that can give rise to civil law rights and obligations between the parties. It is only those objective phenomena which the legal norms specify [as having] the capability to produce civil law results that can be legal facts. For example, our country's law provides that citizens may enjoy the right of home ownership but this does not mean that every citizen has his own home. In fact, a citizen's actual right of ownership to a house is obtained by means of the legal fact of buying or constructing a house, etc.

2. The Legal Consequences Produced by Legal Facts

When legal facts appear, they bring about the following consequences:

(1) The creation of a civil law relationship

For example, as the result of the conclusion of a contract of sale, there arises the rights-duty relationship between the parties requiring the conveyance of the object and the payment of the price. As a result of the infringement of a right, there arises between the one causing the injury and the injured party a rights-duty relationship to pay damages.

(2) The alteration of civil law relationships

For example, as the result of the action of the transfer of an obligation right, the subject of rights in the original obligation relation is changed. Sometimes, as a result of a contract of sale not being performed, the sales relationship may be changed into a damages relationship.

(3) Dissolution of civil law rights

For example, the destruction of material things or the payment of an obligation causes the original ownership right or obligation right to disappear.

3. Types of Legal Facts

Legal facts may be divided into the two major categories of circumstances and acts.

(1) Circumstances

This refers to objective phenomena that are not related to the wills of the parties. For example, the occurrence of a fire may give rise to the liability of the insurance company to pay damages. The passage of time may create or destroy a right to request [something]. The death of a man causes the successor to obtain the right to succeed to the estate, etc. In general, these objective phenomena have legal significance in a specified situation. Therefore they are all legal facts.

(2) Acts

This refers to the actions of persons. It can be further divided into: (1) Actions which have as their purpose the production of certain civil law consequences. For example, the formation of a contract, the signing of a will, the bestowing of a written grant of authority to act as representative. (2) Activity which originally was without the intention to produce legal consequences but which subsequently produces civil law consequences, for example, a negligent action that injures another. Apart from this, the judgments and decisions of courts can give rise to certain civil law consequences. Therefore they must also belong to the [category] of legal facts.

Civil law relations sometimes can come into existence or be altered or dissolved when there is only one legal fact. Sometimes there must be two or more legal facts that are joined together. For example, the establishment of the loan relation not only requires the agreement of the parties, but it also requires the act of the lender [in] giving the lent object to the borrower. Again, the sale of the house not only requires the action of the two parties in signing the contract of sale, it also requires the housing administration office to go through the housing transfer procedure before certain civil law relations can exist. We classify all these legal facts together as factual constituent acts.

III
THE ESSENTIAL ELEMENTS OF CIVIL LAW RELATIONS

Every civil law relation contains the three essential component parts of: subject, content, and object. We call these together, the essential elements of civil law relations.

1. The Subject

The subjects of civil law relations are the parties to civil law relations. They enjoy and assume the rights and obligations specified by the said civil law relations. They can be natural persons (citizens), they can also be juristic persons. They can also be partnership organizations. Under certain specified situations, the state can also appear in the role of the subject of civil law, for example, in issuing government bonds in the name of the state, or when it receives property for which there is no owner or heir. When the state is a civil law subject, it often appears in the name of the state treasury.

In civil law relations, the one who has rights is known as the subject of rights. The one who assumes duties is known as the subject of duties. In most cases, those participating in civil law relations are subjects of rights and they are also the subjects of duties. For example, in a sales contract, the seller assumes the duty to transfer the object of sale to the ownership of the other party. The buyer [*sic*—apparently a misprint for seller] then has the right to demand the payment of the price. On the other hand, the buyer has the right to demand the delivery of the object of sale. At the same time he has the duty to pay the price. In a few cases, one of the parties to a civil law relation only has the right, and the other party only has the duty. For example, in a loan contract the lender only has the right to demand return of the thing when the time arrives. The borrower only has the duty to return, but this is because the lender hands over the borrowed item to the borrower at the time of concluding the contract of loan, and has already assumed his own obligation.

The subjects of rights and duties in civil law relations can be single, or one or both sides can be composed of several persons. In civil law obligation relations, the subject of rights and the subject of duties can both only be specified persons. In ownership legal relations the subject of rights is a specified person. But the subject of duties is not specified and [can be] anyone.

2. The Content

The content of civil law relations consists of the rights and duties of the persons who are parties to the relations. The right refers to the ability of one of the parties to realize certain interests, and the duty refers to the necessity for one party to fulfill the demand for a certain interest, to perform a certain act (or omission). The right and duty are mutually dependent and mutually related. In different civil law relations the content of the parties' rights and duties are also different. For example, the rights of the parties in the sale relation and the lease relation are very different. Even in the same type of civil law relation the concrete scope of rights and duties can be quite different. This is defined by the actual requirements of the parties in the course of production and living, but the common aspects are all determined by the law, and all rely on the power of the state to protect their realization. Civil law relations all rely on the use of force according to law. That is, the social relations of the parties are effectuated and determined by means of rights-duty relationships. To be sure, this is essential for the governing class to establish and maintain the soundness of the social economic order according to its own will.

3. The Object

The object of a civil law relationship refers to the matter to which the rights and duties are directed. If the civil law rights and duties do not have a concrete matter to which they are directed, then, because they have no goal, they cannot be carried out and lose their significance.

However, [the question] what is the object of civil law relations, that is, what is the "matter" at which the civil rights and duties are directed, is something that is much disputed in the circles of scholars of civil law.

Some assert that the object of civil law relations is a "thing" since the direction towards which any civil law rights and duties are directed is expressed as a certain actual interest that is realized on the basis of things.

Others assert that things (including nonmaterial wealth) and actions can both be the objects of civil law. If the object is a property relation it is a thing. The object of an obligation relation is a certain action.

There are also those who assert that the civil law relation is a unified concept. Its object must also be a unified concept. It is not appropriate to take the two different conditions of "thing" and "action" and separately constitute them as objects of civil law. They believe that in a civil law relation, a thing can only serve as the aim, it cannot be the object. Since neither mere things nor actions can serve as the essential elements of civil law relations, it is only when they are brought together to form "an action that realizes a certain material interest" that they can form the object of civil law relations. A civil law object, must, after all, be that which has a certain advantageous result. Thus the object of a sale is the act of transferring the subject matter of this sale. The object of a transportation relation is the act of transporting safely and promptly the thing which is to be transported. The object of an ownership relation is the act of possessing, using, or disposing of an ownership right.

IV
THE TYPES OF CIVIL LAW RIGHTS

The rights and duties of civil law rights are reciprocal. In this division [of this chapter] the types of civil law rights that are discussed are also types of civil law duties. But many institutions of civil law are only named from the point of view of rights. For example, ownership rights, obligation rights, the subject of rights, the object of rights, and the rights of authorship or invention. This is because, in civil law relations, rights usually appear as the dominant aspect. From the point of view of rights, it is easy to reflect directly the scope and the subject of rights. This is advantageous for the protection of lawful rights. Moreover, there are a number of civil law rights that may be discarded by their owners, but duties may not be discarded. Consequently, it is still easier to reflect [in one's analysis] the special characteristics of civil law relations by proceeding from rights.

Civil law rights may be divided into many types according to their nature and special characteristics. Conducting a contrasting study is helpful in advancing in the understanding of civil law. Civil law rights have the following divisions:

1. Property Rights and Personal Rights

Where civil law rights are looked at from the point of view of whether they have or do not have a property content, they may be divided into property rights and personal rights. "Property rights" refers to rights that have a material content or appear directly as an economic interest, such as ownership, obligation rights, and intangible property rights (such as publication rights, patent rights, trademark rights). "Personal rights" refers to rights with no property content which cannot be separated from the person of the subject of rights. For example, rights of the personality (the right to life, health, freedom, one's name, likeness, etc.), rights of status (such as relationship, guardianship, etc. The rights of authorship and invention are also of this type since these rights can only be enjoyed by the author or the inventor.) Property rights can be assigned among the subjects but personal rights are nonassignable.

2. Absolute Rights and Relative Rights

When civil law rights are considered from the point of view of the area they affect they may be divided into absolute rights and relative rights. "Absolute rights" refers to ownership, personal rights, etc. Relative rights are obligations. The difference between the two lies in the fact that the subject of an absolute right usually does not depend on the other party who has the duty to help him by positive action (an act). It is only necessary that the one having the duty not interfere (an omission). That is, he can himself realize his rights. Moreover, the one having the duty is not a specified person. Therefore, the absolute right is also called a right against the world. The subject of a relative right must normally depend on the subject of the duty engaging in an action [that is, performing his duty] and then he can realize his right. Moreover, the subject of a duty is always a specified person, therefore, a relative right is also called a right against a person.

3. Rights to Request and Formative Rights

From the point of view of the use of civil law rights, they may be divided into rights to request and formative rights. The right to request is the right to request someone else to perform a certain act or not to perform a certain act. An obligation right is this sort of right. A formative right refers to the holder of the right being able to rely solely on his own act (such as the act of ratification, the act of authorization, the act of annulment, the act of waiver of rights), that is, rights that can create, change, or destroy civil law rights.

4. Principal Rights and Accessory Rights

Looking at civil law rights from the point of view of their mutual relationships, a distinction can be made between the principal right and the accessory right. The principal right is the right which, as between two mutually related civil law rights, can exist independently. The accessory right is the right which depends on the existence of the principal right for its existence. For example, the pledge right, the mortgage right, the lien right, etc., are all accessory rights for which the existence of the principal right is a prerequisite. The relationship of principal and accessory between the two rights results in the fact that with the assignment or cancellation of the principal right, the accessory right is also accordingly assigned or cancelled.

V
PROHIBITION OF THE ABUSE OF RIGHTS

1. The General Content of the Abuse of Rights

According to the law, a civil law right receives the protection of the law. However, the subject of rights, while exercising his rights, must respect socialist law and morality. He may not abuse civil law rights.

The so-called abuse of rights is the exercise by the subject of a right in a way that exceeds the scope provided by law or morality. It is an act that causes injury to the other person in society. The act of abuse of rights is prohibited by law.

In Roman law, owing to the notion of individual selfishness, the abuse of rights, like the subject of rights, was not a matter that was looked into by the law. At the time of free capitalism, since the principle of individualism permeated civil law, there were no legal limits on the exercise, by the subject of rights, of his rights. The subject of rights could exercise them in any way. After the period of monopoly capitalism, [because of the need of] the ruling class to adjust the contradiction between the rights of the individual and the interests of society, and in order to uphold the interests of the entire capitalist class, there began to appear in continental case law the rule prohibiting the abuse of rights. Therefore, this was ratified by the legislation of several continental systems. However, in the common law systems there was no rule on the abuse of rights.

The civil codes of countries with a system of public ownership all recognize the system of abuse of rights. The Soviet Russian Civil Code of 1922 provides in section 7 that "civil law rights are protected by law except where their exercise violates the mission of the economy and society." Section 5 of the subsequent General Civil Law Legislation, as well as section 5 of the Civil Code of 1964, also contain similar provisions. The Hungarian Civil Code of 1959 provides in section 2.2 that "when, at the time of the exercise of the right, the purpose violates the said right's social aim, particularly when the exercise of the right can injure the state economy, cause citizens to be disturbed, injure the rights and lawful interests of citizens, or [is used] to acquire an unlawful interest for oneself, these are all [instances of the] abuse of rights." It can be seen that countries with public ownership proceeding from [a policy] of upholding society's interests emphatically prohibit the abuse of rights.

In our country's law, article 51 of the Constitution provides: "The citizens of the People's Republic of China, when exercising freedom and rights, may not injure the interests of the state, society, or collectivities nor the lawful freedom and rights of other citizens." The spirit of this rule is that of prohibiting the abuse of rights.

Our country's civil law puts into practice the integration of state and collective interests, brings into realization the unity of the interests of society and the interests of individuals. The civil law wholeheartedly encourages the subjects of rights and the exercise of their rights and protects their legitimate rights. At the same time it also establishes limits on the lawful use of civil law rights. Exceeding limits set by law or morality, and violation of the interests of others or society, [are matters] that the law is concerned with. Consequently, considering matters from the point of view and aim of the general principles of our country's civil law, an action in abuse of rights is forbidden by the civil law.

2. The Essential Conditions of Abuse of Rights

How does one decide if the subject of rights has abused his rights? Considering the point of view of the rules of law, and the decisions of different countries, the standards of decision are not the same. In the main there are the following types: exercising rights and intentionally injuring another; exercising rights without an appropriate interest; selecting a harmful manner of exercising rights; at the time of the exercise of rights, the injury inflicted on the other is greater than the benefit that one acquires; exercising rights [in a way] that does not accord with the aims of society; violating the general principle of the law of delict, etc. In general they may be divided between the "subjective theory" and the "objective theory." In the subjective theory, if, at the time of the exercise of the rights, there is an evil will to exercise an intentional abuse of rights, then this is regarded as an abuse of rights. Under the "objective theory," if, at the time of the exercise of the rights, there is an invasion of the rights of another person and the interests of society, this is regarded as an abuse of rights.

According to our country's judicial experience, for an action to constitute an abuse of rights, it must meet the following conditions.

(1) The right must exist

Abuse of a right first of all requires an existing right. That is, the actor has a civil law right. If the actor does not have a right that he possesses, but is carrying out some action that injures some other person and society, then this is an action of infringement of rights [and not an abuse of rights].

(2) The action exercising the right causes injury to another person in society

Even though the actor has a right which he exercises, if it does not cause injury to another person in society, then this does not constitute an abuse of rights. There are many acts exercising rights that cause injury to other persons in society. For example, a [property] owner who piles up garbage or dirt or poisonous things in front of his door and injures his neighbors. The person who, in using land, blocks ground or running water, and harms the interests of another. The representative who plots with a third person to obtain an unlawful gain and injures the principal. The above instances show clearly an abuse of ownership, the right to use land, the right of representation.

(3) The actor is at fault

Under this rule, the standard for the degree of fault is that the actor has violated the duty set by law. The law provides that the holder of the right in exercising his rights may not exceed the limits set by law and morality. If the actor in exercising his rights exceeds the limits set by law and morality, this amounts to fault. It does not matter whether or not subjectively the actor is intentionally or negligently at fault. Both constitute abuse of rights.

3. The Legal Consequences of Abuse of Rights

The act of abuse of rights is not a true exercise of rights, and consequently does not receive legal protection. Actually this act cannot produce the legal consequences foreseen by the actor. Moreover, when the act of abuse of rights causes injury to the lawful rights of others and society, the law, in order to protect the genuine rights and punish the unlawful acts, must cause the one who has abused rights to assume legal responsibility. Consequently, the parties who have been injured because of abuse of rights, may, according to the methods for the protection of property rights and obligation rights, by means of a law suit, demand that the people's court punish the unlawful act of the actor and protect [them] and, moreover, protect their own lawful rights from being injured.

VI
THE PROTECTION OF CIVIL LAW RIGHTS

Civil law rights are rights whose realization in law is protected by the force of the state. When these rights are unlawfully infringed by others, the parties, by means of a civil action, demand that the state protect them.

In our socialist country, owing to the implementation of the system of public ownership of the means of production, the basic interests of every kind of rights-duty relationship that arises between the parties are identical. Normally the great majority of the rights-duty relationships between the parties can be handled correctly, consciously, and voluntarily by the parties themselves. If there is an act that infringes the lawful rights of another, the actor may, according to law, on his own initiative, pay damages, or, by means of negotiation, arrive at a satisfactory solution. To be sure, this does not mean that there will not be some civil law disputes that arise as the result of disagreements among the parties that cannot be resolved. Under these conditions, if they wish to realize their own lawful rights, it can only be by suing in court or in an arbitration tribunal to have them decide the matter.

Whenever any party's (citizen or juristic person) civil law rights are injured by the unlawful act of another, all may demand protection according to law. This is to uphold the socialist economic order, strengthen the socialist system of public ownership, realize the state's economic plan, and give the necessary assurances to the lawful interests of the citizen. The right to bring an action in court is the basic right of the subject [of rights] given by the state, which he cannot be deprived of. Even if one announces that he has discarded this right, the law does not recognize the effect of the surrender.

Civil law rights are realized in many ways. Civil law rights may also be infringed in many ways. There are many types of actions which a party may bring in court. If the actions in court are classified, the majority fall into the following categories.

(1) An action for performance

This is a suit requesting the court to order the other party to perform some act to bring about the realization of one's own right. For example, the obligee seeks delivery of a thing, the payment of the price or a penalty, damages, etc. The request of the owner of property to have a hindrance in the exercise of his rights removed is also this type of action. An action for performance is the most extensive civil law action.

(2) An action for confirmation

This is an action in which the court is requested to confirm whether some right exists or not. For example, confirmation of ownership to property; confirmation of whether some sort of personal relationship exists; confirmation whether a contract relation is or is not effective.

(3) An action for formation

This is an action to request a court by means of a judgment to form some new right (duty) or to cause some right (duty) to appear. For example, to bring a suit to request the division of commonly held property, or to relieve one from the duty to perform, or to terminate a contract relationship, to dissolve an adoption, to request a declaration of death, etc.

The above types of actions are concrete ways in which the state protects the realization of the lawful rights of the subject of civil law [rights].

Within the field of civil law norms, there are a large number that are optional. That is, the exercise or abandonment of some civil law right can be decided on by the holder of the rights. When some civil law rights are trespassed against, if the injured party does not initiate suit, the court will not decide the matter. These situations, for the most part, involve the rights of citizens among themselves. Since whether or not the citizen exercises these rights does not hinder the general social good, the will of the individual must be respected. However, if the circumstances mentioned above arise between socialist organizations, particularly between organizations with property owned by the whole people, the situation is not the same because their exercise of their lawful rights not only affects the interests of the organization, but has a close relation to the upholding of the state's economic interest, and the economic order, as well as the effectiveness of the state economic plan. Therefore they can not, at will, abandon these lawful rights as citizens can. When a civil law dispute arises among them, and they are unable to negotiate a settlement, they must seek arbitration by an arbitration organ, or bring an action in a court. [Thus] the socialist organizations can distinguish clearly that which is right and wrong, clearly divide up responsibilities and receive state supervision in order to reform their work, and fulfill their responsibilities. When certain civil law disputes between socialist organizations result in very serious consequences for the national economy, the state must intervene. Every level of our country's procuracy is a supervisory organization of the law. It has the right to investigate not merely in criminal, but also, in the same way, in civil cases. This is because in our country's economic sphere all relations are "public." In order to protect lawful civil law rights, the concerned units may support the action. Section 13 of the [Trial] Civil Procedure Code of the People's Republic of China provides that "Organizations, collectivities, enterprises and units, in regard to acts that injure national, collective or individual rights, may support the action of the injured unit or individual in the people's court."

Civil law rights (property rights, personal rights) are protected not only by our country's civil law, but also by our country's criminal law, administrative law, and other related laws.

VII
CIVIL RESPONSIBILITY

1. The General Concept of Civil Responsibility

The content of civil law relations is formed by civil law rights and duties. When the subject of civil law does not perform his duty he may harm the rights of the other party. At the same time he violates a legal rule. Consequently, he must assume civil responsibility.

Civil responsibility refers to the legal consequences incurred when the subject of civil law violates his duty. It is a kind of independent responsibility within legal responsibility. Its special characteristics are:

(1) Civil responsibility is premised on the existence of a civil law duty

A civil law duty arises according to the provisions of law and the agreement of the parties. Actually the duty agreed upon by the parties arises according to law, and, as a result, this duty has legal effectiveness. Section 6 of our Economic Contract

Law provides that "as soon as an economic contract is formed according to the law, it has legally binding force and the parties must fully perform the obligations stipulated in the contract." It may be seen that regardless of whether a duty is prescribed by law or by agreement of the parties, every party must completely perform his own duty. The violation of the duty is a kind of unlawful act and it must be punished by the law.

(2) Civil responsibility is a legal punishment for the violation of a civil law duty

With the use of the form of civil responsibility, there are two forms for the legal punishment of one who has acted illegally. One is directly provided by the law: punishment by action of the people's court. For example, [the court may] order the wrongdoer to assume liability to pay damages. The second is according to the provisions of a contract—the exercise by the parties of the right to impose sanctions given them by the law. That is to say, the parties select and clearly provide in the contract the form and content of responsibility for violation of a contract. When one party breaches the contract, then he is liable according to the contract. If the obligor does not perform, or refuses to assume his responsibility to the obligee, the injured person may demand that the people's court force him to perform or assume responsibility. Since, in the final analysis, civil responsibility is created and determined by the law and is moreover protected by the state's compulsory powers, the existence of civil responsibility is not conditioned on the obligee or injured person bringing suit. As soon as the obligor fails to perform his obligation, the consequences of his responsibility arise.

(3) Civil responsibility is most importantly property responsibility

Since the objects of civil law adjustment are, for the most part, property relations [formed] on the basis of equality and equal value, civil responsibility is principally property responsibility. The property responsibility imposed by the court on the one who acts unlawfully can protect the parties' lawful property interests from being injured. Since the objects adjusted by civil law also include nonproperty personal relations that are related to property relations and which are also of many types, achieving the aims of civil responsibility is not limited to property responsibility. It also includes those forms of nonproperty relations such as signing a statement of repentance or making an apology.

(4) Civil responsibility is a form of independent legal responsibility that is determined by civil law

In our country's feudal system, since criminal law was emphasized and [the importance of] civil [law] was minimized and criminal and civil [law] were not differentiated, cases involving monetary obligations, family, marriage, and land matters were often handled by the use of criminal procedure. Consequently, in fact there was no independent civil responsibility. At present, our country's civil law is an independent body of law. The civil responsibility determined by civil law also forms a kind of independent legal responsibility. It is not the same as criminal or administrative responsibility, nor may it substitute for these kinds of responsibility. Consequently, in practice, civil law can be used independently and it can also be used in conjunction with the other branches of law. Where the one who has acted unlawfully assumes his civil responsibility, he may not avoid the other types of responsibility to which he is subject. He may also not avoid his civil responsibility that he must assume.

Civil responsibility is in conflict with unlawful acts. Moreover, the protection of the civil law must be by means of the weapon of respecting it. The correct use of civil responsibility is of great significance in protecting lawful rights and promoting the performance of obligations. The correct use of civil responsibility can build a normal legal order in the life of society, particularly, in the area of civil law circulation. It is extremely useful in connection with the speedy compensation of the harm received by the injured party, and instructing the wrongdoer in observing discipline and upholding the law, and preventing or diminishing the appearance of unlawful acts.

2. The General Principles of Civil Responsibility

The general principle of civil responsibility is the principle of liability for fault. According to this principle, only when the actor has [committed] a fault is he civilly responsible. If there is no fault, then he is not civilly responsible. In early times, ancient law, such as Germanic law, Babylonian law, etc., all used the principle of liability for the result, which is also called the principle of causing harm. In general, [according to this principle], when the actor causes harm to another, regardless of whether he is at fault or not, he is liable for damages. This is simply described as the principle, "when injury is caused then there is liability." In the Twelve Tables the concept of intention and negligence began to be put forward from the point of view of reducing liability. The Lex Aquilia of 287 B.C. formally got rid of the principle of causing harm, and adopted the principle of liability for fault.

From the beginning of the 19th century, the principle of liability for fault was adopted in the civil codes of continental Europe. Moreover, it was recognized as the general principle. In the French Civil Code of 1804, section 1384 provided: "In the case of an act which causes another to be injured, the person who causes the injury to occur by his own fault is liable to pay damages to the other." [This seems to be section 1382, though the reference is to section 1384.] This rule forms a basic principle of civil responsibility. Section 832.1 of the German Civil Code, enacted in 1900, also recognized this principle. The civil codes of Holland, Italy, Spain, and other countries also adopted the rule of section 1382 of the French Civil Code and made liability for fault the general rule. This rule, together with the unlimited right of private property, and "freedom of contract" were all suited to serve the requirements of the bourgeoisie in the time of free competition, and were a procedure for protecting the interests of the bourgeoisie.

In the common law legal system, since [the law of] torts arises out of case law, there are no general principles of the law of delicts. But at the end of the 13th century there appeared in the common law and in the action of "trespass on the case" the concept of "negligence of failure to pay attention," and in subsequent times there appeared the concept of "intention" and "negligence." In 1932, in England, in the case of Donoghue v. Stevenson [presumably] the common law formally recognized the system of "negligent torts." After this system appeared, it was used not only in "negligent torts" cases, but also in other torts cases. It can be seen that the scope of the principle of negligence in common law was gradually increased.

The civil law of the socialist countries also adopted the principle of fault liability. In 1922, section 403 of the Civil Code of the Soviet Russian Republic provided: "One who causes injury to the person or property of another must bear the responsibility to make compensation for all the injury that was caused; if he can prove that it was unavoidable or that it was an authorized act or if the injury was the result of the injured person's intention or gross negligence he will not be liable." Section 444 of the 1964 Code continues to recognize this principle. Both section 404 of the 1922 Civil Code and section 422 of the 1964 Civil Code make responsibility for a high risk that causes injury to another an exception to the principle of liability for fault. Liability for high risk employs the principle of nonfault responsibility.

From the end of the 19th century to the beginning of the 20th, independent capitalism entered the phase of monopoly capitalism. In this period, since, in the field of industrial production there were frequently industrial accidents, but the principle of responsibility for negligence resulted in [the rule] "whoever has an accident is liable for it," this had the consequence of seriously injuring the interests of the working class and created a worsening in the contradictions between the classes. As a result of the struggles of the working class, and the need of the monopoly capitalists for some relaxation in the class contradictions, some countries, either in the form of case law or of directly promulgated legislation, began to apply nonfault liability in the field of industrial accidents. Gradually no-fault liability extended to traffic accidents, environmental pollution, injury caused by atomic injury, as well as injury caused by defective commodities, etc. Particularly owing to the development, in the societies of that time, of insurance, after the one causing the injury assumed liability, he could, by means of liability insurance, transfer the risk to innumerable other [insured] persons, and cause his own liability to be limited. This greatly promoted the development of no-fault liability. Moreover, it caused the educational value of civil responsibility as a punishment of the wrongdoer to be constantly reduced.

From the point of view of the requirements of the general aim of our country's civil law, and of our country's judicial experience, our civil law has made the principle of liability for fault a general principle. It is only when there is someone who, by his own fault, has inflicted injury by an unlawful act on the lawful rights of the state, a collectivity, or another person that there can be civil responsibility. It is useful so that socialist public property and the lawful rights of citizens can be protected. Parties can be instructed in obeying discipline and obeying the law, and preventing and reducing the occurrence of injury. If civil liability is imposed on one who is without fault, then it is difficult to achieve the aim of educating the parties. However, at the same time that liability for fault has been made a general principle of civil responsibility, it is also necessary to adopt the principle of no-fault liability in special situations clearly provided by law. These exceptions are principally in cases of injury resulting from high risk [activities] and environmental pollution.

3. Two Types of Civil Responsibility

Civil responsibility includes two types of liability, contract and delict.

Contractual liability refers to one of the parties to a contract failing to perform and being liable. Delictual liability refers to a subject of civil law infringing on the property or personal rights of another or on his intellectual property rights. In this book, we distinguish between these two types of responsibility in chapter 18. In chapter 19 there are concrete explanations. Here, there is a general discussion of the differences between the two types of liability.

In every country of the continental legal system, contracts and delicts are regarded as the basis for creating obligations. They are separately called contractual obligations and delictual obligations, or they are called voluntary obligations and nonvoluntary obligations and are placed under "obligations" in the law. Contractual responsibility and delictual responsibility are also separately provided for by obligation law. In common law, the rules that affect contracts and those that affect torts form a system of contract law and a system of tort law. In these two types of law there are provided two different types of responsibility. Even though, in foreign legislation, liability is divided into two types, in practice, because of the requirements of the convenience of the courts in deciding actual cases, frequently the two different types of liability are mixed up.

From the perspective of the requirements of our country's legislation and judicial experience, contractual liability and delictual liability have to be analyzed separately, according to different circumstances, and used as different types of responsibility. Even though both contractual and delictual responsibility are a part of civil responsibility, in the final analysis they are not the same.

(1) The legal basis for using [contractual and delictual responsibility] is not the same

The injured object of a delict is the right—personal, intellectual, or property, etc.—of the other person. In handling cases of delict [infringement of rights] the rules of civil law that are related to delicts are used. But what is injured by an act of breach of contract, is the obligation right of the obligee. In handling it [a breach of contract], it is necessary to make use of the civil law rules relating to nonperformance of the obligation.

(2) The prerequisites for responsibility are not the same

Contractual liability and delictual liability both come into existence as the result of the violation of a duty. But contractual liability is usually the result of a duty intentionally created by the breaching party. When this duty is breached there is already an agreement between the parties. But the delict is the violation of a duty directly imposed by law. When this duty is violated, the parties do not have a rights-duty relationship. A rights-duty relationship only comes into being because of the delictual act of one party.

(3) The conditions for formation of liability are not the same

From the subjective point of view, in the case of contractual liability it is only necessary that there be the subjective fault of the parties regardless of whether it is intentional or negligent. In both cases there is liability. Moreover, this question [of intent or negligence] does not affect the outcome. But in the case of delictual responsibility the degree of the wrongdoer's fault is not the same. There must be differences in the consequences. An intentional delict sometimes amounts to a crime. Looking at the objective requirements, the creation of contractual liability does not require the existence of harm. It only requires the existence of the breach and then there is liability. But in the case of delictual liability there must be actual harm caused to the other party. Only when there is actual harm can there be liability.

(4) The forms of liability are not the same

In contractual liability the most important forms are the contractual penalty and damages. But in the case of delicts the form of contract penalty cannot be used. At the same time that the wrongdoer becomes liable to pay damages he may also be liable for such forms of liability as repentance, apology, etc.

In general, making the proper distinction between contractual and delictual liability is not insignificant for properly using the law and handling disputes of civil responsibility and protecting the lawful rights of the parties according to law.

4. The Forms of Responsibility

Since the actual circumstances in which civil responsibility arises are not the same, as a consequence the injuries are not the same. The forms of liability that are used are not the same. According to our country's relevant civil law rules and judicial practice, the following are the most important forms of civil responsibility.

(1) Damages

When the wrongdoer causes property injury to the other party, then he must make up the economic injury created for the injured party out of his own property. This form of civil responsibility is used both in contractual responsibility and delictual responsibility.

(2) Penalties for breach of contract

Liquidated damages for breaches of contract are also called penalties. This refers to the situation where, according to law, or the prior agreement of the parties, after there has been a breach of contract, the breaching party pays the other party a certain sum of money. This form of responsibility is normally used only in the case of contractual responsibility.

(3) Repentance payment

This is also called a consolation payment. This refers to the liability incurred by the wrongdoer when he violates the rights of the person or rights of the character of the other person, inflicting mental injury on the other person or his relations, for example, slandering another's character and causing him to suffer mental pain. The wrongdoer must pay the injured person a sum of money provided by law to serve as mental consolation. This form of liability is especially important in cases of delict. It is adopted when other forms of liability cannot be used. The amount of the repentance payment can be agreed upon by the parties or determined by the court according to the circumstances.

(4) Removing an impediment, restoring the original conditions, eliminating the danger, and returning the original property

These forms of liability are principally used in cases involving ownership or possession. They are measures for protecting ownership rights and other property rights. But in some circumstances they can also be used in cases of contract liability, for example, requiring the return of property obtained under an ineffective contract.

(5) Fines

The fine is a type of punishment inflicted by the people's court or an arbitration tribunal on the wrongdoer who has violated rules of civil law. A fine is a liability imposed by the state, incurred by the party who has directly violated the rule of law. Consequently, it is not the same as a penalty for violating the contract (or a sum of money for violating the contract) set by the contract for violation and paid to the other party to the contract. The fine is the form of civil law liability assumed by the party when he violates the law. Consequently, it is not an administrative law punishment nor a criminal punishment since it is not the same as the administrative or criminal law fine.

(6) A signed [statement] of repentance

This form is the formal expression of a desire to repent made by the wrongdoer in a manner provided by law. When the circumstances of the illegal acts executed by the wrongdoer are not too odious, and he himself has sincerely repented, or there are other reasons for lightening the treatment of the matter, the court may order a period of consideration and he may be ordered to sign a document of repentance. At the same time that the wrongdoer assumes other types of liability, he may [also] be liable to sign a [statement of] repentance.

(7) Restoring the reputation, eliminating influence, making an apology

When a wrongdoer violates the personal rights or character of another, for example, when he destroys the commercial credit of a certain juristic person or injures a citizen's reputation, the wrongdoer must be ordered to take the measures appropriate to restore the reputation or reduce the influence or apologize.

(8) Stopping the infringement

When a wrongdoer has infringed the property, personal, or intellectual property rights of another, the injured party has the right to demand that the one causing the injury cease the infringement or he may request the people's court to order the wrongdoer to cease the infringement in order to prevent the increase of the infringement.

The above discussed measures can be used singly or they can be used together. But when they are used, the actual circumstances must be considered in order for appropriate ones to be selected.

4 Citizens

I
THE LEGAL POSITION OF CITIZENS

The legal position of citizens refers to every sort of basic right which the state accords to its citizens to participate in civil law activities. It includes the whole field of qualifications of the subject [of rights] and the scope of rights. Every country in the world calls persons who have the qualification of having civil law rights based on their natural condition "natural persons." They are distinguished from juristic persons, but "natural persons" includes foreigners and those who do not have nationality [stateless persons].

The condition whereby a person who has the qualification to be the subject of rights in the natural world has the legal position of a citizen is not something that is bestowed by heaven, nor is it something that comes with birth. It is determined by a particular social form of production. Because of this, after mankind entered the class society in countries of different types, the legal position of [persons] was also different.

In a slave society the slave is a tool of the slave owner— [albeit one] that can talk. In ancient Roman law, "persons" refers only to free men. Only free people have, in law, the legal character of persons. Slaves were seen as "things." They could not have any rights.

It can be seen that in a slave society only a small number of persons had the position in law of being persons, that is, had the qualification to be the subject of rights. But the absolute majority of the total number of persons were slaves and members of the master's household, and either did not have any rights, or did not have the complete capacity to be the subjects of rights. Just as Engels said, "Among the Greeks and Romans inequality of persons was much more evident than any kind of equality. If one considers the ancient Greeks and barbarians, free people and slaves, citizens and wards, Roman citizens and Roman subjects (in a broad sense)—all might claim an equal political position but in the opinion of the ancient people, that would have been madness." [Marx-Engels]

In feudal society, the legal position of the peasants (or serfs) was greatly changed from that of slaves. The feudal land-owning class did not have the life-and-death power over persons that slave owners had. Rather, they recognized peasants as being independent subjects in order to encourage their interest in work. Thus many peasants were placed under feudal exploitation. "The independent economy conducted by the peasants on their own share [of land] was a condition of the existence of the landlord economy. Its purpose was not to assure that the peasants would have the requirements of daily life but to assure that the land owners would have a work force." [Lenin] In a hierarchical feudal society, people had different legal positions because of differences in class, status, job, gender, etc. How many rights a person had, or how great they were, depended on how high his position was in the feudal scale. In the situation in which the landowner had a great quantity of land, the peasants were so bound to the landlord's land that they were almost things that belonged to the land. There were different degrees of dependence in relation to the land-owning class, which was in a situation of exploitation and oppression.

"Equality before the law" was the slogan at the time of the bourgeois revolution. They broadcast the ideas of "heaven bestowed rights" ("sovereignty of the people"). They maintained that men were born equal, that the nation belonged to all citizens, and all the persons in the country were citizens, that all citizens were equal before the law, etc. After the bourgeoisie obtained political power, these slogans were reflected in the constitutions. Moreover, they became a sort of basic principle of the civil law, but the bourgeois revolution merely substituted the capitalist private ownership system and its oppression for the private ownership system and oppression of feudalism. It could not really bring about the equality of everyone before the law. This determined the falsity of bourgeois law.

Under our country's socialist system, since private ownership of the means of production is abolished, and a socialist system of public ownership has been established, in carrying out the principle of distribution according to work, [we] have basically eliminated the origins of the economy that produced inequality, and have established the necessary conditions for equality of all men before the law. Our country's first constitution solemnly declared that "in the People's Republic of China all power belongs to the people" (section 1). Our country's present [1982] constitution reaffirms: "The citizens of the People's Republic of China are equal before the law" (section 33). According to this principle, in our country [people of] every race, without distinction as to sex, or as to whether their employment position is high or low, or their property is much or little, have an equal position before the law. This principle is expressed in civil law matters in that all citizens who are registered as citizens of our country have equal civil law positions and also have the same rights to participate in civil law activities.

A system of socialist public ownership is the economic foundation of our country's citizens having an equal legal position. Consequently, the uninterrupted strengthening and development of our country's socialist public ownership economy will serve as an ever greater material safeguard for our citizens' participation in civil law acts in realizing their own rights.

II
THE CAPACITY OF OUR COUNTRY'S CITIZENS TO HAVE CIVIL LAW RIGHTS [RECHTSFÄHIGKEIT]

1. The General Concept of Capacity to Have Civil Law Rights [*Rechtsfähigkeit*]

The capacity to have civil law rights [Rechtsfähigkeit] is the qualification that citizens must have in order to have civil law rights and to assume civil law obligations. To have the capacity to have civil law rights means to have legal personality. The capacity to have civil law rights is a condition of being a subject of civil law rights.

The capacity to have civil law rights in our country has a socialist character. This is expressed first in the equality of the citizen's capacity to have civil law rights. Every citizen can act as the equal subject of a civil law right. This is a necessary reflection of our country's principle of equality before the law. There can be no limitation or disregard of the capacity to have civil law rights except according to law. Secondly, it is expressed in the identity of rights and duties. The capacity of citizens to have civil law rights includes the capacity of citizens to enjoy civil law rights. It also includes the capacity of citizens to assume civil law duties. In other words, the citizen is the subject of rights. He is also the subject of duties. Citizens have the civil law rights bestowed upon them by the state law. At the same time they must perform the civil law duties required by the state law. This sort of integration between rights and duties changes the separation between rights and duties [that exists in] societies of the exploiting classes. Third, this is expressed as the material guaranty of the realization of the citizen's capacity to have civil law rights. These are all very important indications of the difference between the capacity to have civil law rights in our country and the capacity to have civil law rights in all the oppressing countries.

2. The Content of the Capacity to Have Civil Law Rights

The content of the capacity to have civil law rights refers to the scope provided by the law to the ability of citizens to have civil law rights.

Our country's constitution, apart from providing that citizens have equal rights in the political, economic, and social spheres, also provides, in the field of citizen's property, protection of the citizen's income, savings, housing, and other lawful property rights, as well as the right to succeed to property rights.

In regard to the personal rights of citizens, our country's constitution provides that the personal freedom of citizens of the People's Republic of China cannot be infringed. Citizens have the right, according to law, to personal freedom, to life and health, to their names, to happiness, to their likenesses. There is the right to an occupation [job], which will never be interfered with by the law. There is the right to carry on a trade that is not forbidden by the law. There is the right to form a juristic person that is not forbbiden by the law, as well as the right to discover, develop, and create in the realm of science and art.

In accordance with the development of our country's socialist construction, the capacity of our country's citizens to have civil law rights must become still more substantial and extensive.

At the same time that our country's socialist legal system is bestowing on citizens extensive legal rights, it is also requiring the citizen to assume the duties he is responsible for, and to cherish common property and uphold the common interest and to respect the rights and interests of others. No one may claim the exercise of his own rights as the reason for injuring the state or collective interests or the legitimate rights and interests of other persons, for disturbing society's economic order or for injuring the state's economic construction. Otherwise, the exercise not only does not obtain the law's protection, but must also receive the sanction of the law.

The legal capacity of citizens to have rights and the personality of citizens cannot be separated. Individual citizens can handle, administer, or renounce their subjective rights. For example, they can sell their own property or give it to another person's ownership, but they cannot in any way renounce their capacity to have rights. The capacity of the citizens to have rights, apart from some special provisions of the law, cannot be limited or destroyed by any person or unit.

3. The Commencement and Termination of the Capacity to Have Civil Law Rights

The capacity to have civil law rights and the life of a person are inseparable. For example, the capacity to have civil law rights begins at a person's birth. It ends at his death. After a person is born he becomes a citizen of the state. According to law he has the rights of a citizen until he dies. Therefore every natural person, so long as he is alive, regardless of his age, or the condition of his health, or the degree of his understanding, enjoys equality of capacity to have civil law rights.

(1) The commencement of the capacity to have civil law rights

The capacity of a citizen to have rights is the foundation of citizen's living and carrying on civil law actions. It is the assurance of the citizen's daily life. Consequently, from the birth of the citizen, the law bestows on him civil law rights.

(i) Regarding the concrete time of the commencement of civil law rights, the time for the commencement of a citizen's capacity to have civil law rights in our country must be based on the general opinion of our doctors that the time of "the birth of a living infant" is the standard. The time of birth of the infant must be recorded as proof of birth. From this it can be seen that the capacity of our country's citizens to have civil law rights has no connection with age. Apart from this, the legal capacity of a citizen of our country to marry, participate in collective labor, vote, etc., can only be enjoyed when he has arrived at a certain age according to relevant laws and regulations. But none of these affects the capacity to have civil law rights according to our country's civil law.

(ii) In regard to protection of the fetus, a citizen's capacity to have civil law rights begins at birth. Consequently, we must consider the question of how to recognize the legal position of the fetus that is not yet born. Each country has different rules for this problem, but generally they protect it. Our country's civil courts, in making decisions [on this matter], provide appropriate protection for the fetus. In a succession case, so far as opening the succession is concerned, in the case of the fetus that is not yet born, in general they protect the share the fetus would have received at the time of succession [death].

(2) Termination of the capacity to have civil law rights

The capacity of the citizen to have civil legal rights comes to an end when he dies a natural death or is declared to be dead.

(i) Natural death. Natural death is the absolute end of the citizen's life. Upon the death of a citizen, his capacity to have rights accordingly comes to an end. [In order to determine] the actual moment of death of the citizen, we must take the general medical opinion of the time of death as determinative. After the citizen has died, his legal personality is lost. His marriage comes to an end. The succession of his estate opens.

(ii) Declaration of death because of disappearance without a trace. Apart from dying a natural death, citizens may be declared dead because of disappearance without a trace.

When a citizen has left his residence, and there has been no news of him for a certain period of time, or when he has been in military action or a dangerous accident, and there is no news for a certain period of time, the people's court may, in response to a petition of interested persons, declare him dead. "The Civil Procedure Code of the People's Republic of China" (draft edition) provides a special rule and a special procedure for declaring a person dead who has disappeared without a trace. In a petition filed by interested persons to have a person who has disappeared without a trace declared dead, they must write clearly the facts, the time, and the request, for a determination of the disappearance without a trace. Moreover, there must be a written certification by the security administration of the disappearance without a trace, etc. After the people's court has received the petition, it must publish a notice seeking the person who has disappeared. The period of the announcement is one year. If, after the expiration of the time for the announcement, there has been no news of the one who has disappeared, it may issue the judgment declaring him to be dead. The day when the people's court declares the man to be dead is presumed to be the day when he died. The declaration of death is, from the legal point of view, the end of the legal personality. Therefore the declaration of death gives rise to the same kinds of consequences as a natural death.

(3) The person who has been declared dead appears again

The declaration of death is a type of legal presumption. The person who has been declared to be dead is not necessarily dead. There is still the possibility that he exists or continues to live. When the person who has been declared to be dead reappears, then, according to the provisions of section 135 of our country's Civil Procedure Code (draft): "When a person declared dead reappears, the people's court, upon petition of the person himself, or interested parties, must enter a new judgment annulling the previous judgment." That is, it will be annulled as to its declaration of death. The person who is still living has the right to request return of any of his property that is still in existence from anyone who obtained it without consideration. If his property had been obtained by the state or collectivity without consideration, when this has been sold, then the price of the property has to be given to the person who is still living.

III
THE CAPACITY OF CITIZENS TO ACT
[HANDLUNGSFÄHIGKEIT]

1. The General Concept of Capacity to Act

The capacity of a citizen to act involves a citizen's being able to obtain civil law rights and establish civil law obligations by means of his own acts. The capacity to act includes not only the capacity of citizens to engage in lawful acts, it also includes the capacity of citizens to be responsible for their unlawful acts. For example, the action of a citizen buying a thing obtains for him a property right in a certain thing. Moreover, it establishes a duty to pay the price to the seller. [Another example is the case] when a citizen, through his own negligent act, becomes liable to pay damages for another's injury.

The capacity of a citizen to act and the capacity to have civil law rights are not the same. The capacity to act is not something that every person has, nor does a person acquire it as soon as he is born. The law determines whether or not a citizen has the capacity to act. It will take as a standard the citizen's capacity to judge and determine the consequences of his acts and also reasonably to manage his own affairs. This sort of requirement of the law regarding the capacity of the citizen to engage in acts results from [a desire to] protect the citizen's lawful rights, and to uphold the normal economic order of society. If a citizen does not have the capacity to manage his own affairs independently, and lacks the necessary capacity to judge the consequences of his acts, his civil law acts can be very harmful to him or to the normal economic order of society. In order to prevent these sorts of circumstances from arising, our country's judicial system uses the following divisions of citizens' capacity to act, based on different stages in the development of understanding and different circumstances:

(1) Complete capacity to act

That is, the citizen can, by means of his own independent act, acquire civil law rights and assume civil law duties.

Our country's constitution provides that citizens who reach the age of eighteen have the right to vote and to be elected [to office]. It can be inferred from this that they have the capacity independently to participate in civil law actions and to manage their own affairs reasonably. Therefore citizens over eighteen, in general, have complete capacity to act.

(2) Limited capacity to act

That is, incomplete capacity to act. Although persons who are six to eighteen years of age have a certain ability to discriminate, their intellectual development is still not complete. Their experience of living in society is still not sufficiently rich, so they cannot estimate the consequences of certain rather complicated acts. Because of this, the legal system regards them as persons with limited capacity to act. It permits them to carry on adult acts that are necessary for day-to-day life. They can participate in all civil law relations appropriate for their age. These include civil law rights such as honors and invention, and authorship rights, etc. In the case of civil law actions which they cannot carry on independently, or which are not suitable for them, they must be represented by their parents or other legally appointed representatives. They may also carry them on themselves when authorized by their legal representatives. Otherwise their acts are of no effect.

(3) Without the capacity to act

Our country's judicial practice normally regards those who have not yet attained six years as persons without the capacity to act. That is, they do not have the quality of being able to obtain civil law rights or assume liabilities by their own acts. Since their years are too few, they still do not understand things. Still less can they enter into juristic acts that have an intention and purpose. In order to protect their interests and to secure the development of social and economic order, their capacity to act cannot be recognized. The civil law actions that they must engage in must be carried out by their parents or by their legally appointed representative.

Adults who suffer from mental illness or other sorts of abnormal mental conditions, and who have lost their ability to express their thoughts, and who cannot independently carry on their own affairs, in order to protect their interests and the usual economic order of society, must be determined to be persons without the capacity to act. Our country's Civil Procedure Code [draft] provides a special procedure for determining a citizen's lack of capacity to act. The people's court, on the petition of close relatives of the one suffering, when it has investigated or determined the facts, may decide that the said citizen is a person who does not have the capacity to act. Moreover, it must, according to the law, appoint a guardian for him.

The determination that one suffering from mental illness does not have the capacity to act is only a limit on his capacity to act during a limited period of time. When his mind has returned to normal, and there is the capacity to act independently, then, upon his petition, or that of interested persons, the court, after investigating and determining the facts, must annul the judgment determining that he does not have the capacity to act. Moreover, at the same time, it will cancel his guardianship.

The determination that there is no capacity to act, or the cancellation of [this determination] are both very serious matters. They relate not only to the [question] whether or not an individual can or cannot independently engage in civil law acts but also to the protection of his lawful interests and the maintenance of the social and economic order. Therefore, regardless of whether there is a determination that there is no capacity to act, or a cancellation [of such a determination], both [determinations] must be made completely in accord with the facts.

IV
GUARDIANSHIP

Guardianship is established in order to protect the lawful rights and interests of the person who does not have the capacity to act or has limited capacity to act. Normally a guardian is appointed for a person without the capacity to act. For a person with limited capacity to act a protector is appointed. He may also be called a *bao-zuo* [guardian]. Our country's present legislation does not have different rules for the two, but calls them both guardians.

1. The Purpose of the Institution of Guardianship

The purpose of our country establishing a system of guardianship is to protect minors and adults with mental abnormalities who cannot manage their own affairs independently. At the same time, it is to uphold society's normal economic order. Therefore, the most important responsibility of the guardian is to look out for the person of the one who is under guardianship, and to provide him with intellectual and moral education, to administer the ward's property and uphold his lawful interests, to represent the ward in civil law actions, to obtain rights for him and to establish liability. So far as responsibility for negligent acts by the ward that cause injury to others are concerned, [the guardian is (?)] to assume the liability to pay damages, etc. According to section 17 of our country's marriage law, "when a minor child causes injury to a household, collectivity or other people, the parents have economic responsibility to compensate." This sort of rule is useful in imposing on the guardians a feeling of responsibility, and making them do their work of guardianship well.

The guardian must carefully fulfill his responsibilities, actively upholding the interests of the ward. He may not perform any act that is injurious to his [the ward's] interests. The civil codes of many countries provide that the guardian may not engage in juristic acts with the ward, nor may he represent the ward in juristic acts with his relatives, etc., in order to avoid having the guardian injure the ward. In order to avoid any abuse of the rights of guardianship it is apparent that limitations must be placed on the guardian.

2. Establishment of a Guardianship

In general there are the following three ways of establishing a guardianship:

(1) The guardianship provided by law

This is a guardian directly provided by the law owing to the closeness of the relationship of the nearest relatives. A person assuming the guardian's responsibility is [taken from] those who will most suitably protect the interests of the ward. For example, section 17 of our marriage law provides that "the parents have the duty to discipline and to protect the rights and duties of minor children." From this it may be seen that the parents are the guardians provided by law for their children. Sections 22 and 23 of the marriage law separately provide for the appointment of guardians when the parents are dead or unable to provide for them. Their grandparents, maternal grandparents, or older brothers or sisters who do have this ability have the duty to care for their minor grandchildren, maternal grandchildren, or younger brothers and sisters. From this it may be seen that the guardians of a minor child may be selected from his other near relatives as well as from his parents. According to the spirit of sections 14 and 15 of the marriage law, the guardian who may be decided upon for a person declared to be without the capacity to act must be his spouse, parents, or children.

(2) Testamentary guardian

That is, the guardian provided by the parents in their wills for minor children. The person selected by the parents in their will is naturally someone in whom they have confidence. Consequently, as soon as the will is effective, this sort of designated guardian will obtain confirmation by law. But if the person designated as guardian in the will is not one of the persons designated by law, he may refuse the guardianship.

(3) Appointed guardian

Under circumstances where there is no guardian provided by law, nor a guardian appointed by will, the court or an interested organization may, for the benefit of the minor, or the person declared to be without the capacity to act, designate a guardian. Under our country's judicial practice, it has the right to appoint as a guardian, relatives other than those designated by law, as well as the concerned unit (such as the kindergarten or training institute or units to which the parents or he himself originally belonged).

3. The Dissolution of the Guardianship and Dismissal and Replacement of a Guardian

When the reasons for the guardianship disappear, then the guardianship is dissolved for the ward, for example, when the ward attains adulthood, or the reasons for declaring him to be without the capacity to act disappear, etc. Apart from this, if the guardian seriously violates his responsibilities as guardian, or [if] there is no suitable person who succeeds as guardian, then upon the petition of interested persons, the guardianship may be dissolved and the guardian replaced, after the facts have been investigated and determined by the court or concerned supervisory organizations.

V
NAMES, HOUSEHOLD REGISTRATION, AND DOMICILE

1. Name

A name is a symbol that is used to specify and represent a person. It differentiates a certain citizen from other members of the same society in participating in social activities, exercising rights, and assuming duties. A citizen's name is entered into the household registry when he is born. When a citizen changes his name, it also must be recorded with the household registry organization, and then it is effective. When a citizen's name has been recorded with the household registration organization, it becomes an important personal right of the citizen.

The law protects the citizen's right to his name. The citizen can obtain civil law rights and establish duties only by carrying out juristic acts in his own name. The citizen has the right to use his name and also to prevent anyone else from unlawful use or change of his name. In regard to an act that violates the citizen's right to his name, one must consider how serious it is, and the extent of its influence. Civil responsibility or other legal responsibility will be determined according to law.

2. Household Registration

Household registration is an important problem for a citizen's capacity to have rights and to act. The household register records the citizen's name, birth [date], domicile, relations, death, and other matters. Household registration is for the purpose of establishing the citizen's individual legal position. It is also useful for state control and discipline.

According to the entry in the household registry, the time when a citizen's capacity to have rights and to act begin and ends can be determined. It determines the scope [of the successor's interest] and the sequence of the successors [heirs]. Because of this, household registration is the basic legal condition for determining the legal position of the citizen as a subject of rights.

3. Domicile

Domicile is the essential base, or center, for the life and activity of a citizen. All of the citizen's activities require a certain place. In accordance with economic development, particularly the increased circulation of goods, the scope of people's economic actions grows larger every day. Therefore it is necessary to select one essential place as the domicile of a person's life and actions in order to clarify legal relations. This is quite significant in protecting the lawful rights of citizens, and stabilizing social and economic relations.

According to our country's rules for control of registration and jurisdiction for suit, the citizen must use his place of registration and his domicile for specified political, economic, and legal [that is, lawsuit] actions. If a citizen is absent from his place of registration for a long time, he may be regarded as having changed his domicile, and be domiciled in the place where he has lived for a long time. A minor, or a person determined to be without the capacity to act, is domiciled at the domicile of his guardian. Citizens may change their domiciles, but except where the law provides otherwise, an individual can have only one domicile.

Apart from a citizen's domicile he may also have residences. He may even have several residences. A residence is a place where a citizen stays temporarily [when] the place where he lives is not certain. It may also be a place where he lives apart from his domicile. Specifying the residence may also be important in civil law where there is no domicile or where the domicile has not been checked or known. The residence may be the domicile.

Establishing the domicile has important legal consequences. According to our country's election law for the National People's Congress and local people's congresses, a citizen must participate in elections in his place of domicile. In civil law actions, if the contract does not specify, the domicile may be the specified place to determine if the citizen is missing or to establish the place of performance of an obligation, or the standard for participating in actions in court. In cases involving foreigners, it can also serve as the standard to specify the applicable law. If there is no domicile, it can be presumed to be the place where the party usually lives. If, during certain periods, the party does not live in this place, this does not prevent the use of the presumption. Because of this, the sending of documents or announcements of civil law matters or court decrees—summonses or judgments, etc.—all use the citizen's domicile as the place to which they are sent. When a legal document is not sent in a timely way to a citizen's domicile, the responsible unit or individual must bear the responsibility for delay.

5 Juristic Persons

I
THE GENERAL NATURE AND CHARACTERISTICS OF JURISTIC PERSONS

A juristic person is a form of social organization that has property, that is self-managed, and that can independently enjoy civil law rights and assume civil law duties.

Juristic persons are another sort of subject of civil law rights as opposed to natural persons. They enjoy civil law rights and assume civil law duties in a great number of civil law activities. Juristic persons have the following characteristics.

(1) A juristic person is a social organization

A juristic person is not an independent individual who exists by virtue of birth but is a type of social organization with a certain purpose that is legally protected. A juristic person must have a definite organizational structure, clear functions, and limited authority as well as a scope and form for action. These are the essential preconditions for the juristic person to act as a subject of civil law rights and to carry on [civil law] activities. It is also an essential condition for the state and any supervisory office and society to supervise a juristic person in the carrying on of its activities.

(2) Having property that it manages itself

A juristic person must have property that it manages itself. This is a material basis for a juristic person acting as a subject of civil law acts and extensively carrying on economic relations and activities. The self-managed property of a juristic person refers to state managed enterprises, state organizations, units of social collective ownership, and social groups—every sort of juristic person that has the right to have independent accounting and independent budgeting. In the case of units of ownership by the whole people, this is the state property transferred by the state and placed by the state under the control and allocation [of the juristic person]. In the case of units of collective property, the property is collective property.

Ownership by juristic persons means that one must separate strictly the property owned by the juristic person from that of the members of the juristic person as well as from the property of the organizations that are in subordinate relationship to the juristic person, as well as [from the property of] other juristic persons. As for state juristic persons having property of the whole people, it is necessary to stress the distinction between the juristic person's property and that of the state (state treasury). The limits of the independent rights towards its property, of the juristic person with property of the whole people, are identical to its independent management rights which the state gives it to carry on the management of its affairs. The ownership of the property still belongs to the state. The state supervisory organs still have, in regard to juristic persons with property belonging to the whole people, the power to determine the direction of their management, and thus their scale, and their closing, ceasing, merging, or transfer, etc.

(3) Being able independently to have civil law rights and assume civil law duties

A juristic person acting as a subject of civil law rights must use and enjoy civil law rights and assume civil law liability in its own name. It is a characteristic of a juristic person that its lawful status is realized after it has obtained state recognition; then the independent assumption by a juristic person of a property liability is limited by the property which it can dispose of. That is, it has limited responsibility. Except as otherwise provided by law, neither the state nor an individual assumes responsibility for the obligations of the juristic person.

The three characteristics of a juristic person as discussed above are true for all juristic persons. They are used by every type of juristic person. In considering whether an organization or unit is or is not a juristic person, these three characteristics provide the standard.

II
THE APPEARANCE, DEVELOPMENT, AND USE OF THE INSTITUTION OF THE JURISTIC PERSON

1. The Appearance and Development of the Institution of Juristic Persons

The appearance of juristic persons and the recognition by the law of the institution of juristic persons and their uninterrupted development cannot be separated from a certain social and economic foundation and level of production. Beginning at the stage of the commodity economy and the period following it, commodity production was carried on by individuals. The exchange of goods also developed between natural persons. Consequently the raising of productive forces and the development of the commodity economy required the producers to increase the scale of production and to accumulate capital, carry on frequent exchange of goods, and, as a result, gradually this or that sort of economic system appears. This is essential for all those organizations that have the characteristic of being a subject of civil law. These organizations are the embryonic form of the system of juristic persons. For example, in Europe, in ancient Roman times, the "local self-governing associations" and "association of Roman citizens" and other forms already had civil law rights. At that time there were already some scholars who asserted that "the group had rights and duties independently. These were separate from the individuals who belonged to the group."

When the Middle Ages arrived, many areas developed as city states. Each city appeared in the position of having a "personality." The organizations which had to be formed as a result of economic development also had personality. The organizations which, at that time, were given rights by rulers and kings, and which, moreover, received feudal governing powers and legal protection were educational associations, churches, and other religious groups.

When capitalist society appeared, the hindrances to the development of production by the natural economy were shattered by the enormous advance of productive forces. Every sort of company poured forth in great number. The form of limited stock companies was particularly recognized by the law and was the most important form of juristic person. Some bourgeois scholars hail this. They believe that the appearance of the limited stock company caused what had been conceived by medieval partners as a "mystery" to become reality. The limited stock company is the subject of rights that is the most ideal, the model type which makes it impossible for anyone to have any doubts about its status.

After the victory of the French Revolution, although the position of the juristic person as the subject of civil law rights was clearer, the first bourgeois civil code—the French Civil Code of 1803–04—not only did not provide a system for juristic persons, but even the term "juristic person" had not yet appeared. By the end of the 19th century and the beginning of the 20th, capitalism entered the stage of imperialism. The development of capitalist production became increasingly social and entered into the monopolistic control of large-scale production. The German Civil Code of 1900 had systematic provisions for juristic persons.

After the socialist October revolution under Lenin's own leadership, the Soviet Russian Civil Code that was promulgated in 1923 provided for a system of juristic persons. Continuing down to the present day, the great majority of civil codes include systems of juristic persons.

2. The Use of Juristic Persons in the Capitalist Period

In the period of the rise of capitalism, the juristic person had important uses.

First, juristic persons promoted the strengthening and development of the relations of the commodity economy. The capitalist commodity economy was not the feudal economy of self-sufficiency, but rather the economy developed by free competition. Every sort of capitalist economic organization could act as a juristic person, [and] enjoy every sort of right enjoyed by a juristic person, but [could] only within a certain area assume economic responsibility. This could put the capitalistic economic organization in an advantageous position during the frequent economic movements. It was significant in promoting the strengthening and development of the commodity economy.

Second, the juristic person, in promoting the combining and accumulation of capital, created the conditions for the development of large-scale production. Since it is superior, in comparison with such forms of individual management as do not have the independent status of juristic persons, such as independent businesses or partnerships, because in taking the small capital of individuals and by forming a juristic person like a company, it organized the accumulation of a large amount of capital and greatly increased competitive strength, there was an "astonishing" increase in the scale of production since [companies] could obtain much greater profits than individual managers. This was the material foundation for uninterrupted growth and uninterrupted production on a large scale.

Finally, the system of juristic persons protects the lawful position of non-enterprise organizations. It enables political, cultural, economic, scientific, health, religious, etc., social organizations to obtain the character of being the subject of civil law rights. It facilitates each in realizing its specialized function by carrying on civil law activities.

After capitalism entered [the stage of] imperialism, juristic persons became even more clearly important to the activities of the bourgeoisie.

(1) Monopolistic capitalists could make still more effective use of juristic persons to assume limited [liability] and obtain high interest

The limited liability stock company, a form characterized by Marx as "indicating the modernity of every country in present day economic activity," at this time increased constantly and occupied a dominant position. The use of the limited liability stock company as a juristic person, caused capitalists no longer, as in the case of unlimited liability companies or limited partnerships, to be required to assume total or partial unlimited liability, but separated their individual property from the property of the company. The individual has the right to manage the property of the company but the individual's property is not responsible for the obligations of the company. That is "they are only responsible for the whole amount of their shares and what they dispose of is the entire capital of the company." (Marx-Engels) Moreover losses from investment in one company could immediately be made up by dividends from investments in another.

(2) The juristic person is an essential tool for carrying on capital competition and acquisition

At this time the accumulation and concentration of capital was still more intense than before. Capitalists, by means of trusts, cartels, syndicates, concerns, and multinational parent and subsidiary corporations, and every sort of monopolistic organization, formed a high degree of accumulation and uninterruptedly gobbled up small and medium-sized enterprises in the development of monopoly capitalism.

3. The Significance and Use of Juristic Persons in our Country's Socialist System

In our country's socialist system, it is still necessary to establish a system of juristic persons and facilitate its use by means of legislation. In the midst of the reform of our country's economic system, the basic task is to increase the vitality of enterprises and develop our country's planned commodity economy. To achieve this task, it is necessary to clarify the status of enterprises as juristic persons. As is provided in the Decision of the Central Committee of the Communist Party Regarding the Reform of the Economic System, "Enterprises must truly become relatively independent economic entities and become socialist commodity producers and managers that are independently managed and responsible for their own profits and losses, having the capacity, [arising] from our reform and development, to form juristic persons with defined rights and duties." The significance and use of the system of juristic persons in our country can be explained in the following ways:

(1) It is a legal device to increase the vitality of enterprises

The status of juristic person bestowed by state law on enterprises is designed to make it clear legally that enterprises are relatively independent commodity producers and that managers have their own economic interests and [is designed] to specify the rights and obligations they have according to law, particularly the rights and duties in regard to their independently managed property. This can cause the enterprises to carry out, independently and under the protection of the law, production and management activities. It causes enterprises to become powerful living active organisms which are glowing with inner vitality in economic activity.

(2) It is an effective measure for bringing the civil law activities of the enterprise into the orbit of the legal system

The institution of the legal person requires that the enterprise act within the scope of the rules of law and of the charter of the enterprise. If the enterprise wishes to acquire the status of juristic person, it must comply with the provisions of the law. In particular it must be registered according to law and be investigated and approved by the state organization. When the enterprise has acquired the status of juristic person, it must be independently liable, according to the law, for obligations that have arisen because of its activities, etc. It can be seen that the juristic person is the expression of the use of legal procedures to control the economic activities of enterprises.

(3) It is an organization to guarantee the realization of the basic goal of socialist construction

The basic aim of socialist construction is unceasingly to satisfy the requirements of the people for material and cultural life. State organizations and enterprise units act as state juristic persons and participate in extended civil law activity. In fulfilling the state's economic, cultural, and educational functions, they benefit the people. After the establishment of any sort of scientific, cultural, artistic, etc., association and foundation as a juristic person, it acquires the status of a subject of civil law rights and participates in civil law activities relative to its work. These [juristic persons] are essential for scientific, cultural, and educational activity to develop and flourish.

(4) It is an essential form for developing international economic relations

Because of our country's economic adjustment and rectification, and the carrying out of the policy of opening up, there is ever more frequent contact with foreign economies. Many specialized companies are formed and clearly identified as juristic persons. This is extremely important for making the legal position of enterprises clear, for obtaining faith and credit with foreign enterprises and citizens, and for assuring the development of international economic intercourse on the basis of the principle of equality and mutual benefit.

III
TYPES OF JURISTIC PERSONS

The form of social organization of the juristic person has unceasingly changed and developed in accordance with the development of economic relations. Since every country has a social system that is different, and because legislation that is compatible with each country's situation is different, as well as because of differences of the views of scholars, the types of juristic persons are also not the same.

In capitalist countries of the continental legal system, juristic persons are distinguished in three ways, according to different standards.

(1) Public juristic persons and private juristic persons

This distinction is connected with the distinction made in capitalist countries between public law and private law. Public law juristic persons are juristic persons that have as their purpose sharing the responsibility for the exercise of the state's governing power. They are organizations that include every organization of state power from the central government to the local level. Juristic persons of public law are subject to regulation by public administrative law, or other special bodies of public law. The juristic person of private law is a juristic person that has, as its purpose, the management of the affairs of private persons. It includes juristic persons that are social groups and financial juristic persons. The juristic person of private law is regulated by civil law and other private law.

(2) Juristic persons of social groups and financial juristic persons

The juristic person of a social group is a juristic person that is established by the bringing together of its members (persons). This sort of juristic person may be established with the purpose of obtaining public benefits or seeking profits. When it is established, bylaws must be adopted which provide the purpose, responsibilities, and significant structure of the juristic persons. A financial juristic person is a juristic person that is established on the basis of the accumulation of contributions of funds. This sort of juristic person may only have the purpose of obtaining some sort of common good. At the time it is formed it must be approved by the supervisory office and be registered.

(3) Profit-making juristic persons and juristic persons for the public benefit

A profit-making juristic person is a juristic person that is formed for the purpose of planning to obtain profits from property, for example, every sort of profit-seeking enterprise or company and other economic organization. A juristic person for the public good is a juristic person which is established with the public good as its ultimate purpose, for instance, juristic persons which have the aim of a public social good such as political, religious, educational, technical, and charitable, etc., purposes.

Apart from these there are other sorts of juristic persons that are social groups which are not profit-making juristic persons nor juristic persons organized for the public good such as sports clubs and similar organizations.

IV
THE ESTABLISHMENT OF JURISTIC PERSONS AND THEIR CONDITIONS

The establishment of a juristic person consists of the juristic person going through some procedure and coming into being. Since a juristic person is a social organization that participates extensively in economic activity in its own name, its establishment must be consistent with the interest of the state and be required by society. At the same time, this causes its own lawful interests to receive protection. Since in our country the nature and responsibilities of different organizations are not the same, the following procedures for confirmation [of their establishment] have been adopted:

1. Formation According to Law, Order, or Administrative Regulation

Juristic persons established under these procedures are those that are established under laws of the state legislative organizations, laws, decisions of governments at every level, or instructions and similar provisions from supervisory administrative organizations. For example, [there are] the hydroelectric power industry ministry, the ministries of commerce and foreign trade, economic ministries, and the state committee for reform of the economic system established by the decision of the twenty-second session of the Standing Committee of the Fifth National People's Congress in its "Decision Regarding the Question of Reforming the Organizations of the State Council." Once these organizations are established they obtain the character of juristic persons.

2. Establishment by Means of Examination and Registration

The juristic persons that are formed under this procedure are those for which a petition is filed, and, after checking and approval by the central or local supervisory office, and registration, they acquire the status of juristic persons. Enterprises and social groups are both in this category. Examination and approval are the responsibility of the office that is responsible for supervising the establishment of the juristic person. The registration varies according to the nature of the juristic person. It is carried on by the various departments for supervising industry, commerce, or other offices. The content of the petition for registration includes the name of the enterprise, its location, the name of its responsible person, the day when it begins business, its economic nature, the form and scope of its production [and] management, the amount of its capital, and the number of its staff and workers. An organization which should be registered and is not does not have the status of juristic person. It may not carry on civil law activities in its own name.

3. Establishment According to Standard Provisions and Charters

Juristic persons that are formed under this procedure are organizations that request formation according to the documents having the character of legal norms that determine the nature of their own organizations, scope of activity, and form. After the higher level organization or supervising unit prepares a file, they acquire the status of juristic persons. For example, communes, production teams, production brigades, etc.

Regardless of which of the above described procedures is used to establish a juristic person, the juristic person must first meet certain requirements and then it acquires the status of juristic person. These requirements for juristic persons are set by law and legal rule. The establishment of every juristic person must be carried on in accordance with the law. When an organization that avoids the law and declares itself [to be a juristic person] or when a superior administrative organization authorizes a "juristic person," on its own, [these actions] are without legal effect.

The requirements for juristic persons may be divided into substantive requirements and form requirements. The first four discussed below are substantive requirements. The last is a form requirement.

(1) It [the juristic person] must have a form and scope for production, management, or service activity that are lawful

In every type of juristic person, organization, social unit, [or] association, there is a scope and form for carrying on civil law activities. Enterprises and companies also have their scope and form for carrying on production, management, or service.

First of all, this scope and form cannot violate the nature of the juristic person or the purpose and range of its formation. Because of this, the Party's political organizations cannot engage in commerce; enterprises and companies cannot, without examination, approval, and registration change the scope of their production or management or have one enterprise as the principal managing the others.

Second, this scope and form must harmonize with the property and material resources of the juristic person itself. To take the corporate judicial person as an example, the scope and form of its production management, or its service, must be carried on consistently with its registered capital, its condition, its equipment, its personnel resources in management and subordinate staff (it is necessary particularly that there be a certain number of administrative, financial, scientific, and technical personnel). These requirements are an essential assurance that the juristic person can carry on extensive civil activities within the scope of its activity.

(2) It must have an appropriate amount of property to carry on its activities in fulfilling its responsibilities and achieving its aims

All juristic persons must have a certain amount of property as the material base for their activity. Since they are of different types and sizes the amount of property cannot be the same. For example, enterprise juristic persons and institutional juristic persons are not the same. Industrial and commercial corporations are not the same as advisory companies. But there is a common standard for the amount of property required by dissimilar juristic persons, that is, the standard that the capital [must] be appropriate for the activity. This enables the capital to insure the juristic person's normal activity. In August 1985 the State Council approved The Temporary Rules for Supervising the Registration of Corporations published by the State Administrative Control Office. These specified that a corporation must have the essential liquid capital (not including bank deposits) suitable for the scope of its management activities. In the case of companies in production this could not be less than 100,000 *yuan*. In the case of a corporation that is principally a wholesaler it cannot be less than 200,000 *yuan*. For corporations that are predominately retailers it cannot be less than 100,000 *yuan*. In the case of advisory and service corporations it cannot be less than 50,000 *yuan*. If this requirement for sufficient capital is not met, [the organization] does not have the qualifications to be a corporation.

(3) It must have a sound organization reflecting the independent will of the juristic person

The juristic person is a social organized entity. In order to carry out the management control and the civil law activities that have been set for it, as well to carry out civil law juristic acts, it must operate through the organs of the juristic person. A well established juristic person often has organization provisions or a charter prepared that clearly provides for a sound organization. The organs of a juristic person include the council (board of directors), the general meeting of members (members or staff and workers), or a representative meeting, and other collective organizations. It also includes an organ of individuals who are responsible for representing the juristic person in its most important activities. The organs of the juristic person who represent the juristic person make declarations of intention for juristic acts. They effectuate the work of the juristic person, have authority, and are legally protected. If an association merely hangs up its sign but has no leadership organs, or a group has the name but not the substance [of a juristic person] these [organizations] do not acquire the status of juristic person.

(4) It must have its own name and domicile

The name of a juristic person is the right to personality of the juristic person. Like the name of a natural person, it is a standard for distinguishing among juristic persons. It is essential to clarify the nature and responsibility of the juristic person, and to enable it to engage in management and carry out civil law activities and is also advantageous for the state control of juristic persons.

The domicile of the juristic person is the place where the most important responsible organization of the juristic person is located. It is quite important as regards the juristic person's own activities and in regard to its economic relations of many kinds with outsiders, as well as in regard to jurisdiction for suits and so forth. The "brief-case corporation" which does not have the name of a juristic person, or, although it has a name, has no fixed domicile, cannot be recognized as a juristic person.

(5) It must act in accordance with the legal procedures for registration

After an enterprise juristic person, association juristic person, contribution juristic person, etc., has met all substantive requirements it still must carry out the registration procedures according to law. When it acquires a certificate it then becomes a juristic person. When the state's control registration office handles this matter it must examine the charter and substantive requirements for regulation of the juristic person, item by item. If it is accurate, then it is recorded. If it is false, then the [further] procedures are not followed. This shows the importance of the state carrying on supervision and investigation of juristic persons by means of registration.

V
THE JURISTIC PERSON'S CAPACITY TO HOLD RIGHTS AND CAPACITY TO ACT

1. The Juristic Person's Capacity to Hold Rights

The juristic person's capacity to hold rights is the juristic person's right to participate in civil law relations and to obtain civil law rights and assume obligations. Even though the juristic person, like the natural person, is a subject of rights and duties, the juristic person is an entity organized by society. It is not a living entity like a natural person. Consequently, when the juristic person's capacity to hold rights is compared with that of the natural person there are the following differences.

(1) The beginning and end of the capacity to hold civil rights are not the same [for natural and juristic persons]

The natural person's capacity begins with birth and ends with death. The continuation of life is a condition for its existence. The juristic person's capacity to hold rights begins with the establishment of the juristic person and ends when it winds up or dissolves. If the juristic person, because of adjustments or bad management, and so forth, decides to wind up or be dissolved, then it is necessary, in connection with the time for liquidating its property (for accounting), that the juristic person's property and obligations (both owing and owed) be completely liquidated. After this has been done, the juristic person is still regarded as being in existence. It is only when the juristic person is completely liquidated that the capacity to hold rights ceases. In West Germany, Japan, etc., contract law and regulations regard this as the juristic person's "artificial existence."

(2) The scope of the capacity to hold rights is not the same

A juristic person is a kind of social organization. It cannot have the capacity to enjoy certain rights that presuppose a citizen's personality, to adopt, for example.

(3) The limitations on the capacity to hold rights are not the same

The capacity of citizens to hold rights is general, equal, uniform. Normally there is no difference between the capacity of one citizen and that of another to hold rights. The scope of activity of juristic persons is not the same. Each has a different capacity to hold rights. The capacity to hold rights is determined by the scope of its activities. The capacity to hold rights of a juristic person is determined by its purpose and by the scope of its activity. A juristic person does not have the right to act contrary to its purpose nor to go beyond the scope of its activities.

2. A Juristic Person's Capacity to Act

The capacity of a juristic person to act is its ability to obtain civil law rights and assume civil law duties by means of its own acts. The capacity to act of the juristic person is not the same as that of the natural person—closely connected with his age and mental condition. It has its own special characteristics. These are expressed as:

(1) The commencement and termination of the capacity to act

A juristic person's capacity to act begins at the same time that it acquires the capacity to hold rights. That is, after the juristic person is established according to the prescribed procedure, it acquires the capacity to hold rights and also has the capacity to act. When the juristic person is dissolved, its capacity to hold rights and its capacity to act both lose their condition precedent and they come to an end at the same time.

(2) The scope of the capacity to act

The scope of a juristic person's capacity to have rights and its capacity to act are the same, that is, the scope within which they can, by their own acts obtain rights and assume duties. [This scope] cannot exceed the scope of the limitations on their capacity to hold rights; otherwise the acts of the juristic person are ineffective. Moreover, it must assume the appropriate legal liability.

(3) Putting into effect of the capacity to hold rights

The natural person's capacity to act is, in general exercised by his own acts. But the juristic person's capacity to act in general is realized by means of the juristic person's organs. The juristic person's organs are divided into those which are individuals and those which are collectives. "Individuals" refers to the responsible person of the juristic person such as the factory director, the administrator, the head of the commune, the director of the school, chairman, and so forth. "Collectives" refers to the commune members' congress, the membership assembly, the representative assembly, the administrative committee, the board of directors, the executive council, and so forth. These have the right to represent the juristic person in executing acts. The juristic person's organs, and the limitations of their scope, are set by law, provisions, and the charter.

There are two ways in which the juristic person's organs exercise its capacity to act.

(i) The organs exercise civil law acts directly. The juristic person's organs are its lawful and natural representatives. They constitute a unified subject of rights together with the juristic person. There is no relationship of principal and representative. The juristic person's organs participate in civil law relations in accordance

with the intention of the juristic person. In regard to outsiders a juristic act executed in the name of a juristic person is its own act. Consequently, the juristic person is completely liable for all the lawful acts executed by its organs with third parties (such as signing contracts). This includes liability for damages for injuries caused to third parties. If the organs of the juristic person conclude an unlawful contract that violates laws and regulations (including a contract which a third person knows or should know exceeds the limitations of the rights of the juristic person), this cannot be legally effective for the juristic person. The juristic person has the right to cancel the liability that has been assumed.

(ii) The juristic person may execute civil law juristic acts by means of representatives commissioned by its organs. The civil law juristic act executed by the juristic person may also be executed with third persons by individuals or organizations that are not attached to the organs of the juristic person (staff and workers, commune members, assembly members, or any other citizen or juristic person). These natural persons or juristic persons who receive appointments to act as representatives are representatives of the juristic person. When they execute civil law juristic acts with third parties in the name of the juristic person, the [general] rules of representation are applied.

VI
THE ALTERATION OR DISSOLUTION OF A JURISTIC PERSON

1. The Alteration of a Juristic Person

Change or alteration in the juristic person means an important change and alteration of the juristic person's organizational structure and nature, scope of activities, property or name, domicile, subordination relations, and so forth. From the point of view of domestic juristic persons, this kind of change is often inseparable from adjustment, reform, or rectification of the economic or administrative system.

(1) Change in the organizational structure of juristic persons

This change often takes the form of merger or division.

(i) Merger. (1) A new juristic person is formed from merging two or more juristic persons; (2) one juristic person is merged into another juristic person.

(ii) Division. (1) A juristic person is divided to form several juristic persons; (2) a portion of a juristic person is separated out to form a new juristic person.

(2) Change in the nature, scope of activities, or property of a juristic person

(i) A change in the nature of a juristic person. This refers to the case when a change of circumstances requires a change in the nature of the juristic person as

provided at the time it was formed, for example, [when] an enterprise, because of joint management, changes its system of ownership.

(ii) Change in the scope of activity of a juristic person. This refers to situations where, because of the requirements of production, management, or work, a new scope of activity replaces the old, as when an enterprise changes its products and carries on a shift in production.

(iii) Changes in property. This refers to a change in capital while [the juristic person] is an operation.

(3) A change in name, domicile, or dependency relations.

(i) Change in the name of the juristic person. The name of the juristic person is the name it has selected to carry on juristic acts. If there are reasons requiring a change in this name than this is name change, as when a factory or store changes the factory or trade name.

(ii) A change in domicile of the juristic person. This refers to a juristic person which, because of a move and so forth, changes its registration from that of its original domicile. As, when a coastal enterprise moves to the interior, a certain service unit leaves and moves to a new location.

(iii) Changes of subordination relations. This means [that] because of a change in the system and so forth, there has been a change in the subordination relations of a juristic person. For example, a state managed enterprise is changed to a local state-managed enterprise. The juristic person of a certain province is changed to the juristic person of a neighboring province and so forth. The change in the juristic person must be checked, authorized, and registered according to law.

2. The Termination of the Juristic Person

The termination of a juristic person refers to the situation where the status of the juristic person as such ceases to exist. The causes and manner of termination of a juristic person in general have the following characteristics:

(1) Dissolution according to law.

A statute or administrative regulation orders a dissolution, usually because of a change in the system of the state organization, or because the task of the juristic person has already been accomplished. When juristic persons are formed by laws, legal rules, or administrative regulations, dissolution is taken care by the same procedures.

(2) Because the juristic person's acts violate the law, or legal rules, or violate the purpose of its formation by carrying on management or [other] activities that are against the law and it is ordered to be dissolved by the superior office or has [its status] revoked.

(3) Cooperatives, learned societies and similar organizations are dissolved when it is so decided by their members [delegates] at a meeting, according to the provisions of their charters, and [the result] is then reported for approval to the office having jurisdiction. Industrial and commercial enterprise will, according to the governing rules, petition to cease activities and get permission.

(4) Because the capital is not sufficient for the obligations, there is no way to pay obligations, and [the juristic person] is declared bankrupt.

(5) Other reasons

Regardless of whether the termination of a juristic person falls within one of the above categories, whenever the decision to dissolve is made there must be an announcement. Moreover, there must be a specialist designated by the supervisory organization (a specialist organization) or an organization [named] by the juristic person itself to liquidate (settle). The organization [this person] will complete the work under the direction of the supervisory organization or the people's court. The liquidating organization must make a thorough investigation of the property of the juristic person, verify all of the obligations that are owed and owing, [and] prepare a balance sheet of assets and liabilities. Surplus property remaining after liquidation will be transferred to the superior office or to another juristic person in accordance with the law or the charter in order to avoid property losses. The juristic person's satisfaction of obligations will be carried on within the scope and manner provided by law. In liquidating the property of bankrupt juristic persons, it is not possible to select unpermitted methods because [the juristic person] is a state or collective juristic person. Their circulating fixed capital must be placed with the funds available for satisfying obligations.

VII
THE NAME, DOMICILE, AND PRODUCTION MARK

1. The Name of the Juristic Person

The name (tradename) of the juristic person is a mark differentiating it from the other juristic persons. It must indicate the direction of the activity and the subordination relations [of the juristic person] in order to cause others to distinguish it.

A juristic person has the right to the exclusive use of a name that has been registered. If this sort of right to exclusive use by the juristic person is infringed upon by another by means of false use or defamation, it has the right to seek the protection of the court and request the cessation of the infringing act and damages for any injuries caused by the infringing act.

2. The Domicile of the Juristic Person

Usually the domicile of the juristic person is the place where the organs of the juristic person are located. The organs of some juristic persons are extremely large and they have branches everywhere, even in foreign countries, so it is even more important [in such cases] to specify clearly the location of the domicile.

The domicile of the juristic person is something that cannot be omitted from the examination and registration of the juristic person. It shows the place where the juristic person carries on important economic activities. The juristic person sets up a bank account in that place. Moreover, it affects the performance of obligations, jurisdiction for suit, the place for settling accounts, and so forth. Consequently, it has great legal significance.

3. Production Marks of the Juristic Person

Production marks are marks of the enterprise placed on goods or packages which show their basic characteristics. The most important matters contained in them are the name of the enterprise, its domicile, the specifications of the goods, special aspects, function, etc. The production mark is a state procedure for controlling the quality of goods. It is also a means for [dealing with] the enterprise's liability to the consumer.

A juristic person carrying out production management has the right and duty to have a production mark on the goods or the package.

VIII
STATE SUPERVISION OF JURISTIC PERSONS

Juristic persons act as subjects of civil law rights. They participate voluntarily in civil law activities and form economic relations with other subjects of rights. This may have a great direct influence on the entire social economy. In order to stabilize the social and economic order, and to make sure that the circulation of lawful property rights is not infringed, the state must supervise every kind of activity engaged in by juristic persons [to determine] whether or not it is lawful. The content of the state's supervision of the juristic person is very broad. The measures of control are often expressed in legal norms. Although these legal norms lie within the range of administrative law, in view of their use and purpose, they can be regarded as a constituent part of the civil law regarding the system of juristic persons. The system of state control of juristic persons can be divided as follows:

(1) Supervision by the administrative office in charge

This refers to the determination by the superior level administrative control office whether enterprises within its jurisdiction have completely fulfilled the planned task or whether contracts are in harmony with the state's plan or the requirements of law as well as the investigatory supervision regarding prevention of the closing, suspension, merger, or transfer of enterprises (Temporary Provisions on State Industrial Enterprises sections 38, 21 promulgated by the State Council on 1st April

1983). The administrative supervisory office may also, in accordance with the law, promulgate administrative rules and measures in order to supervise the activities of the enterprise juristic person.

(2) Supervision by the office of industry and commerce

This refers to the investigation and supervision, by every level of the industrial and commercial administrative offices, of the industrial and commercial enterprises within their jurisdiction. Every industrial and commercial enterprise must submit to the industrial and commercial office concerned, the essential documents, accounts, report forms, and other relevant materials. Every level of the industrial and commercial organization, based on the rules for the control of industry and commerce, exercises, according to law, control over enterprise and juristic persons. Moreover, in the case where the management activities of the enterprise juristic person violate the law, it has the right to criticize and admonish, impose fines, or notify the bank to freeze an account or even to order suspension.

(3) Bank supervision

This involves the bank's supervision over whether or not the enterprise juristic person's use of and settling of accounts with its funds are lawful, as well as over production and management. Our country's banks or financial institutions may also have the administrative control function of being responsible for supervision of the nation's currency. Consequently, at the same time that an enterprise juristic person submits reports to superior supervisory offices, it must send production plans and financial plans, together with statistics on the carrying out of its plan, and the accounting reports, to the bank where it has an account, in order to receive monetary supervision by the bank.

(4) Taxation supervision

The taxing authorities have the right to investigate and supervise the monetary accounting affairs and tax payments of the enterprise juristic person. The enterprise must make reports of the facts in connection with the investigation of the taxing authorities. Moreover, it must submit the relevant data on fiscal receipts and cannot refuse or hold back [information]. The enterprise juristic person must pay taxes according to law. If it evades taxes it will receive punishment according to law.

In addition, the state auditors at every level are responsible for carrying out supervision over the receipts and expenditures of enterprise juristic persons. Section 4 of our country's Constitution clearly provides [*sic*, actually, article 91.1]: "The state council establishes an auditing body to supervise new auditing of revenue and expenditures of all departments under the state council and of the local governments at different levels and those of the state financial and monetary organizations and of enterprises and undertakings." According to this provision, our country's auditing authority must also exercise supervision over enterprise juristic persons.

The state, by means of the law, gives to every economic control office the right to supervise the activities of enterprise juristic persons. This is an essential measure for fulfilling the state's economic functions. It is possible by means of every kind of control measure to make maximum use of the activity of enterprise juristic persons and conscientiously to ensure the state's unified leadership over the activities of juristic persons in order to develop as quickly as possible our country's planned commodity economy.

6 Partnerships and Joint Ventures

I
THE GENERAL CONCEPT AND SPECIAL CHARACTERISTICS OF PARTNERSHIPS AND JOINT VENTURES

Partnerships and joint ventures are joint entities voluntarily formed by two or more citizens or juristic persons using their property and skills in which there is joint labor and management and which have civil law rights and assume civil law duties.

The partnership is usually a form of contract provided for in the civil codes of many countries. This is the embodiment of the partner's intention to obtain a joint agreement. But the joint entity that is formed according to the agreement—the partnership or joint venture—in order to realize its own purpose in the course of carrying out its activities, extensively participates in many types of civil law relations. This causes them [the partnerships and joint ventures] to form an independent subject of civil law rights that is located in between citizens and juristic persons.

Partnerships and joint ventures have the following legal characteristics.

(1) Partnerships and joint ventures are jointly organized by two or more citizens or juristic persons

Partnerships that are organized by two or more citizens are manifestly not the same as independent proprietorships. Independent proprietorships are independently managed by the individual citizen. Partnerships are managed by the joint management of citizens. Normally the law sets a figure for the lowest number of citizens who can organize a partnership and clearly provides that it must be two or more persons. The fixing of the highest number is handled by different methods. The legal rules of some countries provide that the partners in a partnership enterprise may not exceed ten or twenty persons. But the majority of countries do not have any limits on the maximum number of partners since the number of organizations with large numbers of members which do not organize corporations but instead, organize partnerships, is not, after all, very large.

A joint venture is usually formed by two or more juristic persons. For example, [it can be] any sort of joint body in which individual juristic persons jointly invest funds and engage in joint management and sign an agreement on the basis of equality and mutual advantage. The relevant rights and duties are provided for by the contract. In our country, many of the loosely formed joint relations entered into by juristic persons among themselves, as well as a number of cooperative management ventures, are, for the most part, joint ventures.

(2) Partnerships and joint ventures are based on the voluntary joining of those participating

Partnerships and joint ventures are created according to agreements of the participants; the investment, labor, management, distribution, etc., are all matters that are agreed upon. Regardless of whether the agreement is reached by discussion initiated [by the parties] themselves or by the introduction of someone else, all, in the end, are based on mutual trust after deep consideration of the pros and cons.

Partners and parties to a joint venture are not the same as shareholders in a limited liability stock company. The interests of the shareholders are closely connected with the number of shares which they have subscribed to. They are concerned with the fluctuating value of the share prices. It is seldom asked which shareholders organized the corporation. They do not have direct contracts with each other. They [often] do not even know each other. Mutual consideration and trust are out of the question.

(3) The joint contribution and management of those participating in partnerships and joint ventures

In order for partners or joint ventures to succeed in realizing their joint intention and establishing the organization they must contribute capital according to the charter or the agreement. They contribute the material basis required for the joint venture. The capital [contributed] includes cash, property, equipment, or buildings, or land. They also may contribute skills or labor (such as cooking, tailoring, repairing skills, and so forth). The proportion of time and the manner of capital contributions by the partners is usually clearly provided in the charter or agreement. If there is no ratio for contributions concretely provided, the civil law of every country has provisions that those participating contribute equally.

Joint management refers to an enterprise which is jointly managed by the partners or joint venturers. Thus, activities which are only joint, and are not under joint management, do not have the special characteristics of joint management. For example, several citizens who jointly contribute to the purchase of the building or other important pieces of property related to the production of articles of daily life, have a joint relation, [as do] the parties to a joint venture who have merely made a joint agreement [but] have not formed a new economic entity. In these cases there is no partnership entity. In our country, the parties who are forming a partnership organization must themselves participate in the labor, or the production or management activity of the partnership. If it is necessary to ask for help or include an apprentice, this must be handled in accordance with the state provisions.

(4) Partnerships and joint ventures are the subjects of civil law which are situated between citizens and juristic persons

Every country's civil law basically makes only natural persons and juristic persons the subjects of civil law. Some countries recognize partnerships as juristic, some countries place them in the category of natural persons. We believe partnership organizations have their own characteristics, so they are different from natural persons and from juristic persons. First of all, individual proprietorships use individual names for all civil law juristic acts. Enterprise juristic persons, on the basis of the organizations established by their charters, carry on civil law activities with others. No shareholder who has not been granted a special right can independently carry on activities with others in the name of the juristic person. But the partnership organization may carry on civil law activities within the scope of its legal functioning in its own name. At the same time, partners often have the same rights. Second, an independent proprietorship has unlimited liability for obligations. Among enterprise juristic persons there are limited liability companies and limited liability stock companies both of which have the special characteristic that liability for the obligations of the organization is limited to the entire capital of the company. But partnerships and partners must, without a contrary provision of law, be liable jointly and without limit for their obligations. The joint venture also has its own characteristics. It may be seen that partnerships and joint ventures are organizations that are situated between natural persons and juristic persons. They must have a special position as the subjects of civil law rights.

Partnerships which participate in civil law acts are of long standing. After the appearance of simple commodity production, in the stage where individual persons carried on commodity production and management, owing to the limitation of capital and capabilities of all kinds, when they wished to extend the scale and benefits of production, then they had to follow the path of the accumulation of capital and joint management. The earliest form may have been joint management and control by members of the household in connection with privately owned property. Subsequently, there gradually developed an association of individual proprietorships or a directly managed partnership enterprise. A large number of Sino-foreign businesses such as workshops, handicraft factories, as well as commercial and transportation businesses, are partnership organizations. At present these partnerships have developed from associations among citizens to associations among juristic persons. The associations among juristic persons assume an ever increasing importance in the economic life of society. Even though partnerships and jointly managed organizations are rather loose associations of individual persons, their resources are much richer than those of the individual proprietorship and they are simply more convenient—flexible—than corporations, in organizing and raising capital to manage. Consequently, partnerships and jointly managed organizations can continue to exist without decline. Not only in ancient times and modern times, but even at the present in capitalist and socialist societies, though corporations exist in great number they [partnerships and joint ventures] maintain great vigor and occupy an important position.

II
THE FORMATION OF PARTNERSHIPS AND JOINT VENTURES

The formation of a partnership organization requires, first of all, the formation of a charter or agreement by the partners. This should clearly provide for relevant matters, including, in general: the name of the partnership organization, the nature of the partnership activity, and its domicile, the names of the partners, their ages and domiciles, the total capital and the types, quantities and value capital contributed by the partners (including its monetary value), the term of the activity, the procedure in final accounting, compensation for labor, and a ratio or standard for the distribution of profits, the responsibilities of the partners, the scope and limits of rights, entry into the partnership and departure from it, and the methods of handling termination of the partnership, as well as other important matters. As for the form that must be used in the charter or agreement, the rules of different countries are not the same. We believe that in order to prevent internal disputes among the partners and external disputes between the partnership and other subjects of [rights], it is best to use the written form. The formation of joint ventures is in accordance with the Temporary Measure for Promoting Economic Joint Ventures.

Can there be legal consequences when the partnership organization established by the charter or agreement of partners carries on independent civil law activities with the outside? Some countries recognize them and give them legal protection. Other countries require that the registration procedures for formation be followed. They make this a procedure that must be followed by partnerships for dealing with third persons. Our country has used the system of registration for over thirty years. In the Temporary Provisions for Privately Managed Enterprises promulgated by the Finance Committee of the State Council in March 1951, it is provided that, "fifteen days after receiving the investment of each partner, the partnership must send to the industrial and commercial administrative control organization the required documents in order to be established and registered. The documents will include the matters that are to be registered: the partnership contract; certified documents showing complete payment of capital, contributions, or supplementary assurances; certified documents showing examination and approval of the business; if any of the partners are not adults, certificates or ratification by their representatives, etc. In April 1983, it was provided in Certain Provisions on Cooperative Management in Urban Areas promulgated by the State Council that when a partnership petitions to start operations, it must wait for examination and approval of the charter or agreement as well as the household registration of the members. The petition for registration is made to the local control organization for commerce and industry. When it has been examined and approved, and the approval has been given to the enterprise, it may engage in business. The establishment of a joint venture is governed by the Provisions for Control or Registration of Commercial and Industrial Enterprises.

III
THE MANAGEMENT AND CONTROL OF THE PROPERTY OF PARTNERSHIPS AND JOINT VENTURES

The partners and parties to a joint venture may contribute capital in the form of funds, things, and other types of movables together with buildings, fields and other types of immovables, as well as technology, and so forth, to constitute their share of property for establishing the organization. The property and property rights and benefits that are required in the course of business belong to the whole partnership organization. They are the property of all the organization, although the common property comes from the individual property of the partners. The charter or agreement specifies the share of each partner, but while the partnership continues, the individual partner cannot treat the property that was invested (in the partnership) as he would treat his individual property prior to investment, or after he had withdrawn from the partnership. The common property of the partnership is under the unified use and management of the partnership organization. At the same time, without a clear provision in the charter or agreement that one or several persons exercise certain functions, the entire body of partners have the common right to manage and control and supervise the work of the partnership organization. The partnership organization is normally carried on by its responsible person or designated partner. When there is a major question regarding the orientation of the management, final settlement, changes, dissolution, etc., of the partnership organization, it is necessary that the matter be discussed by all the partners and a unanimous decision obtained. Then it can be carried out. The lawful civil law activities of the partners and the partnership organization are effective in regard to the entire body of partners, but in the case of the action of a partner in using partnership assets seeking to obtain private gain, he must personally assume legal responsibility. The law has the same sort of provision for parties to a joint venture.

The profits from the operation of a partnership organization are in every country, for the most part, divided according to the provisions of the partnership charter or agreement. In our country, it is provided that after the partnership organization has paid its annual tax, the surplus must be allocated in four parts to the surplus reserve fund, the public welfare fund, the labor dividend, and the capital investment dividend. The obligations of the partnership are settled out of the property of the partnership. If that is insufficient, the partners are jointly liable. If any one or all of the partners receive a demand for payment from an obligee, then all are liable to pay all or part, unless the law has a contrary provision.

IV
ALTERATION OR TERMINATION OF A PARTNERSHIP OR JOINT VENTURE

During the course of the activity of a partnership or joint venture, circumstances may change. For example, the orientation of production may change. There may be an increase in the invested funds, there may be a change in the name or residence, or increase or decrease in the organization's members, or a change in the responsible person in a joint venture, and the responsible managing partners, and so forth. After these changes have been approved by the participants, they will petition to the industrial commercial administrative control office in regard to changes in the charter or agreement. In regard to changes in membership of the organization, it must be recognized that the newly admitted partners have the same liability as the existing partners as to obligations that arose before they became partners. Partners who withdraw from the partnership are liable for the obligations that arise before they withdrew. Only in this way can the interests of third parties be protected.

Partnerships and joint ventures are terminated for the following reasons:

(1) The time limit set in the partnership or joint venture agreement arrives

When the partners or the parties to the joint venture accumulate capital and establish the partnership, there is usually a time limit set for the duration of the operation of the partnership or joint venture. When the time limit arrives, unless the partners or parties to the joint venture unanimously agree to continue the organization and extend the time for production and operation, all activities of the partnership or joint venture must cease.

(2) The partners or members of the joint venture unanimously agree to dissolve

Regardless of whether the partners or members of the joint venture lose their basis of confidence in each other, or the operations of production are not good, or for similar reasons, it is only necessary for the partners or members of the joint venture who do not wish to continue the partnership or joint venture to obtain a unanimous decision of those participating at [a meeting] of the whole body; then the procedures for termination of the business can be carried out.

(3) The purpose of the partnership or joint venture has already been achieved or cannot be realized

The former occurs when, for example, the target plan for the production of goods by the partnership or joint venture anticipated in the charter or agreement has already been completed. The latter occurs, for example, when the goods do not sell, or the raw materials have been consumed and [more] cannot be obtained.

(4) Termination because of administrative regulations

In regard to a partnership organization that has been established and registered which, without cause, has failed to commence operations for a comparatively long time (say six months), the industrial and commercial administrative office having jurisdiction has the right to cancel the registration. In addition, in the case of a partnership or joint venture which is defective that engages in production management and which, within the time set for reorganizing the enterprise has not reformed, the supervisory office has the right to order it to cease.

(5) Termination by judicial decision

Normally, when the capital of a partnership or joint venture does not satisfy its obligations and it does not have the ability to settle its obligations, then, upon the request of an obligee or obligor, and after a reorganization that does not work, when a court has investigated the facts, it may declare it to be bankrupt and dissolve the partnership or joint venture.

When all the members of a partnership or joint venture voluntarily petition for dissolution, or the state or the state administrative control office or the people's court, according to law, announces jurisdiction, in every case there must be an announcement. At the same time, there must be a final accounting of the partnership or joint venture. The person carrying on the accounting will be selected by the partners jointly, or will be appointed by the office having jurisdiction, and [will] work under the supervision of the court.

The responsible work of the party settling the accounts is, in general: to (1) finish up the work and dispose of the property; (2) make a settlement of the claims held by and owed to the organization being liquidated; (3) divide up the surplus or deficit; (4) divide up the remaining property. The person settling the accounts must first, on the basis of a thorough investigation of all of the property, prepare a balance sheet and inventory and send it to all of the partners and offer it to the obligees [of the partnership] for examination. After this, he must settle one by one all claims by and against [the organization being liquidated], and handle claims differently according to their nature and whether or not there is security. Finally, after settling all the claims of and against [the organization being liquidated] the remaining property of the partnership or joint venture must be used first, to return to the participants their investments. If there is any more, it will be distributed to the participants proportionately to their contributions to the partnership.

If the partnership or joint venture property is insufficient to settle the obligations [of the organization] and repay the investments of participants, all those participating must make up the deficiency proportionately according to their contributions. If there are participants who are unable to pay their shares, the others who are jointly liable by law or agreement must be equally liable for that person's share.

7 Property [*Sachen*]

I
*THE GENERAL CONCEPT OF PROPERTY [THINGS—*SACHEN*]*

The "thing" that is studied by the science of civil law refers to a material object, other than a person, that occupies some definite space, and that, moreover, can be controlled and utilized by human power. It may be a natural thing that has not been processed, or it may be a thing that has been manufactured by labor. It may have a definite form. It may also not have a definite form. Regardless of what sort of thing it is, if it is essential for men in production or in their daily lives—anything that brings about material benefits to the individual and society—it is a thing that is studied by civil law scholars.

The important meaning of things in civil law is not only that the most important objects of adjustment by civil law are social relationships based on the possession and transfer of the material means of production—thus, the great majority of civil law relations involve property [things], but also [depends on] the direct relation that the nature of certain characteristics of things has to whether civil law relations can come into existence, or what form those that come into existence will have, as well as what subjects [of law] they will be created between. In brief, the significance of different kinds of property in civil law as well as their position in civil law relations is different in societies of a different nature as well as in societies of a similar nature. This is because, in the final analysis, this question is determined by a particular society's material mode of production and the will of the ruling class.

II
DIFFERENT TYPES OF PROPERTY

In our country, in order to strengthen socialism's system of common ownership of the means of production, and to push forward the rate of development of the national economy, gradually to raise the people's living standard, and maintain the economic order and social peace, and to protect the personal security of the people, it is necessary that use be made of laws and regulations in regard to the regulation of property [things] of different sorts, and that there be clear rules for the area in which each kind of property circulates and for its participation in civil law circulation. According to the rules of our country's law and regulations, property [things] may be divided into the following types:

1. The Means of Production and the Means of Consumption

[The question,] who owns the means of production is the basic standard for differentiating types of societies. The different economic classes are also an important basis for differentiating different types of societies. Because of this, the differentiation of the means of production and the means of consumption is an important division of "things" in law. According to our country's constitution and other rules of law, the means of production basically belong to the whole people or to collectivities. A few forms may belong to peasants and individual workers. But the great majority of the means of consumption belong to citizens. This reflects the basic feature of our country's socialist system. This sort of division of property has great meaning for civil law. It is expressed in the systems of ownership, obligations, and contracts.

2. Fixed Assets and Circulating Funds

The precise types and amounts of capital that are assigned to state organizations and to social organizations are determined according to the responsibilities assigned to them by the state. As regards the most important fixed assets, they [the organizations] normally do not have the right to increase or decrease them on their own without the permission of the supervisory organization. Normally, these fixed assets are allocated according to administrative laws and regulations in accordance with administrative procedure. They may not be transferred in accordance with civil law. Recently, the autonomy of enterprises has increased and state managed enterprises have the right to sell or lease idle fixed assets. The receipts are still added to the fixed assets. Circulating funds may be transferred in accordance with civil law.

3. Property that Circulates and Property with Limited Circulation

This refers to whether or not property that is being circulated has restrictions, and, if so, the extent and differentiation of the restrictions.

Circulating property refers to property which the state permits to be circulated by the subjects of ownership rights among themselves according to the system of civil law autonomy. The range covered by this sort of property is very broad. Many civil law activities that are carried out between citizens and between juristic persons and between [citizens and juristic persons] that create civil law relations are often carried on with this sort of property as the purpose.

Property of limited circulation refers to property which, according to law and regulations, is subject to different limitations on circulation within the range of civil law circulation. Property of limited circulation may be divided as follows:

(1) Natural resources and natural goods and commodities exclusively owned by the state

Our country's Constitution clearly provides that minerals, running water, and forests designated by law as national forests, wastelands, and other sorts of land and sea resources, all belong to the [category of property that is owned by] the whole people. Apart from this, railroads, airlines, post and telegraph communications, and other enterprises and their facilities constitute the life blood of the state economy and they may only be owned by the state. These properties may, in accordance with administrative procedures be allocated to state organizations and enterprise units to carry on the development of their utilization and economic supervision, but they may not transfer the ownership rights to collectives or individuals by means of civil law procedures.

(2) Land

Land is an important means of production. Urban land belongs to the state. State owned land may only be allocated by administrative procedures. Land that is used for agriculture belongs to people's communes or to agricultural cooperatives in collective ownership. No organization nor individual may engage in the sale or lease of land.

(3) Property that is subject to planned procurement and supply

Goods subject to planned procurement in the agricultural sector (unified state monopoly purchase) and goods subject to unified purchase (assigned purchase) are those which use the plan as the basis for their purchase and sale contracts. The state, in regard to three products with great importance for the national economy and the people's livelihood—grain, cloth and oil, from the fifties on—has carried on planned procurement and marketing. It promulgated a number of laws and orders to regulate them and to provide that production units (state farms or people's communes) in disposing of their produce, after [taking care] of the portion [needed] for their own living purposes and storage for future use, would sell a fixed quota to the state. Units or individuals that had not fulfilled their unified purchase responsibility could not sell on their own.

In the case of many commodities under unified state procurement, such as sorghum, silk, tea, sugar, tobacco, vegetables, fruits, medicine, etc., usually the production units, after fulfillment of their required quotas, have the right to sell [the rest] on their own.

In recent years, in accordance with the development of production, and the improvement in market supplies, there has been a gradual reduction in the types of quantities of commodities subject to state procurement and distribution. Beginning in 1985, aside from specific goods, the state has not sent down to the peasants state procurement or distribution and procurement responsibilities. Important agricultural products like grain and cotton are also no longer the object of unified [state] procurement.

In the case of commodities in the industrial sector which are subject to commodity-allocation planned supply and marketing, such as steel, coal, lumber, cement, every sort of machine tool, etc., if the quantity is within the planned allocation, it will serve as the object of exchange when two socialist organizations enter into a contract for supply between themselves. Neither party may violate the plan, fail to perform the contract, or freely transfer the goods and materials that were to be supplied.

(4) Gold and silver

From the establishment of the state, our country carried out unified control of gold and silver through the People's Bank of China. According to the June 1983 Provisions for Controlling Gold and Silver, promulgated by the State Council, [the terms] "gold" and "silver" include: gold and silver produced by mining and as by-products from smelting gold, gold and silver bars, pieces, ingots, dust, gold and silver coins, articles made of gold and silver, and gold alloy, as well as the products of industrial chemistry containing gold and silver, gold and silver residues, waste, waste liquid, and scrap. In our country, gold and silver are under unified management by the People's Bank of China. The state permits units and individuals to have gold and silver, according to law, but they may not use it in calculating prices. It is forbidden for there to be private sale of gold and silver, or use of it as security for a loan. When it is sold, only the People's Bank may be the purchaser. It may not be sold to any citizen or organization. All of the gold and silver produced by organizations of the whole people, or those that are in collective ownership, as well as the surplus gold and silver of those units that require gold and silver to use as raw materials, may not be sold on their own, nor be mutually exchanged, nor retained for use. It must be sold to the People's Bank. With state permission, in certain cities, shops can be established to produce and sell gold ornaments, but it is forbidden to resell the gold at a profit.

(5) Weapons, ammunition, and explosives

In order to protect the security of the state and the stability of the social order, the circulation of these items in civil law relations is the subject of strict limitation. According to relevant rules of law, arms and ammunition used by the army, police, and militia are controlled by promulgated administrative rules. When non-military units buy military firearms, sport firearms, hunting rifles, and injection guns, they units buy military firearms, sport firearms, hunting rifles, and injection guns, they must be purchased with the permission of the supervisory bureau from the designated unit. Apart from this, no unit or individual may engage in the purchase and sale of firearms, ammunition, gunpowder, detonators, and other blasting materials. They will be distributed and procured by the State Material Ministry. It is forbidden to engage in private sale.

(6) Narcotic medicine and other powerful narcotics

Narcotics include opium, morphine, cocaine, and other toxic drug substances that may easily become addictive that are designated by the Ministry of Health. The "Provisions for the Control of Narcotics" issued by the State Council in September 1978, provides that the production, supply, and use of narcotics must be strictly controlled. The production units do not have the right to sell or use them. Specially designated suppliers must have received permission from the Ministry of Health. Hospital units that require them all must have the permission of local health offices. The amount sold is also limited. Juristic persons and citizens may not supply or obtain narcotics without this permission. The state also strictly controls the supply and acquisition of powerful narcotics. The restriction on the civil law circulation of these materials assures the proper supply of the needs of hospitals and scientific research, and protects the life and health of the people.

(7) Historical and cultural objects

This is a general term for cultural objects that have historical, artistic, or scientific value. According to the "Temporary Provisions for the Administration of the Protection of Cultural Objects" promulgated by the State Council in March 1961, and the "Announcement Regarding the Strengthening of the Work of Protecting Historical and Cultural Objects" promulgated in May 1980 and the "The Law of the People's Republic of China for the Protection of Cultural Objects" passed by the Fifth Session of the National People's Congress on 19 November 1982, together with other laws, historical and cultural objects may not be traded on the black market. When individual citizens sell their personally collected cultural objects, it must be to units designated by the state to purchase cultural objects. It is strictly forbidden to export them privately; it is strictly forbidden to sell them at a profit; it is strictly forbidden to sell them privately to foreigners, in order to prevent the people's cultural inheritance and the state's treasure and property from receiving irreparable loss. In addition, the state also strictly controls items that are seriously harmful to the establishment of a civilization with a spirit of socialism (such as reactionary and obscene tapes, video cassettes, etc.) and strictly forbids units and individuals from copying, recording, or selling them on their own.

4. Specified Things and Generic Things

Specified objects are objects that have independent special characteristics. Other painting, etc. Generic things are types, each of which has the same characteristics—things which may be specified by means of type or specifications or calculations based on length, capacity, or weight, for example, certain grades of rice or cement. A generic thing may be substituted for the same type of thing, but when the generic thing has been separated from the mass of the same type of things to become the object [of the transaction], then it acquires the quality of being specified.

The division into these two types of property has a great deal of legal significance which appears in three areas:

(1) In concluding a sales contract the time at which ownership will pass in these two cases is regulated differently by the legislation in every country

Because of the dissimilar natures of specified property and generic property, the ownership to a specified thing passes at the time of the conclusion of the contract, whereas in contracts for generic things, ownership passes when the property is transferred.

(2) The requirements for a demand for return of the object of the contract are not the same

When a contract is entered into in which the object of the contract has to be returned (such as a contract for the lease of a dwelling), when the contract comes to an end, that which is returned must be the original specified object. In the case of some other contracts (such as the contract of a loan for consumption), if, at the time the contract is entered into, the object is money or grain, or some such generic thing, when it is concluded it is only possible to demand the return of a number or measure of things of the same quality. It is not permitted to demand return of the original item.

(3) The responsibility after the object of the contract has perished is not the same

When the object of an obligation is a specified item, and prior to performance of the obligation it is destroyed, the obligor may avoid the responsibility of transferring the object of the contract, but when this inflicts injury on the other party, he must pay damages. If the object of the contract is a generic thing, the obligor must still deliver the same grade of the generic thing if it perishes prior to the time for performance.

5. Movable and Immovable Property

Movable property refers to things that can be moved [physically]. Immovables are things that cannot be moved or whose economic value will be injured if they are moved, for example, land and buildings. The French Civil Code makes the division between these two types of property the basic division of property, and has very extensive provisions for immovable property. The Civil Code of Soviet Russia does not make the division between movables and immovables. In our country, the decisions in cases have consistently recognized the different character of these two types of property. The differentiation of these two types of property is legally significant. Thus, the requirements for the transfer of ownership and the establishment of rights are not the same. For example, in the case of the transfer of an immovable house by sale, gift, mortgage, or *dian* [a type of secured transaction], registration procedures in the building supervision office must be carried out for there to be legal effect. If, in the case of movables, a civil law juristic act is executed, then, except in the case of automobiles and ships, it is, in general, not necessary to carry out registration procedures.

6. Principal Things and Accessory Things

The principal thing is a thing whose essential use is to provide the realization of a definite economic purpose by its independent existence. Accessory things are things which have only an accessory use in connection with the use of a principal thing. The relationship of the two is like the lock and the key, the boat and the oar. The former is the principal thing, the latter is the accessory. The laws of many countries make this differentiation. The legal significance of the differentiation between these two types of property is that when the law or contract does not have a contrary provision, the accessory thing must follow the principal thing. For example, if the parties enter into a contract for the sale of a complete set of goods, the seller must deliver to the buyer the odd fittings along with the main object.

7. Divisible and Indivisible Things

"Divisible things" refers to things which, after having been divided, do not lose their economic utility. For example, grain, oil, liquor, etc. Indivisible things are the things which, after division, do not conform with their economic use, or clearly decrease in economic value. For example, a cow, a bicycle, an article of clothing, etc. The legal significance of this differentiation and these two types of things is:

(1) In the case of property relations, the manner of dividing the shares of common owners is not the same. When the property is divisible, in dividing property, a common owner may divide the actual thing. When splitting property, in [the case of] indivisible things it is only possible for one party to get the thing. The others get compensation in money.

(2) In the case of obligation relations, when there are a number of obligors and obligees whose rights and duties are not the same, and the object of the obligation is a divisible thing, the obligors and obligees have the right to benefits and the duty to bear the burdens according to their shares. When the object is an indivisible thing, the obligees or obligors have joint obligation rights and bear joint duties.

8. Property [Things] Which Can Be Consumed and Property [Things] Which Cannot Be Consumed

A consumable thing is something which, after one use, is destroyed or changes its original form. For example, raw materials, fuel, and food stocks, etc. Nonconsumable things are things which realize their economic value by use over a long period of time and gradually wear out. The legal significance of the difference between these two types of property lies in their relation to the nature and content of contract relations. For example, consumable property can only be used as the object for contract of a loan for consumption. Nonconsumables can be the object of a contract of lease or a loan.

9. The Original Thing and Fruits

The original thing is the thing that produces benefits. Fruits are benefits which the basic thing produces. Fruits may be divided according to their manner of acquisition. There is a difference between natural fruits (fruit from trees, the young of an animal mother, etc.) and legal fruits (the interest from a loan, rent from a house, etc.). The significance of the difference between the original item and the fruits lies in the fact that, except where the law or agreement between the parties provides otherwise, the owner of the original thing has the right to obtain the ownership to the fruits. When the ownership of the original thing is transferred, the right to obtain the fruits is transferred at the same time to the new owner.

III
MONEY AND NEGOTIABLE INSTRUMENTS

1. Money

Money is a special object of civil law relations, a type of thing having a special use in our country. Money is every sort of *ren min bi* [the Chinese currency] issued by the People's Bank of China marked with an amount in money (paper money, coins, every sort of commemorative money).

Under a capitalist system, money can become the capital of possessing another person's uncompensated labor. In our socialist country money serves as an important means of calculating and supervising the production and circulation of commodities, developing the national economy, and improving the people's economy. In civil law relations, money serves as a procedure for making payment provided by law in contracts of sale, lease, hire, loan, transport, insurance, etc., and in other lawful acts. It also serves as damages, as well as a legally designated means for making supplementary payments in the final accounting in civil law relations.

According to the November 1977 Decision Regarding the Carrying out of the Supervision of Cash of the State Council, all money owned by state enterprises, institutions, organizations, groups, ministries, schools, and collective economic units, except for limited amounts in a cash reserve, must be placed in the People's Bank of China. They may not retain it themselves. In the economic relations and activities between juristic persons and organizations, except where, according to a special provision of law, they may make use of cash, they must settle accounts by means of transfers through the People's Bank of China. Money serves as a means of payment only in accounting. It need not be used in circulation. But the establishment of civil law relations between juristic persons and citizens, or between citizens, basically still makes use of cash as the method of payment.

Within our country, unless there is a contrary provision of law, *ren min bi* are the legally designated means of payment. The circulation of all foreign currency is forbidden.

2. Negotiable Instruments

Negotiable instruments are also a form of property. They are a type of written instrument that serves to create and prove a certain property right. The realization of the property right requires the presentation of the negotiable instrument. Consequently the negotiable instrument is not the same as the ordinary certificate of an obligation right (such as the appointment of a representative, or a loan receipt). A certificate can prove whether or not some right of a certain person exists or not. It does not have in itself the character of a negotiable instrument.

Negotiable instruments can be divided into those in the name of a person [order instruments] and those that are not in someone's name [bearer instruments]. The former have the [personal] name or [business] name of the holder of the right written on them, as order checks, drafts, cashiers' checks, bills of lading, etc. The latter do not have the name of the person owning the right written on them. Rather whoever bears the instrument has the property right as in the case of government bonds, treasury bonds, etc.

In our country the assignment of negotiable instruments must be carried on under the rules of individual statutes.

IV
FOREIGN EXCHANGE

Foreign exchange is the money of a foreign state. There are negotiable instruments in foreign exchange, orders for payment in foreign exchange, and other items that use foreign funds. In order to uphold our country's interests, and uninterruptedly increase the receipts of foreign exchange, to economize on payments, and strengthen the control of foreign exchange, in December 1980, the State Council promulgated Temporary Provisions for Foreign Exchange Control of the People's Republic of China. They provide that the People's Republic of China carries out the aim of state centralized control and unified management. The specialized bank for managing foreign exchange is the Bank of China. That is, within the boundaries of China, unless the law or rule provides otherwise, all receipts by Chinese or foreign organizations or individuals of foreign exchange must be sold to the Bank of China. The Bank of China will sell needed foreign exchange under an approved plan. The sale, mortgaging, or circulation of foreign currency is forbidden. In order to control foreign currency the State Council has given to the Bank of China authority to issue Foreign Exchange Certification (for short, Foreign Exchange Certificates). The circulation of foreign exchange certificates is regulated by special provisions.

8 Juristic Acts

I
THE GENERAL CONCEPT OF JURISTIC ACTS

"Juristic Act" refers to a lawful act based on the declaration of intention by the subject with the purpose of producing civil law consequences. It is a simplified term for civil law juristic acts.

Juristic acts are the broadest and most important legal facts. The great majority of civil law relations are produced, altered, or dissolved by means of juristic acts. We may regard them as a legal device frequently used by people who have the intention to organize production and exchange. The study of juristic acts has great significance.

From what has been said above about the definition of the juristic act it has the following characteristics:

1. A Juristic Act Must Take the Declaration of Intention as Its Essential Condition for Formation

The declaration of intention refers to the action of the actor expressing his intention to others to demand the carrying on of a juristic act in a definite form. It may be seen that a declaration of intention requires two elements. One is the actor (the subject) who must have the intention to obtain certain specified civil law consequences. That is, he has a purpose in his heart. This is the place where all civil law juristic acts begin and come back to. But if the intention of the actor remains in his heart, this stage of activity does not have legal significance. Another element is required, namely, the act of expressing his internal intention to the outside by means of a certain form. This causes others to understand. If this is not the case [that is, there is no declaration of intention] there is a possibility that there will be no legal consequences. The legal consequences produced by a juristic act are all determined by the content of the declaration of intention. Consequently, the declaration of intention is the basic element of the juristic act. If there is no declaration of intention, there is no juristic act.

However, the declaration of intention is not the same as the juristic act because, under many circumstances, if there is only a declaration of intention on one side, the expected legal consequences are not produced.

2. The Juristic Act Must Be Capable of Giving Rise to the Expected Legal Consequences Expected by the Actor

Whether or not the legal results contemplated by the actor will be produced is another test to determine whether or not this sort of act constitutes a juristic act. In human activities there are certain acts that do not have the purpose of creating a civil law consequence. Those acts are not juristic acts. Some acts, although they are expected to have consequences, do not have the anticipated consequences (the promised agreement is not obtained, for example). In some cases, although there are legal consequences, these are not the purpose that was anticipated by the actor (for example, the consequence of causing someone to be injured). These acts are not juristic acts. Generally, juristic acts are not all acts that give rise to legal consequences, but [include only] those acts whose legal consequences conform to the actor's purpose and demand.

3. Juristic Acts Must Be Lawful Acts

The lawfulness of the juristic act refers to its content (purpose, motive) being recognized by law. At the least, it is not prohibited by law. Apart from this, [the notion] includes the requirement that the form of the act correspond with the law. It is only when the content of the act and its form do not violate the legal rule that it will receive protection by the state, and thus create legal consequences which the actor wished to obtain. The juristic act is thus, in essence, a sort of lawful act since what it reflects must be the proper requirements of our country's social and economic production and life. On the other hand, in the case of those acts that use the form of a juristic act in seeking an unlawful purpose by making use of economic oppression or the oppressive use of the power of office, causing injustice to others' acts, etc., the legal consequences not only do not conform to the expectations of the actor, they are often contrary to what he intended. None of these sorts of acts are juristic acts.

II
TYPES OF JURISTIC ACTS

1. Unilateral and Bilateral Juristic Acts

The unilateral juristic act is one which can be formed when there is a declaration of intention by only one party. This sort of juristic act does not require the agreement of the other party, to be legally effective. For example, the execution of a will, the rejection of succession rights, the cancellation of a grant of agency, the ratification of an authorization for representation, and so forth. Bilateral juristic acts require that there be declarations of intention by both parties that are in agreement and then there can be a legally effective juristic act. This sort of action is also called a contractual act. Contractual acts can also be divided into two types. (a) The concrete aim sought by the intent of the two parties is the same, as in the case of an act [creating a] partnership when all have a common aim, an act [creating] a joint venture, etc. (b) The concrete aims sought by the intentions of the parties are not the same, for example, the sale. The aim of the seller is to acquire the price. The aim of the buyer is to acquire the goods. The contractual acts constitute the majority of acts that are juristic acts. They are much more significant than unilateral acts. They are an important legal system within the civil law. The bilateral acts are what are studied in the field of contracts.

2. Gratuitous Juristic Acts and Nongratuitous Juristic Acts

In the case of gratuitous juristic acts, one party gives the other party a certain advantage. But the other party merely receives this advantage. He does not pay any return consideration, as in a contract of gift, a contract of loan for use, a contract for an interest free loan for consumption, etc. These contracts may be regarded as a form of disposing of one's own property according to his intention in connection with its return. Although in this sort of act there is no question of a reciprocal price, still it requires that the wills of the two parties be in agreement before it can become effective. In the case of a nongratuitous juristic act, one party gives a certain advantage to another party, and the other party must then make an equivalent counter payment. This sort of act is the most common among civil law actions. For example, the sale, lease, hire, etc., are nongratuitous juristic acts.

It is only in bilateral juristic acts that there is a difference between gratuitous and nongratuitous juristic acts. All unilateral juristic acts are gratuitous acts. Some acts, from their nature, can only be nongratuitous and some can only be gratuitous. If one that is nongratuitous is changed into one that is gratuitous or vice versa, then the nature of the act changes. For example, contracts of sale or lease are both nongratuitous. If they are gratuitous, then the former becomes a contract of gift, and the latter is changed into a loan for use. Apart from these, there are some juristic acts that can be either gratuitous or nongratuitous, for example, deposit, representation, the loan for consumption, etc. In these sorts of contracts, whether or not there is consideration is decided by the parties. If, in the contract, there is no clear provision, then most often it is regarded as being gratuitous, as this sort of contract arises for the most part among citizens and has the character of being one of mutual assistance.

3. Promissory Executory Juristic Acts and Real Juristic Acts

Promissory juristic acts are formed when one party's declaration of intention is reciprocated by the other party's promise (also a declaration of intention), and are those in which the rights and obligations are those agreed upon by the parties. For example, the contract relations of sale, loan, and hire are formed when the declarations of intention of two parties agree because of promises. This sort of act is by far the most important among bilateral juristic acts. The real juristic act refers to the juristic act in which, in addition to agreement between the two declarations of intention, it is still necessary that there be a transfer of a thing before the juristic act comes into being. Therefore it is also called a real contract. In other words, if there is an act without a transfer of a thing, but merely an agreement of the two parties' intention, the creation of a rights-duty relation still cannot arise. For example, contracts of gift, bailment, loan for consumption, and transport, etc., are also regarded in law as real contracts. The reason these contracts require the delivery of a thing before they can become effective is because of the nature of the contract or particular aspects that have been decided on. For example in the case of a gift, even if the donor has made a declaration of intention to make a gift, this is in the group of gratuitous contracts, and prior to delivery of the thing, [the donor] must be permitted to cancel at his option. In the case of contracts for a loan for consumption, deposit, and carriage, the reason for the contract is the delivery of the thing. Only then can it be established. This is because the law requires one party to assume the duty. If there is no act of delivery of the thing, then there is no corresponding performance.

4. Juristic Acts With Required Forms and Juristic Acts Without Required Forms

Juristic acts with required forms are those for whose formation the law requires a form. For example, supply contracts between enterprises under state management on the basis of a plan, as well as other contracts that cannot be immediately settled, must be in written form. Or, again as in the case of a contract of sale of a house between citizens, there is not only a written form requirement, [but] it must also be registered in the housing administration before the transfer is effective. Juristic acts without required forms may use any form. For example, the oral or written form may be selected by the parties themselves. In general, a contract of sale between citizens that is performed immediately [on both sides], or a contract of loan between citizens is of this kind.

5. Principal Juristic Acts and Accessory Juristic Acts

The principal juristic act is an act which does not rely on the existence of another legal relationship before it comes into existence, for example, an act of contract for a loan. An accessory juristic act is one which depends on the principal juristic act. The establishment of this sort of juristic act requires the existence of the other legal relations. [An] example [is] the act of guaranty of an obligation.

6. Independent Juristic Acts and Supplementary Juristic Acts

An independent juristic act is one for which the actor relies on his declaration of intention in order for it to be established. A supplementary juristic act is one in which a certain juristic act requires a declaration of intention of another before it comes into being. The said supplementary declaration of intention then becomes a supplementary juristic act. Examples [include] the consent of a statutory representative to the act of a person with incomplete capacity to act, or the ratification by the one being represented of an act of a representative that exceeds his authority—these sorts of juristic acts.

Juristic acts can also be classified from other points of view.

III
FORMS OF JURISTIC ACTS

The form of the juristic act refers to the form by which the actor expresses his internal intention to the outside. If the content of the intention did not make use of a certain form to be expressed to the outside, then there would be nothing to indicate its existence. Outsiders could not be aware of it or establish a civil law relation with it.

As to the form required for a juristic act, since circumstances differ, [the forms] differ. In the case of some juristic acts, one or both of the parties may freely select the form. It [the act] is then legally effective. In the case of some juristic acts a form provided by law must be used before [the act] is effective.

According to the rules of our country's current civil law norms, and the general principles of every country's civil legislation, acts may be divided into those using oral and those using written forms. In addition, in a number of situations the law also recognizes the actor's silent [implicit] method of expressing his intention. Consequently, silence is also a form for juristic acts. The division is discussed as follows:

1. The Oral Form

The oral form uses the method of speech to make the declaration of intention. It includes face-to-face conversations and arranging things by telephone. All of these are juristic acts for which the law does not require the written form to be used. In all [such cases] the oral form may be used. The oral form is simple to use. Usually when the price is low, or when a juristic act can be settled or concluded on the spot, the parties may, if they wish, elect this form. But the disadvantage of the oral form is that there is no written record. If a dispute arises, it is not easy to obtain good evidence. Consequently, the oral form should not be used for juristic acts when the consequences are great, the content is complicated, or when a certain period of time must elapse before it is settled.

2. The Written Form

The written form may be divided into the general written form and the special written form (including the notarized form, the certificate of inspection, and certificates of examination, verification, and registration).

(1) The general written form.

This means to use a written form to express the intention of the parties. A juristic act for which there is a written form has the advantage of having evidence that can be examined. Moreover, the rights and duties of the parties are specified and disputes can be avoided or decided. When the written form is used, the parties can write it themselves or can get someone else to write it for them. But, in order to explain that the content is what is intended by the actor, the actors must sign and seal the document. The written juristic act may consist of one document or a combination. A juristic act which comes about by means of an exchange of letters or telegrams also comes within [the category] of a juristic act that uses [the written form].

In our country, important juristic acts between socialist organizations all must use the written form. As provided in section 3 of the Economics Contract Law, "except for those which are settled immediately, economic contracts must be in written form." Consequently, all important juristic acts between enterprise units and collective organizations, must, according to the provision of the law, be in written form. Also, according to the rules of the local housing offices of our country, the sales and leases and other juristic acts [related to] houses also must employ the written form.

(2) Special written forms

These are divided into:

(i) Notarized forms. This refers to the parties giving their written juristic acts such as contracts, wills, and so forth, to the state notarial office having authority according to the provisions of the Temporary Provisions for Notaries of the People's Republic of China, and requesting notarization and obtaining a notarized document. A notarized juristic act acquires exceptionally strong probative force, both as to its facts and as to its legality.

(ii) Certificate of inspection. This refers to the case of the industrial and commercial supervisory office which, acting according to its supervisory authority, investigates and issues an inspection certificate in regard to the legality of a contract. Frequently the parties may decide whether or not to require that a juristic act have an inspection certificate. However, if the law provides that a certain contract be inspected by the industrial and commercial administrative supervisory office, or by the notarial office, then there must be an inspection certificate or notarial certificate according to law, before the juristic act is legally effective.

(iii) Certificates of examination, verification, and registration. That is, the law provides that certain juristic acts must have the full form of being examined, verified, and registered by the superior organization. Thus, in many foreign

contractual acts, the written contract must be submitted to the superior organization to be examined, verified, and authorized. Some juristic acts require the procedure of examination, verification, and registration. For example, the acts of selling houses, ships, and certain types of motor vehicles, and the [act] of creating certain types of juristic persons, all must go through the procedure of examination, verification, registration. In the cases of the juristic acts discussed above, it is only when the above procedures have been followed that the acts are effective.

3. The Form of Silence

In all of the above juristic acts, the actor expresses his intention to others by means of a positive clear, direct, form. It could be called an explicit form. The form of silence is opposed to these explicit forms. It is not like the explicit form in which the intention can be learned from his direct declaration of intention. Rather, it can only be learned from an indirect declaration of intention by means of a presumption or according to presumptions based upon the customs of daily life.

Silence may be divided into two types. The first is where the actor has done some "act." For example, the lessor, after the expiration of the lease term, has continued to receive payments of rent from the lessee. It is assumed that he consents to a continuation of the lease. When the former and subsequent wills have conflicting provisions, the conflicting provisions of the subsequent one are regarded as cancelling the provisions of the former, etc. Another type is accomplished by the means of "omission"—that is silence of the actor. Normally silence cannot be used as a declaration of intention. It is only when the law has a special rule that the circumstance can serve as a declaration of intention. For example, according to our country's rule for settling accounts, if the paying party, after having received the bank's voucher of having made payment for him, if, after the passage of a certain period of time, he does not dishonor this payment, he is regarded as having authorized payment.

Silence, as a declaration of intention, must have some limits. There cannot be broad interpretation of this matter.

IV
CONDITIONS FOR THE EFFECTIVENESS OF JURISTIC ACTS

Juristic acts must meet the following conditions in order to be considered legally effective, and, moreover, capable of producing the legal results anticipated by the actor.

1. The Actor Meets the Requirements [Standards]

In order to carry out a juristic act it is necessary that the actor meet certain requirements:

First, the actor must have the capacity to act. In regard to natural persons, persons without the capacity to act (minors, persons declared to be without the capacity to engage in legal acts, or a person who is not in his right mind and is unable to understand the meaning of his acts) cannot execute juristic acts that are legally effective. But law and custom do not prevent persons without the capacity to act, or persons with limited capacity to act, from engaging in a few actions that are compatible with the requirements of their years. With regard to juristic persons, when one engages in juristic acts it must act by its representatives (or by someone commissioned by it within the scope of action provided in its charter and bylaws). But the law does not prevent a juristic person from engaging in certain juristic acts which, although they are not within the scope of its responsibilities, are necessary in order to protect its existence and activities.

In addition, when the juristic act relates to disposing of certain rights, the actor must be a person with a capacity to dispose of those rights. For example, the owner of a house has the right to dispose of (sell) that house. A lessor of the said house only has the right of possession and use of the said house. He does not have the right of disposition, and thus he cannot dispose of (sell) the said house.

2. The Declaration of Intention Must Be in Accordance with the Actual Intention of the Parties

Normally the declaration of intention is in accordance with the subjective intention of the actor. But there are also occasions when, for objective and subjective reasons, it happens that there is a difference between the declaration of intention and the actual intention. If a juristic act arose out of duress, fraud, or misunderstanding, this would be the result. In those circumstances the decision as to whether the juristic act is lawful and effective would depend upon whether there is agreement between the declaration of intention and the actual intention of the actor. This sort of doctrine is not applied in the case of a negligent actor's expression of his intention to outsiders. All persons who have the capacity to act must, under ordinary circumstances, be responsible for their declarations of intention. They cannot rely on the declaration of intention having been made unintentionally or being something that they did not completely understand or estimate sufficiently, etc., and in this way fail to assume the responsibility. But if the declaration of intention has arisen because of the strength of an outsider (most importantly that of the other party), for example, if, because of the threats or fraud of another, someone makes a declaration of intention, if the act is regarded as valid because of the outward appearance, this is obviously unreasonable. This is because the most important aim in establishing the system of juristic acts is to assure that when parties participate in economic activities they can achieve their real intentions. Because of this it is only when there is agreement between the real intention of the actor and its external expression that it can be affirmed to be lawful and effective.

3. The Content Does Not Violate the Law and Public Morals

Since juristic acts are recognized and protected by the state, unless their content is lawful they cannot be legally effective. But if the purpose or the price violates a legal rule, or a contractual act violates an order under the plan, or a testamentary act deprives minor children of their lawful share of inheritance, etc., these are all unlawful acts. Although these acts have legal significance, and can give rise to legal consequences, they cannot give rise to the legal result contemplated by the actor, since they are contrary to law.

The determination as to whether or not the content of the act is lawful must first of all be based on whether it lies within the provisions of the existing law. However, no legal provisions of any period that relate to the acts of persons can provide for everything without any gaps. Consequently, when there is no concrete provision to deal with a matter, it is necessary to go first to the spirit of the Constitution and to the basic principles of civil law legislation.

The consequences brought about by moral norms are not like the consequences brought about by legal norms that have the force of the state behind them. But in the case of civil law activities, if the content or purpose of an act violates the principle of social morality, then this is enough to cause the action to be regarded as being without effect, because an immoral act does not receive the recognition or protection of socialist law.

4. [It Must Be in] Accordance with the Legally Designated Form

For the juristic act to be effective, it is not only necessary that the content of the juristic act be lawful but the form in which it is expressed must also be in accordance with legal rules. When the law has rules and states certain requirements as to what sort of form must be used for certain juristic acts, these rules are compulsory. Parties have no right to select [any other form]. If they do not follow the form that is decreed, the juristic act cannot come into being. These are certain measures that the state has taken in intervening and supervising the carrying out of certain juristic acts and in order to protect the socialist order.

V
CONDITIONAL JURISTIC ACTS AND JURISTIC ACTS WITH A TIME LIMIT

1. Conditional Juristic Acts

Legal norms establish special conditions for some juristic acts. Moreover, when the occurrence of this condition is made the basis [for determining] whether or not the juristic act is effective—the establishment of rights and duties, their alteration, or dissolution—then this is a conditional juristic act. If a party includes in advance a purchase contract to buy certain material in the future from another party, but in the contract there is a condition that it will come into effect within sixty days if a certain scientific test is successful, this sort of contractual act is a conditional juristic act.

The utility of a conditional juristic act lies in the fact that it can progressively cause the actors' intentions to have legal significance. For example, A's motive in wishing to buy low quality coal from B is the hope of reconstructing the boiler to use low quality coal so as to be able to reduce construction costs. But if the technology for converting the boiler fails, then the poor quality coal has no meaning for it. Under normal circumstances the juristic act (declaration of intention) can only indirectly reflect the party's needs, it cannot reflect the motive for the said needs. In other words, the actor's motive cannot serve as the basis for the coming into being of the rights-duty relationship. In order to solve this problem, it is only necessary to have the motive for the juristic act serve as a condition of the contract. In this way the actor can first of all be assured that he will get the thing he needs (the test is successful), and he will avoid the purchase of something he does not need (the test is unsuccessful) and thus avoid a condition that will be anticipated to cause trouble.

A condition in a juristic act is a specially designated fact that can be a natural phenomenon and it can also be a human action. But in order to serve as a condition, it must at the same time have the following characteristics: (a) at the time the juristic act is executed (the contract is signed) it must not yet have happened; (b) it can happen; (c) whether it will happen and when it will happen cannot be known in advance; (d) it is selected by the parties. A fact decreed by law (for example, a change in the plan, irresistible force), as well as facts required by the nature of the act (as, in the case of a contract of insurance, the insured's accident) are not this sort of condition.

There is a difference in the conditions of juristic acts between conditions precedent and conditions subsequent. The former refers to the case in which, although the rights and obligations in a juristic act are already fixed, their effectiveness is in a state of suspension. That is, the obligee cannot exercise his right to make a demand. The obligor still does not have the duty immediately to perform his duty. Only when the condition has occurred does the above discussed rights-duty become effective. The second refers to a juristic act that is already effective but when the condition occurs, the rights-duty relation is dissolved.

Apart from this, it is possible, from another point of view, to divide conditions into positive and negative conditions. The former are those which make the happening of a certain fact the occurrence of the condition. The latter refers to the non-happening of a certain event as a condition. But regardless of whether they are positive conditions or negative conditions, they can be either conditions precedent or [conditions] subsequent.

Once a conditional juristic act is established, it is binding on the acting party. Afterwards, whether or not the condition occurs must be left to the natural unfolding of the events. The actor must not, for its own advantage, or in bad faith, promote or hinder the happening of the condition. Normally, when a condition has been brought about by bad faith it must be regarded as not having occurred. When it is prevented from happening by the bad faith it must be regarded as having occurred. The purpose in law of this sort of claim is to protect the parties' lawful rights. This makes the conditional juristic act of positive use in civil law circulation.

2. A Juristic Act with a Time Limitation

When a juristic act has clearly provided a time limit which makes the passing of a certain period of time the prerequisite for the effectiveness of the juristic act (that is, the creation or destruction of the rights and duties), this juristic act is a juristic act subject to the condition of time limits.

The significance of time in certain juristic acts is not clear, as in the case of an act of immediate sale, an act of gift, etc. In these sorts of juristic acts, the rights-duty relationship is created, realized, and concluded almost at the same time. But in the great majority of important civil law juristic acts, the element of time is extremely important. For example, in a long-term material-planned supply contract, the times for the transfer of products are specified. In capital construction contracts there is a time specified for beginning work and for completing work. Moreover, in contracts of lease, loan, deposit, transport, etc., the obtaining of rights and the performance of obligations have a direct relation with time. Performing contract obligations according to a time limit is an indispensable requirement for the state in connection with the socialist economy in coordinating production and marketing activities, fulfilling responsibilities of the plan, strengthening and speeding up capital turnover, and improving economic results.

From the point of view of the use of a time period in connection with the effectiveness of juristic acts, a division can be made between a "suspensive time period" and a "resolutory time period." When a suspensive time period is provided in a juristic act, it [the juristic act] becomes effective when the time period arises. That is, although the rights-duty relationship has already been specified prior to the arrival of the time limit, it is still postponed and temporarily does not take effect. The obligee only has the right to demand performance from the obligor upon the passage of the suspension. (For instance, in the case of an obligation relation with a time set for repayment, when the agreed-upon time occurs, the obligor must immediately repay the obligation.) Consequently, a suspension of time is also called a "beginning time." When a resolutory time is provided, a juristic act's effectiveness is annulled upon the passing of the time. That is, the effect has already come into being as a result of the rights-duty relationship established by the juristic act and continues until the end of the resolutory time (for example, in the case of a lease relation, with a specified time period, [the lease] is annulled when the time has elapsed). Consequently, a resolutory time period is also called an ending time. Even though, like conditions, time periods are used to suspend or terminate rights-duty relations, they are not the same. The parties cannot know in advance whether a condition will or will not occur. They act as though the condition will occur or will not. But in the case of time, the parties can know in advance of an act [that] the time will certainly arrive.

The times that are set in juristic acts may be set in the following ways. (1) The parties may designate a certain calendar date (for example, 1 January 1982) to be used as the date for determining when rights and duties are created or dissolved. (2) They may designate a certain period of time (for example, from 1 January 1982 until 1 June 1982) to indicate the period of time during which the rights and duties exist or do not exist. (3) They may set up a time determined by an event that is certain to occur (for example, the termination of work on some project), or [by] a time period [that is certain to occur] (such as the period between the time of entering the station and leaving the station). (4) The time when a party makes a request may determine the time (as when the entruster collects the deposited object, when, in an obligation where no time is set, the obligee demands performance of the obligation).

As regards the calculation of time, according to the general rule, if the time is to be calculated by the hour, the calculation is from the moment of beginning. If the calculation is by the day, week, month, or year, the day of beginning is not included in the calculation. The calculation begins on the following day. If the last day is Sunday or a holiday, then the first working day after the holiday is the final day of the time. The end of the last day is midnight. If there is a provision for business hours, the time ends at the conclusion of business activity.

If the time is not calculated continuously according to the calendar (as, three months after the note arrives, three years after making the agreement), one month is calculated as thirty days, one year is 365 days.

VI
INEFFECTIVE CIVIL LAW ACTS AND THEIR CONSEQUENCES

[Until this point of the chapter the only term used has been *fa lü xingwei*—juristic act. Here it changes to *minshi xingwei* which I translate as "civil law act." Where *fa lü xingwei* occurs it is translated as "juristic act."]

1. The Bases for the Ineffectiveness of Civil Law Acts

An ineffective civil law act is one which does not fulfill the conditions of the juristic act and therefore cannot give rise to the expected civil law consequences. An ineffective civil law act does not possess the special characteristics of the juristic act. Therefore, it is not a juristic act. It is also not a type of juristic act.

Under the following circumstances there are what can be regarded as ineffective civil law acts.

(1) The actor is not qualified

This includes (a) the actor who does not have the capacity to act or temporarily has lost the capacity to act; (b) the actor who does not have the qualifications of a juristic person but uses the name of juristic person, or, although it has the qualifications of juristic person, the act exceeds the limits of its power; (c) the disposition of property by a person without the lawful right to do so. This includes a person who engages in civil law acts for another where no authority has been given but he acts on his own.

(2) The content of the act is unlawful

In order to maintain the socialist economic order, and to protect the lawful rights of citizens, it is necessary to determine strictly according to the principles of socialism, whether or not an act is within lawful limits. In reference to the related provision in the 1922 Soviet Russian Civil Code, Lenin clearly pointed out that it is not merely the juristic acts that directly violate the law that are to be regarded as without effect, but juristic acts that violate the interests of the laboring masses of workers and peasants also must be regarded as being without effect. In civil law acts in our country it is not only acts that clearly violate the letter of the legal norms that must be regarded as being without authority, but also all acts whose content injures the common interests, violates the social order, or offends against socialist morality, must be regarded in the same way—as civil law acts that are without effect.

Among civil law acts in general, it is only when there are objective facts that violate the law that there can be the basis for regarding them as constituting acts that are without effect. It does not matter whether the said act has resulted from intention or negligence or from defective knowledge of the law. In all cases it is ineffective.

(3) Acts that do not comply with the form designated by law

See section IV.4 of this chapter.

(4) The declaration of intention is not genuine

The fact that the declaration of intention is not the same as the actual intention of the one who makes the declaration is an important basis for the invalidity of civil law acts. The following types are the most important.

(i) A simulated civil law act. A simulated civil law act is one in which there is the form of the lawful [act] but the actor does not really intend the act to bring about legal consequences. This sort of act does not really have the nature of a juristic act. It is without effect.

(ii) Sham civil law acts. In the case of a sham civil law act the actor executes a juristic act with the intention to conceal some act. The sham juristic act does not reflect the actor's real intention. Consequently, it is without effect. Among these there are two types of circumstances. One is the case where the concealment has

the purpose of violating or avoiding the law. For example, to use a gift to conceal speculation; in order to avoid the compulsory execution process of a court, pretending to transfer property by gift. In another kind of case, the concealed act is not a violation of the law. For example, A wishes to lend his house to B to live in, but proceeding from the belief of a certain type of person he conceals the act of gift by signing a purported lease and concealing the true loan for use. In handling sham civil law acts, regardless of which of the above types is selected, all must be treated as sham acts. If the concealed juristic act violates the law, then this act is without effect. If necessary, it is possible to affix [criminal] responsibility. If the sham act is not in violation of the law, it must be treated as the juristic act it was really intended to be. For example, in the example given above, the relationship between A and B must be handled as a loan for use and not as a lease.

(iii) A civil law act that is induced by fraud. Fraud is an act with the purpose of causing the other party to have a false belief. A civil law act which is executed as a result of the fraud refers to one party intentionally establishing a false set of circumstances, and covering up the true, in order to cause the other party to be caught in a mistake and then execute a civil law act. This sort of act has the following characteristics: (1) the fraudulent act must be intended by the actor; (2) the method of fraud can be positive (as to make false words appear true); it can also be negative—silence (when the seller intentionally fails to declare the defects of the item sold to the buyer). The purpose in both cases is to cause the other party to be deceived; (3) the party who is defrauded executes the act entirely as a result of the false idea. That is, if he had understood the true facts he would not have agreed to enter into this sort of civil law act.

Civil law fraud can also include criminal swindling, but the fraud that causes an act to be without effect does not necessarily include criminal law swindling. Any evilly intentioned act that has the purpose of causing the other party to become mistaken is a fraudulent act, and in civil law these are all the basis for making acts invalid.

(iv) A civil law act which is executed because of threats and coercion. "Threats" means to cause someone to be afraid and to execute an act because of injury that is to be inflicted in the future. A civil law act which is executed because there have been threats and coercion is a civil law act which is executed because of threats. The threats can be directed against the physical body (as, injury or killing) or they can be moral (as, rumors, slander); it may also be directed at property (setting a fire, destruction of a thing). Threats may be directed at the person himself, they may also be directed at the individual's relatives, but they all must be unlawful, significant, and possible actions. On the other hand, threats that are lawful, trivial, or very unlikely to occur, cannot result in acts induced by threats.

Coercion and threats are not the same. Coercion is violence and force applied directly to the person (such as taking into custody or striking); coercion is forcing [someone to do something] by means of circumstances which are actually happening. A threat is coercion by means of future harm.

Regardless of whether there were threats or coercion, both constitute the basis for declaring a civil law act to be without effect.

(v) A civil law act that results from the representative of one side plotting with an evil intent with the other side. This sort of act is one in which the agent betrayed his principal by privately colluding with the other to carry out an infringement on the lawful rights of the principal. The agent has the legal duty of being required to uphold the interests of the principal and to bring about the realization of the principal's intention. Under the circumstances discussed above, he has injured the interest of the principal and violated his intention. Therefore, this sort of act is invalid.

(vi) A civil law act which is executed because someone takes advantage of another's emergency need and clearly violates justice. This act is one in which one person forces another to act contrary to his own intention and to accept especially unfavorable conditions, and [thereby] himself receives and obtains a great advantage. This is clearly unjust. This sort of act [is like the act induced by] threats or coercion entered into by one party because of the other's pressure. For example, the "*Bawang* contract" [*Bawang* is a despot who rules by force; hence, presumably, a contract imposed by force], and the usurious contract are typical examples of the form of this sort of act. If, because of a sort of urgent need that is common in production or daily life, one is willing to accept conditions that are not very just in a civil law act, if they do not exceed the limits permitted by law, it will be regarded as being effective.

(vii) A civil law act that proceeds from a serious misunderstanding. A serious misunderstanding refers to the case where one party makes a serious error in understanding a major provision of the juristic act. If the error had not been made, [that party] would not have entered into this sort of juristic act—for example, if he thinks a price of 100 *yuan* is ten *yuan*. Although both fraud and mistake are based on civil law acts that are executed on the basis of a mistaken understanding, in the former the actor himself made the mistake. In the latter the other party causes the mistake. Misunderstanding does not include mistakes that are simply ones of motive. For example, the motive of the purchaser of a certain pesticide is to get rid of a certain kind of insect, but in fact, another type of insect appears that causes this pesticide to be useless. The sort of juristic act that is made on the basis of one's own mistake of judgment is not a civil law act that is the result of a serious misunderstanding.

Among the four bases that are set out above, for deciding that a civil law act is ineffective, the first three can be determined on the basis of objective conditions of the act. In the case of the final one, since it is closely connected with the mental activity of the parties, until this sort of mental activity has been revealed, the outsider has no way to evaluate it, because the objective appearance of both parties can often be in accordance with legal rules. There must be a petition to annul by an interested party and it is only when the court has determined to issue an annulment and promulgated it that it is possible to confirm that the civil law act is without effect. Therefore this sort of act is called a voidable civil law act. It must be pointed out that the persons who are permitted to petition for its annulment include not only the one who was injured, and the one who was mistaken, but also include interested third parties. If one party or both parties are socialist organizations, and moreover there is a clear injury to the interest of the state or the people, the investigative organizations [procuracy] must have the right to initiate action to determine whether the said acts are effective.

Sometimes only a portion of a civil law act is ineffective. If the invalid part is discarded, and this has no influence on the remainder, then the ineffective part is annulled, and the remainder is effective.

2. The Consequences of an Invalid Civil Law Act

Civil law acts that are invalid. Invalid civil law acts have no legal force ab initio. But this does not mean they are without legal effect. According to the circumstances, invalid civil law acts still may give rise to administrative consequences or criminal consequences or civil law consequences. Below we will speak of civil law consequences.

(1) Both parties withdraw

Where there is an invalid civil law act (including a civil law act that has been annulled), if the actor did not intentionally injure the other party's interests when he violated the law, then each party must return to the other the property he has received. This causes the property relations to return to the condition that existed prior to the execution of the act. For example, if both actors do not have the capacity to engage in acts or if both parties are defective in legal knowledge, so that the act that is executed does not meet the legal form requirements; or an act results from a serious misunderstanding—in all these cases there must be restitution. If the act discussed above causes one party to be injured, the party who is at fault (if he is a person with the capacity to act) must be liable for damages to the other party. For example, if a person with the capacity to act knows, or should know, that the other party does not have the capacity to act, and engages in an act that causes the other party to be injured, he must pay damages to the other party. When a civil law act is executed because of a serious misunderstanding and causes injury to the other party, the party who was mistaken is liable to pay damages.

(2) Unilateral restitution

If the ineffective juristic act consists of one party intentionally infringing on the interests of the other party, and violating the law, this gives rise to the consequence of a unilateral duty to repay. If one party, with evil intent, makes use of threats, coercion, fraud, and the other person's urgent needs, or colludes with the other party and executes a civil law act, and the parties have already performed it, then the party who is in violation of the law must return the property which he has received from the other party to that party. The property which the injured party has received does not have to be returned to the other party, but is received by the court to be paid into the Treasury. Because he intentionally used means contrary to the law to injure the other party, the actor loses his right to demand that the other party return the property which he has given him.

(3) Returning the amounts obtained by both parties to the Treasury

When a juristic act has resulted from the intentional violation of the law by both parties, since their act is one that injures society, neither has any right to get back the property paid to the other party, but they must return to the Treasury the property which they have both received. Where the parties have engaged in serious violations of the law, not only must the property which they have received be paid over but the property which it has been agreed to deliver, but which has not yet been delivered, must be paid into the Treasury.

(4) Compulsory purchase

This method is normally used when the parties have violated a rule and sold a small quantity of jointly purchased materials. This act violated the law or local administrative rules, but it was minor and the handling of this sort of act must be by means of compulsory purchase by the designated organization in accordance with the posted schedule of state purchasing prices.

In the case of the above four types of civil law acts that are without legal effect, apart from the civil law consequences that have to be assumed, this does not exclude criminal liability of the actors for any consequences. If the act violates the criminal law, then it is necessary to proceed to affix criminal responsibility.

9 Representation

I
THE GENERAL CONCEPT OF REPRESENTATION

1. The Definition and Legal Characteristics of Representation

Representation is a type of civil law relationship. In the relationship of representation, the representative executes juristic acts with third persons in the name of the one being represented, within the limits of his right of representation. The legal consequences of these acts are directly borne by the person being represented. For example, a cooperative A, appoints B, a corporation, to represent it in ordering five water pumps. The B corporation, within the scope of the rights bestowed on it, signs a contract with enterprise C in the name of the cooperative A to purchase the five water pumps. This immediately creates a contract between the cooperative A and the enterprise C for five water pumps. The act of representation of the representative is legally effective as to the one being represented. The parties to the act of representation are the one being represented [A] and the party dealt with by the representative [C] and not the representative [B].

Representation relations all have the following legal characteristics:

(1) The act of representation is carried on in the name of the one being represented

The responsibility of the representative is to act for the one being represented in executing juristic acts. It is only when the representative acts in the name of the one being represented in executing acts of representation that he can bring about rights and duties for the one being represented. The use of the name of the person being represented means that the legal consequences of the act of representation relate back to the one being represented. If the representative executes a juristic act in his own name, this sort of act is the representative's own act and not an act of representation. This characteristic of representation is the point of difference between the representation relation and brokerage. In the case of a brokerage office or a commission shop that sells goods on commission, the one commissioned carries on the buying and selling in his own name.

(2) The act of representation must be an act with legal significance

The act executed by the representative must be an act that can give rise to legal rights or duties. That is, it must be an act that can have legal consequences, for example, representing the principal in signing a contract, performing an obligation, or carrying on a lawsuit. Because of this, the representative in completing his act of representation must normally involve third parties. That is, he makes a declaration of intention to a third party or receives a declaration of intention from a third party. This special characteristic of representation is the basis of the difference between representation and an act that is undertaken as the result of a commission to manage, for example, such acts as straightening out materials for another, reading and revising a manuscript, carrying out calculations, estimates, and so forth. All of these are not civil law representation relations.

(3) The representative independently makes declarations of intention within the scope of authority given him by the principal

An act of representation is a juristic act and the declaration of intention is the heart of a juristic act. Therefore the representative, in the act of representing, according to the scope of the grant of authority and the circumstances, has an independent right to make a declaration of intention. That is, he has the right to decide himself how to make a declaration of intention to a third party, or whether or not to accept a third party's declaration of intention. This special characteristic of representation is the basic difference between a representative and a mediator, a transmitter [of information] and a witness.

A mediator is also called an introducer. His responsibility is to introduce two parties to establish a legal relation. He serves the function of intermediary. He does not take part in the legal relations of the two parties. He does not need to make a declaration of intention independently. The transmitter only takes the declaration of intention of one party, and from beginning to end, transmits it to the other party. Even less does he need to make a declaration of intention. As for the witness, he is the certifier [prover] of a legal relationship. His only function is to prove the existence of the said relationship. He does not participate in making the declaration of intention for a juristic act. He also does not participate in the legal relationship.

(4) The legal effect of the acts of the representative relates directly to the principal

The acts of the representative within the limits of his right of representation are regarded in law as the acts of the principal. Therefore, although the representative act arises between the representative and the other person, the effects of this act extend directly to the principal. That is to say, the rights or duties created by the representative act relate directly back to the principal. They include responsibility for injury caused by the representative in carrying out his responsibilities of representation.

From the above it can be seen that the representative relationship includes the representative, the person being represented [the principal], and their relations to third parties.

2. The Development and Significance of the System of Representation

Representation constitutes an independent legal system. It is the result of the development of a high-level commodity economy.

Following the development of the exchange of commodities, men, because of their health, location, or knowledge, often needed to carry on activities through the representation of others. Late Roman law already had rules of this type for representation.

Following the development of a capitalist commodity economy, the exchange of commodities was frequent. Social life grew more complicated daily. People could not take care of everything personally, but had to get assistance from others. This was particularly due to the difficulties and limitations arising from the individual's health, knowledge, and ability, as well as time, place, and so forth. So there was a still greater necessity to rely on representation by others to bring about the realization of one's own rights. As far as capitalist companies and enterprises are concerned, with their constant trade and the expanded activity of professional management, it was difficult to manage by relying solely on their organizational structure. Making use of the form of commissioning representatives to carry on management activities and participate in the circulation of civil law matters was not only absolutely essential but was also completely economical. By means of representation, a company or enterprise could, at the same time, in different places, and even in different countries, carry on many business activities, breaking the barriers of time and space, and greatly increasing its power to compete or monopolize. The system of representation was adapted to the objective needs of a capitalist commodity economy and gradually formed a sort of independent civil law system. The French Civil Code of 1804 and the German Civil Code of 1900 had different systems of rules for representation. This caused the system of representation gradually to hasten to perfection and to form a constituent part of civil law.

Our country also recognizes the system of representation. The Economic Contract Law of the People's Republic of China, the Patent Law of the People's Republic of China, the (Trial) Code of Civil Procedure of the People's Republic of China, as well as many concrete economic rules, all have important rules for representation relations. Our country's system of representation harmonizes with the objective requirements of the development of the socialist economy. It expresses the relationships of mutual help and working together between men in a socialist society.

Using our country's system of representation with its special characteristics greatly facilitates citizens and juristic persons exercising their civil law rights. It is of great significance in enabling the realization of the civil law rights of citizens, juristic persons, and other subjects of civil law rights, greatly facilitating society's economic activity and fulfilling our country's construction of modernization.

3. The Scope of Application of Representation

The scope of application of representation is exceptionally broad. Both citizens and juristic persons may, by means of the act of representation, execute juristic acts and other acts having legal significance in order to realize their own rights and to perform their own duties. The activities of representatives include, most importantly, the following:

(1) Representation to carry on all kinds of juristic acts

[Examples include] representation in sales, leases, hire, [work contracts], transport, loan, the performance of obligations, etc.

(2) Representation to perform certain financial or administrative obligations

[Examples include] representing a juristic person in registration, or in the registration of trademarks, or in paying taxes, and so forth.

(3) Representation in a lawsuit

According to the (Trial) Code of Civil Procedure of the People's Republic of China it is possible to use a representative in a civil law suit. A party who, because of lack of capacity to act, or limited capacity, or because of the circumstances of location, time, or health, is unable to appear personally in court to carry on the suit, may be represented in the carrying on of the suit by his representative appointed by law or by his commissioned representative.

However, representatives cannot be used for every juristic act or act of legal significance. Those actions that require personal performance such as writing a will, registering a marriage, adopting children, etc., may not be accomplished by representation. Those personal obligations, such as an agreement [to produce] a manuscript, or to execute a painting, or to perform [in a show], that are owed to the promisee cannot be satisfied by representation.

II
THE BASIS FOR THE CREATION OF REPRESENTATION AND THE TYPES OF REPRESENTATION

Representation is created by legal facts that can give rise to a representation relation. The legal facts that can give rise to a legal relation are: the appointment by the parties, statutory rules, and directives of concerned state supervisory organizations. A distinction is made among appointed representatives, representatives by operation of law, and designated representatives.

1. Appointed Representatives

An appointed representative is one who acts as a representative on the basis of an appointment by the principal represented. The principal bestows the power of acting as representative on the representative by means of a declaration of intention to appoint. This is called an act of appointment. The act of appointment is a unilateral act. It only requires the unilateral declaration of intention of the principal to make the grant of authority effective. That is to say, it only requires the unilateral act of appointment by the principal in order for the representative to obtain the authority to represent.

The legal relationship that operates on the basis of the appointment of a representative may be a relationship based on a contract of appointment, a relationship that arises from a labor contract, or a partnership relationship, or a relationship arising out of a job.

The form by which the principal grants authority may be oral or in writing. The written form of a grant of authority to represent is called a letter of appointment as representative or a certificate of appointment. This is a legal document that shows clearly that the representative has the authority to represent.

The act of the principal in granting authority must be directed towards the representative. It may also, at the same time, be directed towards the object of the representation [that is, someone with whom the representative is dealing]. The declaration of intention of the principal granting the authority to represent to the representative, when directed to the opposite party, also has legal effect. Under these circumstances, when the authority is cancelled, the principal must notify the other party. Only then is the cancellation of the authority to represent effective. The authority to represent may be given to one person or to several. When there are several representatives, the scope of authority of each representative must be clearly indicated at the time of the grant of authority. If the law or the one granting authority does not have a special provision, then this [situation] is regarded as several representatives carrying on a joint representation. Moreover, they are jointly responsible.

2. Representation by Operation of Law [Statutory Representation]

Representatives by operation of law are representatives created by direct statutory rule as a basis. The most important representatives by operation of law are those appointed to represent persons without the ability to act or with only a limited ability to act, for example, in the case of a blood relationship between parents and children. Our country's marriage law provides that the father and mother are the statutory representatives of their minor children. In the case of organizational relations between a union and its members, our labor law provides that unions represent their members in signing collective agreements and in participating in lawsuits that relate to labor disputes, etc.

3. Designated Representatives

A designated representative is one who becomes a representative by a direct administrative order from a state supervisory organization or by the designation of a court. Since state supervisory organizations or the people's courts are able to use regulations and orders to appoint one person to act for another person, this is still based on the rules of state laws and policies. Therefore, appointed representatives come within the area of statutory representatives designated by operation of law.

According to law, one who is designated as a representative may not refuse [the appointment] without cause.

4. [Appointing] a Sub-representative

The [term] "sub-representative" refers to the case when a representative transfers to a third person the carrying out of his representation. Therefore it is also called the transfer of a commission or re-representation.

Since a representation relationship is strictly personal, the representative normally must himself complete the act of representation. It is only when it is within the authority granted by the principal, or under emergency circumstances for the benefit of the principal, that the representative may transfer his commission to a third party for execution.

When a sub-representation is established, the representative must first obtain the consent of the principal. When this is not possible, then, when the matter is over, he must notify the principal, and, moreover, inform him of the essential circumstances related to the sub-representation in order to protect the interests of the principal and to strengthen the system of representation.

When the representative transfers his authority to a third party to carry on the representation, a representation relation comes into existence between the representative and the sub-representative—a second representation relationship. In order to increase the responsibility of the representative to select the sub-representative, the representative bears responsibility to the principal for the actions of the sub-representative.

III
CERTIFICATE OF REPRESENTATION

1. The Nature and Use of a Certificate of Representation

The certificate of representation is called a letter of appointment as representative or the letter granting authority [to represent]. It is a legal document issued by the principal that shows clearly the authority of the representative to represent. Our country's Economic Contract Law provides that in concluding a contract by representation it is necessary first to obtain the appointing unit's certificated grant of representation, and then sign the contract in the name of the appointing party, and within the scope of the authority granted; only then does it directly create rights and duties vis-à-vis the appointing unit. Our country's (Trial) Code of Civil Procedure provides that in order to appoint another to represent one in a suit, it is necessary to present to the people's court a letter of authority to represent signed or sealed by the person making the appointment. It may be seen that a certificate of representation is the proof of the representation. Based on the certificate of representation, the representative can, within the limits of the representation, carry on civil law acts for a third party in the name of the principal. The principal then has the duty to bear the legal consequences.

To show unequivocally whether or not the representative has the right to represent is not only of concern for the representative and the principal, but also for the other parties to acts carried on by the representative. Therefore a certificate of representation is very significant in the relationship of representation.

In the appointment of a representative, the effectiveness of the certificate of representation comes directly from the act of the principal granting authority. Because of this, it happens that if, for some reason, the contract of appointment of the representative does not come into existence or loses its effectiveness, there cannot, because of this, be any influence on the representative's power to represent. For example, a contract of representation that is induced by fraud loses its legal effectiveness, but the contract of representation is not necessarily without effect. That is, a certificate of appointment of representation that has not been cancelled remains effective. The representative acts of the representative are still legally effective as to the principal. Therefore the civil codes of every country, in general, provide that if the principal cancels a representation or the representative abandons it, then the representative must return the certificate of representation. The representative has no lien on the certificate of representation. This is in order to ensure the full utility of the system of representation. It is also advantageous for protecting normal economic relations and the interests of a good-faith third party.

2. The Content of the Certificate of Representation

In order to have the representative relationship established on a stable and reliable foundation, the certificate of representation must clearly show the name of the representative, the nature of the representation, the scope and time period for the representation. The principal must sign and seal the certificate of representation.

The certificate of representation may make a grant of authority to represent [the principal] in the execution of a particular juristic act or it may indicate a certain person who will be the other party to the juristic act. There may also be a certain matter in which to carry on representation, such as the establishment of a purchasing agency or a selling agency between two juristic persons in a certain business. Our country's (Trial) Code of Civil Procedure provides that the representative for litigation, in order to admit [liability], abandon or amend a complaint, carry on a settlement, bring a suit or appeal it, must have a particular grant of authority from the principal. In general, the right of representation is limited to what is clearly and unmistakably stated in the certificate of representation. This is required when the representative is dealing in a representative capacity with third parties. It is advantageous for making clear the rights, duties, and responsibilities of all parties to the representation.

3. The Form of the Certificate of Representation

A certificate of representation is not limited to a certain form. In a statutory representation, although the authority to represent is dependent on a provision of law, when the representative designated by statute and another party engage in a juristic act, the other party has the right to demand that the representative tender his certificate of being a representative. Usually a household registration book or a certificated document prepared in the household registry organization or a related organization can be used as a certificate of representation.

In a commissioned representation, a grant of authority between juristic persons or between juristic persons and citizens must, in general, be in written form, that is, a written grant of authority to act as representative. In order to make the responsibilities unequivocal and to avoid subsequent disagreements that might arise, the certificate appointing a representative must be notarized in accordance with the statutory rule, or the nature of the act of representation, or the agreement of the parties. It is only after notarization that it can take effect. It must be signed and sealed by the representative of the juristic person and sealed by the notary.

In the case of the representation normally used by citizens in daily life, the grant of authority may be made orally or in writing, but in order to protect the normal carrying on of the representation relation, and to prevent disputes from arising in important civil law matters, it must be in written form to be valid.

IV
THE END OF A REPRESENTATION RELATIONSHIP

A representation may come to an end because of one of the following reasons.

(1) One party dies or there is declaration of death, or a juristic person is dissolved

A representation relation is a kind of civil law relationship that is strictly personal. If the party acting as the subject of the civil law relation dies or is dissolved, the representation relation is then dissolved because of the loss of one of the subjects of the legal relationship.

(2) The representative loses the capacity to act

In a representation relation it is the representative's duty to act as a representative in executing a juristic act. If the representative loses the capacity to act, or is declared to have lost the capacity to act, he loses the ability to represent others in executing juristic acts. The relation of representation must, in consequence, dissolve.

(3) The reason for constituting a statutory representation disappears

If, in the midst of a representation, a reason for establishing the representation disappears, the representation must, accordingly, disappear. For example, if a minor arrives at the age of majority, or if the declaration that the principal does not have the capacity to act is dissolved, and the guardianship is dissolved, the reasons which gave rise to the representation having disappeared, the relationship of representation loses its basis for existence and is dissolved.

(4) The cancellation and resignation of the right of representation

In the commission of representation the principal has the right to cancel a representation and the representative also has the right to resign the representation. These acts of cancellation or resignation are all unilateral acts. They require only that there be notification of the other party and the legal effect of the right of representation is destroyed. This is because the relationship of representation is founded on the basis of mutual trust. Moreover, in order to accomplish a certain act of representation, once this presupposition has changed, it follows that the parties may dissolve the relationship.

In the case of the cancellation of the authority to represent, and the resignation of the representative, there must be notification of the other party in order to avoid causing injury to the other party. Otherwise, if this is not done, [then the one failing to give notice] must assume responsibility for any property injury that the other party suffers. Notice of the cancellation of the representation and resignation of the representative must still be given to the other party, or a third party must be informed in the same manner that he was informed of the grant of authority, in order to protect the interest of the other party or the third party. The principal cannot avoid his responsibility for a juristic act entered into between the representative and a good-faith third party prior to cancellation or resignation of the representative authority because of the cancellation or resignation.

(5) When the task of representation has been completed or the time period for the representation has come to an end

After the representative has completed the work designated by the principal, the principal acquires the civil law rights obtained for him by the representative, and assumes the civil law duties that have been created. The representation relation between the representative and the principal is then said to be at an end. The representative must immediately notify the principal of the completion of the job or give him a report.

If a representation relationship has a time limit, after the time for effectiveness of the representation has expired, if the one being represented has not continued the grant of authority, the representation relationship is dissolved.

V
REPRESENTATION WITHOUT AUTHORITY

1. Representation Without Authority and the Basis for Its Coming into Being

A representation without authority occurs when one who has no authority to represent another executes a juristic act in the name of another, such as when one who has not received a grant of authority carries on some matter with legal significance for another. For the most part, representation without authority arises in the following circumstances.

(1) The representation relation is already dissolved

The representative who, after the representation expires, or after the task of the designated representation is completed, still executes a juristic act in the name of the principal, is a representative without authority. [Similarly, representation without authority can arise in] a representation subject to a condition subsequent. If the condition occurs and the representation is dissolved, under these circumstances representative acts executed by the representative are all representation without authority.

(2) The representative exceeds the representative authority

Although the representative and the principal have a representation relationship, the representative only has the rights of representation within the limits of the authority to represent. If the representative on his own, without authority, executes an act which exceeds his authority to represent, the portion in excess is an act of representation without authority.

(3) Representation when the authority to represent has not yet been bestowed

When the grant of authority has not been made, or there is no direct legal provision or particular order of the state's supervisory organization, and the representative on his own executes a juristic act, this is representation without authority.

2. The Legal Consequences of Representation Without Authority

(1) "The principal" has the right to ratify (recognize) [the representation]

The unauthorized representation is not legally effective against the "principal," but if the "principal" subsequently ratifies the act, then the unauthorized act becomes an authorized representation and is effective as to the "principal." The right to ratify by the "principal" has retroactive effect. That is, once the principal has ratified, the representation relation is regarded as having taken effect from the beginning. If the principal does not make a declaration of intention of ratification, the unauthorized act of representation is clearly designated as an act without effect, and it does not give rise to any legal force against the principal.

The declaration of intention of the "principal" ratifying or refusing to ratify the unauthorized act of representation may be made to the unauthorized representative or to the other party.

(2) The other party has the right to give a deadline or to cancel

Along with the right of the principal to ratify, there is a reciprocal right of the other party to the unauthorized act of representation to set a deadline for the "principal." That is, he may notify the "principal" to state within a certain time whether or not he ratifies the act. If the "principal" delays his ratification for an unlimited period of time, this places the other party in a very insecure condition, and causes him to suffer injury. If the "principal" exceeds the time limit, and does not make a definitive reply, he is regarded as having refused to ratify after he loses the right to ratify.

Prior to the principal's ratifying the unauthorized act of representation, the other party has the right to cancel. That is, to renounce the juristic act executed with the representative without authority. This is an essential consequence of the equality of the rights of the other party with those of the "principal." If there were only the right of the "principal" to ratify, and no right of the other party to cancel, then it would be difficult for the other party's interests to obtain equal protection. Therefore, the other party, prior to ratification by the principal, may on his own cancel all or part of the action that was executed with the representative without authority. However, if, when the other party executes a juristic act, he already knows that the representative is without authority he loses his right to cancel.

(3) The duty to pay damages of the representative without authority

If the actions of the representative without authority have not been ratified by the "principal," and if there is no way to prove that he has authority, the representative must bear the responsibility for his own acts. That is, he should pay damages for any injuries suffered by the other party from the unauthorized act. The scope of the damages [is determined] by applying the general rule of damages of obligation law. The representative without authority must pay damages for injuries that the "principal" receives from his unauthorized act of representation. Requiring the unauthorized representative to assume liability to pay damages is beneficial to the strengthening of the system of representation, and the social and economic order, and the lawful rights of third parties.

10 Prescription

I
GENERAL DISCUSSION OF THE SYSTEM OF PRESCRIPTION

1. General Concepts and Significance of Prescription

The system of prescription is a system whereby, after a certain set of facts has gone on for a certain period of time, there are certain legal consequences. The civil law of countries with a system of private ownership divides prescription into acquisitive prescription and extinctive prescription. In every case in which, after a specified set of facts has gone on continuously for a specified period of time, a right is acquired, it is called acquisitive prescription. In every case in which, as the result of a particular set of facts having gone on continuously for a certain time, there is the loss of a right it is called extinctive prescription. In general, a certain set of facts and the passage of a certain period of time, are the two conditions for the establishment of prescription. They are separately discussed as follows.

First, prescription requires the existence of a certain set of facts as an essential condition. In the case of acquisitive prescription, the fact of actual possession of another's property is the condition. In the case of extinctive prescription the fact of not exercising a right is the condition. If these sets of facts do not exist, then, regardless of the passage of time, in both cases there cannot be the legal consequences of prescription.

Secondly, the passage of time is also a necessary condition for prescription. It is only when there is a certain set of facts that continue for a definite period of time that the legal consequences can arise. Therefore, prescription is established after the passage of a certain period of time. To be sure, if the certain set of facts does not exist one cannot have prescription just because of the passage of time. There must be the union of the specified set of facts and the passage of a specified time period; then prescription takes place.

Prescription is a legal fact recognized by state law. When prescription is established, the legal consequences of changes in rights and duties naturally come into being regardless of the objective decision of the parties. Therefore, prescription belongs to the category of a legal fact [that is called] an "event."

Prescription and the preclusive term [*Ausschlussfrist*] are different. The preclusive term refers to the time for exercising the right. That is, the law provides certain time periods [terms] for the exercise of certain rights. When the term is exceeded, this will result in the extinction of that right. For example, section 15 of the Contract Provisions for the Purchase and Sale of Industrial and Mineral Products provides that when the external appearance and type of the products, the model, specifications, design, and color, do not conform to the rule, if the supplying party has sent the goods and arranged for their transportation, the party requiring the goods must, within ten days after the arrival of the goods, tender a written [statement] of variances. If he does not tender a written [statement] of variances within the specified time, the goods that have been sent must be regarded as conforming with the rule. In this case, the ten-day term is a preclusive term. If the said term is exceeded, the right of the requiring party to present a written [statement] of variances because of defects is extinguished. The difference between prescription and the preclusive term lies in the fact that in the case of the preclusive term, there is no question of suspension, cutting off, and extension, but in the case of prescription there can be suspension, cutting off, and extension. The preclusive term merely provides a period for the continued existence of the right. If the period is exceeded, the right is completely extinguished. But in prescription, acquisitive prescription is only aimed at the problem of the acquisition of rights. That is, it works so that after the extinctive term is completed, the right of the holder of the right is not completely extinguished. In addition, the term of prescription is usually longer than the preclusive term.

The principal significance of prescription is to assure the order of social economic life. If people do not exercise their subjective rights for a long time, and the law, moreover, recognizes their validity for an indefinitely long period of time, this will inevitably lead to obligation rights from a long period before (this sort of obligation relation has often already been forgotten by the obligor) suddenly [appearing and thereby] changing the previous economic order. In order to protect the previously settled conditions of economic life, the law's provision of a system of prescription is absolutely essential. Secondly, the fact that the law does not give protection to rights that have exceeded the period of prescription is advantageous in that it encourages the obligee to exercise his rights immediately. It causes the rights and duties between the subjects of civil law to be immediately settled in order to encourage further circulation in civil law matters and the development of the social economy. Moreover, carrying out a system of prescription can also avoid disputes over obligations of a long time previous from arising. Often, in these sorts of disputes, because of the lapse of time, proof is difficult to discover and check. So, although the obligee has a right, often it is difficult to produce proof, so that it is difficult to decide the truth or falsity of the case. Therefore using a system of prescription is valuable to a court in deciding case.

2. The Historical Development of Prescription

The origins of prescription are in Roman law. In Roman law acquisitive prescription and extinctive prescription were two dissimilar systems. Acquisitive prescription began in the Roman law of the Twelve Tables. Extinctive prescription was established in the law developed by officials in deciding cases. The former is derived from possessory prescription, the latter began in procedural prescription. In the middle ages the Glossators brought these two institutions together and placed them in the general category of "prescription." In modern times, whenever a capitalist country promulgates a civil code, some, following the Glossators, place prescription in the general part (such as France and Japan). Others place extinctive prescription in the general part and possessory prescription under property (Germany).

Soviet scholars deny the reasonableness of acquisitive prescription. They believe that to acquire a property right by possessing another person's property for a long time, even if the possession is open and peaceful, is to violate the standards of socialist common life. Therefore, in the general part of the 1922 Civil Code of the Russian Soviet Republic, only procedural prescription is provided for. Section 44 provides that "the right to bring suit is extinguished if suit is not brought within the time period described by law." However, the civil law of the Democratic Republics of Germany and of Hungary both have provisions on acquisitive prescription.

For a long time, in the civil law theory and civil law legislation of our country, acquisitive prescription was not recognized. We believe that the actual requirements of our economic activity are that a system of acquisitive prescription should be established.

So-called acquisitive prescription is also called possessory prescription. It refers to the possessor without a right who, on the basis of his intention to own, in good faith, openly and uninterruptedly occupies another person's property. After the lapse of the period set by law, he acquires the ownership of the said property according to law. The essential requirements of acquisitive prescription are: (1) The possessor who has no right possesses on the basis of his own intention to own and is not regarded as guarding or making use of someone else's property. (2) The possessor without right must act in good faith. That is, when the possessor without right occupies another person's property, he does not know nor is he charged with knowing that the said property belongs to someone else. (3) The possession by the possessor without right must be open, uninterrupted, and for the period of time provided by law. Only then can he obtain, according to law, the ownership right.

Acquisitive prescription and procedural prescription supplement each other. Each is indispensable. When the procedural prescription has expired, the obligor may avoid the duty that he was required to fulfill but he cannot, by means of procedural prescription, acquire the ownership to the object in question. But the holder of rights also cannot enjoy the ownership rights to the said property. This might result in the said property being under no control for a long period. This would be disadvantageous to the stability of the social economic order. Consequently, the law, at the same time that it provides for procedural prescription, must provide for possessory prescription in order to make certain the ownership of property. In actual life, providing a system of acquisitive prescription is also advantageous for causing the owner of property to care for his own property painstakingly, to exercise his rights promptly, and to maximize the economic utility of his property. To be sure, a special principle of protection is selected based on the property of a socialist country. In general the system of acquisitive prescription is not used in connection with state property.

II
PROCEDURAL PRESCRIPTION

1. The General Concept of Procedural Prescription

Procedural prescription refers to the case where the obligee does not exercise a right during the prescriptive period and thus loses the right to request the court, in accordance with civil procedure, to compel the obligor to perform his obligation. Therefore, in fact, procedural prescription is extinctive prescription.

After the establishment of extinctive prescription in Roman law, every country subsequently made use of it, but the legislation of different countries in regard to the legal consequences of extinctive procedure was not the same. In the civil codes in some countries, it is provided that after the expiration of the period of prescription the holder of rights loses his substantive rights. Some countries provide in their civil codes only that after the expiration of the period of prescription the one having the duty has a defense. That is, the one having a duty has the right to avoid performance. The provisions of the 1922 Russian Civil Code, in connection with prescription, actually provide for the extinction of the substantive right to bring suit, that is, the right to win a lawsuit and not the procedural right to bring suit.

The particular characteristics of procedural prescription are:

(1) After the prescriptive period has expired, the one holding the right may still bring suit in court demanding that the one having the duty perform [it], and the court must accept the suit. After accepting the suit, the court must decide on the basis of whether or not a good reason for the delay in bringing the suit exists, whether or not to protect [the right]. If there is no good reason for the delay in bringing suit, it may reject the suit on the basis of the period of prescription having expired.

(2) After the expiration of the prescriptive period, if the one having the duty initiates performance of the obligation, the obligee still has the right to receive it. After that, the obligor may not demand a return [of the performance] on the basis that he did not know that the time for prescription had passed.

The important purpose of prescription is to uphold the stability of all social economic relations. Therefore, legal rules in regard to prescription are in the realm of compulsory legal rules. Unless there is a different special legal rule, every organization and citizen must obey them. Agreements between the parties to lengthen or shorten the prescriptive term are without effect.

2. Types of Procedural Prescription

Procedural prescription can be divided into ordinary procedural prescription and special procedural prescription.

(1) Ordinary procedural prescription

Ordinary procedural prescription is also called long-term procedural prescription. Usually it is provided for by a single rule in the civil code. It is used for ordinary civil law rights. The rules for the term for ordinary civil law prescription are not the same in the legislation of different countries. Speaking generally, in capitalist countries relying on Greek and Roman law, there is a relatively long term, even several times ten years. Socialist countries have a relatively short time, generally not more than five years.

Our country's civil law legislation still has no special rule regarding the usual procedural prescription. In our country's world of legal science it is generally believed that the subjects of a civil law relationship are not the same. Each is also not the same in respect to the aim which it wishes to achieve and in its influence on the national economy. Procedural prescription must provide different periods of time that are in harmony with these [conditions]. Thus for [disputes] between citizens, five years, for [disputes] between a citizen and juristic person, three years, and for a [dispute] between juristic persons, two years, etc. This point of view is somewhat more in harmony with our country's actual conditions. It can be offered as a reference when [the matter] is legislated.

(2) Special procedural prescription

Special procedural prescription is also known as short-term prescription. Its term for prescription is shorter than the ordinary period. It is used for certain legal relations that require prompt settlement. Based on a special law, it prevails over the principles of general law. Special procedural prescription also prevails over ordinary procedural prescription. In general, special procedural prescription is provided for by a civil code or in separate laws. For example, section 61 of the Patent Law of the People's Republic of China provides: "The period of prescription for infringing a patent right is two years, calculated as beginning from the day when the holder of the patent or an interested party knew or should have known of the infringement." Section 8 of the Inheritance Law of the People's Republic of China provides: "The time for beginning suit over disputes over inheritance rights is two years, calculated as beginning from the day when the one inheriting knew or ought to know of the infringement of his rights. But when twenty years have passed after the opening of the succession, a suit may not be brought." Apart from this, there are also provisions for special periods of prescription in the transport, insurance, and other laws.

3. Calculating the Beginning of the Running Time of Procedural Prescription

The term of prescription is normally computed from the time the right can be exercised. This is because it is only when the possessor of the right can exercise it and is remiss in exercising it, so that the prescriptive term is exceeded, that the holder of the right must bear the legal consequences [of prescription]. If there is an obligation right whose time [for exercise] has not yet arrived, the holder of the right still has no right to make a demand. Procedural prescription consequently is not calculated from the day the right comes into existence. If, at the time a civil law right comes into existence, the holder of the right already has the right to make a demand, procedural prescription naturally must begin to be calculated from this time. But the basis for this is not that the right came into existence, but that the right to make a demand could then be exercised. Consequently, since the types of obligations are not the same, the moment when the prescriptive period begins to run is also not the same. According to differing circumstances, the methods of computation can be roughly divided as follows: (1) In the case of obligation rights subject to a condition precedent, the time commences from the time when the condition takes place; but if the right to demand specifies a time period, then the time of prescription is computed as beginning from the time this period is completed and the right to demand may be exercised. (2) In the case of an obligation with a time for commencement, when that time arrives, the prescriptive term begins to be computed. (3) In the case of an obligation in which the time for settlement [payment] has not been specified, [the term] begins to be computed from the time when the obligation is established, but when the time for settlement [payment] is specified the time for computation begins when that time arrives. (4) In regard to an action for damages, generally the time for computation begins when the harm was done. If the injured person does not know of the time of the injury, or that someone was injured, the time for beginning the computation for procedural prescriptions begins at the time he knows, or should have known, that the injury occurred and that it injured someone. Even though there are a number of differences in the point at which the time for computing the prescriptive term begins and the type of obligation discussed above, actually one still takes the time at which the holder of the right may exercise his right as the time for beginning the time for the running of procedural prescription.

III
SUSPENDING, CUTTING OFF, OR PROLONGING PRESCRIPTION

1. Suspending Procedural Prescription

(1) The general concept of suspending procedural prescription

The suspension of procedural prescription refers to the occasion when, while the period of prescription is running, a certain event or condition specified by the law arises which prevents the holder of the right from exercising his right. Therefore, the law provides for the temporary suspension of the running of the period of prescription. The period of time that has already run is still in effect. When the matter which caused the holder of the right to be unable to exercise his right ceases, prescription continues to run. The intervening period of time during which prescription was temporarily halted is not computed in the time [for the running of] prescription in order to make sure the holder of the right has the time required to exercise his right.

However, the answer to the question of what the legal consequences are if specified matters should arise during the time prescription is running, is not exactly the same in every country. The German Civil Code has two types of rules, according to the nature of the obligation. In one type, if the legally designated matter arises at any time during the time that prescription is running, it can have the consequences of suspending it. With the other type, it is only if the matter arises during the last six months of the time for the running of prescription that there will be the consequences of suspending prescription. The Civil Code of the Russian Soviet Republic provides that "it is only if the [matter arises] during the last six months of the [period of prescription] or continues into that time that suspension can take place. If the said prescriptive term does not amount to six months then it may be suspended during the entire time of prescription." The Japanese Civil Code also has a similar provision. Our country still must await the enactment of legislation to provide a rule. But we believe that the idea that regardless of when during the period of prescription the matter that causes suspension arises, in all cases it may give rise to the consequences of suspension of prescription, is not necessarily appropriate. If the cause for suspension arises and ceases before the last six months of the period of prescription, then although this may reduce the prescriptive period for the holder of the right after the cause for suspension has ceased, the holder of the right still has six months of the period of procedural prescription. According to the conditions of our country's communications and transportation, and the [way] courts are set up, this is enough time to enable a holder of rights to bring suit in a court. Therefore, there is no need for a suspension of prescription. To provide that the legal consequences of suspension of prescription arise only if the cause of suspension arises within or continues into the last sixth months of the period is advantageous for protecting the lawful rights of the holder of the rights. It is also useful in encouraging the holder of rights actively to enforce them, it avoids complicating legal relations. Thus it is suitable for achieving the purpose of procedural prescription.

(2) The bases for suspension of procedural prescription

Usually the bases for suspending prescription are brought together in a civil code. Therefore they are also called the legally specified bases for suspension. In our country, the bases for suspension of prescription still await civil law legislation, but according to scholarly theory and statements, the holder of rights must have [these bases] when there are circumstances that are unforeseen and which he cannot overcome, which prevent him from exercising his rights, for example: (1) unforeseen circumstances such as natural disasters, wars, etc., which are beyond human power to resist; (2) the holder of rights loses the capacity to act or has only limited capacity to act, and has no legally designated representative; (3) after succession begins, there is no definite successor or executor, etc. Just because the reasons that prevent the rights holder from exercising his rights are a sort of objective cause that cannot be attributed to the rights holder, the law recognizes these reasons as having the power to suspend prescription and protect the lawful rights of the holder of rights.

2. The Cutting Off of Prescription

(1) The general meaning of the cutting off of prescription.

The cutting off of prescription refers to the fact that during the period of prescription the happening of a certain matter hinders the running of prescription and even causes the prescriptive time that has already run to be without effect. After the basis [for cutting off prescription] has ceased, the period for prescription begins to run [once more].

The cutting off of prescription and the suspension of prescription are both complete bars to prescription, but the suspension of prescription is a temporary bar, the cutting off of a prescription is a complete bar. The causes that can serve as the basis of cutting off prescription are certain acts of the parties. When these acts appear prior to the running of the prescriptive term, the result is the cutting off of prescription.

(2) The bases for cutting off prescription.

The bases for cutting off prescription are normally all provided for in a civil code. Therefore, they may also be said to be the legally designated bases for cutting off prescription. According to the nature of the system of prescription, the following acts may be said to be those which are legally designated as the causes for cutting off prescription.

(i) Acknowledgment. This is the declaration of intention of the one having the duty, made to the holder of the right, recognizing the existence of the right. The result of this action is to cause the rights of both parties among themselves (once again) to be clearly settled. Therefore, every country's civil law provides that acknowledgement [by the one having the duty] is one of the bases for cutting off prescription. The manner by which the obligor acknowledges the obligation need not be restricted to a specially designated form. For example, the obligor seeks an extension of the time for delivery, or makes a partial delivery, or proffers a guaranty of performance of the obligation, or pays interest, or rent, etc. All of these [acts] may be regarded as acknowledgements. Because of the acknowledgement, the cutting off of prescription is effective. This is definite and unconditional and is thus the strongest basis for cutting off of prescription. The obligor's declaration of

intention to the obligee acknowledging the obligation, makes the cutting off of prescription effective. The acknowledgement must be made while prescription is running. After the term of prescription is complete, the acknowledgement cannot give rise to the cutting off of prescription.

(ii) Demand. That is, the holder of the right makes a demand in the form of a declaration of intention for performance of the duty to the one owing the duty. This refers only to a demand made outside a lawsuit for the expedition of the performance of the obligation by the obligor. The act of the holder of the right requesting performance by the obligor thus changes the circumstance of his not having exercised his rights. Consequently it is a reason that prevents prescription from running.

(iii) Bringing suit. That is, the holder of the right, by bringing a lawsuit, demands that the obligor perform his obligation. The action of the holder of rights in going before the court and bringing suit is a forcible means by which the holder of rights demands that the obligor perform his obligation. It must be regarded as the exercise of his rights. Therefore, bringing suit is one of the important methods of cutting off prescription. On the day the holder of the right brings suit in court the period of prescription is cut off. If the suit that is brought before the court by the holder of the right is rejected by the court, or is voluntarily withdrawn, then it cannot be effective to stop prescription. But the complaint sent to the obligor can be regarded as a demand on the obligor. Therefore it can give rise to a cutting off of prescription on the basis of a demand.

Apart from this, the announcement of a suit or a request for enforcement of performance [of the obligation] are generally regarded as having the same effectiveness in stopping the running of prescriptions as bringing suit.

3. Postponement of Prescription

The postponement of prescription refers to a court giving a suitable prolongation to the term for the prescription of an action. If the obligee has not exercised his rights within the period of prescription, and there are none of the bases for suspending or cutting off prescription provided for by law, but the court, after investigation, believes that there is a good reason for the failure to exercise the rights when the suit is brought after the expiration of the prescriptive term, it may, on considering the concrete circumstances, appropriately prolong the period for completing prescription in order to protect the party's legitimate rights. We believe that our country's legislation, when determining the rules for the existence of prescription, must give the court the power to decide whether or not to prolong the period of prescription on the basis of whether or not there is good reason for it to fill the gaps in the legally designated bases for prescription. But the court must exercise strict control in regard to this sort of prolongation. Otherwise it could be a violation of the purpose of establishing a system of prescription.

II PROPERTY

[*Chapters 11–17 Omitted*]

III OBLIGATIONS

18 The General Statements of Obligations

I
THE CONCEPT AND MEANING OF OBLIGATIONS

1. The Concept and Special Characteristics of Obligations

An obligation is a civil law relationship between specified persons. One party to the obligation has the right to demand that the other party perform or not perform a certain act. The other party has the duty to satisfy the said demand. Owing to the fact that the manner in which obligations arise are different, in some obligations only one party enjoys the right and does not assume the duty. The other party has a duty and does not enjoy a right. In the majority of obligations both parties enjoy rights and assume duties and the two parties' rights and duties are mutual and reciprocal.

Obligations form an important part of the civil law's adjustment of property relations. In recent times every country regards obligations as the most important field of law within civil law. It is only in the names [given it] that there are differences. Some call it obligations or obligation law. Some call it the law of obligations, some call it the law of obligation rights and duties, some call it the law of obligation rights and duties relations, but in content there is no great difference. When obligations, property rights, and property rights relations are mentioned together, they are usually called obligation rights or obligation law relations. These differences in names do not influence or change the content of obligations.

The most important property relations adjusted by civil law are ownership rights and obligation rights relations. These two kinds of property relations are part of civil law relations. Ownership and obligation rights are two basic property rights. In a society of a commodity economy, the ownership right itself is the foundation and prerequisite for obtaining obligation rights. If the subject of civil law does not have any rights to the ownership of property, he cannot transfer the said property rights and create obligation relations. At the same time, after the obligation relation arises, it frequently leads to the transfer and acquisition of ownership rights. Ownership rights are also the consequence of the realization of obligation rights. This explains clearly that ownership rights and obligation rights are closely related to each other but obligation rights are not, when all is said and done, the same as ownership rights. This is shown in three areas:

(1) The subject of an obligation

The subjects of an obligation are the parties to the legal relation of the obligation. Among the parties there is one party who has the right to demand that the other party do or refrain from doing something. This is the subject of rights. He is called the obligee. The one who is the subject of the obligation to perform or refrain from performing a certain act as demanded by the other party is called the obligor. In the case of mutual and reciprocal obligations, both parties to the obligation are subjects of the right to make a demand, thus both are obligees and obligors. Citizens and juristic persons can both be the subjects of civil law. One or both parties may be single or [composed of] several [persons]. The state is a special civil law subject. Naturally it has the characteristic of being the subject of an obligation.

The obligation right relation is a civil law relation between specified subjects. It is not merely the obligee who is specified, the obligor is specified, too. Whenever an obligation relationship is established, regardless of the basis of its establishment, its obligor is *ipso facto* determined. The obligee's right to demand [performance] is only effective as to a particular obligor. Consequently, it is often called a right against persons [*in personam*]. The property relationship is not the same. It is a civil law relationship with a specified subject of rights and an unspecified subject of duties. The owner of property is the subject of the right. Everyone else has the duty not to infringe on the exercise by the owner of his ownership rights over the said property. Consequently, all of the unspecified people besides the owner are the subjects of a duty. Consequently, the ownership right is often called a right against the world [right *in rem*].

(2) The content of an obligation

The content of an obligation includes the rights enjoyed by an obligee and the duties assumed by the obligor. That is, the obligation right and the obligation duty. The content of an obligation is determined by the actual scope of the performance of a particular act or the nonperformance of a particular act, which causes it to be determined. The performance of a specified act is also called the performance of a positive act. Nonperformance of a certain act is also called performance of a negative act. Since their scope is already determined, the two are both called specified acts. In real life the obligee often requires the obligor to perform an act in order to achieve his own purpose. Therefore, the realization of the obligee's rights must rest on the obligor's act.

The ownership right is not the same. The owner has the rights of possession, use, and disposition over the things he owns. He can directly exercise control over the things he owns. He does not need help from anyone else's act to realize his own right. Everyone except the owner has the duty not do something. That is, they may not perform any act that would interfere with or injure the owner's exercise of his rights.

(3) The object of an obligation

The object of an obligation is the common aim of the obligee's right and the obligor's duty. In common parlance the object of an obligation can be a thing, as in the contractual relationship of sale or lease. In those cases the objects are things. It also can be an act, as in the contractual relation of hire and transport where the object is the proffering of labor, [or] the action of finishing a certain work, or sending a passenger or goods to a certain destination.

The ownership relation is a possessory relation between the subjects of civil law in regard to material goods. Because of this, its object is limited to things, but according to the rule of law, there can be only one ownership right to one thing. That is, one thing, one right. Thus the ownership right itself is exclusive.

The difference between ownership and obligation rights is also seen in the way they are protected by law. When the obligee's obligation right is protected, he can generally only seek damages or payment of the penalty for breach from the obligor or a third party. But when his ownership right is infringed, the owner can request an affirmation of his property right, the restoration of the original conditions, return of the original thing, and removal of the impediment.

2. The Historical Evolution of Obligations

The history of obligations is very old. Owing to the differences in the periods of social development and the differences in each country's legal system, there are also differences in the rules regarding obligations. To understand the process of development of the creation of obligations, comparing different historical periods and obligation systems in different types of countries is helpful in understanding the nature and use of obligations.

Marx pointed out, in discussing the circulation of goods, [that] "the status of obligee or obligor . . . arose from the circulation of simple commodities," "the class struggle in ancient times for the most part took the form of a struggle carried on between the obligees and obligors. In Rome this sort of struggle ended in the bankruptcy of the common people who sank into slavery. In the Middle Ages this sort of struggle [resulted] in the bankruptcy of the indebted feudal lords, whose political power followed their economic base and was lost, and together they came to an end." Until the arrival of a capitalistic society, "the relations between obligees and obligors took a monetary form—and what was reflected was nevertheless a still desperate conflict in the conditions of economic life." This penetrating statement summarizes to a high degree, and, moreover, clearly reveals the process of the establishment and evolution of obligations under the conditions of private ownership: they begin with the simple circulation of commodities accompanying private property. The creation and appearance of classes and nations, the long historical development, and the stages of slave society and feudalism, reflect from beginning to end the opposition and struggle between classes, particularly in the capitalist societies where the commodity economy rose to its highest stages. Labor was transformed into a commodity, money was transformed into capital and then was turned into a tool of aggression. The capitalist class, by means of obligation relations, obtained the commodity of labor in completely extracting surplus value from the hiring of the bodies of the workers and consequently creating an intense conflict between the bourgeoisie and the working class. Because of this, it can be seen that in a society of private ownership, obligations originate and end as a legal system that reflects and serves a system of oppression.

Actually, obligation relations already existed prior to the development of written law. In the 18th century B.C. the Babylonian Code of Hammurabi provided rules for sales, leases, loans, and the obligation of slavery, and so forth. It can be regarded as the earliest pioneer legal system that recognizes obligations in written law. In the sixth century B.C. when Solon, the ruler of Athens, carried on a political reform, he proclaimed the abolition of the system of slavery of the clans and nobility in regard to the common people. The law of this time already had rules for free obligations (contractual obligations) and unfree obligations (the obligations arising out of injury to a person or property). Moreover, in economic life, the pledge was well developed. The [legal] devices that guaranteed obligations—earnest money, mortgage, and guaranty, etc.—gradually became widespread. In Ancient Rome the country inherited the economy, government, and culture of Greece and the countries of the East. "The Law of the Twelve Tables" constituted the starting point of the subsequent development of Roman law. They brought together customs that already existed, and provided rules on the relation of obligor and obligee. Moreover, they were extremely strict with regard to the obligor who could not fulfill his obligation. Subsequently, the *Corpus Juris Romanum*, the great collection of Roman law, was compiled and published. It was the most complete body of law, which reflected a high degree of development of simple commodity production. Its rules regarding obligations, contract, and so forth, are quite complex, and serve as the basis for much capitalist private law legislation in subsequent times. The French Civil Code is [one] that took Roman law as its base and blended [with it] the custom of that time. In view of the great significance and use of the system of contract for the development of capitalism, in the said French Code, the provisions on contract (obligations) and the related relations of guaranty occupy almost half of the provisions of the code. From this can be seen the degree of its thoroughness and its careful system. The French Civil Code has had little amendment. Up until now it is still the law of France. It has had an enormous impact on the civil law legislation of every capitalist country in the last 200 years.

The Soviet Russian Civil Code, which was promulgated after the Soviet

October Revolution, is the first socialist civil code of modern times. When Lenin promulgated this code, he supplied guidance. This code has rules on obligations. It has many provisions on contract. All show the spirit of Lenin's instructions. Its publication and application reflect the objective existence of commodity relations and the objective importance of taking a system of obligation rights to stabilize the social and economic order. It was, in consequence, necessary to deny the fallacy that appeared after the October Revolution that, in a socialist system, commodity production no longer existed. In 1964, the new Soviet Russian Civil Code appeared. Obligations still form an important part of it. The Soviet Russian Civil Code has been very influential in the field of civil law in other countries with systems of public ownership. The Hungarian and Mongolian civil codes adopted the style of the Soviet Russian Code. There is a special part in the codes on obligations. Yugoslavia promulgated an Obligation Relations Law in 1978.

In our country's past when the term responsibility was used, it referred to owing money to someone. Sometimes it referred to lending money. In the "*Xiao-Cai Tian-Guan*" part of the *Book of Rites* there is the statement "Let responsibility be decided by means of the parts of the record." "Responsibility" is "obligation." "The parts of the record" is the certificate of olden times. The record is a document. "Parts" means one [document] divided into two. The obligee took the left [part of the] certificate and the obligor took the right. The ancient books of the *Zuo Zhuan*, *The Warring States*, the *Shi Ji*, the *Han Shu*, etc., all have references to obligations in the historical period of slavery. By the time of the Tang, the ruling class collected the legal experience of the period after Qin-Han and prepared a model feudal code, the Tang Code. This is the earliest extant code and had great influence on subsequent feudal royal dynasties. It had "miscellaneous rules" that apply to obligations. In regard to sales and loans they required that there be a contract established within a certain period of time. The obligor has a duty to perform according to the contract. If there was a violation, then he would be sentenced to a criminal penalty according to the degree of seriousness [of the offense]. After this, the Song, Yüan, Ming, and Qing Dynasties took the Tang Code as the standard. The law of degrees and regulations was thus based on following and taking over these rules. Obligation law went directly back to "miscellaneous law." It was only because of changes in times and circumstances that there were changes in this content. There were changes in style. At the same time they adopted laws and imperial orders and carried them out together. That is, when necessary, they used the methods of orders substituting for laws in order to carry out the will of the ruling class down to the end of the Qing. When the "Draft Qing Civil Code" was drawn up, this was the beginning of the division in our country between civil and criminal law. In it there was an "obligation law" section. This draft was never promulgated. The Empire fell, but from it [the draft] one can see the tendency of civil law and the reception of western influences. After [the foundation of the republic] the Guomindang government promulgated a civil code of over 1000 articles. Obligation law constituted half of it. It principally followed the German and Japanese codes. Its nature nevertheless reflected the semi-colonial, semi-feudal economic relationships [in this country]. In the revolutionary base areas, under the leadership of the Chinese Communist Party, the people's political power, based on the development of the revolutionary situation and changes in class relationships, has provided every sort of necessary policy and legal norm to adjust every sort of social relationship. So, in February 1942, the "Shanxi Gansu Ningxia Provisions for Protecting Personal and Property Rights" were promulgated. This met the needs of the war of resistance against Japan. They were enacted to uphold and strengthen the national anti-Japanese united front. In them there were provisions on obligations. After the founding of the new China, among the laws, regulations, provisions, and rules which the People's Government continuously enacted, it progressively enacted a legal system in the field of obligations and contracts, etc., under the new historical conditions. It was very useful for restoring the country's national economy, carrying out social reform, promoting the reform of the economic system, and national economic development.

From the sequence and general picture of the historical development described above, it can be seen that the creation and development of obligations meets the objective requirements of the development of a commodity economy. All in all it reflects and serves different historical periods and the will and requirements of the ruling class of countries with different systems. Moreover, all in all it is useful to the maintenance of social and economic order under the particular historical conditions. It is established in an important position in civil law.

3. The Particular Characteristics and Application of Our Country's Obligation Rights

Our country's system of obligation rights is an important constituent part of the civil law. It is constantly adapting to the needs of the development of the commodity economy, is progressive, established, and strengthened. In our country's economic reform of recent years, owing to the policy, abroad, of opening to the outside, and internally, [of] enlivening the economy, the exchange of commodities is constantly more active, every type of capital accumulation and partnership, as well as [contracts of] hire, deposit, transport, brokerage, commission agency, social services, insurance, etc., are part of the third commercial movement also developed. The products of science and technology are also transferred for compensation. Capital construction carries out the systems of investment—compensation and bid contracts. The circulating capital of enterprises changed from treasury allocations to bank loans. These all require that our country's civil law use the legal form of obligation law to be made secure in order to protect the production management and economic circulation, which are beneficial to our country's economic development, banning and punishing activity that injures the social and economic order and harms the public interest, in order to protect the development of our country's planned commodity economy.

Our country's system of obligation law is the legal system that reflect's our country's planned commodity economy. It requires obedience to state planning arrangements, and carries out the principle of equality and mutual benefit, compensation of equal value, relying on the law of the market to adjust commodity supply and demand relations in order to fulfill all of the needs of production, work, and the people's livelihood. It develops many kinds of economic and management forms, and affirms the carrying out by the economies of the whole people, collectivities, and individuals among themselves, of cooperative management and economic association on a basis of voluntariness and mutual advantage. It protects every kind of economic entity carrying on competition among themselves using proper procedures in order to raise more speedily the productive force of society. Within economic organizations, by means of certain legal forms (such as contracts), it establishes every kind of economic responsibility system, uniting the interests of the state, collectivity, and individuals, and bringing together responsibility, rights, and interests to increase and strengthen the activity of economic organizations, strengthen and extend the sense of responsibility of the workers and make full use of their activity and creativity. These norms that were discussed above are concretely realized in every kind of obligation law norm and serve as a guide for every obligation act. At the same time, they serve as the special characteristic of our country's obligation law.

Another characteristic of our country's system of obligation rights realizes the requirements of the norms of socialist morality. Under the conditions of socialism, every obligation relation is created on the basis of the unity of interests of every subject of civil law. Thus it can rely on the parties to an obligation to be acutely conscious of jointly realizing the aims of the obligation. Consequently our country's system of obligation law is permeated by the norms of socialist morality, as in advocating and encouraging justice and trustworthiness, in being united in mutual helpfulness, and taking up the cudgels in a just cause in wholehearted devotion to the public good, and other noble characteristics and actions in order to promote the realization of the aim of every obligation, in this way, conscientiously observing the law on the basis of morality, using law as the background for the development of the moral way of doing things. They both [the parties] work together without coming into conflict. They complement each other. This can cause the obligation to receive reliable and effective protection. Moreover, it is profitable for upholding the normal social economic order, fostering good social tendencies.

The special characteristics and application of our country's system of obligations enables it to be of great utility in the development of our country's planned commodity economy and in the harmonious realization of our country's socialist modernization.

II
TYPES OF OBLIGATIONS

In the handing down of civil law, obligations have complicated characteristics of many kinds. It is extremely important to sum up these different types of obligations, according to definite standards and types, in order to understand and study the nature, characteristics, legal effectiveness, and mutual relationships of these different types of obligations. Obligations can be divided according to different standards into the following different kinds.

1. Obligations for Specified Things and Obligations for Generic Things

Based on the dissimilarities among the objects of obligations, one can divide obligations into obligations for specified things (which may be called specified obligations) and obligations for generic things (which are also called generic obligations).

An obligation for a specified thing is an obligation whose object is a specified thing. The object of the obligation already exists at the time the obligation comes into existence or is already specified. Moreover, it is particularly specified and cannot be substituted for by another thing, for example, an antique, a machine that one has already started to use, a house that is located at a certain place, and so forth. When used as the object [of an obligation], these all have the character of being specified. The particular characteristic of this type of obligation is that the obligor must perform his obligation by delivering the particular thing specified by the obligation. Unless there is a different provision in the statute or contract, the ownership of the specified thing is transferred at the time the obligation arises. If the specified thing is accidentally destroyed or injured prior to transfer, the obligor is relieved from the duty of transferring the specified thing, but he is liable for damages for the loss.

If the object of the obligation is a generic thing, then this is an obligation for a generic thing. The object of this sort of obligation is a portion of the same type of thing, or an item which is processed and manufactured in accordance with the same type of specifications and quality as this type of thing. When the obligation arises, this portion which serves as the object of the contract has not yet been actually determined. At the moment of performing [the obligation] by transfer [of the thing], this portion is then separated from the mass (in the case of a product then [the crucial time is] when it is manufactured). It then becomes the object. If it is an obligation whose object is a definite quantity of the same type of goods, or steel of the same standard, or cement, or food products from one batch, or publications, then it is this type [of obligation]. The generic obligation is much more widely used than the obligation for a specific thing. For instance, the great majority of contracts of sale, supply, purchase and sale of agricultural sideline products are generic. The particular characteristic of this type of obligation is that the obligor must perform his obligation by delivering goods that meet the specified requirements of the generic obligation. The property interest in generic goods is transferred at the moment of delivery. If, prior to the delivery, the generic thing is destroyed, [unless there are] special circumstances the obligor is not discharged from the duty to deliver the thing.

2. Unitary and Multiple Obligations

Since the number of the subjects of obligations are not the same, obligations may be divided into unitary obligations and multiple obligations. When the subjects of the obligation—the obligee and the obligor—are each a single person, this is a unitary obligation. When the obligee and obligor, on one or both sides, are several persons, it is a multilateral obligation. In the case of the unitary obligation, the obligee exercises the right and the obligation is performed by the obligor. The right and duty are reciprocal. The obligation relation is simple and clear. Obligations with multiple parties are different. If there are several obligees, several obligors, or both sides have multiple parties, then different rights and duties relations may arise between the entire group on both sides, or between one subject of one side and the subject on the other, and among the several persons on one side. The circumstances are thus somewhat complicated. According to the differences of the scope of the rights and duties of each of the several subjects, and their mutual relationships, multiple obligations can be divided into obligations by shares and joint obligations.

In an obligation by shares, each of the subjects of the obligation enjoys rights and assumes duties according to his share (the share or shares may be equal or unequal). If there are several obligees, each has the right to demand payment [performance] for the share of the right he has. This is an obligation right according to shares. An obligee by shares does not have the right to demand payment of the whole obligation. He also cannot, without a grant of authority to represent, act for other obligees in receiving performance. If there are several obligors, each has the duty to perform a share of the obligation according to his share. An obligor by shares is not liable for performing the whole obligation, unless there has been a transfer of the obligation. He is not liable to satisfy the duties of the other obligors. Unless the law or contract provides otherwise, most multiple obligations are of this type.

In the case of joint obligations, the several subjects of the obligation have joint rights or are jointly liable. Any of the several subjects has the right to demand the entire performance, or has the duty to perform the entire obligation. If there are a number of obligees and each has the right to demand the whole, this is a joint obligation. If there are several obligors and each has the duty to perform the whole, this is a joint obligation duty. In joint obligations, joint obligation duties are more common than joint obligation rights. Every obligor who is liable for the whole obligation cannot avoid liability and shift responsibility to others or avoid the duty to perform the whole because one of the joint obligors dies, disappears, does not have the ability to pay them, and so forth. If the law or agreement of the parties creates this sort of obligation, this causes the obligee, in exercising his rights, to obtain, in effect, a guaranty. The joint obligation extends to a many-sided rights-duty relation, particularly when the joint obligor has a heavy responsibility. Consequently, the joint obligation must be in accordance with the law or a contract before it can come into existence.

When, in the case of a joint obligation, one or a small number of the obligors performs the whole obligation, or one or a small number of obligees receives the whole performance, a new rights-duty relationship accordingly arises among the several subjects. If, in the case of the joint obligation relation, one of the obligees receives the entire performance of the obligation, the rights of the obligees [as to the original obligor] are then destroyed. Accordingly, the original obligee who received the performance of the obligation becomes a new obligor. He is liable to deliver to the other obligees (new obligees). Each must get his share of the obligation. If it is a joint obligor, and one of the obligors performs the whole, the obligation of the joint obligors [to the original obligee] is destroyed. Consequently, those who were originally bound to perform the obligation become new obligees. They have the right to demand that the other joint obligors (the new obligors [of the new obligation to reimburse]) each pay his own share of the obligation. The above discussion reflects the special characteristics of the joint obligation. That is, the joint obligation may, because of laws or transfer, become an obligation by shares.

3. Simple Obligations and Elective Obligations

Obligations can be divided into simple obligations and elective obligations, according to whether or not the parties can choose the content of the obligation. An obligation in which the content of the obligation is limited, so that the parties have no choice, but can only demand or be liable to perform an act or omission, is a simple obligation. If the content of the obligation provides several acts that may be performed or omitted, and the parties can select one from among them, this is an elective obligation.

The elective obligation exists in order to encourage circulation. They are set up to satisfy the parties' needs. When the right of selection belongs to the obligee, this is the right to elect the obligation. If it is the obligor [who has the right to select], this is the right to elect the obligation duty. When there is a provision for election and it is not clear to whom the right of election belongs, it is usually regarded as [the right to] elect the duty. The nature and content of the elective obligation are made explicit by legal rule or by contract. The purpose of the obligation, the time and place, and manner of performance, including even the methods of providing relief if the performance is unsatisfactory, can all be subject to election. For example, in a sale relationship, the two parties agree, or else the seller agrees beforehand, that if the quality of the goods sold does not meet the standard, the buyer has the right to demand exchange or return. This sort of obligation of a contract of sale, giving the buyer a right to elect, is a common selection obligation.

After the selection has been made, an elective obligation is changed into a simple obligation. When, in the case of an elective obligation, owing to the fact that it is impossible to turn over the responsibility to the parties and supply an area for election, and there only remains one possibility of effectuating [the contract], it becomes a simple obligation. For example, in a transport contract, the obligor may select between rail transport and water transport. Subsequently, because of floods, the rail line is cut off. There is no other transport to select except water. At this point the elective obligation becomes a simple obligation.

As indicated in the above discussion, these are several important kinds of obligations. Apart from these, obligations may also be divided according to whether it is the principal obligation or a subsidiary obligation, the entire obligation or a partial obligation, a divisible obligation or indivisible obligation, a labor obligation or a monetary obligation, etc.

III
THE BASES FOR OBLIGATIONS COMING INTO EXISTENCE

The coming into existence of an obligation means that the subjects of civil law have, according to the rules of civil law, created an obligation rights-duty relationship. The obligation relation, like other civil law relations, requires certain legal facts for its creation. Because of this, the legal facts designated by the norms of civil law as being capable of creating an obligation are the bases of an obligation coming into being.

The bases for an obligation coming into being are very broad. Many of the countries which use codified law place the provisions on obligation as a special part of the civil code. Moreover, the important bases for any obligation coming into being are clearly provided for, but the classifications and content [of obligations] are different.

According to the socialist nature and special characteristics of our country's obligations, the most important bases for independently creating obligations may be divided as follows:

1. Obligations that Arise Out of Contracts

Contracts [*he tong*] which are also called agreements [*qi yue*] are agreements between subjects of civil law rights as to the creation, alteration, or termination of civil law rights-duties relationships. The contractual act is a juristic act which is [the result of] of mutual declarations of intention by two or more persons that are in agreement. The formation of any civil law contract means that an obligation relation has been created between the parties. The actions by which citizens, in order to satisfy the material and spiritual requirements of life, or in a comradely way, supply each other's needs to carry on civil law activities, the economic intercourse and coordination frequently engaged in by juristic persons according to the requirements of production, management, and development, are, for the most part carried on by means of all sorts of contracts. The greatest number of obligations are those created by contract. Consequently, contract is the principal juristic fact that creates obligations.

Among the different types of contracts, the economic contracts which are entered into between socialist organizations for the purpose of realizing certain economic aims are especially significant. They are of immense utility in assuring the carrying out of the state plan, regulating market supply and demand relations, linking up production supply, transport, and sale in developing production, and enlivening the economy and insuring the socialist direction of economic activity. The Economic Contract Law of the People's Republic of China provides the rules for the problems connected with these contracts.

2. Obligations that Arise Out of the Infringement of Rights [Delict]

An infringement of rights is an action that unlawfully invades and injures socialist public property, or the personal or property rights of citizens. The person who is injured by an act that is an infringement of rights has the right to demand compensation for the injuries. The one who executes the action that infringes on rights and injures another, has the duty to make compensation to the injured person for his losses. The rights-duty relationship which is established by the infringement of rights is an obligation that arises out of an infringement of rights. Owing to the fact that it arises out of someone being injured, the content of the obligation is concentrated on compensation for the injury. Consequently, it is customarily called the "obligation from injury to another" or "the obligation for damages."

An act that invades rights is a type of unlawful act. The legal norms violated by acts in violation of the law are not the same. The responsibility of the actor and the treatment and punishment it receives are accordingly different. The obligation that arises out of an infringement of rights shows clearly that the said act violates a civil law norm. The actor must be liable for the civil law responsibility that arises out this act—he must pay damages for the injuries to property [that are] received by the other. The law recognizes that an obligation rights-duty relation arises out of the act invading rights between the one who is injured and the one who caused the injury. The purpose is to protect social common interests and the citizen's lawful rights and interests, to uphold the correct social order, and to eliminate the consequences of unlawful acts. At the same time, this sort of recognition is of positive significance in regard to strengthening and clarifying discipline, increasing and strengthening the people's acceptance and respect for law, and preventing the occurrence of acts violating the law. However, the nature of the acts that infringe on rights and those that injure the social order are not the same. Apart from imposing civil responsibility according to law, it may also be possible, because of a violation of administrative law, or criminal law, to impose administrative responsibility or criminal responsibility, since to cause someone to assume civil responsibility for invasion of rights does not mean that he may not, according to the law, be liable administratively or criminally. On the other hand, to impose administrative or criminal liability on someone does not prevent him from being liable in civil law.

The most important obligation duty which must be assumed because of an infringement of rights is to make compensation for the economic injury received by the injured party. If the infringement of rights did not cause the injured party to receive an economic injury, the one who caused the injury must assume liability in other ways. If there is a violation of a citizen's personal rights, such as a right to his name, likeness, or honor, the one causing injury must assume the responsibility to cease the infringement, make an apology, and eliminate the effects [of the act], etc. The duty to pay damages for harm occasioned by an act that is an infringement of rights and the liability to pay damages for injuries for failure to perform a contract are not the same. The contract obligation is an obligation that already exists. When the contract comes into existence the obligation arises. The duty to pay damages is a consequence that arises when the duty to perform the contract is not fulfilled. The scope and manner of the damages must be handled in accordance with the provisions of the contract for violation of the agreement or statutory provisions that are relevant to contracts. The obligation arising from the infringement of rights is a newborn obligation. The act of infringement of the one causing the injury is the basis of the obligation. The payment of damages is the content of the obligation. It is also the civil law liability that must be assumed by the one who causes injury. The scope and manner of making compensation are handled by the legal rules of civil responsibility for infringement of rights.

3. Obligations Arising Out of Unjustified Enrichment

Unjustified enrichment means without any legal basis—without having agreed to execute a contract and also not enjoying any right based on law—to cause someone else to suffer injury and obtain enrichment [a benefit]. When the facts of unjustified enrichment arise, the one whose interests are injured has the right to demand that the one who received the benefits return his right to the benefits. The one who received the benefits is liable to return the benefits he received. This rights-duty relationship established between the parties on the basis of unjustified enrichment is the obligation that arises out of unjustified enrichment. The law affirms that the unjustified enrichment is the basis for the formation of an obligation. Its purpose lies in assuming that the property interests of the state, collectivity, and individual do not receive harm. The requirement that the one receiving the benefit return the unjustly received benefits is essentially a means of restoring the original conditions and correcting the inequitable abnormal property relationship that has come into existence.

4. The Obligation that Arises Out of Management of [an Action] Without Mandate [*Negotiorum Gestio*]

[The action of] management without authority refers to the situation where someone who has no legal basis—no grant of authority and no legally imposed duty—manages the affairs of another. The manager voluntarily, on his own initiative, carries out management activities for the benefit of another. This very moral act deserves to be held in high esteem and to be encouraged. For this reason, the law recognizes a rights-duty relationship arising between the parties where there is management [of the affairs of another] without authority [mandate]. Thus the manager has the right to demand compensation for essential expenditures made in managing the affair. The one whose affair is managed has a duty to compensate the one who manages for the said expenditures. This sort of rights-duty relation is the obligation of managing [the affairs of another] without mandate.

The one who manages the [affairs of another] is one who has not received a grant of authority when it can be presumed that the principal's intention would be [that he] carry on [these] management activities. Because of this it is not the same as the commissioning [of a representative]. Rather, the purpose of the act of management and its results are all planned for the benefit of the principal. The manager is, thus, actually placed voluntarily in the position of the principal to represent him in the management of this affair. Because of this, it only requires the principal's ratification and then the rules of commissioning [representation] law can be used. This causes the management [of affairs] without mandate to have legal effect as a commissioned representation from the moment it came into being. The management [of affairs] without mandate and unjust enrichment have certain characteristics in common as to form. For example, in both cases, one party receives a benefit. Moreover, the one who receives a benefit both receives benefits and bears a duty. Essentially, however, they are not the same. The purpose of the manager is to cause the principal to receive a benefit. The law affirms that the principal has the duty to compensate for the necessary expenditures. This is complementary to the principal's right to enjoy that which he has when he has already received a benefit. At the same time, it is a protection and encouragement of the manager's lawful advantages and his spirit of warmth and sincere service to others. In the case of unjust enrichment, one party has been injured, but the injured party basically has no desire to cause the person who obtained a benefit to receive any advantage. The law affirms that the one who received the benefits must be liable to return the improperly received benefits. This is respecting and protecting the actual intent and lawful rights of the injured person. At the same time, the benefit obtained by the one who received the advantage is not justified and ought to be returned to its owner. But the retained unjust enrichment does not cause the one who has benefitted to receive any injury. The management [of the affairs] of another without authority is completely unlike the infringement of the rights of another. The former is a voluntary act solely for the benefit of another, the latter is an act in violation of the law that causes injury to another. If an obligation arises from management of the affairs of another it must be analyzed from the standpoint of the purpose and manner of the management, its results, and other points of view, in order to ascertain its nature and classification correctly.

5. Other Bases for Creating Obligations

What was discussed above were the most common or comparatively typical bases that give rise to obligations. Apart from these, obligations can arise on the basis of other reasons such as certain unilateral juristic acts implemented according to law, as well as moral acts which, according to the principles of socialism, should receive legal protection, which can form rights-duty relationships between the parties concerned. These are also, in consequence, the bases for creating obligations.

There are relatively few obligations created by unilateral juristic acts. Since the rights-duty relationships of these obligations are determined by a unilateral intention and act, they must have a basis in law before they can be established. Moreover, usually it is a matter of the actor giving the other person a sort of right, not causing him to assume a duty. For example, a testamentary gift is a unilateral juristic act that causes an obligation to arise. Citizens, according to the provisions of our country's Inheritance Law, have the right to bequeath all or a portion of their estates to the state, a collectivity, or an individual. When a citizen uses a will to affirm the testamentary gift or bequest relationship, this is a unilateral juristic act. It causes the legatee, after the testator's death, to have the right to demand the bequeathed property. The executor of the will has the duty to transfer the bequeathed property to the legatee.

The protection of the obligation relation that arises out of a citizen's lawful act according to the principles of socialism refers to certain special circumstances. For example, when a citizen, in order to protect public property, or the person or property of another, causes himself to receive harm, the related unit or person who receives benefits must be liable to compensate him for his loss. For this, an obligation relation arises. This sort of action of rescuing others is often taken under emergency conditions and is essential in order to protect the person of another, or public or private property. The injury received by the actor is not only to property. Sometimes there can also be injury to his person. He may be wounded or disabled or fall ill. He can even sacrifice his life. These sorts of outstanding character and elevated action shown in readiness to take up the cudgels in a just cause, to be so devoted to public service as to lose one's own interests, sacrificing oneself for others, are much to be prized. Moreover, our country has always advocated and promoted this general atmosphere [of heroism, etc.]. Law serves as a standard to lead men in carrying on the actions of normal social life. It has a great deal of utility in arousing and educating. It should support and protect this sort of act and cause those who act for the public and others, and are injured, to receive the necessary compensation. This sort of act which creates obligations and at the same time also receives a certain amount of protection from administrative, labor, and other bodies of law will have an active influence on the creation of a culture with a socialist spirit and in developing an atmosphere of socialist morality.

IV
PERFORMANCE OF OBLIGATIONS

1. The General Concept of the Performance of Obligations

The performance of obligations occurs when the subject of an obligation, according to the provisions of the obligation, completely and appropriately performs a prescribed act or does not perform a prescribed act. To speak concretely, the subject of the performance of the obligation, in accordance with the rules of law or contract, on the basis of a proper object, at the proper time, in the proper place, using proper methods, completes an act or omission to act [literally, non-act]. Simply speaking, it is an obligor completing the act or omission specified by the obligation.

The obligation reflects the development of property. Regardless of whether it is in accordance with the requirements of law or contract, its purpose is to develop socialist construction, to fulfill the needs of the people, to keep the channels of circulation unimpeded, and protect the stability of the social order. Only when the obligation is performed, can its purpose be fulfilled. Obligations between socialist economic organs that arise to realize the duties under the state economic plan are actually the division of work by the parties under the plan. By means of legally effective obligation relations that carry out cooperation and mutual help, each segment in economic activity is made to be linked up reasonably. This causes maximum use to be made of the material and financial resources of the state and collectivities in order to serve together the needs of the whole society. This sort of obligation relationship which is related to the economic plan and the people's livelihood or overall interests, requires the obligor scrupulously to abide by [the principle] of trustworthiness, conscientiously to perform the obligation, and at the same time requires the obligee to assist and receive the obligor's performance in order to assume the responsibility for completing the state plan together. However these kinds of obligations that come into being by being based on the provisions of the directive plan are of limited number. Moreover, in the spirit of reform in the system of planning, the scope of this kind of directive plan will begin to diminish. On the other hand, the obligations which are established by the voluntary action of two or more parties reflect the complexity of society's needs and are innumerable. According to the development of our country's commodity economy it is necessary to make horizontal economic relations increase greatly and constantly. Every kind of obligation relation will, accordingly, increase to an appropriately large number. These kinds of obligation relations which are founded by reference to the directives of the state plan or completely formed by the adjustment of the market are indispensable for developing the national economy and fulfilling the needs of the people for material and cultural life. The realization of the object of every obligation is of great significance in protecting the carrying out of the plan and causing the commodity economy to grow normally. Consequently, the law requires that in every obligation, after its formation according to law, the parties must strictly perform their duties according to the provisions of the obligation.

2. The Legal Requirements for Performance of Obligations

An obligation is a rights-duty relation whose realization the state enforces by means of compulsion. In order to ensure the realization of these sorts of rights and duties, and to arrive at the established purpose of the obligation, the law sets out the general requirements for performance. Complete performance includes actual performance and correct performance.

(1) Performance in Fact [Actual Performance]

Performance in fact is performance according to the aim provided in the obligation.

The object of the obligation may not be arbitrarily changed nor may paying a penalty sum or damages substitute for performance of the contract. This is determined by the socialist nature of our country's obligation law. In our country the obligation is a most important means of bringing about the nation's economic plan. It carries out every type of economic interchange. It is the commonly used legal device for fulfilling society's need for production and the people's material and cultural needs for living. Implementing the requirement of actual performance makes maximum use of obligations in the area of circulation, and, at the same time, it can cause the parties to adopt an attitude of being conscientious and responsible and of strictly respecting the rules of the obligation and actively performing their own obligations. If one permits the parties to perform in a way that is not provided for, or not in the way agreed on, or to perform in some other substitute way, if [the performance] is in accord with the principle of exchange for equal value in form, it seems that the obligee has not received any injury, but since the original requirements have not been obtained or satisfied, the purpose of the obligation has not, in fact, been achieved. From the point of view of consequences, it will certainly cause property, supply, transport, and sales to get out of line, and create confusion in the economic order. It will influence the development of production and the raising of living standards for the masses. Consequently, actual performance is a normal requirement for every type of obligation. It must be strictly observed. Only under special circumstances is it permitted to use the device of property responsibility, as in using monetary compensation for the price or damages, to substitute for actual performance. The so-called specially provided circumstances are such circumstances as the case where a specified thing which is the object [of the obligation] has perished and actual performance is impossible. Or [when], because of the delay, the obligor's actual performance is no longer of any interest. When an obligation provided by law is not performed, there can be liability only for damages (the rules for transport of goods generally provide that if the goods are lost there is only liability for damages). Apart from these exceptions of limited scope there are also situations [where substitute performance] has to be allowed when certain circumstances come about.

Our country's system of obligation rights particularly enforces actual performance. This clearly shows how different it is from the capitalist obligation law system. In a capitalist society, owing to the fact that the government is not involved in production, periodic economic crises cannot be avoided. [Moreover] because of the existence of unemployment and currency fluctuations, obligation relations can very easily be seriously damaged. Actual performance lacks a firm foundation for general realization. At the same time, the establishment of obligation relations by the bourgeoisie is for the purpose for making a profit. It is only necessary that it be possible to plan on a profit. Even if there is no actual performance they are not concerned, to the extent that there is speculative trade. If this is regarded as lawful, there is no need of actual performance. Thus in the case of the system of obligation rights under capitalism, there cannot and need not be, as there is in our country, a strong emphasis on, and requirement of, actual performance. From this it can be seen that the requirement of actual performance is a special characteristic of our country's socialist obligation rights system. At the same time, it is a distinguishing feature from all those systems of oppressive obligations.

To be sure, carrying out the principle of actual performance also proceeds from the facts. If the object of the obligation can be bought on the market for money, then using money to substitute for the thing will not harm the interests of the state or of the parties. Therefore the obligor must be permitted, by paying a contract penalty or damages, to substitute for performance. According to section 35 of our country's Economic Contract Law, when one party breaches the contract, and "the other party demands that he continue performance," this means that the election of actual performance is up to the obligee. A court or arbitration tribunal may also proceed from the factual circumstances and decide whether or not the obligor must actually perform.

(2) Correct performance

Correct performance is to require that the subject, object, time, place, and manner of performance all be proper. It is a concretization of actual performance. It is the standard for determining if the performance is complete. When there is a dispute between the parties over the obligation, the responsibility can be allocated according to whether or not the performance is proper.

(i) The subject of performance. The subjects of performance are the persons who perform and receive performance of the obligation. An obligation is normally performed by the obligor for the obligee; the performance of the obligor is normally received by the obligee. According to the nature of obligation as well as the rules of law and contract, some obligations must be performed personally by the obligor, as when the agreement provides for a special person writing or painting or performing. In these cases [the obligation] must be performed personally by the one requested. There are some obligations in which performance must be received by the obligee, as in the case of manufactured products that are supplied under a state product allocation plan. Apart from obtaining the special permit required by law, the party requiring [the products] must himself receive the supplying party's performance. However, if the nature of the obligation as well as the law and contract provisions do not conflict with it, a third party may also perform in the place of the obligor, as in substituting in paying the rent for a dwelling, or substituting for someone in registering a trademark. A third party may also substitute for the obligee in receiving the performance, as when someone sends a sum of money to a shop, orders goods, and indicates clearly that they are to be sent to a third party. The third party can then receive the performance. When the obligee demands that the obligor perform an obligation for a designated third party, he cannot cause the obligor to receive harm in consequence. After the obligor performs for the third party, the obligation relation is terminated.

In the circumstances [discussed] above, the third party is not the subject of the obligation. If the third party takes the place of the obligor, and does not perform or does not perform properly, or if the third party in receiving performance for the obligee causes harm to the obligor, the other obligee or obligor is liable.

(ii) The object of performance. The objects of the performance of obligations are different. Generally they may be classified as things [property] (including money) and actions (such as offering labor, doing work, etc.). The essential condition of performance of the object is that the nature of the object must be consistent with the requirements [of the obligation], as in the case of the quality of products, which must correspond with state standards or standards that are agreed on. In contracts in which it is agreed that [goods will be furnished] according to a sample, a sample is the standard of quality. In the case of furnishing labor or doing a job of work, in the same way it is required that it be done in accordance with the standard provided by rule or agreement in order to assure quality. If, at the time the obligation is established, the quality requirements have not been clearly provided, then performance must be in accord with the medium quality standard for that type of goods, labor, or work. In regard to other matters, such as quantity, price, honorarium, etc., performance must be in accordance with the performance decreed by law or agreement. Since the packaging law has not yet been enacted, if one party required that packaging be in accordance with the nature of the things or has some other special requirement, this should be clearly provided for in the contract, and the parties must conscientiously respect [the provision].

(iii) Time of performance. The time of performance means the time at which the obligor performs for the obligee, and the time at which the obligee receives the performance. The time of performance is sometimes provided concretely, as a particular year, month, day, etc. Sometimes a period of time is provided. The parties to the obligation will, according to the times set by law or the contract, perform the obligation and accept the performance. This is proper performance. If there is no clear provision as to the time when the obligation is established, the obligor may perform the obligee at any time. The obligee may also demand performance at any time, but he must give the necessary time to prepare. In a contract with two obligations, unless there is a contrary provision, both parties must perform at the same time. There are two types of breach of [an obligation] to perform on time. One is when the party exceeds the time for performance or the time for receiving the performance. This is called delayed performance. The parties are liable for any injury caused by delayed performance. In the second, the time has not yet arrived, and the obligor performs the obligation. This is called advance performance. The obligor may perform in advance in the following circumstances: if, by law or contract provision, he may perform in advance, he has the right to perform in advance, and the obligee must immediately accept [the performance]. If advance performance does not violate the nature of the obligation, the obligee must permit the advance performance. If the advance performance could have a bad influence on the carrying out of the state plan or injure or make difficulties for the obligee, then it cannot take place without the consent of the obligee.

(iv) The place of performance. The place of performance is the place where the obligor performs his obligation and where the obligee receives performance. The place of performance has a direct influence on expense and the time of performance. When there is a dispute over formation, it is a basis for [determining] liability. For these reasons it has great actual significance for both parties. Performance, or acceptance of performance, that takes place in places specified by the law and in the contract by the parties to the obligation, or in the places determined by the nature of the obligation, is proper performance. If the law or contract does not provide a specified place for performance, it may be performed in accordance with the following provisions: in cases of the transfer or repair of a building, in the place where the building is located; in the case of payment of money, in the domicile of the obligee or his residence; in other cases the domicile or residence of the obligor.

(v) The manner of performance. There are many types of obligations and their nature and special characteristics are quite varied. Consequently there are also many ways of performing obligations. It is not possible or necessary to make them completely uniform. For example, an obligation can be performed completely at one time and can also be performed in parts at different times. There can be performance by selection of the method of delivery of the object of the obligation directly to the obligee. There can also be the selection of delivery by post or shipment [by carrier]. The methods of performance are specified by the parties in accordance with the special characteristics of the object and content of the obligation. If this is already provided at the time the obligation comes into being, one party may not on its own change [its performance]. Performance in accordance with the method provided is proper performance.

Among the methods of performance, total performance at one time and performance in installments both have direct advantages and disadvantages for the parties. Attention must be paid to establishing which is correct as an aid in allocating responsibility. If the law or contract does not have a special provision, in general, complete performance at one time is required. The obligee has the right, when the obligor tenders partial performance, to refuse to accept it. However, when, in the case of an obligation in shares, one obligor has performed his share of the performance, this cannot be regarded as an installment performance but as a total performance. If the law or contract clearly provides for performance in installments, and a performance at one time would injure the other party, then the obligee has the right to refuse to accept total performance at one time.

V
NONPERFORMANCE OF AN OBLIGATION

1. The General Nature of Nonperformance of an Obligation

Nonperformance of an obligation means the subject of the obligation has not completely and properly performed a certain action or omission as provided by the obligation. Bluntly speaking, if, according to the rules of the obligation it is required that something be done and it is not done, or that something should not be done and it is done, in both cases there is failure to perform an obligation. If the supplier does not tender goods to the recipient, or the borrower in a loan for use, contrary to the terms of the loan, transfers it to another to use, then these are all failures to perform obligations.

As a general proposition, the failure to perform an obligation and the performance of the obligation are complete opposites. Consequently, any violation of the requirements of the obligation constitutes nonperformance. This [nonperformance] may be divided into complete nonperformance, partial nonperformance, and improper performance. To take transport of a thing as an example, if a carrier does not deliver the transported object to the consignee at the designated place, this is complete nonperformance. If the carrier only delivers a portion of the objects to the consignee at the designated place, this is part performance. If the carrier delivers the entire shipment to the consignee at the designated place, but, owing to improper care, it has been damaged, this is improper performance. Looked at from a different point of view, partial nonperformance and improper performance often overlap. As in the above example of partial nonperformance, there is also improper performance as to the quantity. The improper performance in the above example was also partial nonperformance in terms of quality. These differences in viewpoint that result in different determinations do not affect the fact that they are [both] nonperformance of obligations. There is also no difference in civil responsibility.

Formation of obligations and their performance are naturally of great significance to the national construction and to the life of the people. The nonperformance of obligations has a bad influence on production, work, and daily life. It directly injures the interests of the obligee to the extent of causing injury to social material wealth. In order to avoid the negative consequences, the parties must maintain a conscientious and serious attitude when voluntarily entering into an obligation by negotiating. They must, in the spirit of seeking truth from facts, consider their actual needs and performance capability. Then they must cause the obligation to be formed on a practical and reliable foundation. After the obligation has been formed according to law, it must be observed strictly and scrupulously abided by. [Each] must seek to perform his own obligation completely and properly. When it is impossible to perform an obligation or to perform it fully, then he must immediately notify the other party of the circumstances in order that they may together choose effective measures to prevent the appearance and spread of harm.

2. Conditions of Liability for Nonperformance of Obligations

In the case of nonperformance of an obligation, the obligor must, according to the provisions of the law or contract, assume appropriate liability. For example, he pays a penalty or damages, etc. This sort of civil law ability is legally effective. It is only necessary to set a certain condition which must then be carried out according to the provisions. The most important conditions for assuming liability for failure to perform an obligation are that there be a causal connection between the obligor's nonperformance and the injury received by the obligee, and that the obligor be at fault and not be able to perform.

The causal connection between one party's act and the other party's injury forms an objective condition of liability, for example, [when] the supplying party has not, as provided, sent the materials to a factory. This causes the factory to stop work while it waits for materials, and it is injured. The nonperformance of the former [party] is the cause of the injury to the latter [party]. The causal connection between the two is completely clear. The obligor must be responsible for the injury that he has brought about. But in present day life, conditions being terribly complicated, it requires careful investigation and analysis to determine whether or not the injury results from the obligor's failure to perform. Sometimes it is necessary to use modern scientific techniques to carry on the investigation before it is possible to make a sure judgment.

The fault of the obligor is an important condition for the liability of the obligor. Section 32 of our country's Economic Contract Law provides: "When one party, by his fault brings it to pass that the economic contract cannot be performed, or cannot be completely performed, the one who is at fault is liable for the breach of contract." The law provides that nonperformance of an obligation must give rise to liability. This is chiefly aimed at the obligor's fault that brings injury to the interests of another or the public. Ordering him to be responsible for the consequences may prevent the injury from ever happening, or cause the injury created by the fault to be remedied. Fault includes intentional and negligent [fault]. Intentional [fault] means that the obligor knows that the failure to perform will harm the interests of the other party or the public and he still has the intention to do it or permits it to happen. Negligence means that the obligor must foresee and is able to foresee the harmful consequences of nonperformance, but as the result of excessive self-confidence and carelessness and laxness he did not take the necessary measures to prevent [the events]. This makes it impossible to perform the obligation and inflicts injury on others. The difference between intention and negligence is not terribly significant in civil law responsibility. Generally speaking, it is only necessary that the obligation not be performed and that [this lack of performance] not have a legal basis, and it can be presumed that the obligor is at fault. For civil responsibility it makes no difference whether the fault is intentional or negligent. Although the question of whether or not the obligor is at fault is a subjective requirement, at the time of making the determination, it must be done on an objective basis. When there is a dispute, it is only when the obligor can prove on the basis of sufficient objective facts that he was not at fault and had a lawful ground for [his action], that he can escape liability for nonperformance. The most important bases for avoiding liability are the following:

(1) Irresistible force

Section 34 of our country's Economic Contract Law provides that irresistible force can serve as a condition for avoiding obligations. The so-called irresistible force means force which it is impossible for men to foresee and which they cannot resist. It includes natural phenomena (such as wars, etc.). When the occurrence of these irresistible causes makes it impossible to perform the contract, one party must immediately notify the other party, and, according to the circumstances, avoid liability partially or wholly.

(2) The fault of the obligee

When the fault of the obligee makes it impossible to perform the obligation, this may relieve the obligor of liability. If both parties are at fault, then, according to the Economic Contracts Law Section 32, on the basis of the circumstances, the liability must be split between the parties.

(3) The fault of a third party

When the fault of a third party makes it impossible to perform an obligation, the obligee and obligor are both free of fault, but according to the law of every country, one of the parties must first be liable, and then, according the legally provided procedures, seek compensation from the third party who was at fault. Section 33 of our country's Economic Contracts Law provides that when, as the result of the fault of a higher level leading body or the organization that is in charge of the business, the contract cannot be performed, "the one breaching the contract must first pay the contract penalty or damages. The matter will then be handled by the higher level leading body or the organization in charge of the business."

Altogether, the obligor, in all the situations in which the law permits him to escape liability if he is not at fault, need not bear responsibility for the failure to perform.

3. The Consequences of Nonperformance of an Obligation

The consequences of nonperformance of an obligation refers to the fact that when the obligation is not performed the obligor must be liable. According to the actual requirements of performance of an obligation, if, when there is no performance, the obligor still has the capacity to perform and the obligee still needs the performance, the obligee has the right, under the procedures for forcible execution, to demand forcible execution. As for the obligor, he has assumed liability for the consequences of nonperformance. Moreover, he cannot escape the fact that he still has a duty actually to perform. On the other hand, when he assumes the duty of actually performing, he cannot escape the fact that he is still liable for the consequences of nonperformance. The most important consequence of nonperformance is the payment of the penalty for breach, or damages.

The payment of a penalty is a kind of compensatory legal judgment against the obligor for nonperformance of an obligation. It is only necessary that the obligor not perform. It does not matter whether or not the obligee is injured, or whether the injury is large or small, in every case the penalty must be paid. If the penalty is insufficient to compensate the other party's injury the obligor must still pay damages for the remaining amount. The amount of the penalty, as well as its proportion, and the time and manner of payment, must all be provided for by law or contract.

Damages are a legal procedure of compensation [which must be carried out] on the basis of the principle of compensating for the actual injuries suffered. The actual injuries include the reduction in value of the property of the obligee by the failure of the obligor to perform, as well as the injury caused to the obligee by losing an advantage he surely would have obtained. If the law of contract has a special provision on the scope or method of compensation of damages for injury these must be carried out according to the rule.

Liability for the penalty and liability for damages are not the same. The payment of a penalty is not conditioned on the existence of actual injury. Consequently, even if the nonperformance of the obligation does not result in injury, the obligee still has the right to demand that the other party pay the penalty. In fact, the amount of the penalty may exceed the actual injuries. But damages are conditional on the actual harm that was caused. The penalty is something that is agreed to by the parties at the time the contract is entered into or provided by law, while damages are computed according to the actual injury after the breach by a party. Consequently, the payment of the penalty is a much easier proceeding than the payment of damages. This is especially the case for contracts where there is no way of computing the injury caused by the breach. By having the penalty serve as liability for the breach of contract, it is possible to avoid the difficulties of proof if a conflict arises. The reduction of the complications of the claim for damages is an advantage to the court or arbitration tribunal in settling a case as soon as possible.

The most important actions whereby a party does not perform an obligation and is liable to pay the penalties and damages are of the following types:

(1) Delayed performance

In the case of obligations which are not performed on time owing to the fault of the obligor, it is the obligor who is in delay. This is also called occasioning delay, and the time of delay is computed from the time when the period for performance is completed. The consequences of the obligor's delay are:

(i) He will pay a penalty to the other party in accordance with the provisions of the law or contract. According to Section 35.5 of the Provisions for Contracts of Purchase and Sale of Mineral and Industrial Products, reference must be made to the rules on delay of the People's Bank of China, the ratio between the value of the portion that is delivered late to the whole must be calculated and the obligor compensated with the penalty. If the penalty is insufficient to compensate the obligee for his injury, then the remaining amount must be supplied. At the same time, [the obligor] must continue the obligated performance.

(ii) The obligor must assume liability for fluctuations in the price of the object of the obligation because of a delay in performance. According to Section 17 of the Economic Contracts Law, when the price rises, performance will be in accordance with the original price, when it falls, in accordance with the new price.

(iii) If, owing to a delay in performance, performance of the obligation has ceased to be of interest to the obligee, the obligee has the right to cancel acceptance of performance, and, moreover, to demand damages for injuries. Under these circumstances the obligee must immediately notify the obligor of his decision to refuse acceptance. When the obligor performs prior to receiving notice, the obligee must accept it.

(iv) In the case of a delay in the performance of an interest-bearing monetary obligation, interest runs at the legal rate and must be added for the period of delay. If the obligee fails, without legal basis, to accept, or does not tender to the obligor the agreed upon assistance, causing the obligor to be unable to perform on time, this is the obligee's delay. It is also called delay of acceptance. The consequences of the obligee's delay are:

(a) When the delay makes it impossible for the obligor to perform, this destroys the liability of the obligor [to perform].

(b) When a penalty is paid according to the provisions of law or contract to the other party, according to section 36 of the Provisions for Industrial and Mineral Products Purchase and Sales Contracts, if, upon the tender of goods, the picking up of the goods is not timely, it is necessary to refer to the relevant rules of the People's Bank of China on delay. Then, in the proportion that the delayed portion of the price bears to the total, the contract penalty should be paid to the obligor. In the case of effectuating the shipping of the goods, or having them sent, [when] because of the delay of the obligee injury results and there is a fine by the Transport Ministry, the obligee is liable. If the penalty is insufficient to compensate for the injuries received by the other party (including storage and insurance charges) [the one causing the delay] must make up the difference.

(c) In a case of an interest-bearing monetary obligation, the obligor escapes the duty to pay interest for the period of delay.

(2) Improper performance

"Improper performance" refers to the situation where the object of the performance does not correspond with the quality required by the provisions in the contract. Usually it is called a defect. In the case of improper performance, the obligee has the right to tender a written statement of the variances. According to section 15 of the Provisions for Industrial and Mineral Products Purchase and Sales Contracts, the obligee must make an examination or test within the time provided in the contract and tender a written statement of variances. If the external appearance of the commodities, their type, model, nature, and color do not correspond with the contract, the written statement of variances must be tendered within ten days or within the time agreed on by the parties. In the case of certain defects in commodities which appear after certain necessary installation and operation, in general, the written statement of variances is to be made within six months after the day when operations began. If the written statement of variances is not made within the prescribed time, the performance of the obligor is regarded as having been in conformance with the contract.

The liability of the obligor for improper performance is:

(i) When, even though the object of performance is defective the obligee agrees to use it, he may reduce the price or negotiate the price in accordance with the quality. If the obligee cannot use it, then, according to the actual circumstances, the obligor must repair it, exchange it, or take it back. Moreover he is liable for any expenses thereby incurred. If it cannot be repaired, exchanged, or taken back, he is liable for the penalty and damages.

(ii) When the packaging is not in accordance with the contract, the obligor is liable for its return and repair or repackaging. Moreover he is liable for any expenses incurred thereby. If, because of the packaging which is not in conformity with the contract provisions, the obligor suffers harm, he is also liable for damages.

(3) Incomplete performance

"Incomplete performance" refers to the case where the obligor performs only a portion of the performance. When there is incomplete performance, the obligor has already performed a portion, and he reduces his liability appropriately. But because he has not performed completely, this is still an act which is a type of nonperformance of an obligation, and, as a consequence, the obligor cannot avoid his liability according to law. According to section 17 of the Provisions on the Purchase and Sale of Agricultural Sideline Products, when the quantity supplied is less than that provided in the contract, and the party requiring it still has need of it, this [missing] amount must be supplied. The supply of the [missing] part will be handled according to the provisions for transporting goods. This explains that when there is incomplete performance, the obligee has the right to demand continued performance. At the same time that the obligee continues performance, he is still liable for breach of contract for incomplete performance. If the obligee does not demand that the performance be continued, he may annul the contract and, moreover, demand that the obligor pay the penalty or damages.

(4) Inability to perform

"Inability to perform" refers to the case where the obligor cannot perform or cannot perform completely. If a cause recognized by the law as avoiding liability makes the obligation permanently incapable of being performed, the obligor is relieved from his obligation to perform. But he must immediately notify the obligee that the obligation cannot be performed. If the legally recognized cause only temporarily prevents the obligor from performing, the obligor must continue performance when the said cause ceases to exist. If the performance cannot be accomplished because of the obligor's fault, the obligee has the right to demand that the obligor continue performance.

(5) Refusal to perform

"Refusal to perform" refers to the obligor failing to perform without a valid reason. When there is refusal to perform, the obligor has intentionally violated the law; consequently he must be legally liable. The obligee has the right to annul the contract and to demand that the obligee pay the penalty or damages. At the same time he may demand that a court compel the obligor to perform his obligation.

VI
CHANGES IN OBLIGATIONS

1. The General Concept of Changes in Obligations

An obligation is based on certain legal facts, and if the subject, content, or object is changed, this is called a change in the obligation. This sort of change can arise between citizens, between juristic persons, and between juristic persons and citizens. The change in the obligation is only a change in part of the obligation. There must be a lawful basis for it to be effective.

(1) The change in the obligation is a partial change on the basis of a still existing obligation

At the time the obligation comes into being, its subject, content, and object are all ascertained. When, afterwards, there is a change decided on by the parties, owing to the subjective intention of the parties, or to objective circumstances, and the key elements of the obligation are changed, this gives rise to a change in the obligation. These sorts of changes to obligations take place in special circumstances and are a continuation of the obligation that already exists. What are not the same are [those matters in which] changes are made in its concrete form. Consequently a change in the obligation is not the same as a substitution obligation [novation]. In the case of a change, the continued existence of the obligation is the basis for the obligation relationship both before and after the change. The obligation retains its same character. In the case of a replacement, the original obligation is dissolved, and a new obligation comes into being. There is no intrinsic relationship between the two obligations.

(2) A change in an obligation must have a legal basis

At the time it comes into being, an obligation is based on the law or an agreement. The validity of the obligation depends on its having a lawful basis. It is the same for the change in the obligation. Only when it has a lawful basis can it be effective. At the time the obligation is amended, since the original obligation has been extended, the legal basis on which it came into being naturally continues to have legal force, but this basis does not, and cannot, substitute for the basis of the change in the obligation. Actually, a change in an obligation has a completely different basis for coming into being, otherwise there would be no need to change the obligation. Consequently, a lawful basis is an essential condition for the validity of an amendment to an obligation coming into existence. As regards the question whether the payment of a penalty or damages belongs to an amendment to an obligation there are, at present, still differences of opinion. This payment and damages naturally have a lawful basis. But their basis was already determined at the time the obligation came into existence, and it is only when the obligation has not been properly performed that these consequences must be borne. Consequently, in essence, they must not be regarded as amending obligations.

A change to an obligation is not a common practice, but it may be helpful to the parties in exercising their rights, in performing their duties, and in fulfilling their needs. When objective circumstances change, it is also useful to select measures of change in order to avoid or diminish harm. Because of this, the law gives them [changes] approval and protection.

2. The Bases for Changes in Obligations

There are many bases for changes in obligations. The following are among the more common.

(1) Because of a change in the law or a plan

An obligation may be changed as a result of a legal rule. For example, according to the rules of contractual guaranties, the guarantor, after satisfying the obligation, has the right to demand compensation from the one guaranteed. According to the Inheritance Law, if an heir does not accept the estate, the other heirs have the right to divide the share of the inheritance that was rejected. Changes in state plans can give rise to changes in obligations. Moreover, these are important bases for the changes of contracts between juristic persons. In order to realize overall balance in the state economy, when changes occur in the objective conditions, revisions amounting even to abolition of important parts of the state plan are difficult to avoid. When there are changes in the state plan, then contracts that are based on, or entered into, in accordance with the plan, must undergo appropriate changes. For example, some enterprises, in accordance with the aim of state economic adjustment, carry out mergers or transfer production. As to certain products, owing to the discovery of latent qualities and innovations and reforms, there is greatly increased productive capacity. Great unforeseeable changes arise in connection with foreign trade. All of these can give rise to changes in the state plan, and the obligations that are related to the plan must also be changed accordingly.

(2) Because of agreement between the parties

Agreement between the parties, that is, a common declaration of intention of the parties, is a usual basis for the creation of obligations. In the same way, this is the usual way of changing obligations. It is necessary only that the parties not violate a legal rule, and that they form an agreement to change an obligation according to legal procedures and forms, and this sort of juristic act will be effective, for example, [when] after a contract of sale is made between manufacturing enterprises, and, owing to changes in the market requirements, the two parties agree to change the nature of the product, the standards, quality, the place of delivery, etc., [or when] in a loan relationship between citizens, owing to the request of one party, the other party permits a delay, and there is an agreement for a delay in the time for repayment. All of these cases give rise to changes in obligations.

(3) Because of irresistible natural disasters

An irresistible natural disaster is a condition for avoiding liability for failure to perform. After the natural disaster has occurred, if the obligor still has some capacity to perform or can compensate in some other way, and at the same time it does not harm the interests of the obligee, the obligor must be permitted to make appropriate changes in his performance based on the actual changes of the circumstances. This is advantageous in reducing property losses both to the parties and to the public. For example, when owing to hail, there is a reduction in the vegetable crop, the delivering unit may agree with the procuring unit to reduce the originally agreed-upon quantity of vegetables, or to deliver different products.

3. Types of Changes in Obligations

(1) Change in subject

An agreement for the transfer of rights or duties from the obligee or obligor to a third person may give rise to a change in the subject of the obligation. Section 27 of our Economic Contracts Law provides that when one of the parties merges or is divided, the parties that remain after the change assume or divide the duties to perform the obligation and enjoy the necessary rights. After the change in the obligation, the assignee of the rights in the obligation becomes the new obligee. The one who assumes the obligation becomes the new obligor. The content of the obligation and the object or the nature of the obligation are preserved or do not change. The legal facts that give rise to this sort of change in the subject of the obligation vary according to whether it is the obligation rights or duties that are transferred.

The transfer of obligations is also called the cession of obligations. This is the bilateral juristic act of the obligee assigning the right and the third party receiving the assignment. When the two parties arrive at an agreement, the assignment takes effect. The assignee then takes over the position of the obligee and becomes the new obligee. This sort of change in the obligee has no influence on the duty of the obligor. Consequently, it normally does not require the consent of the obligor, but notification of the transfer of the obligation right must be made immediately to the obligor. Otherwise, if the obligor performs towards the original obligee, he [i.e., the original obligee] may not refuse to accept the performance. When the obligation is transferred, guaranties and other accessory rights are transferred along with it. For example, a mortgage, a guaranty, and other forms of security interests, as well as the right to interest which is accessory to the [principal] obligation, as well as the right to a penalty if the obligation is not performed and a right to damages demand, etc., also follow the transfer into the hands of the third party. A transfer of an obligation that is transferred by the intention of the obligee is permitted by law, but [this transfer] has, as a prerequisite, that it not violate the laws and the state plan, as well as the special agreement of the parties. At the same time, some obligations that have a close relationship with the person, such as an inheritance right or a right to demand support money, etc., may not be transferred. Apart from transfer by agreement, transfer may also be effected through a direct provision of the law. For example, after a joint obligor performs the obligation, he has the right to demand reimbursement from the other obligors.

The transfer of an obligation duty is also called the assumption of an obligation. It is the bilateral juristic act of the transfer of the duty by the obligor and the assumption by the transferee, but whether or not this sort of agreement to transfer an obligation is effective will be decided according to whether or not the obligee agrees, since the obligee is not a party to the agreement, and whether or not the third party who is assuming the obligation has the capacity to perform the obligation and is trustworthy are directly related to the obligee's rights. Consequently, it is only after the obligee's consent that this agreement can be effective in regard to him. After the obligee has consented to the transfer of the obligation, and it is effective, the one who has assumed the obligation then occupies the position of the obligor and is the new obligor. When the obligation duty is transferred, if there is a duty that is included in the obligation, such as the duty to pay interest, a penalty for nonperformance, and damages, these are also transferred with it. But other persons (not those who have assumed obligations) who have made guaranties of the obligation (such as a guaranty, mortgage, etc.) did so on the basis of the original obligor's understanding and trustworthiness. Consequently, unless they have given their approval, these [duties] are not transferred along with the transfer of the [principal] obligation. The transfer of the obligation duty is a right of the obligor, but the exercise of this right has, as a prerequisite, that it must not violate the rules of the law and the state plan, nor injure the rights of the obligee. Apart from this, the third party may, of his own volition, agree with the obligee on a transfer of the obligation. This sort of agreement already has the consent of the obligee and operates for the benefit of the obligor. Consequently, it does not require the consent of the original obligor to come into existence. But the obligor has the right to cancel the above agreement.

(2) Changes in content

"Changes in content" refers to changes in the rights and duties between the parties.

The great majority of obligations are based on objective needs, but along with the fact that objective circumstances are changing constantly, sometimes it is necessary to make appropriate changes in the content of the obligation in order to maintain the interests and fulfill the needs of the state, the collectivity, or individuals. There are two types of changes in content. One is when there is a change in the content of a contractual obligation, that is, when the parties to the contract, after the formation of the contract, make changes, supplements, and classifications in the contract provisions because of changed conditions, with the result that the content of the contract changes. After the contract has been amended, the parties must perform according to the provisions of the amended contract. But that portion of the performance that took place prior to the amendment is still effective. The second type is a change in the content of noncontractual obligations. For example, because of changes in the intention of one party, his actual requirements, or his ability to perform, there may be an increase or decrease in damages for injuries. If the bases of the content of the obligation change, if there is no violation of the law or state plan, then upon the agreement of the parties, or the declaration of intention of one of them, it can be changed.

(3) Changes in object

A change in the object is a change in the aim of both the obligation right and the obligation duty. It is closely connected with a change in the content of the obligation. They condition each other. The determination of and change in the rights and duties of the parties must refer to and make use of the object of this obligation. The determination of and changes in the object must also influence and be realized in the parties' rights and duties. This is determined by the special characteristics and nature of the obligation. Consequently, the change in the object of the obligation often follows along with the change in the content. The causes and bases for the change are also the same.

VII
TERMINATION OF AN OBLIGATION

The termination—also called the ending—of an obligation means that the rights-duties relationship of the obligation has come to an end because of a legal fact. The most important legal facts that give rise to the termination of an obligation are of the following types:

1. The Obligation that Is Terminated by Performance

When the obligor has completely and properly performed the obligation by bringing about the act or omission provided by the obligation, he has fulfilled his own duty, and caused the obligee's right to be realized so that the purpose set by the obligation is achieved. The obligation relation is also terminated. The performance of the obligation can come about as a simple brief proceeding (as in the use of a sale which is accomplished immediately by the payment of ready cash). It can also be expressed as a complicated and comparatively long-term proceeding. But regardless of whether it is simple or complex, it is only necessary that the obligation be performed [literally: paid] and that the obligee has received it [the performance]. The obligation relation then comes to an end because of performance. Since the performance corresponds to the purpose of the obligation coming into existence, this is also the most common reason an obligation is terminated.

2. The Obligation that Is Terminated by Setoff

Setoff occurs when both parties are mutually obligated to each other and the two obligations mutually offset each other and are extinguished. Setoff operates as a means of extinguishing obligations. It can also cause both parties' obligation rights and interests to be realized, and can also save labor, time, and expense [that would be used in] actual performance. Consequently, it need only fulfill definite conditions, and one or both parties may use it as a method of terminating an obligation. Both parties must be obligors and for the same type of prestation. That is, the object of both obligations is the same type of thing or money. If there is a difference in amount [that is, one party's obligation is smaller than the other] then there is setoff for the lesser amount. The remaining amounts remain as an obligation right and duty. Both obligations must be due for performance, or if one party whose performance is not yet due voluntarily surrenders his time advantage, the nature of the obligation must be such that setoff is possible (for example, furnishing labor and engineering designs, shipping goods, etc., by their nature are obligations that may not be offset, [in fact] and so they cannot be offset [in law]). In real life, the great majority of setoffs are monetary obligations. Monetary obligations between socialist organizations, according to the rule, are to be performed by settling accounts through a bank. If the two parties who are mutual obligors use the method of setoff to terminate the obligation relationship, then in the same way, they must carry out transfers through the bank in which they set up accounts. This sort of termination of an obligation can also be regarded as reciprocal performance by the two obligors.

3. Termination by Means of Deposit

Deposit refers to the case where the obligee, without proper grounds, refuses to accept the performance or the obligee has disappeared and his location is unknown and it is difficult to perform. Then [in such a case], by certification from a notary, or a decision by a court, [the obligor] would deliver the object of the obligation to the supervisory organization to keep. After the obligor has made the deposit, his duty is then satisfied, and the obligation is accordingly terminated. The deposit is useful for preventing and taking care of the situation where an obligation is suspended for a long period of time. It is also a protection for the lawful rights of the obligor.

Deposit must have a lawful basis. It is only when, at the time that performance is tendered, and the obligee without reason does not accept, or when the obligee's address is not clear, or when the obligee is temporarily undetermined (as, when several persons claim an obligation right, and a dispute has arisen) and similar circumstances which cause there to be no way to perform the obligation, or for it to be very difficult to perform the obligation, that it may be used. Usually there must also be a certificate by a notary or a checking and approval by a judicial organization in order for it to be effective. Under circumstances where it is possible, the obligor must notify the obligee after making the deposit. Otherwise he will be liable for any injuries that are thereby incurred. When an effective deposit is made, the original obligation is terminated. The obligor is separated from the obligation relation; the obligee then has a right to demand the object of performance from the one who is keeping it. But he must be responsible for the risk of natural injuries to the object of the obligation that occur during the period of deposit. Moreover, he is liable for the expenses of custody or auction, etc., for the period of deposit. When the subject of the obligation right is unclear, or the obligee has disappeared or his whereabouts are unknown, usually the related organization will use the technique of public announcement to solve the problem.

4. Termination of an Obligation Because of a Legal Rule or Administrative Regulation

An obligation may be terminated by the direct rule of law. For example the Methods for Handling Disputes over Agricultural Obligations in New Areas promulgated in the early part of the founding of our country provided: "Obligations incurred before Liberation that are owed by peasants and other workers to landlords are all cancelled." Circumstances of this sort are very rare. The state selects compulsory procedures to cancel out obligation relations directly only in case of a very special need. Obligations can also be cancelled as a result of administrative regulations, for example, [when] a supervisory organization promulgates an administrative order changing or cancelling the production quotas for certain planned products, or orders certain enterprises to stop production, change production, merge, close down, etc. These administrative regulations adjusting economic activities or economic relations cause certain obligations to be terminated that certain units which are responsible for carrying out responsibilities mutually have with each other or between themselves and other units or individuals to be terminated. As to the consequences that result from these terminations, they must be handled according to the relevant policies and legal norms. However, in the termination of an obligation by administrative order, it is necessary to protect and respect the interests of the parties. In regard to parties who are harmed by the termination of the obligations, they must be given suitable compensation.

5. Obligations that Are Terminated by Remission

"Remission" refers to the case where the obligee abandons his obligation right and cancels the obligor's liability. When an obligation has been remitted, the obligation is then terminated. At present our country still does not have any rules clearly providing for remission. However, in practice, the termination of obligations by remission does occur. Moreover, it is necessary only that [this remission] not violate rules of law, and that it not be inconsistent with the nature of the obligation, and then it will be recognized by law, for example, [when, in an obligation] between citizens, the obligee, out of mutual friendship, remits the obligor from his duty. Obligations between socialist organizations do not normally use remission, because in the case of obligation rights created by law it is not only that the obligee may exercise rights, at the same time he also has duties that must be fulfilled to the state and society. Moreover, to permit remission would also influence economic accounting and the turning over of profits to higher authorities. It could even hinder the carrying out of the country's economic plan.

In order for a remission to be effective, there must be a declaration of intention by the obligee. The obligation that is remitted may be an existing obligation, or a conditional obligation, or an obligation subject to a time limit. It may be remission of the entire obligation or remission of a part. When it is only remission of part of the obligation, only a portion of the obligation is terminated. When the obligation is terminated because of remission, the accessory obligations are also terminated accordingly.

6. Termination of an Obligation Because of Merger

"Merger" refers to the case where the rights and duties of one obligation are, for some reason, united in one subject. The two subjects of the obligation have become one. Is not possible to exercise the obligation right or to perform the obligation duty to oneself. Consequently, the obligation is terminated following the merger. Although merger can occur between citizens, in our country it occurs primarily between juristic persons. For example, two enterprises that were originally in an obligation rights-duty relationship merge. The new enterprise has both the status of the original obligee of the original obligation and of the original obligor. The obligation, because of merger, is terminated.

Apart from the reasons discussed above, obligations may also be terminated for other reasons, for example, agreement between the two parties, dissolution of a juristic person, death of a party, decision of an arbitration body or court, an unintended situation that makes performance impossible, etc.

VIII
GUARANTY OF OBLIGATIONS

1. General Concept of the Guaranty of Obligations

The guaranty of an obligation is for the purpose of supervising and urging the obligor to perform his duty. It is a kind of legal procedure for insuring the realization of obligation rights. It has its own special content, form, and characteristics. It is an important kind of legal system.

After the one furnishing the guaranty and the obligee have formed a guaranty relationship, it is [established] on the basis of the original obligation relationship. Moreover, it fills out certain rights-duty relationships. Its purpose is to cause the obligor to perform his obligation strictly, and, as far as possible, to prevent the obligor's failure to perform from harming the obligee. Since the guaranty obligation is an accessory obligation, its purpose is to insure the performance of the principal obligation. Consequently, the creation and existence of the guaranty obligation is premised on the existence of the principal obligation. If the principal obligation is amended or terminated, the guaranty obligation is amended or terminated accordingly.

The system of guaranty is very old. There had already appeared early in slavery societies, such types of guaranties as pledge, pawn, earnest money, and so forth. The guaranty obligation in which the obligor used his own person as security is an important early form of guaranty. Upon the arrival of the capitalist society, the system of guaranty obligations had an even fuller development with an even more extended field of use.

In the society of private ownership, the guaranty of obligations is an important tool for protecting the exploiters and maintaining the system of exploitation. In our country, contracts of guaranty serve the maintenance of the socialist economic order. The guaranty of obligations between socialist economic units is useful for strengthening contract discipline and discipline of the plan. Guaranties of obligations between citizens are to protect the lawful rights of citizens. In foreign trade obligations guaranties are to ensure the security of international trade and are an important form for promoting Chinese foreign trade.

2. Methods of Guaranteeing Obligations

The methods of guaranteeing obligations are also called the forms of guaranteeing obligations. According to the rules of our country's civil law, and economic practice, the important forms are as follows:

(1) Suretyship

(i) The forms of suretyship and the formation of suretyship. Suretyship is a contractual form of obligation guaranty. According to the contract of suretyship the surety assumes the liability towards the obligee of the principal contract that the obligor of the principal contract will perform.

The contract of suretyship is an accessory contract. Its establishment of a surety is premised on the existence of the principal contract.

The contract of surety uses a third party other than the parties to the principal contract as guarantor. The parties to the contract of surety are the surety and the obligee of the principal contract. The obligee of the principal contract is also the obligee of the contract of surety. The surety is the obligor of the contract of surety.

Normally the contract of suretyship is negotiated and entered into between the surety and the obligee. If the law has [special] provisions [for a particular use] it is handled according to the law. For example, section 6 of the Temporary Measures for the Signing of Contractual Agreements by Organizations, State Enterprises, and Cooperatives of the former Government Administrative Council of 1950 provided: "Contracts must have a surety. Suretyship takes the guaranty by the superior organization or supervisory organization as a principle."

In the contract of suretyship, the surety and the obligee negotiate and establish the scope of the liability of the surety. The scope of the liability of the surety for the obligation of the obligor may be agreed on by the parties. The surety may be liable for the whole obligation duty or only for a part of the obligation duty. When the scope of the guaranteed obligation has not been clearly determined, it is presumed that the surety has assumed liability for the whole obligation.

The liability of the surety to the obligee is of two types: secondary liability and joint liability. In the case of secondary liability, when the obligor of the principal obligation does not perform a contract it is necessary first to make a demand on the obligor of the principal obligation to perform. When the principal obligor does not perform, the surety will then perform in his place or be liable for damages. Joint liability means that the surety bears joint liability together with the principal obligor. The obligee can demand that the obligor perform or pay damages, and he can also demand that the surety perform or pay damages. There is no prescribed order [for making demands for performance].

According to section 15 of our country's Economic Contract Law, "When the party [whose performance is assured] does not perform, the surety unit is jointly liable for damages." The "joint liability" referred to is clearly secondary liability. This is a secondary obligation.

(ii) The relation of the surety and obligee. The surety must be liable in accordance with the rules of the contract of suretyship. When an obligation is added after the contract is established which the surety has not agreed to guarantee, the surety is not liable as surety. After the contract of surety comes into being, if the principal obligation is reduced, the obligation of the surety is also correspondingly reduced.

When the surety is two or more persons it may be agreed among the sureties to share the surety liability. This is called joint suretyship. The joint sureties may agree to bear the liability for the guaranty in shares. They may also agree to be jointly liable as sureties. When the law or contract has not clearly provided a rule, it is presumed that the sureties are jointly liable.

(iii) The relation between the surety and the principal obligor. After the surety has performed the principal obligor's duty to satisfy the obligation, the surety can then, within the scope of its performance, [for example, payment] take the place of the obligee. He has the right to demand compensation from the principal obligor. After the surety who is jointly liable has satisfied the obligation, he has the right to seek compensation from the other sureties.

If the surety and the principal obligor are jointly liable, after the surety has performed towards the obligee, he must immediately notify the obligor so that the obligor will not perform a second time. On the other hand, after the obligor performs, he must also immediately notify the surety.

If the obligee brings an action against the surety, the surety must notify the obligor to participate in the action in order to have the obligor bring forward the necessary defenses. If the surety does not notify the obligor to participate in the action, and unnecessary harm results, the obligor has the right to reject the surety's claim for compensation.

(iv) The determination of the surety's liability.

(a) The surety's liability is terminated because of the termination of the principal obligation.

(b) When it is provided that the surety bears a surety's liability for a limited time, if the obligee does not, within a specified time, make a demand for satisfaction [of the obligation], the surety is relieved of his liability as surety.

(c) If the parties have not provided a time limit for the suretyship, if, after the time for satisfaction of the principal obligation provided by law or when an ultimatum of the surety has expired, the obligee still has not brought an action [for satisfaction] of the obligation, the liability of the surety is terminated.

(2) Penalties

(i) The general concept of penalties. In order to guarantee performance of the obligation the parties agree that if one party does not perform he must pay to the other party a certain sum of money (cash). This is called a penalty.

The penalty is established to insure performance of the obligation. When the obligor does not perform the obligation he must, according to the rules, pay the penalty. Early in Roman law there was a penalty contract or a fine contract. In carrying out their civil law, most countries recognize the penalty for breach of contract.

The penalty is generally used in obligations arising out of contracts. In our country, among the frequent provisions in the agreements of the parties, there are some which are called fines for breach of contract, or penalty sums for breach of contract, or fines for exceeding the time, and so forth. They are all penalties for breach of contract in nature.

Penalties are divided into penalties by operation of law and penalties that are agreed on. Penalties by operation of law refers to penalties whose amount and ratio are directly provided by law. For example, in section 35 of the Provisions for Purchase and Sale Contracts for Industrial and Mineral Products, it is provided that "where the supplying party cannot deliver . . . the normal penalty will be used where the portion of goods that is not delivered is from one to five percent of the total. The special penalty will be used where the portion that cannot be delivered runs from ten to thirty percent of the total." The agreed-upon penalty refers to the penalty agreed on by the parties to the contract. If the law has not provided a statutory standard for the penalty, or, although it has provided a standard for the penalty, it is not concrete and clear, the parties may agree upon and set a penalty provision. The penalty set by the parties may not exceed the entire amount of the contract. It also may not set the penalty ratio too low. Otherwise, the people's court or an arbitration tribunal has the right to reduce or cancel the agreed-upon penalty.

(ii) The legal nature of penalties. In theory there are different views on the nature of the penalty. The laws of all countries regarding penalties are not the same. The French, German, etc., laws of the continental system have two different types of rules regarding penalties. One is the punishment penalty; the other is the penalty of damages.

The penalty that is a punishment refers to the penalty that is agreed upon by the parties as having the nature of the punishment. When the obligor does not perform his obligation, the obligee, apart from being able to demand the payment of the penalty, may, at the same time, demand performance of the obligation or [damages for] the actual injury caused by the failure to perform. It may be seen that the most important special characteristic of the penalty as a punishment is that it is in addition to performance or the payment of damages for the actual loss. The obligor has to make a payment—i.e., a payment beyond the actual injury.

The damages penalty is also called the penalty in which the amount of damages is agreed on in advance. The amount of this penalty is first agreed upon by the parties. When the obligation is not performed, the obligee need only prove that the obligation has not been performed as a fact. It is not necessary to prove the amount of the injury or that there was an injury. It can simply demand the amount agreed upon as a penalty. When the obligee has demanded the amount of the penalty he cannot at the same time ask the obligor to pay damages for the actual injury. This sort of penalty enables the parties to avoid the expense, time, and effort required to compute the actual injury.

Whether the penalty is a punishment or [constitutes] damages is something that is determined according to the parties' agreement if the parties have agreed on it. If they have not agreed on it, the rules of some countries presume that the penalty is to be regarded as a sum agreed on in advance for damages.

Section 35 of our country's Economic Contracts Law provides: "When one party violates an economic contract, he must pay the penalty to the other party. If the injury caused to the other party by the violation exceeds the amount of the penalty, he must pay damages to compensate for the inadequate amount of the penalty." According to this provision it is clear that when the penalty exceeds the actual injury or there is no injury, the penalty will be paid, but if the actual injury exceeds the penalty, the breaching party must supplement the amount that is short. This sort of provision to a certain degree increases the liability of the breaching party. It is quite valuable in protecting the lawful interests of the injured party and is useful in enforcing contract discipline.

The penalty is not only a form of liability for nonperformance, it is also a form of guaranty of the obligation. By virtue of the prior agreement of the parties or the direct provisions of the law, the parties are supervised and caused to fulfill the performance of their duties according to the provisions of the obligation.

(3) Earnest money

Earnest money means that in order to assure the performance of a contract one of the parties pays the other party a certain sum of money (cash).

The payment of earnest money is usually prior to formation of the contract. It also may be subsequent to formation and prior to performance. But it is not paid when there is a breach. This is the difference between earnest money and a penalty.

The amount of earnest money does not exceed the total amount of the contract. The actual amount is negotiated and agreed upon by the parties.

The most important purpose of earnest money is to assure performance of the contract. Consequently, earnest money is a form of obligation guaranty. However, the actual purpose of the earnest money and its utilization are not the same. If one considers dividing earnest money according to the purpose of the parties, there are four types: (1) *Formation earnest money*. That is, to consider the payment of earnest money as a condition for the formation of the contract. (2) *Evidentiary earnest money*. That is, the payment of the earnest money serves as proof of the formation of the contract. (3) *Violation [of the contract] earnest money*. This is the earnest money that serves as damages for nonperformance. (4) *Abandonment earnest money*. This is the earnest money that serves as a condition for freedom to abandon the contract.

According to section 14 of our country's Economic Contracts Law, the earnest money in an economic contract is violation [of the contract] earnest money. The violation [of the contract] earnest money is to provide in advance the amount of damages. After the payment of the earnest money, the party who paid the earnest money is liable for nonperformance of the contract. He cannot demand return of the earnest money. If the one who received the payment of earnest money is liable for nonperformance of the contract, then, according to principles of justice, he must return double the earnest money.

Earnest money is also an advance payment for a contract. If the contract is performed, the earnest money serves as a part payment. Even though earnest money served as advance payment it is not the same as advance payment. Advance payment is provided by the contract. A portion of the price is paid prior to performance of the contract. After performance of the contract, there is payment of the remainder of the price that is left over after the advance payment. If it is not possible to perform a contract, then it is necessary to return the advance payment. The advance payment does not serve as a guaranty of the obligation.

Since the earnest money has the nature of an advance payment it is related to the question of the control of funds. The payment of earnest money in a contract between socialist organizations may not violate the financial and economic system.

19 Obligations Arising from Acts that Infringe on Rights [Delicts]

I

THE CONCEPT AND CHARACTERISTICS OF OBLIGATIONS ARISING FROM ACTS THAT INFRINGE ON RIGHTS

1. The Concept of the Act that Infringes on Rights

An act that infringes on rights is one of the sources from which obligations arise. It is an act whereby the actor unlawfully infringes on the property or personal rights of others. When an act that infringes on rights causes an injury to property, an obligation relation arises between the one who has acted unlawfully and the injured party. In this sort of obligation relation the injured person is the obligee and the one causing injury to the other is the obligor. The injured party has the right to demand that the other party who caused the injury compensate him for the loss caused thereby and the one causing the injury bears the obligation to make appropriate compensation to the other party.

In the earliest times, the injured person and his blood relatives responded to solve [the problem of] the harm done to him by the act that infringed on rights by revenging themselves on the one causing the injury. But with the development of human society, revenge by the blood relatives of the injured person was gradually replaced by compensation with property. According to the Records of Qin Jian [the bamboo slips of the Qin Dynasty], unearthed in Shihudi of Hubei province, in our country's laws of the Qin Dynasty there were already some provisions regarding compensation in damages. Ancient Roman law divided acts in infringement of rights into private delicts and quasi-private delicts, and provided specific amounts of damages and the methods of calculating them. These provisions had a profound influence on the written law of later periods. The French Civil Code of 1804 inherited the structure of Roman Law. It labelled an act in infringement of rights as "an obligation that does not arise out of agreement" and put acts in infringement of rights in the third section entitled "The Ways of Obtaining Property." It used acts in infringement of rights and quasi-delicts to replace the private delict and quasi-private delict of Roman Law. The German Civil Code of 1900 treated acts in infringement of rights as an independent source of obligations and arranged delicts in the second section under "The Law of Obligation Relations," thus laying the foundation for the modern law of acts in infringement of rights. In the countries of Anglo-American law, torts are an ancient independent legal system that has enjoyed a long history. In these countries, relations arising from tortious acts have been adjusted through precedents and individual statutes. In the U.S.S.R. and East European countries, acts in infringement of rights are placed in the Obligation Section of their civil codes. They are referred to as "Causing Injury to Others." The position of acts in infringement of rights in those countries is second only to obligations arising from contracts. In the judicial practice of our country, obligations arising from acts in infringement of rights are called "obligations to pay damages."

2. The Characteristics of Obligations Arising From Acts in Infringement of Rights

Because the nature of the social system and the conditions of our country are different, obligations arising from acts in infringement of rights in our country bear the following legal features.

(1) Civil liability arising from acts in infringement of rights is a type of legal sanction

That is, the law makes the wrongdoers bear certain legal consequences for their acts that harm the public interest of society or the lawful rights and interests of other citizens. Since the areas of law affected by unlawful acts are different, their legal sanctions may be divided into the different methods of civil law sanctions, criminal law sanctions, administrative law sanctions, etc. Although they are all created to maintain the social order and protect the public interest of society, and the lawful rights and lawful interests of individual citizens, they are different legal systems, and the differences among them are quite clear.

(i) Differences in the manner of bearing liability. Criminal law sanctions and administrative law sanctions are not confined to economic sanctions (penalties and fines), and their economic sanctions are purely punitive in nature, whereas the sanctions in the law of acts that infringe on rights are civil law sanctions. They are mainly economic sanctions that are compensatory in nature.

(ii) Differences in the degree of enforceability. Criminal law sanctions and administrative law sanctions must be carried out once they are ordered by judicial or supervisory organs, whereas, subject to the condition of not violating the rules of law and socialist moral norms, the parties may negotiate civil law sanctions among themselves, or the matter may be settled through a third party. The injured

party may also waive his right to demand damages from the other party.

(iii) Differences in the principles of handling [cases]. Civil law sanctions are determined according to the principle of compensation of equal value. Thus the amount of damages is equal to the actual loss suffered by the injured party. But the property sanctions of a criminal law and an administrative law nature are not premised and based on the actual value of the property loss.

(iv) Differences in the place to which the property taken by way of sanction will be returned. Damages in civil law are entirely used to compensate for the property loss that has occurred and are paid to the injured party. But the fines and confiscation of property of criminal law sanctions and the penalties and confiscations of administrative law sanctions must be handed over to the State Treasury and become property of the State.

From the explanations of the above four differences, [it follows] that in handling disputes over injuries from acts in infringement of rights, and in imposing sanctions on the wrongdoer, criminal law and administrative law sanctions cannot substitute for civil law sanctions, and civil law sanctions cannot substitute for criminal law and administrative law sanctions. Instead, one must, in light of the concrete situation, apply one of them alone or apply them together.

(2) Civil law liability for injury from acts in infringement of rights is property liability

The wrongdoer must assume legal responsibility for the injuries to property resulting from his own acts or omission that violate legal rules. The civil law liability for acts in infringement of rights can arise at the same time as administrative and criminal law liability. It can also arise alone. But regardless of whether the unlawful acts of the wrongdoer can, at the same time, give rise to several types of liability, if there is an injury to property, he must be liable for it in civil law. Section 31 of our country's Criminal Code clearly provides: "When a criminal act causes another to suffer economic loss, the one who commits the crime, in addition to receiving criminal law punishment, must, according to the circumstances, be sentenced to compensate the economic loss." As mentioned above, civil law liability is a kind of independent legal system. It is only by using the method of adjusting property relations, according to the legal rule, forcing the one causing injury to make use of his own property to make up the property injury suffered by the other person—for the property injury caused by the act in infringement of rights—that socialist property and the lawful interests of citizens can be protected in adjudging the violation of the law.

(3) Civil responsibility for acts in infringement of rights is the legal means for dealing with infringements of ownership rights and personal rights

Civil responsibility for acts in infringement of rights and civil responsibility for breach of contract are both property liability, but they are two different kinds of civil responsibility. They differ in their presuppositions and scope of application. Civil responsibility for the act in infringement of rights is directed at the unlawful infringement of the lawful rights and interests of another, such as ownership, personal rights, intellectual property rights, etc., and the legal system that is formed thereby. What are protected are rights that are directly provided and created by law outside of contract relations. But in contractual relations, the rights created by the parties in their contract are what are protected.

3. The Importance of Correctly Understanding and Handling Disputes over Acts in Infringement of Rights

Civil law disputes arising from acts in infringement of rights account for a considerable portion of all civil cases. At the present time, these disputes mainly arise from fights, traffic accidents, accidents in medical treatment, environmental pollution, etc. These illegal acts not only cause direct injury to socialist property and the lawful rights of citizens, but they also harm public morality, endanger the social order, influence stability and unity, and are injurious to the establishment of the Four Modernizations. If these disputes are not settled in a timely and proper way, this may cause the contradictions to intensify and even give rise to criminal cases. From the experience of deciding cases, in the case of disputes in infringement of rights, there are, at the same time, acts which seriously violate the criminal law and constitute crimes. Consequently, establishing a legal system of civil responsibility for acts in infringement of rights and making use of the civil law procedures for damages to cause acts in infringement of rights to be restrained and punished, is very significant for effectively upholding the socialist economic order, protecting the establishment of socialist modernization, teaching citizens voluntarily to observe discipline and honor the law, and prevent unlawful acts from occurring.

II
THE ESSENTIAL CONDITIONS FOR CIVIL RESPONSIBILITY FOR ACTS IN INFRINGEMENT OF RIGHTS

Civil responsibility for acts in violation of rights is a kind of legal liability. For it to come into existence, certain elements must be present. Those elements are the constituent elements of civil responsibility for acts in infringement of rights. Usually, the following four elements must exist concurrently.

1. The Objective Existence of Actual Injury

Property loss is a prerequisite to the existence of civil responsibility for acts in infringement of rights. Therefore, the objective fact of the property loss suffered by the injured party becomes the prerequisite and basis of this sort of civil responsibility. If the act has not caused any loss, it cannot constitute an act in infringement of rights, and the actor does not bear civil responsibility.

The loss or injury referred to here is injury to property. As to personal injury, this also refers to property loss resulting from personal injuries. For example, medical expenses incurred in treating the injuries, loss of wages, etc. If the personal injury does not result in a property loss, for example, an infringement on a citizen's right to his name, right to his reputation, right to honor, right to his likeness, or when there is an infringement of the name, reputation, credit, etc., of a juristic person, administrative law or criminal law and other methods will be used to protect [the affected interest], and the people's courts or the basic legal organizations may take active measures and order the wrongdoer to cease the infringement, restore the reputation, eliminate the influence, or make apologies. When necessary, it may also use methods of providing consolation and give the injured person economic compensation.

Property loss includes both direct loss and indirect loss. Direct loss refers to the reduction in property presently owned by the injured party, for example, damage to the property of the injured party or the expenses incurred by the injured party for medical treatment after the injury. Indirect loss, also referred to as "benefits which might have been obtained," is the income that the injured party would normally have received, but, because of the injury, could not obtain, for example, the loss of income resulting from absence of work while being hospitalized.

2. The Unlawfulness of the Act in Infringement of Rights

An actor is only liable for his unlawful acts. If the act that caused personal or property injury is unlawful, then the actor is liable to pay damages for the injury he caused. Otherwise he is not liable. In short, the unlawfulness of the act is an essential condition for establishing liability for acts in infringement of rights.

In determining the unlawfulness of an act in infringement of rights, one should use as criteria not only the Constitution and civil law rules that are effective at the present time. It is also necessary to use, as a basis, socialist moral norms. An unlawful act may not only be a positive act of commission; it may also be a negative act of omission. The former is an act which is prohibited by law and the latter is the omission of an act which is required by law and morality.

Usually acts that injure others' property or person are unlawful acts. However, there are certain acts that, although they cause injury to others, are lawful acts. Under such circumstances there is no liability to pay damages. They may be classified as follows.

(1) An act authorized by the work of [the actors]

For the protection of the public interest of society and the lawful rights and interests of individuals, the law allows workers to "injure" the property or persons of others where it is necessary in carrying out their duties. This kind of act is lawful, and there is no liability to compensate for the injury that is caused. For example:

firefighters may, in order to prevent the fire from spreading, pull down buildings near the fire. Those working to prevent epidemics may burn the clothes used by people who have carried contagious diseases for the purpose of eliminating the contagious disease. A surgeon performs an amputation on a patient; a policeman fires at and injures fleeing criminal offenders, etc.

(2) Legitimate acts of defense

Legitimate acts of defense are those which are exercised against one who is committing an injurious and unlawful act, to prevent or lessen the injuries that may be produced by him, in order to protect the public interests of society or the lawful interests of oneself or others. Legitimate acts of defense are protective in nature and are, thus, a sort of lawful act. The one who is fighting back is not liable to pay damages.

But defense must be legitimate and reasonable. It is not permitted to abuse this right by excessive retaliation. An act of defense that is excessive is an unlawful act, and the one who exceeds the proper limits of defense is liable for the injury caused thereby.

As for the essential conditions for constituting an act of legitimate defense, refer to the related provisions in the criminal code.

(3) Emergency acts to avoid danger

Emergency acts to avoid danger are emergency measures taken that inflict a lesser degree of harm on others when it is unavoidable in order that the public interest of society and the lawful interests of oneself and others will not receive still greater harm. For example, a ship may, if it encounters a dangerous storm en route, in order to protect its passengers, throw overboard all or part of its cargo; to avoid being hit by an automobile, a person may turn over a stand at the side of the road, etc. Emergency acts to avoid danger are lawful acts. If the danger was not caused by the actor, he is not liable to pay damages for the injury caused by his act. If the danger was created by a third person, the third person who caused the danger shall be liable to pay damages.

For the essential conditions required to constitute the emergency for avoidance of danger, refer to the related provisions in the criminal code.

3. The Causal Relation Between the Unlawful Act and the Injury

The causal relation between the unlawful act and the injury is one of the essential conditions for civil law liability and it is also one of the most complex among the four.

Causal relations or causation refers to a necessary relationship between objective phenomena of the natural world and society. That is, when a phenomenon occurs, it is under such conditions that it must be caused by another phenomenon that already exists. The former phenomenon is called the result and the latter the cause. The necessary objective relation between the two is called a causal relation. The causal relation is objective. It is determined by the internal rules of the phenomenon. It is not shifted according to the subjective intention of men. For example, the driver who violates traffic rules and knocks down a pedestrian, causes him to be injured. The causal relation between the driver's causing of trouble and the pedestrian's injuries exists objectively and is direct. Consequently, in holding [someone] civilly responsibile for an act of infringement of rights, it is necessary that the related circumstances and objects undergo objective analysis and, proceeding from the facts scientifically, study of whether or not there is an essential causal relation between the act in infringement of rights and the injury. But it is not possible to rely only on superficial phenomena and make subjective assumptions.

We begin, in the spirit of seeking truth from facts, by analyzing the causal relation, beginning with the result to trace the cause. That is, we take a specific injury as a result, and try to find out objectively what caused the injurious result. Investigating the causal relation is an essential step. Its purpose is to determine whose act (or omission) caused the injury. Then, on this basis, we proceed to determine who must be civilly liable for this injurious result.

Causal relations are an objective process. Usually they are clear and easy and not difficult to determine. But sometimes there are complicated situations and a certain injurious result may well have been caused by several related causes (a chain of causal relations and results) and finally come about. Each of these causes has to be examined regardless of whether it is part of the course of a natural phenomenon or the act of a person, otherwise we would not find out the actual manner of the appearance of the injury. If there are some actions by several persons among the causes, then these actions are the objects we must search for in analyzing the causal relations. Moreover, according to the actual circumstances, we must separate the causes and conditions. From many causes [we must] sieve out and select the essential cause, from the parties' actions, distinguish the principal and subordinate [causes], from many [causes] that harm people, differentiate the serious and not so serious, in order to determine whether or not there is civil responsibility and the objective basis for how much. However, we cannot, from this, determine who is liable for the injurious result regardless of whether the acts were those of several persons or just one, since the simple causal relation is only one of the essential elements of liability for the injury. To determine finally who is liable for the injurious result, one has to continue the investigation to be sure whether the other elements are present.

4. The Actor's Fault

Usually, to be liable in civil law for the injurious result, the actor has to be subjectively at fault for his own acts and the injuries which they caused. The fault here refers to the state of mind of the actor when he decided to act, which may be both intentional and negligent.

When an actor foresees the consequences of his act, and he still intends them to happen or permits them to happen, this is called [an] intentional [act].

If an actor should have or could have foreseen the consequences of his act, but did not actually foresee them, or, although he foresaw the consequences, he believed [on no strong basis] that the consequences would not occur, this is called negligence. The determination whether the actor acted negligently has to be based on whether the actor should have and could have paid attention [to the consequences of his acts] and did not do so. Since there are differences in time and place, and conditions, and the objective environment changes constantly, the standard of what people can and should pay attention to also never stops changing. Therefore the standard of what is to be paid attention to varies with changes in time, place, and the surrounding circumstances. The actor's age, level of education, special expertise, work experience, level of skill, the amount of responsibility in his position, etc., are all to be conscientiously ascertained, but it is not possible to make a subjective abstract determination. In regard to people who have different occupations and who have different levels of skill, such as doctors and nurses, engineers and ordinary workers, master workers and apprentices, the degrees [of care] which they can and should observe are different. They do not have the same requirements and cannot be treated the same.

The three requirements discussed above all constitute the objective requirements of civil law liability. The fault of the actor is a subjective element of civil law liability. Its significance lies, on the one hand, in the fact that it deters and prevents failure to observe the law and discipline, and [prevents] disregard of the safety of [others'] person and property and other wrongful acts. On the other hand, it encourages and supports a spirit of active initiative among the masses of the people to carry on their work freely and boldly. The distinction between intentional and negligent fault in criminal law is very important in determining the nature of the crime and the appropriate penalty. But the distinction usually has no effect on the determination of the scope of civil law liability, for the scope of the actor's liability for acts in infringement of rights is determined solely according to whether there is injury or how great the injury is, and not by whether or not the actor acted intentionally or negligently. In civil law, sometimes negligence is divided into ordinary negligence and gross negligence. This kind of division in judicial practice is made according to the degree [of care] particularly required of the actor. If, under certain circumstances, the law requires that the degree of care that a certain actor is required and able to exercise be higher, and the actor does not comply with the higher requirement, but does not violate the standard of care that ordinary people are required and able to observe, then this is ordinary negligence. If the actor had not only failed to comply with the higher degree of care required of him by the law but did not comply with the general standard [of care] which all men are required and able to observe, then this is gross negligence.

In the adjudication of civil cases, the degree of fault of the actor has, in most cases, no actual significance in determining the existence of civil responsibility. But under certain circumstances, the degree of fault becomes the main basis for determining the liability to pay civil law damages. The three situations listed below are these types of situations:

(1) Mixed fault

If the occurrence or aggravation of injury is not only because of the actor's fault, but also because of the injured party's intentional [act] or gross negligence, this constitutes mixed fault. Since, in the case of mixed fault, both the actor and the injured party are at fault for the occurrence of the injury, how much of the responsibility each must bear must be determined according to the degree of the fault of each of them. The portion that was caused by the injured party's fault should be borne by the injured party himself.

(2) Jointly injuring another

When two or more persons cause injury to others, this constitutes jointly injuring others. The basic characteristics of jointly injuring others are: (1) the several actors subjectively had the common intention to cause injury, or there was joint negligence, that is, they were all at fault jointly; [and] (2) their unlawful acts are in fact the objective causes of the injurious result. [The actors], who caused the injury together, are jointly liable to the injured party for damages for his loss of property. The liability for payment of the entire amount of damages is apportioned among those causing the injury according to the degrees of their respective fault. The joint liability towards the outside of those causing injury together and the apportioning of liability among themselves are two different kinds of liability and should not be confused or substituted for each other. This is so because the purpose of the obligation arising out of an act in infringement of rights is to protect the lawful rights and interests of the injured party.

(3) Injury caused by the injured party's intentional act or grossly negligent act

If the injurious result was principally caused by the intentional [act] or gross negligence of the injured party, and the person causing the injury was only guilty of ordinary negligence, the one who caused the injury may be relieved from liability to pay damages. If both the injured party and the one causing the injury acted intentionally or were grossly negligent so as to cause the injury, this constitutes mixed fault, and there is no question of relieving the one causing the injury from liability.

III
SEVERAL SPECIFIC TYPES OF CIVIL RESPONSIBILITY FOR ACTS IN INFRINGEMENT OF RIGHTS

The four elements of civil responsibility for acts in infringement of rights discussed above must, in most cases, be present at the same time to subject the actor to liability for an act in infringement of rights. None can be missing. Otherwise, it is not possible correctly to recognize the civil responsibility of the actor for the injury. However, under the special situations set out below, related organizations or staff may be liable even if the four elements are not present at the same time, or some additional element may be needed to subject related organizations or staff to liability.

1. The Liability of Persons Without Capacity to Act or With Only Limited Capacity to Act for Causing Injury to Others

Persons without the capacity to act or with only limited capacity to act cannot appreciate the consequences of their acts and the implications thereof. They lack the ability to handle their affairs carefully, so they cannot be responsible for their own acts.

"Persons without capacity to act" usually refers to infants and persons who are mentally ill. According to the Marriage Law, and other relevant laws and regulations, the civil law activities of the person without capacity should be carried on by his statutory representatives or by guardians appointed by law to represent him. If an infant or a person who is mentally ill causes injury to others, civil responsibility for damages will be borne by this statutory representative or guardian. With such provisions, the injured party's property loss will be compensated and his lawful rights and interests will be effectively protected. Moreover, this will cause the guardian to be more responsible [in the exercise of his duties], and will prevent the injurious acts of persons without capacity to act from occurring.

A person with only limited capacity to act possesses a certain power of discernment. If he also has an independent income, he must, together with his statutory representative, be jointly liable for the injuries caused by his unlawful acts.

When a person with intermittent mental illness becomes [mentally] ill, his mind loses its normal state. He cannot understand the consequences of his acts and he cannot control his own acts. For instance, an epileptic is not liable for the injurious result of his acts done when he was under the influence of epilepsy. But this requires a scientific appraisal and the obtaining of collateral evidences. As for a person who caused injuries to others by rendering himself temporarily unconscious by excessive drinking or the use of narcotics, he shall be held liable for the injuries because he himself was at fault. This is not one of the special situations discussed above.

2. Liability of State Organizations for Injuries Done by Their Staff Members

State agencies are liable for the injuries caused by their staff members who are carrying on their official functions only under the following conditions: when (1) there is clear provision of the law; (2) the acts of the officials are clearly improper. Only then is the state organization liable for this sort of injury. For example, firefighters who, in the course of fighting fires, pull down buildings that should not be destroyed; or when official public security personnel, who in carrying on their work, drive a car and run into someone, causing the other person to suffer a property loss. [In such cases] the state organizations concerned must bear responsibility to make appropriate compensation in light of the actual circumstances.

3. Liability of Juristic Persons for Injuries Done to Others by Their Employees

Juristic persons carry on their activities in relation to outsiders through their employees. Therefore, juristic persons should be held civilly liable to make compensation for the acts infringing on rights committed by their employees when acting within the scope of their employment. But the liability of a juristic person does not result in excluding the liability of the employee. The juristic person may impose a certain liability on its employee based on the degree of his fault, and his economic circumstances. If the activity carried on by the employee has absolutely no relation to the business of the juristic person, then the [employee] himself is liable for the injury he caused.

4. Liability for Injuries Caused by Domestic Animals

When a domestic animal causes injury to the property or person of another [person], the owner or person in charge of the animal must bear civil responsibility to compensate for the injury. But if the incident was caused by the fault of the injured person, the owner or person in charge of the animal is not liable. If the incident was purposefully provoked by a third party, the third person shall be liable to make compensation.

5. No-fault Liability for Injuries Resulting from Extrahazardous Activities

Under normal circumstance, the determination of civil responsibility requires fault. If we do not make fault a necessary element of liability to pay damages for injury, this will certainly influence and limit the normal exercise of citizens' rights and the fostering of the development of enterprises. This is the general rule of modern civil law legislation. But with the rapid development of socialized large-scale production, particularly with the appearance of large-scale and hazardous industries which might frequently cause injury to others, if the principle of fault liability were still insisted upon, the injured persons would often be unable to obtain compensation. From the late 19th century to the early 20th century, there appeared in the legislation of some capitalist countries, on the strong demand of the workers, the rule of "no-fault liability." That is, in certain situations, the person who caused damage to others was liable to make compensation even if there was no fault on his part. The 1838 Railroad Enterprises Act of the Kingdom of Prussia first provided:

"Railroad companies shall be liable to make compensation for injury to persons and things carried by them and to other persons and things which are caused by their transport activities. An enterprise that is likely to cause injury to others, even though the owners are absolutely without negligence, may not avoid liability because there is no negligence." Subsequently, in 1839, the principle of no-fault liability for the activities of hazardous industries was extended to the mining industry by the Mining Law. The principle of no-fault in the last century in every country functioned as a principle for handling special acts in infringement of rights. It first appeared in Germany, Austria, Switzerland, and other continental-law countries. It was called "causal liability." In countries of the Anglo-American law systems it is called the principle of liability for the "result." That is, whether or not the one who causes injury is liable, depends only upon whether there is an injurious result. If there is an injurious result, even if there was no fault, he is civilly liable. In the Soviet Union, hazardous industries are called ultrahazardous activities, and no-fault liability is called "liability for danger." The Obligation Law of Yugoslavia terms the principle of fault "subjective liability," and uses it as the principle for ordinary acts in infringement of rights. It terms causal liability "objective liability," and uses it for civil responsibility in the case of special acts in infringement of rights.

The legislative and judicial practice of our country recognizes no-fault liability resulting from the carrying on of ultrahazardous activities. Ultrahazardous activities refers to activities involving the upper atmosphere, high tension, or high pressure, inflammables, explosives, toxic materials, radioactive materials, etc. Under present technical conditions, even when these activities are managed with great care, they may still cause injury to the life, health, and property of others. Consequently, those entities which engage in these activities are liable for injuries resulting from their ultrahazardous activities when others are injured as the result of carrying them on. Even if there was no fault, civil responsibility and obligation to make compensation will be imposed. Such a rule will help to make the organizations and individuals engaging in extrahazardous activities more responsible for, and careful with their work, and make them constantly improve technological safety measures in order to protect the security of the properties and persons of others. But, if injury is intentionally caused by the injured person, then the organizations and individuals engaging in dangerous activities are not liable to make compensation.

6. Liability for Causing Injury to Others as the Result of Environmental Pollution

The main task of environmental protection is to ensure a rational utilization of natural resources in the construction of socialist modernization, to prevent the destruction and contamination of the natural environment, and to try to create a clean and agreeable environment for life and work, in order to protect the people's health and promote economic development. However, with the development of production by heavy industries and urban construction, mining and industrial areas are constantly expanding; plants and factories stand everywhere like trees in a forest. As a result of this, the phenomenon of the contamination by the "three wastes" [waste gas, waste residue, and waste water], etc., appeared. This not only threatens the health of the people, but also causes unnecessary harm to nearby farmers' fields, running water, buildings, etc. Consequently, the number of disputes over injuries caused by environmental pollution is increasing. At the present time, those enterprises and institutes which, against state law, release excessive amounts of waste gas, water, waste residue, waste water, particulates (particles), radioactive matter, or which violate control standards for noise, vibrations, stench, etc., are civilly responsible to make compensation if, by so doing, they cause injury to others. If the violation is serious and causes grievous consequences, they must also bear administrative and criminal liability.

IV
THE SCOPE AND METHODS OF COMPENSATION FOR INJURIES CAUSED BY THE INFRINGEMENT OF RIGHTS

1. The Scope of Compensation

The determination of the scope of civil responsibility to make compensation must be made in accordance with the following principles:

(1) The property loss should be fully compensated

Civil responsibility for acts in infringement of rights is property liability. The scope of this liability—whether it is large or small—is not determined by the degree of fault of the actor, but the liability to make full compensation is determined by the extent of the property injury. The purpose of law in establishing civil responsibility is, on the one hand, to punish the wrongdoer, and, on the other hand, to compensate for the loss suffered by the injured party.

The whole loss includes direct loss and indirect loss. The one causing the injury must make compensation to the injured party not only for the direct diminution in the [value of the] property, that is, the value of the injured party's direct loss. He must also make compensation for lost income advantages that would have been received, that is, the indirect loss.

(2) The principle of compensation for property loss caused in cases of personal injury

The actor must make full compensation for the whole loss suffered by the injured party in the case of injury to property. In cases of personal injuries, there is compensation for all the property loss suffered by the injured party as a result of the injury to the person. If, when the one causing the injury is criminally or administratively liable because his criminal and administrative liability are being pursued, it does not mean he avoids civil liability.

(3) The economic situation of the parties should be taken into consideration

After it has been determined that the one causing the injury is subject to civil responsibility in accordance with the constituent elements of civil responsibility, in concretely determining the amount of the damages, the economic situations of the parties should be considered. If the financial condition of the one causing the injury is fairly good, and he is able to compensate, he should be ordered to compensate for the entire injury. If the actor's economic situation is not good, and full compensation of the loss by him will cause him and his family to fall into great difficulty in their lives, or make it difficult for him to maintain a normal way of life, it is necessary to work on both parties, and providing the consent of the injured party is obtained, [the damages] might be appropriately reduced or eliminated, taking into account the concrete circumstances. When necessary, the problem may be solved through social relief.

2. Methods of Compensation

The injuries caused by acts in infringement of rights are divided into losses to property and the expenditures incurred as a result of injuries to the person. Injuries to property occasioned by unlawful infringement of another's property or intellectual property [should be remedied] first by return of the original property or restoration of its original condition. If the original property has been destroyed, or its original condition can only be restored with great difficulty, compensation may be made with an object of the same quality or the amount of money assessed according to the actual value of the injured property.

As to compensation for losses incurred in cases of injury to the person, the matter must be handled differently according to the following three types of circumstances.

(1) Ordinary injuries

Injuries that can be healed through medical treatment and which do not render the injured person disabled are called ordinary injuries. In handling this type of case, one should look to the medical certificates, and the receipts issued by hospitals to the injured person, to determine the amount of damages according to the concrete situation and actual needs, for example, medical bills, hospital fees, the expense for a food allowance while hospitalized, and expenses for nourishment, as well as expenses incurred for necessary trained nursing care, necessary travel expenses to see doctors, the lost wages of workers, and lost income from labor of peasants, etc.

The purpose [of compensation] is to facilitate the injured person's ability to get well soon and to restore his ability to manage his own affairs and to work, by means of medical treatment and nourishment.

(2) Disability of the person

Disability refers to those serious injuries received by the injured person that cannot be completely healed and result in the loss of all or part of the [injured person's] working capacity. If the injured person suffered serious injury, but it is difficult to say whether he will be disabled, the injury should first be treated as in the case of ordinary injuries. When the condition of injury becomes stable, and it is clear that the injured person is disabled, then the case should be handled as a disability case. In the handling of the disabled person, the amount of damages which the one who caused the injury must pay in compensation should be determined in light of the degree to which [the injured party] has lost the ability to work, whether there is a reduction in his original salary and whether the injured party is entitled to the benefits of labor insurance, and according to the relevant state regulations.

(3) Death

If the deceased is a minor who had no independent income, the actor should, apart from paying the funeral expenses, if it is necessary in light of the concrete situation, also, in order to comfort the family of the deceased, pay a certain sum of money as consolation to the head of the family of the deceased. If the deceased was the main person who was responsible for the support of the family, the actor should pay to the deceased's family, besides medical, funeral, and other expenses of the deceased, a compensatory sum of money which is proper in light of the financial responsibility which the deceased had taken towards his family before his death. But the total sum for living expenses should not, in general, exceed the standard of living in the area.

If the injured person had an insurance contract with an insurer, and the injured person [or his family] seeks damages because his person is injured or he dies, this does not affect the right of the injured person, as the one protected, to ask for insurance benefits from the insurer.

If the party that caused the injury is a socialist organization, the damages it pays should not be counted as production cost, but should be paid from the after-tax profits or the portion of profits retained by the enterprise or from the enterprise fund. It must itself be liable and cannot transfer the liability to others.

20 Unjust Enrichment and Management of Affairs without Mandate [*Negotiorum Gestio*]

I
OBLIGATIONS THAT ARISE OUT OF UNJUSTIFIED ENRICHMENT

1. The General Concept of Unjustified Enrichment

The obtaining of an advantage which causes injury to another and has no legal basis is unjustified enrichment. The coming into being of unjustified enrichment has no legal basis. Therefore, although it is an accomplished fact, it receives no legal protection. Moreover, the appearance of this fact between the parties forms a civil law rights-duty relation. This kind of civil law relationship of unjustified enrichment is the obligation created by unjustified enrichment. The party whose property was injured as a result of the unjustified enrichment is the obligee, who has the right to demand that the other return the advantage, and the one who obtained the improper advantage because of the unjustified enrichment is the obligor, who has the duty to return the benefits that were received. For example, the lender receives a payment of a sum of money that has already been paid, the buyer receives an excess of quantity of goods from the seller, one who is commissioned to transport something mistakenly delivers it and the other party receives it. Although the reasons that give rise to these facts are not the same, all create the obligation of unjustified enrichment between the parties.

2. The Necessary Conditions for the Creation of the Obligation of Unjustified Enrichment

(1) The requirement that one party receive an advantage

One requirement of unjustified enrichment is that one party actually receive a benefit. If one party causes the other party's property interest to be injured, and he himself has not actually received any benefit, then even though the law makes him liable to pay damages, this does not constitute unjustified enrichment. Consequently, one mark of the difference between the obligation of unjustified enrichment and other obligations is that one party receives a benefit.

One party receives an advantage. In general, this means that the one who receives the benefit obtains unjustly some particular property, for example, if a cashier negligently and erroneously, pays out ten *yuan* bills in place of five *yuan* bills. Half of what the payee receives is unjustified enrichment. But sometimes, the one who receives the benefit performs an obligation improperly and avoids [a duty] and is thus enriched, for example, [if] a cashier in a tax office, by virtue of a mistake in computation, reduces the amount of a taxpayer's tax. This [benefit] which the taxpayer received as the amount he should have paid and did not pay is unjustified enrichment. In the above two payments, one party either increased his own property through another's payment or benefited by having his property not reduced because he did not perform. In fact there is no difference. In both cases the benefit received is unjustified enrichment.

(2) It is necessary that the other party be injured

[Another] requirement of unjustified enrichment is that one party be injured. If one party receives a benefit, but the other party is not thereby injured, then this is not unjustified enrichment. If someone uses waste water from a factory or mine to irrigate or collects the manure of the cattle of another to use as fertilizer, then even though in both cases one party obtains a benefit, the other party is not injured. Hence, in both cases, this is not unjustified enrichment.

Usually, when one party is injured, it is because the benefit which the other party receives caused his property to be injured, but sometimes there can be a case where one party's acquisition of benefits causes the other party not to receive what he ought to have received. In the former case the property of the one who is injured is caused to be diminished when it ought not to be diminished. In the latter, the property of the injured party does not increase when it ought to increase. These two situations are the reverse of the situation discussed above. The payment received by the payee which was half again too large caused the cashier's unit to be injured in the amount of the excess payment. In the case where the taxpayer paid too little, this caused the taxing office to be injured in the amount of their diminished receipts.

(3) There must be a direct relation between the benefits that are obtained and the injury that is suffered

The obligation of unjustified enrichment arises from the receipt of benefits by one party that causes harm to another. That is, there is a direct conflict of interest between the two sides which forms a rights-duty relationship between the parties. Consequently, a direct causal relation between the harm and the benefit received is an essential condition of unjustified enrichment.

In the obligation of unjustified enrichment the cause of the receipt of enrichment by one side is the result of the other side being injured. That is, if the same facts result in one side receiving a benefit and the other side being injured, then there is a direct causal relation between the two, and this is unjustified enrichment.

(4) There must be no basis in law

No basis in law means that one party obtains a benefit without having a lawful cause or right. This is one of the elements of establishing the right of unjustified enrichment. If the receipt of a benefit by one party and of an injury by the other has a legal basis, the parties' rights and obligations are naturally recognized and protected by law. They are also not unjustified enrichment. For example, the benefits received by the obligor from the injury to the obligee resulting from the running of civil law prescription is not unjustified enrichment.

"No basis in law" means, in general, that when the party who was enriched obtained the benefit, there was no legal basis (for his doing so), nor any legal right. If the original obligor makes another payment of an obligation that has already been paid, and the original obligee receives [the benefit], unjustified enrichment is created. However there are occasions when it may be that at the time the benefit is received, there is a legal basis, but subsequently, this basis, owing to some circumstance, ceases to exist. In these circumstances it is possible for unjustified enrichment to come into existence, for example, [when] one party gives the other party a pledged article as a means of performing the contractual [duty of giving] security. When the contract is completely performed, the right of pledge no longer exists. If the original pledgee continues to possess the item, unjustified enrichment arises. Consequently, it does not matter whether the lack of legal basis existed at the beginning or that it was lost subsequently. In both cases, there is unjustified enrichment.

3. Handling Obligations of Unjustified Enrichment

When unjustified enrichment has been established, the rights-duty relation is established between the parties. The injured person has the right to demand the return of the benefit, the person who received the benefit has the duty to return the benefit he received. The so-called return of the advantage includes return of the original thing and interest produced by profits received from the thing.

However, it can be seen that the formation of the obligation of unjustified enrichment in which the recipient of benefits must be civilly liable to return the benefits he has received, which have caused injury without a legal basis, is not the same as the [liability] arising from unlawful infringement of the rights of another person or property. The latter is an unlawful act. The actor being required to bear civil responsibility to pay damages, is a sort of legal system. Because of this, in regard to the handling of unjustified enrichment, apart from providing that the one who receives benefits must return those benefits in order to protect the lawful rights of the injured person, it may also be decided whether or not the liability of the recipient of the benefits is large or small according to his knowledge (of the circumstances), and there are [resulting] differences in the scope of what benefits must be returned.

The most important three types of circumstances that may appear are the following: The first is where the person who receives benefits does not know the circumstances (this is also called good faith). That is, when he acquires the benefits he does not know the unlawful basis for the acquisition and in this way receives them. The scope of his duty to restore is limited to the portion of the [benefit] that is still in existence. If the benefit has ceased to exist, then he has no duty to return. The so-called remaining portion is not limited to the precise form of the original item. If the form changes, and the value of the property still exists and may be used as substitute compensation, then this is still the remaining portion. The second [circumstance] is when the one acquiring the benefit knows the circumstances (this is also called bad faith). That is, at the time he obtains the benefit he well knows that he is obtaining a benefit without a basis in law. Then he must be completely liable to return the benefit. If, because of some unintended reason, the property no longer exists, he still does not escape the duty to return. The third situation is that in which the one who has received benefits does not know the circumstances at the time he received them, but he learns them subsequently. Under these circumstances, taking the period when he knows as the boundary, then divide the period into the time before and after that time, and allocate the scope of the duty to return accordingly.

The reasons the law provides the bases discussed above are: the lawful interests of the injured person must be protected, but unjustified enrichment is often caused by the injured person. Consequently, in some circumstances, the injured party must bear a certain responsibility. If the one who receives the benefits does not know of the circumstances [when] he receives them, and he himself is without fault, but he caused injury to another, he has a certain [limited] degree of liability. If he knows the circumstances, but still causes injury to another through inattention, he must bear the entire responsibility. This way of deciding according to the circumstances and differentiating the methods of handling the cases accordingly is advantageous for upholding the seriousness and justice of the law. It is also helpful in preventing the development of unjustified enrichment.

In practice, it is necessary to pay attention to the differences in the circumstances of unjustified enrichment, and its differences from other types of obligations, and thereby determine the content and scope of the parties' rights and duties.

II
OBLIGATIONS THAT ARISE OUT OF MANAGEMENT OF AFFAIRS WITHOUT MANDATE [NEGOTIORUM GESTIO]

1. The General Concept of the Obligation of Management Without Mandate

When someone manages the affairs of another without a basis in law, this is management of affairs without a mandate. The one who manages the affairs of another is the manager, the one whose affairs are managed is the principal.

Management of affairs without mandate occurs when a manager who has not received a grant of authority [mandate], and who has no legally imposed duty, undertakes an action on his own which is designed to benefit another. The law recognizes the institution of management of affairs without mandate. It is quite significant for developing the practice of socialist morality and constructing a spiritual civilization. The manager in the case of management of affairs without mandate is the obligee. He has the right to demand compensation for necessary expenses incurred in managing the affair. The principal is the obligor. He is subject to the duty of compensating the said expenses, for example, looking after and nourishing, for the other, domestic animals that have strayed; paying the rent, water, or electricity for a neighbor, and causing injury to himself. These matters are those that cause the obligation of administration without mandate to arise between the manager and the principal.

2. The Necessary Conditions for Forming the Obligation of Management of the Affairs of Another Without Mandate

(1) The necessity to manage the affairs of another

The management of someone else's affairs is an essential condition of management of affairs without mandate. If a concrete analysis is made of this requirement, the source of the special characteristics of management of the affairs can be seen. It is necessary, first of all, to limit the rights-duty relationship that can be established on the basis of the affairs that are to be managed. If, after a snow, in order to make matters more convenient for those going along [the road], ice and snow are cleared from the road, this sort of labor for the common good cannot establish management [of affairs] without mandate. Second, it must be done objectively in order to benefit others. If one carries out one's own affair, mistakenly regarding it as that of another, so that the purpose is for another's benefit, this also cannot give rise to management [of affairs] without mandate. But management [of the affairs] of another is not limited to matters which are entirely those of others. If one repairs the wall of a courtyard or a path to water that is used in common by oneself and another, there can be management [of the affairs] of the part that belongs to the other. Third, the affair that is managed cannot be limited to a simple act of management. For example, if a person is absent and one buys for him [his quota of] rationed goods that are of limited quantity, [requiring] a certificate available within a certain grace period, or acts for him in transferring a train or boat ticket that is about to expire, etc., these acts of transferring ownership are also acts of management and may serve as the bases for the obligation of management of affairs [without mandate].

(2) There must be the intention to benefit another

The intention of the manager to benefit another is an essential element of management [of the affairs] of another without mandate. The intention to confer a benefit on another may be determined from the motive and results of the act of management. So far as motive is concerned, the action of the manager must be performed with the purpose of aiding the other. So far as results are concerned, the advantage received from the act of administration must finally return to the ownership of the principal. In consonance with these conditions, even if the actor is mistaken, e.g., if he mistakenly believes A's matter to be B's and undertakes an act of management, this does not affect the creation of an act of management [of affairs] without mandate. It is only that the principal is not the same. If the manager and the principal can both receive benefits from the act of management, there can be management [of the actions] without mandate of the portion received by the principal. If these conditions are not met, as if one repairs another person's property for his own use, in general, management [of the affairs] without mandate does not come into being. If these conditions are violated, not only is it not possible to establish management [of affairs] without mandate, but according to the circumstances, unjustified enrichment or even infringement rights may be created. The so-called benefit includes the right which the act of management causes the principal to receive directly. At the same time, it may include the principal avoiding or reducing a loss and indirectly receiving a benefit. It may be a benefit received in fact. It may also be at the same time a legal benefit (for example, performing for another support obligations required by law). Management [of affairs] without mandate is not the same as the management of affairs by virtue of a commission. The intention of the manager to act for the benefit of another does not need to be expressed; it can still establish management of affairs without mandate.

(3) It must not have a legal basis

The concept of no basis in law includes the case where the manager has not received a commission and also has no statutory duty. It is one of the essential conditions of management [of affairs] without mandate. If the one managing the affair receives a commission he has a contractual duty. If he has a legal duty imposed by the law, then this is a basis at law. An action taken as a result of this cannot be management [of the affairs] without mandate. For example, a citizen or juristic person manages some affairs for another on the basis of a commission relationship or a guardian carries on a civil law act for a person without the capacity to act under a guardianship relation, the State Lost and Found Office, acting on the basis of its official function as the representatives of the owner of the lost property in managing the lost property, etc., are none of them management [of the affairs of another] without mandate. The difference between the management of the affairs of another without mandate and [with] mandate is, most importantly, that the management of the affairs of another has no basis in law. Consequently, after subsequent ratification of the management by the principal, the rights-duty relationship of the parties may make use of the relevant rules for mandate.

3. The Handling of the Obligation that Arises from Management of the Affairs Without Mandate

When management of the affairs of another without mandate has arisen, a rights-duty obligation relation is then created between the parties. The manager has a right to demand reimbursement for necessary expenses incurred in the management. The principal has the duty to repay the said expenses. The so-called necessary expenses include the expenses directly incurred in carrying on the matter, duties undertaken for the benefit of the principal, as well as injuries directly received by the actor in carrying on the work. The amount is determined by the actual circumstances. But it may not exceed the advantages received. The management of affairs is a moral act carried out with the intention of aiding another and the principal is directly benefitted. Therefore the principal should be liable for the necessary expenses incurred by the manager. The manager, apart from demanding necessary expenses, may not request from the principal an honorarium or seek an honorarium in a disguised form. Otherwise, the basis and meaning of management of the affairs without mandate would be lost.

In order for management of the affairs without mandate to have a reliable basis, and so that there will be no disputes among the parties, the manager, in carrying out the management, must be conscientious and must have the purpose of seeking the advantage of the other person. For example, the manager must carry out the management according to the clear or presumed intention of the principal. He must select suitable methods of administration in order to reduce expense and avoid loss. He must immediately give notice to the principal of the circumstances of the management and transfer to the principal any advantage obtained. These are united with the purpose of the manager to benefit the other. They are also consistent with the right of the manager to make demands [for reimbursement of expenses for example]. Except where the bad faith or gross negligence of the manager might lead to a different opinion, the principal may not, on the pretext of the violation of his intention or injury to his interest, refuse to perform his duty.

21 Obligations Arising Out of Contract

I
THE GENERAL CONCEPT OF CONTRACT

The contract (agreement) is a juristic act based on a unified declaration of intention establishing, changing, or terminating a civil rights-duty relation. On the basis of this definition it can be seen that the contract has the following legal characteristics.

(1) The contract is a juristic act among two or more parties

The contract must be [the result] of declarations from two or more subjects of civil law rights. Then it is established. The agreement of the declarations of intention is the important indication of the difference between the contractual act form and the other important juristic acts. For example, when the testator executes a testamentary act, there is only one unilateral juristic act, and then it is established. It does not require negotiation and agreement with the heir. Therefore, it is not a contract.

(2) A contract is an agreement as to a civil law rights-duty relationship that is established, amended, or terminated by the parties

[Examples include] the agreement of the buyer and seller as to the purchase and sale of some type of commodity, or the agreement between the consignor and the carrier as to the shipment of some goods. The contract may also be an agreement to change some civil law relationship. For example, after the contract of sale has been formed, the parties, because of their actual requirements, [may] agree to change the color and type of the goods and the time for payment. This changes the rights and duties that were originally established between the parties. The contract may also be an agreement to terminate a civil law rights-duty relationship that already exists. For example, after a contract of hire has been formed, because of changed circumstances, the commissioning party and the commissioned party decide to stop processing some item, and, thus, terminate the originally established rights-duty relation.

The contract is an agreement to establish change or terminate his civil law relationship between the parties. It can give rise to definite civil law consequences. This is the basic point of difference between contracts and ordinary agreements. For example, when people carry out certain agreements on the activities of social intercourse, no legal rights-duties relation arises. A violation may receive a certain censure from public opinion, but there is no civil law liability.

(3) A contract is formed by the parties on the basis of equality

It is formed by independent subjects of civil law independently and voluntarily. Consequently, the parties are equal in the contractual relation. The equality of the legal positions of the parties is the basic difference between contractual relations and establishing an administrative relationship: one giving orders and one being given the orders on the basis of ordering and obeying.

According to the special characteristics of contracts, the parties who establish a contract, regardless of differences in administrative levels or the relative size of the enterprise units, occupy a position of equality between themselves. Neither party may impose his will on the other.

(4) The content of the contract is legally effective

Contracts established according to law are legally effective. This is expressed in the fact that the provisions in the contract that provide what both parties must do in performing the contract provide all the legal duties of the parties. [If they do not perform they] receive legal punishment. Once a contract has been formed, neither party can change or terminate it on his own without the other party's consent.

II
THE EVOLUTION OF THE SYSTEM OF CONTRACTS

The system of contracts has already had many thousands of years of history. The contract is the legal form for the exchange of commodities. The system of contracts developed along with the commodity economy. Marx said, "First there was trade and then the legal system developed from this trade. This factual relationship which was produced by means of trade and out of the midst of trade subsequently took the legal form of contract."

1. The System of Contract in Slave and Feudal Societies

In the *Zhou Li* [the Book of Rites] there is already a record of contracts. The *Zhou Li–Tian Guan-Xia Zai* says, "Decide the weighing of responsibility on the basis of the *Fu Bie* [a sort of deed]"; "decide sales on the basis of the *Zhi Ji* [a sort of security instrument]"; "decide gifts on the basis of the *Shu Qi* [a sort of deed]." The *Fu Bie*, the *Zhi Ji*, and the *Shu Qi* are different written contractual forms for the loan, sale, and other relationships. The oldest extant code in the world today, the Babylonian Code of Hammurabi, already had rather detailed contractual rules. Roman law also had relatively complete contract rules.

In the slave society, a slave could not be the subject of a contract, but was the object of sale or lease relationships between slave owners. Ancient Rome had the system of a patriarchal household. The paterfamilias had the power of life and death over the members of his household. While the paterfamilias was alive, the sons of the family were not the subject of rights and did not have the right to enter into contracts or dispose of property.

A clearly distinguishing mark of the contracts of ancient times is their formalism. The Code of Hammurabi provides that, under certain circumstances, one who obtained property without a written document had committed a crime. "The right to bring an action cannot come from a pure agreement [*nudum pactum?*]" is a principle of Roman law. That is, if the contract is not formed according to a legally designated form, one could not use the legal process to enforce it. Roman law provided many forms for the formation of contracts so that in the later phases of the slave society, because of the requirements of the developing commodity economy, the contract forms were finally simplified.

In the slave and feudal societies, each country's rulers selected certain forms for certain relations to carry on different degrees of intervention. For example, the Code of Hammurabi had detailed provisions for the prices of goods, the interest on loans, the rent for rented objects, as well as every kind of remuneration for labor, and so forth. In our country, in ancient times, the requirements of strict forms in all the royal dynasties, were, in the same way, relatively strict. The Tang Code provided that in the case of the sale of land, houses, slaves, and cattle, within three days of the transfer, there must be the execution of a *shi quan* [a kind of bond]. If the three days were exceeded, and none was executed, the buyer received thirty strokes of the light bamboo and the seller twenty.

2. The System of Contract in Capitalist Societies

Capitalist societies are the most advanced societies of a commodity economy. [Their appearance] also marked the time of the greatest advance of the system of contract. The development of the capitalist society went through two stages—free capitalism and monopoly capitalism. In these two phases there were differences in contracts.

In the stage of free capitalism, because of capitalism's requirements of free competition, "freedom of contract" formed a basic principle of the contract law system of the capitalist class. According to this principle, whether the contract was formed or not, the form of its execution, the content of the contract, the selection of the other party, were all matters that were left to the parties to decide. The state interfered very little.

The principle of freedom of contract was of great importance in encouraging competition and development in the capitalistic economy. However, this kind of outward appearance of freedom of contract could not cover its class nature. Therefore, when entering the stage of monopoly capitalism, the principle of freedom of contract underwent great changes. In the fields of legislation, adjudication, and contractual practice, there were revisions in the principle of freedom of contract. After World War I, the capitalist countries all promulgated a series of compulsory special regulations directly interfering with the operation of a social economy, which greatly limited the principle of freedom of contract. In the courts, there appeared the principle of "change in the situation." From scholars, there appeared the theory of "formation of rights by courts." The concept of the contract being "equivalent to law" was smashed. The performance of contracts and liability for breach were no longer, as they had been previously, predetermined by the will of the parties. This was the expression in the legal sphere of governmental interference in the economy in the phase of monopoly capitalism.

3. The System of Contracts in a Socialist Society

The system of contracts in a socialist society is a new type of contractual system. Its development and changes in different countries are all closely connected with the theory and practice of the socialist commodity economy.

The socialist society envisioned by Marx and Engels was one that did not have the production of commodities and did not have currency. For the first few years after the October Revolution, Russia lived in a condition of imperialist military intervention and civil war. A temporary communism was carried out. Economically, there was strictly centralized administration. There was unified allocation of materials, and the receipt and accumulation of surplus grain. The buying and selling of grain were forbidden. Under these circumstances, the use of contracts was restricted to a very small area.

After the war, in 1921, there began to be a return to a period of a national economy. In 1922 the Civil Code of Soviet Russia was promulgated. In it, more than half of the provisions were devoted to contract relations. Afterwards, supply and procurement contracts, capital construction contracts, advanced purchase contracts, and other forms of contracts [appeared]. The contract system of the Soviet Union harmonized with the centralized unified planned economy. A specialized characteristic is the strict state supervision of the contract relation, particularly the use of the compulsory contract as a tool for carrying out the economic plan.

In the first year of our country's formation, our country at the same time selected the Soviet models of that time, and in the fields of agriculture, handicraft, and capitalist industry and commerce, carried on the phase of socialist reform and creatively made use of contracts. Since the overthrow of the Gang of Four, contracts have had a new development.

A socialist contract system is established on the basis of commodity relations based on a foundation of public ownership. The objective norms developed by socialist commodity relations determine the essential nature of the existence of a system of contracts. Socialist economic planning determines the close relations between the system of contracts and the national economic plan. The system of contracts directly or indirectly serves to realize the general purpose of the socialist economic plan. This is the essential point of difference between the socialist system of contracts and the contract systems of countries of the exploiting classes.

III
THE NATURE AND FUNCTION OF OUR COUNTRY'S SYSTEM OF CONTRACTS

1. The Nature of Our Country's Contract System

Our country's contract system is a socialist contract system. It is essentially different from the contract systems of countries of the exploiting classes.

First, the nature of the contract system is determined by the nature of the economic relations which it reflects. Our country's system of ownership of the means of production is composed principally of ownership by the whole people, and collective ownership of the laboring masses. At the same time, there is also private ownership subject to the condition that there is no exploitation of man by man. The commodity relations that are formed under this form of ownership system are socialist commodity relations. The contract system is then the legal means for socialist commodity exchange.

Second, the subjects of contracts in our country are: enterprises of ownership by the whole people and collective ownership, organizations, associations, and laborers. Their relations with each other are on the basis of equality and mutual assistance. Although each subject has rights and interests, their relations with each other are based on the essential unity of interests.

Third, the socialist nature of our country's socialist economic contract system is reflected in its aim. [The purpose of] our country's contract system is to uphold the socialist economic order, to strengthen and develop socialist public ownership and to protect the lawful interests of citizens, and to fulfill the material and cultural needs of the people.

2. The Function of Our Country's Contract System

(1) The use of the contract system in socialist reform

In the stage in which agriculture, the handicraft industry, and capitalist industry and commerce underwent socialist reform, every kind of contract was used. This was effective in fulfilling the socialist reform of the system of private ownership of the means of production.

In the period of socialist reform of agriculture and the handicraft industry, supply and marketing cooperatives, state managed commerce and mutual help in agricultural organizations, and agricultural production cooperatives used contracts among themselves. Agricultural aid groups and agricultural producers' cooperatives obtained advance payments, the means of production and the means of daily life, by means of contracts. The purchase price of commodities was also protected, thus reducing the exploitation of private commerce, and usury. Reducing or cutting off the relations among agriculture, handicrafts, and capitalism, and promoting the cooperative movement, created advantageous conditions for the socialist reform of capitalist industry and commerce.

In the phase of socialist reform of capitalist industry and commerce, a number of contract forms were used: state processing orders [with private firms], state monopolies for purchase and marketing, commission selling, and so forth. The conclusion of contracts between state managed enterprises, and supply and marketing cooperatives and privately managed enterprises on the basis of state requirements, fixing a rights-duty relationship between the parties, enabled the capitalists to obtain a profit. This uses the capitalist economy, on the one hand, for the advantage of the national economy and the people's livelihood, and on the other hand, it also limits any [activity] that is not advantageous to the national economy and the people's livelihood. The state, by means of the contract system, in different stages controlled the process of production by privately managed industrial enterprises and the activities of privately managed commercial enterprises. It partially restricted the anarchistic situation developed by capitalist management. In this way the system of contract was an effective legislative tool in carrying on socialist reform of capitalist industrial and commercial enterprises.

(2) The use of contracts in the construction of socialism

(i) The system of contracts is useful in strengthening the national economic plan. Contracts between socialist organizations are useful for the national economic plan. This is expressed in the following ways:

First, the contract is a device for making the economic plan concrete. Our national economy is a socialist planned economy. All economic intercourse between units which makes use of contracts puts into effect the aims of the state's directed plan. This sort of performance of a contract formed directly according to the state economic plan fulfills the actual carrying out of the state economic plan. Accordingly, the contract is a tool for carrying out the state economic plan.

Second, the contract specifies the essential bases of the state economic plan. Contracts between enterprises for production, supply, transport, and sale reflect the essential data of the requirements for economic development. Consequently, they are an essential basis for formulating the state economic plan. Third, the contract is a means for making the state economic plan accurate. When contracts are concluded between enterprises according to the plans, it is possible that certain defects in a plan will appear that result from not following the facts. Under these circumstances the enterprises have the right and duty to present proposals for revising the plan to the control organization and to make the target of the plan conform to the facts. When, in performing contracts and carrying out the plan, new circumstances are encountered, and it is not possible to perform a contract, and it is necessary to amend the plan, the proposal of the enterprise to the control organization to change the plan makes the plan's activity change in accordance with the objective facts.

Fourth, the contract is an essential complement to the state economic plan. Except for actions which enterprises are required to take under the state directive plan, many of the enterprise's activities come under the state's leading [as opposed to directive] plan, or are decided directly by market requirements. Economic contracts entered into by enterprises based on market requirements constitute an important supplement to the state's economic plan.

(ii) Contracts are useful for bringing about specialized cooperation. Following the development of social productive forces and advances in technology, the social division of labor becomes ever more detailed. Specialized cooperation constitutes an essential trend for socialized large-scale production. Specialization requires cooperation. Cooperation fulfills specialization. The contract is the link for cooperative activity among enterprises. By means of this link, thousands of enterprises are brought together, and all the different parts of the national economy form a unified whole, causing the great machine of the national economy to turn round in a rhythmic way.

Previously, owing to the fact that the system of contract was incomplete, contracts lacked essential legal effectiveness. Cooperation among enterprises lacked essential legal protection. This encouraged a number of enterprises into the tendency of forming their own systems. Conscientiously carrying out the contract system, clearly defining the rights and duties between and among enterprises strengthens the responsibility of enterprises towards each other and offers a legal guaranty for specialization.

(iii) Contracts are useful for strengthening economic accounting and improving economic administration. Enterprises that carry out economic accounting rely essentially on the strength of the individual enterprise. At the same time, they require certain external conditions. In carrying out a system of contract, the enterprises clearly provide for their mutual rights and duties and a violation of a contract entails property liability. This gives the enterprise the need, at the time it enters into a contract, to carry on economic accounting. It makes the formation of the contract occur on the basis of feasibility. After the contract is formed, it strengthens economic accounting and actively creates the conditions for performing the contractual duty.

(iv) Contracts are useful for the state's guidance of agriculture, and for carrying out the plan, and strengthening the economic relations between town and country. The state carries out planned procurement for essential agricultural commodities, but it cannot rely solely on administrative regulations to do this. It is better to use

the system of contracts. The state economic offices concerned conclude agricultural sideline products procurement contracts with agricultural units of collective ownership and with peasants concretely putting into effect the state's agricultural production plan and the agricultural sideline products procurement plan. At the same time, the economic offices concerned must still form purchase and sale contracts for industrial and mineral products with agricultural units of collected ownership and peasants, supply necessary agricultural means of production and means of daily life, and fulfill the requirements of peasants for production and daily life.

(v) The system of contracts is useful for opening the economic and technological flow to the outside. Foreign trade contracts are legal procedures for foreign economic regulation. They are useful for promoting economic and technological circulation. They are useful for increasing foreign exchange. They are useful for using foreign capital, attracting technology, and speeding up the Four Modernizations.

(3) The utilization of contracts in fulfilling the needs of citizens for material and cultural life

In our country, the requirements of the citizens for material and cultural life, as well as medical and health care and other social welfare, are provided in part by the state or social organizations to the citizens without compensation. As the socialist economy develops, the portion that is gratuitously granted can increase accordingly. But for a long time citizens will rely principally on the income from their own labor to satisfy the requirements for material and cultural life. Moreover, they use contracts to do this. For example, to purchase consumer goods, the processing and repair of articles of daily use, the renting or borrowing of housing and articles of daily use. The use of all means of transportation, loans of money, savings deposits, property insurance and life insurance, public utilities, services of daily life, travel services, cultural and physical education, entertainment, and so forth, are all carried on the basis of exchange of value by means of nongratuitous contracts. This kind of contractual relationship between equals is a civil law relation that receives state protection. It is an indispensable legal tool for fulfilling the constantly increasing requirements for material and cultural life.

IV
THE TYPES OF CONTRACTS

Social, economic, cultural, and property circulation are of many types and these determine the many types of contracts. The list of contracts is very large. [When observed] from different points of view, contracts can be divided from into many types. Carrying out the classification of contracts on the basis of their legal characteristics, one can see the special conditions for the formation, and the elements of their legal effectiveness, for contracts of different types.

1. Planned Contracts and Unplanned Contracts

According to whether or not the contract is based on the directive plan, the contract can be classified as a planned or unplanned contract. A contract which is formed directly as a result of the state directive plan is said to be a planned contract, for example, a supply contract, a capital construction contract, etc. Contracts which are not directly based on a state directive plan are called unplanned contracts.

The difference between planned contracts and unplanned contracts is that the parties with planned contracts must form the contract in accordance with the state plan. It is the right of the parties to form the planned contract. It is also the duty of the parties to the state, which must be fulfilled. The content of a planned contract must be based on the plan. Parties may negotiate within the scope of the planned provisions. When the planned responsibilities change, the contract will change or terminate accordingly. When a planned contract violates the plan, it will give rise to the legal consequences of an invalid contract. The content of a nonplanned contract is negotiated and determined by the parties.

2. Consensual Contracts and Real Contracts

A contract can be classified as a consensual contract or a real contract according to whether the object is [to be] delivered. When the parties have agreed on the essential provisions and the contract then comes into existence, this is a consensual contract. If, apart from the agreement between the parties, it is still necessary to deliver the object, this is called a real contract.

The difference between a consensual contract and a real contract is significant for determining the time when the contract becomes effective. The law determines which contracts are consensual and which are real. Within the scope permitted by law, the parties may negotiate and decide.

3. Contracts Requiring a Form and Contracts Not Requiring a Form

Contracts may be divided into those which require a form and those that do not, according to whether a special form is required for the formation of the contract. Contracts that require a form are those that require the execution of a special form before they can be formed, for example, the requirement of a writing, the requirement of a verification or notarization, proof by a third person, or the checking or approval by a concerned organization. A contract that does not require a form is one that does not require a particular form for formation. The contracts requiring forms that are specified by law are called legally designated form contracts. When the law does not require a form, but the parties have required the execution of a particular form, it is called an agreed-upon form contract.

The significance of the differentiation between contracts that require forms and those that do not, is that in the case of a contract that requires a form, until the specified form has been executed, the contract does not come into existence. In principle it has no legal effect.

4. Bilateral and Unilateral Contracts

Looking at the contract from the point of view of the nature of the rights and duties of the two parties, contracts can be divided into bilateral and unilateral contracts. If the two parties to the contract assume mutual duties, it is called a bilateral contract. In a bilateral contract the rights and duties of the parties are mutually related. For example, in the contract of sale, the seller has the duty to deliver the object [of the contract] to the buyer. He has the right to demand that the buyer pay the price. The buyer has the duty to pay the price and the right to demand that the seller deliver the object. From this it can be seen that in a bilateral contract, one party's duty is the other party's right. Therefore, the bilateral contract is one where both parties have duties and both parties have rights. Since contracts are essentially economic relations based on exchange of value and mutual interests [whose purpose is] to adjust the circulation of commodities, by far the majority of contracts are bilateral, for example, sale, supply, procurement of agricultural sideline products, lease, hire, etc.

If, in a contract, one party only assumes obligations and the other party only enjoys rights, this is called a unilateral contract. For example, the contract of loan. After the contract of loan is concluded, the lender has the right to demand repayment. The borrower has the duty to repay.

The significance of the difference between bilateral contracts and unilateral contracts [is this]: in the bilateral contract there are legal consequences that do not exist in the unilateral contract. Looking at the order of performance between the two parties, if the law and the contract have not provided that one party has the duty to perform first, a party who has not himself performed does not have the right to demand that the other party perform. Looking at the contract in the light of the existence of an irresistible force which makes it impossible to perform the contract, when one party cannot perform because of an irresistible force, he has no right to demand that the other party perform. If the party has already performed, he must return what he has received to the other party. If one considers the situation when the contract cannot be performed because of the fault of the parties, if one party has already performed, when the other party is unable to perform because of his own fault, the first party may demand that the other party perform the contract, pay damages, or rescind the contract.

5. Nongratuitous Contracts and Gratuitous Contracts

A contract can be classified as gratuitous or nongratuitous according to whether the transfer of contracts rights is made on the basis of an exchange of consideration of equal value. If the one who enjoys rights must compensate the other party with the price (including paying the price, completing a job of work, or offering to perform labor in some manner), this is said to be a nongratuitous contract. For example, contracts of sale, exchange, lease, etc., are all nongratuitous contracts. When, in a contract, one who enjoys a right does not have to compensate with a return price, this is said to be a gratuitous contract. For example, the contract of gift, the loan for use, interest-free loans, and so forth. Some contracts may be either gratuitous or nongratuitous, for example, contracts of commission, deposit, and so forth.

Normally, socialist organizations, apart from special circumstances where there is gratuitous assistance, enter into nongratuitous contracts with other socialist organizations on the principle of an exchange of values. Gratuitous contracts are mostly used between citizens and between citizens and socialist organizations.

The significance of the difference between gratuitous and nongratuitous contracts lies in the fact that the extent of the parties' obligation is not the same. Speaking generally, the liability of the obligor in a nongratuitous contract is relatively heavy. The liability of the obligor in a gratuitous contract is relatively light. For example, in the case of a nongratuitous deposit, when the deposited property is injured or destroyed by intention or negligence, the bailee is liable for the entire injury. In the case of injury to or loss of the deposited object as the result of negligence, although the bailee cannot avoid liability for the property, he will be evaluated leniently.

6. A Contract Entered Into by a Person for His Own Benefit and a Contract Entered Into for the Benefit of a Third Person

Normally the parties enter into a contract to achieve a certain economic goal. They themselves enjoy the rights and are liable for the duties. But under some circumstances, one party does not enter into the contract for himself, or someone he is representing, but for the benefit of some third person. For example, in the case of life insurance or property insurance contracts, the one taking out the insurance indicates the name of the beneficiary in the insurance contract. Thus, the contract is entered into for the benefit of a third party. In this kind of contract, the beneficiary has, according to law, the right to demand payment of the insurance or damages.

In principle, contracts entered into for the benefit of a third party can only give the third party certain benefits. It cannot cause the third party to assume any liability. Just because of this, the formation of this kind of contract does not require notification of the third party or the consent of the third party.

The most important legal characteristic of this kind of contract is that the third party has an independent right. From the inception of the contract the third party may independently enjoy the rights provided by the contract. When the obligor does not perform, the third party has no right to demand [performance].

The third party may accept or refuse to accept the contract for his own interest. When he refuses to accept, the party who is concluding the contract for the benefit of the third party himself enjoys the rights under it. According to law they are enjoyed by his heirs or successors.

7. The Principal Contract and Subordinate Contracts

The principal and subordinate contracts are contracts that have principal and accessory relations. The contract which does not require another contract as a prerequisite—which has independent existence—is a principal contract. A contract that requires the existence of another contract as a prerequisite for it to come into existence is called a subordinate contract. For example, mortgages and pledges are subordinate contracts. Subordinate contracts take the existence of the principal contract as a prerequisite. If the principal contract is altered or terminated, in principle, the subordinate contract is altered or terminated accordingly.

8. The Basic Contract and the Contract to Make a Contract [*Vorvertrag*]

Depending on whether, at the time of the contract, there is or is not a prior agreed-upon relationship, the contract may be called the basic contract or a contract to make a contract [*Vorvertrag*]. The contract to make a contract is a contract in which the parties to have agreed to enter into a contract in the future. Therefore, this sort of contract is also called a preagreement. The basic contract is a contract whose formation is the performance of a contract to make a contract. The duty of the parties to the contract to make a contract is to form the basic contract. If there is a violation of the contract to make a contract, and the basic contract is not formed, then [the one violating] assumes property liability.

There is a practical significance to the difference between a contract to make a contract and the basic contract. For example, the agreement of the parties to establish a real contract is a contract to make a contract.

9. Contracts With Names and Contracts Without Names

Contracts can be divided into those with names and those without names, according to whether the law provides a name.

Named contracts are those to which the law gives a definite name and for which, moreover, it provides rules for the content.

In actual economic life, contractual relations become complex. Only in the most commonly seen contracts can the law provide clear differentiation of the rights and duties of the parties according to a definite standard and give names to contracts. Those contracts for which there are clear provisions, are named contracts or model contracts. Contracts without names are those to which the law has not given a definite name, that is, contracts other than named contracts. The content of contracts without names need only not violate the law. They have the same legal effect [as named] contracts. For example, if A and B agree together that A will give a certain thing to B and B must do some particular work for A, [this contract has no name but is valid].

The significance of the difference between named and nonnamed contracts lies in the fact that the law that is used in the event of disputes is not the same. In the case of a named contract, a dispute must be handled in accordance with the provisions of the law relating to the said contract. In the case of disputes that arise in contracts without names, the matter can be handled by reference to the rules for a similar named contract. If there is no similar named contract to which reference can be made, it is handled according to the general contract rules and the basic principles of civil law.

V
THE FORMS OF CONTRACTS

1. The Principle of a Form for Concluding Contracts

The form of the contact is the declaration of intention by which the parties form a contract. The law has provisions requiring the use of forms. In the case of certain contracts, the parties must act in accordance with these rules. When the law has no provisions, the parties may establish or agree to a contract as they wish. But when the rules of the form of the contract are appropriate for its content, [these rules] may impel the development of the contract relation, or may influence the development of the contract relations. Therefore, in determining the form of the contract, the following three principles must be considered:

(1) It should be advantageous for the development of the economy

In determining the form for a contract, it is necessary, first of all, to consider the requirements of the socialist economic plan. In regard to a contract which is formed directly in accordance with the state plan, it is necessary to choose rather strict forms in order to strengthen contract discipline and assure the completion of the national economic plan. For the form of contracts for the transfer of commodities outside the plan, particularly the form of contracts between citizens, the requirements are not as strict, causing the parties to have a margin for free selection. This serves to speed up the circulation property.

(2) Strengthening the socialist economic system

For a long time, our country's system of contracts has not been completely established. Contract discipline has been weak. In order to strengthen the legal system, for a certain period it is essential to have strict form [requirements] as to a number of contracts, particularly economic contracts.

(3) Work out measures to suit local convenience

Our country's area is very extensive and its conditions are complex. It is not necessary that there should be unified requirements for contract forms.

The two important forms for contracts are the oral form and the written form. The written contract is divided into the ordinary written form and special written forms.

2. The Form of Oral Contracts

The use of oral communications (including the telephone) to make the declarations of intention and conclude a contract is called the form of oral contracts.

The most important use of oral contracts is in contract relations which are immediately settled. For example, commodity contracts of sale between retail commercial establishments and their customers, sales at country markets, sales that are immediately settled between socialist organizations, are all oral contracts. Contracts between citizens such as loan, deposit, commission [mandate], etc., which are not immediately settled, frequently use the oral form.

Oral contracts are convenient and quick to use. Consequently, the form has an extensive use in every country's economic life. The form of oral contracts is also used in international trade.

The shortcomings of the oral contract are that when there are disputes, it is difficult to produce proof and not easy to allocate responsibility.

3. The Form of the Written Contract

When the declaration of intention that forms a contract is made by means of a written instrument, it is called a written contract. The particular advantage of a written contract is that there is something to be examined. It is advantageous for the supervisory organization and the control organization to supervise and examine when disputes arise. It is relatively easy to affix responsibility.

Written contracts are the important form of contract for socialist organizations in their economic relations. Section 3 of our country's Economic Contract Law provides: "Except for those which are settled immediately, economic contracts must be in written form. Documents, telegrams, and charts agreed upon by the parties as changing the contract are also included as constituent parts of the contract."

Written contracts do not normally require any type of specially designated form. But they must include the names of the juristic persons and citizens, the rights, duties, and responsibilities of both parties, the date when the contract was executed, the signatures or seals of the parties. When a juristic person executes a written contract it must affix the public seal of the juristic person. Moreover, in addition, the signature or seal of the juristic person's agent or representative [must be affixed].

Some contracts do not state clearly in writing all the rights, duties, and responsibilities of all the parties but refer to the basic provisions of the contract provided by the supervisory ministry. The certificate of the transport of goods [bill of lading] of the Ministry of Transport is the written form of the contract of transport. The rights, duties, and responsibilities of the parties are all governed by the provisions of the supervising ministry's transport regulations.

Apart from properly signed written contracts, there are certain other contracts which the law expressly provides [are to be considered as] written contracts: those concluded by letter, telegram, and telex.

The certificates which are given in daily life by the contractor to the one ordering the work, such as passenger tickets, and so forth, must be regarded as a simple form of contract. The rights, duties, and responsibilities of the parties to this kind of contract are usually governed by the regulation of the control ministry concerned.

According to the provisions of law, some contracts must be examined and verified by the parties, notarized, verified by a third party, or examined and registered in the organization concerned. These are special forms of written contracts.

Examination and verification is a system of examination and control of contracts established by the organization in control for contracts entered into between socialist organizations. The examining and verifying organizations will investigate to determine the status of the subjects of the contracts, the lawfulness of the content, the accuracy of the facts, whether or not the provisions of the contract are complete, clearly defined, and reasonable, and whether they are feasible. [Contracts] that conform with the requirements of the law will be given a signed certificate. For those that do not, the parties may be required to renegotiate and execute a new contract. After a contract has been examined and verified, the supervisory organization also must supervise its execution.

In regard to contracts entered into at trade fairs or trade markets by trade organizations of business ministries that are not in the same line of work or in the same locality, by custom these will be examined and verified by the fair or market organization. If the market or fair organization personnel are not the supervising organizations of the parties signing the contract, the one carrying out the examination will not have the character of a supervisor, but the proceeding will be in the nature of verification by a third party.

Notarization of a contract is authentication of a contract by a state notarial organization. After lawfully examining [the contract], it signs a certificate. Once the contract has been notarized, it may be used to prevent disputes, reduce lawsuits, and protect the parties' lawful interests.

When there are several parties, they can agree to certification by a third party. This is a form frequently used for relatively important contracts among citizens. Juristic persons may also use this form.

There are some contracts which require examination and approval by the supervising organization before the contract is effective. This [form] is chiefly used in important economic contracts. For example, supply contracts performed according to the material allocation plan and capital construction payment contracts entered into according to the capital construction plan require checking and approval by the supervising organizations. Sino-foreign joint management agreements and contracts, contracts for the importation of technology and equipment, etc., all require checking and approval by the supervising organization. This sort of investigatory procedure for the formation of contracts reflects the requirements of our country's planned economy.

There are a number of contracts that require registration in the supervisory office before they are effective. The sale and purchase of motor vehicles by our country's juristic persons and the purchase of houses by citizens require registration according to the rules. Only after registration with the supervisory office is the contract effective according to law.

VI
THE FORMATION OF CONTRACTS

The procedure of forming the contract is a procedure [whereby] the parties arrive at an agreement regarding the provisions of the contract. It is divided into the two phases of offer and acceptance. In practice, many contracts take the form of making a bid or inviting bids. Nevertheless, making or inviting bids are ways in which offer and acceptance are actualized.

1. Offer and Acceptance

(1) The offer

The offer is the tender by one party to the other of a conditional contract. He hopes that the other party will make a declaration of intention accepting it. The party who makes the offer is the offeror. The other party is called the offeree. The offer includes the following.

(i) The offer is a kind of proposal to form a contract. It must include the essential provisions that the contract needs in order to be formed. It must be given to the offeree. If it is not a declaration of intention that meets these conditions, it is not an offer.

The offer is not the same as an invitation for an offer. An invitation for an offer consists of one party requesting the other party to make him an offer. After the person to whom the request has been made makes the promise [i.e., the offer], the contract can then come into existence [by acceptance, but it is not yet in existence]. The offer is not the same. When the offer is accepted by the offeree, then in principle, the contract may be formed. According to the practice in our country, if the law has no clear provision, the following fact situations are regarded as invitations to offers: (1) advertisements; (2) the commodities laid out in the market with prices; (3) a commodity price list; (4) the announcement of an invitation for bids or a sheet with an invitation to bid.

The offer has a definite legal significance. The oral offer is legally effective as soon as it is understood by the offeree. Nonoral offers are effective when they reach the offeree. After the offer is effective, the offeror may not retract or amend the offer. In [legal] theory this is called the binding effect of the offer. [This rule exists] because within the time that the offer is effective the offeree may have, because of the offer, refused another similar offer, or failed to make an offer to another, or already have taken certain steps in performing the contract. If the offeror retracts or amends the offer at will, the offeree may, in consequence, be injured.

After the offer has become effective, the offeree has the right to accept (that is, he receives the offer and forms a contract). Unless the law has some other provision, the offeree has no duty to accept. If the offeree does not accept, unless there is an exception provided by law or some other rule, he also has no duty to notify the offeror.

After the offer arrives, if the following conditions exist, it loses its effectiveness and the acceptance is noneffective.

(i) Rejection of the offer. That is, the offeree notifies the offeror of his intention not to accept within the time for acceptance. Even though the offeree has not directly rejected the offer, if he has suggested certain changes to the terms of the offer as a condition for forming the contract, under these conditions, the original offer is regarded as having been rejected and ceases to be effective. At the same time, this sort of declaration of intention of changes in conditions must be regarded as the offeree making a new offer to the original offeror (also called a counter-offer).

(ii) The time for acceptance expires. (1) When a time is provided for an offer, and the offeree has not accepted within this time, the offer ceases to be effective. (2) When there is no time limit for acceptance set out in the offer, if it is an oral offer (including [an offer by] the telephone), if the offeree does not immediately accept, the offer then ceases to be effective; if the offer is by letter or telegram, and the offeree has not accepted within a reasonable time, the offer ceases to be effective. The so-called reasonable time includes time for the offeree to consider and time for the letter or telegram to arrive.

(iii) Retraction of the offer. Prior to the offer becoming effective, the offeror may retract the offer he has made. But the notice of retraction must arrive prior to the arrival of the offer or at the same time. After the retraction of the offer, the offer is not effective as to the offeror, but if the announcement of the retraction is delayed in arriving, it [the retraction] is not effective. If the offeree, prior to receipt of the delayed announcement of retraction, has already accepted, the offeror may not refuse to form the contract.

(2) The acceptance

Acceptance is the offeree's declaration of intention to accept the offer. That is, the offeree replies to the offeror [conveying] his desire to form a contract in accordance with the provisions of the offer. Because of this, the acceptance must agree with the offer. If the offeree changes the conditions of the offer in the reply, this kind of reply does not constitute an acceptance but is regarded as a new offer.

When the acceptance becomes effective because the offeror has received it, the contract is formed. In the case of oral acceptance, this is when the offeror understands it. The time for the effectiveness of a nonoral acceptance is when the announcement gets to the offeror. But the expression of acceptance must arrive within the time for acceptance. If the time is exceeded, the acceptance is noneffective.

If normally the announcement of the acceptance could arrive, but it has arrived late because of delays in transmission, the offeror must immediately give notice to the offeree of the circumstances of the delayed arrival of the acceptance, so that the offeree will not be injured because of preparations to perform a contract and so forth. If the offeror does not give immediate notice of a delay in arrival of the acceptance, the acceptance will be regarded as effective.

The acceptance, like the offer, may be retracted if the retraction arrives at the same time or prior to acceptance. But a delayed retraction of acceptance is not effective as a retraction of acceptance.

(3) The time of the establishment of the contract

The determination of the time when the contract becomes effective is important for determining the rights, duties, and responsibilities of the parties.

Generally speaking, when the parties have agreed upon the provisions, the contract is formed. Since the forms for concluding the contract are different, the legal rules are also different and there are differences in the time when it is concluded.

When the form of the offer is by dialogue (oral or by telephone), the offeree must accept immediately and the contract is then formed. If the parties agree on a time for acceptance or the offeree accepts within that time, the contract is formed.

As for the time for formation of a contract, when the offer is by letter or telegram, the standard time is the time of receipt by the offeror. That is, when the offeror receives a signed letter or telegram of acceptance.

If the law or contract provides that there must be investigation and verification, notarization or certification by a third party, or examination or registration of the office concerned, the contracts are formed after these procedures are complied with.

In addition, when the law or agreement between the parties so provides, if the offeree has not rejected within the prescribed time, and accepts by silence or has expressed his agreement with the offer by actions, as by sending goods, paying the price, etc., then, on the day following the day provided or agreed upon for the acceptance to be made, the contract is formed.

2. Bids and Invitations to Bid

(1) The invitation to bid

The invitation to bid refers to the one making the invitation following a particular procedure and publishing certain standards and conditions in order to request the bidders to bid. The subject of the bidding could be the sale of goods. It could also be capital construction or some kind of cooperative affair, etc. From the legal point of view, the invitation for bids is a sort of attempt to attract offers. It does not have the effectiveness of an offer. The person inviting bids may accept or not accept the bid when it is made to him (by the other). This is because the declaration of intention inviting bids cannot give rise to the effectiveness of a contract that must be executed between the one inviting bids and the bidder.

Usually the one inviting bids makes an announcement inviting bids. The invitation is made by means of publication in a newspaper or publication that advertises the invitation. After the announcement of the invitation to bid, the one invited to bid must tender a request. When the one inviting bids receives the request, he will first need to conduct an investigation as to the status of the bidder. Subsequently, within the specified time he will send the bidding materials to those selected to participate in the bidding. The bidding materials are prepared by the one inviting bids. In general they include: the written invitation to bid, the requirements of the one inviting bids, the circumstances that must be understood by the bidder, the rules for the bidding, the technological and quality requirements, and so forth. The one inviting bids must assure the precision and correctness of the technological diagrams and materials that are furnished in order to enable the bidder to compute the price according to these diagrams, and, after bidding, to organize production according to the diagrams.

Prior to the formal opening of the bids, the one inviting the bids must specify the estimated price of the object of bidding, that is, the bottom bid, in order to enable there to be a comparison with the bid prices and [this] constitutes an important reference to those participating in the bidding.

(2) The bid

A bid is the bidder's quoted price sent to the one inviting bids and is his agreement to the conditions provided in the documents of the invitation to bid. A bid is the concrete proposal of the bidder to the one inviting the bids to conclude a contract in accordance with the latter's requirements. After the bid, the bidder has the duty to enter into a contract with the one inviting bids. But the one inviting bids has the rights of an offeree. He (it) may select from among the bidders one or several persons to perform a contract with him. Apart from the necessity of selecting the most advantageous in accordance with the invitation announcement, he may also discard all the bids and issue a new invitation.

The bidders who participate in the bidding, after seeing the invitation, must, in general, tender their requests to the one inviting bids within the time set in the invitation, according to the announcement, in which [the bidder] makes a statement in detail on his own ability to complete and perform the contract according to the specifications of the invitation. When his request has been approved by the one inviting bids, and after the bid documents have been received, he must, in accordance with his own management and administrative level, prepare the cost proposal and send it within the prescribed time to the one inviting bids, to compete in the bidding.

(3) Opening the bids, reviewing the bids, deciding the bids

(i) Opening the bids. This refers to the one inviting the bids at a certain time and at a certain place, and in the manner provided, making public all of the bidding materials (including the bid letters), publishing the names of the bidders, the bid

prices, and other matters. Normally, the opening of the bids is participated in by the bidders, the person inviting the bid, the bank, and administrative control office, and the notarial office. The one inviting the bids will announce in everyone's presence the names of the bidders and the bid prices. After the bids have been opened, the bidders cannot change their bids.

(ii) Consideration of the bids. This refers to the one who invited the bids examining, distinguishing, and comparing in detail the bids submitted by the bidders until he has decided on the bid. The consideration must be secret. The successful bidder will be determined by means of consideration and selection of the most advantageous conditions [in the bid].

(iii) Decision on the bid. This refers to the selection of the bidder on the basis of consideration of the bids [above]. Normally the decision is made the day the bids are opened. A day for deciding on the bids can also be set for a time after opening the bids. Once the decision has been made, the one inviting the bids must immediately notify the successful bidder that he is the successful bidder. Afterwards, the one inviting the bids and the successful bidder begin to negotiate and establish the contract.

The bidding invitation system is the outcome of the conditions of a commodity economy, in a society with a commodity economy where maximum use is made of the laws of competition. Inviting and making bids are a method of competition. Recently, in the reform of the construction business, the system was energetically promoted with good results. Practice proves that putting into practice the system of bidding is useful in encouraging enterprises to develop a reasonable type of competition among themselves. It is very significant in lowering the cost of living, assuring the quality of commodities, and raising economic benefits.

VII
ESSENTIAL PROVISIONS OF CONTRACTS

1. The Concept of the Essential Provisions of Contracts

If it is impossible to perform the contract if a particular provision is missing or unclear, that provision is an essential provision of the contract. Consequently, essential provisions of contracts are provisions without which the contract cannot be formed. Contract provisions other than essential provisions are called ordinary provisions.

This is not to say that ordinary provisions in contracts are not important, just that if ordinary provisions are missing or are unclear this does not affect the formation or the validity of the contract.

There are three bases for determining the essential provisions of a contract. One is the legal rule. If there is a concrete rule requiring a particular provision in a contract, then [the contract] must be formed in accordance with the legal rule. The second is to make the determination according to the nature of the contract. If the law does not have clear rules on the essential provisions of the contract, the matter may be determined by the nature of the contract, for example, in a contract of sale, the quantity and price of the object of the contract, in a contract of transport, the place of destination and the cost of transport. In each case, the nature of the contract determines the essential provisions. The third is the determination [of the meaning of the contract by looking at] the intention of the parties. Apart from provisions required by law or the nature of the contract, when the two parties agree, or one party insists on the necessity of a clause, this is also an essential clause, for example, [when] the buyer demands that the seller must send a certain commodity to a particular place before he will buy the said commodity. In this way the buyer has proposed to make the place of delivery an essential provision of the contract.

2. Essential Provisions of Ordinary Contracts

Since the nature of different contracts is different, the necessary provisions that they require are not the same. Normally the object, price, and term are regarded as essential provisions of the contract. However, these items are not central provisions for all contracts. For example, a gratuitous contract has no price. Contracts for the loan for use and the loan for consumption do not all have determined time limits. Some provisions are used in the great majority of contracts. We call them the essential provisions of ordinary contracts.

(1) Object

The object of the contract is the object towards which the rights and duties of the contract parties are directed. For example, in a contract of sale, the seller delivers the agreed-upon commodity; in a contract of hire, it is the work needed by the contractor; and in a transport contract, it is the transport labor offered by the carrier, and so forth. If there is no object, the rights and duties have no basis. The contract then cannot be performed. The determination of the object not only requires specifying the classification of the object, but also requires clearly specifying the quantity and quality. If only the category of the object [is set out] in the contract and it is impossible to specify the quantity and quality, then it may be that, because the object is not clearly specified, there is no way to perform the contract.

(2) Price or fee

The price or fee is a consideration in money (sometimes a thing) which one party pays to the other party for the commodity he has delivered, the work he has done, or his labor. The price or fee is an essential provision in a nongratuitous contract. If, in a contract of sale, there is no price specified, then one cannot use some other method to specify the amount of the price. This contract of sale cannot be performed.

(3) Term

The term of a contract is the time element in the formation of a contract. Relying on it, the time for the commencement, realization, and termination of the rights-duty relationship of the parties can be determined. If there is no term provision in the contract, and there is no other way of determining the time clearly, the contract cannot be formed.

When the law or contract have no clear rule as to certain provisions, the essential provisions must first be determined by reference to the nature of the contract. If the contract lacks the essential conditions, the contract must be regarded, in principle, as not having been formed. The parties can agree to add the essential provisions but this is actually a new formation of a contract.

If a contract's essential provisions already exist, but the ordinary provisions are not complete, the contract must be regarded as having been formed. As to the incomplete ordinary provisions, these can be determined from the nature of the contract or they can be supplemented as agreed on by the parties. But no party can use the reason that the lack of an ordinary provision makes it impossible to perform as a basis for cancelling a contract that includes the essential provisions.

22 Contracts of Sale, Exchange, and Gift

I
THE GENERAL CONCEPT OF THE CONTRACT OF SALE

1. The General Concept and Special Characteristics of the Contract of Sale

A sale is an agreement whereby one party, the seller, transfers ownership of property to another party, the buyer, and the buyer accepts the property and pays for it.

According to the definition, it can be seen that the contract of sale has the following legal characteristics:

(1) Transfer of the ownership of property by a seller to a buyer is the main characteristic and legal consequence of a contract of sale.

Therefore, in a contract of sale, a seller's ownership of property is terminated because of the sale; the buyer's ownership of an object begins because of the sale. A seller is usually the owner of the property he sells. A seller transfers the ownership right of the property to a buyer through the receipt of the necessary payment. This kind of monetary exchange is the typical legal form for the exchange of commodities. It reflects the objective requirements of the exchange of commodities. This legal characteristic of a sales contract causes it to be differentiated from a contract of lease or a contract of loan in which one party only gives his property to the other party for temporary use, and does not transfer the ownership to it.

Since the owner of the property of a unit of property owned by the whole people is the state, and not each unit, in the case of a contract of sale between units of property owned by the whole people, only the right of management and control of the property can be transferred, and not the ownership.

(2) A contract of sale is a bilateral, nongratuitous contract in which the rights and duties of both parties are reciprocal

The performance of his duty by one party is conditional on the performance by the other party of his duty. The buyer performs his duties of paying a certain amount of money and receiving the ownership of the object. The seller enjoys the right to receive payment, but loses the ownership of the property. This characteristic differentiates a contract of sale from a contract of gift. Although the ownership of the property is also transferred, there is no consideration. The donor only fulfills his duty. He does not enjoy any rights [in a contract of gift].

A contract of sale is a nongratuitous contract in which a seller delivers the object to the buyer and the buyer transfers the price to the seller. This distinguishes the contract of sale from contracts of loan (for use), the gratuitous mandate, and the non-interest-bearing loan. The latter contracts are formed on the basis of the principle of gratuitousness.

(3) A contract of sale is an executory contract

Unless otherwise regulated by law or agreed to by the parties, a contract of sale is formed and produces legal consequences when the main terms of the contract have been agreed to by the two parties. Each party to the contract must bear the liability agreed to in the contract. This characteristic differentiates a sales contract from a contract of loan, a transport contract, and a contract of deposit which are real contracts. They are formed not upon the agreement by both parties, but upon the delivery of goods; then they become binding.

2. The Nature of the Contract of Sale

A contract of sale is the legal form for the exchange of commodities. In a society of production and exchange of commodities, there are appropriate contracts of sale with different natures. Therefore, the nature of the contract of sale reflects the nature of the exchange of commodities. If one departs from a particular society's economic situation, there is no way to understand correctly the nature of a sales contract in the society and its function in social and economic life.

The capitalist society is a highly developed society with a commodity economy where everything is turned into a commodity. Capitalists who seek for high profits not only carry on exchange by making raw materials and products into commodities, but the labor force that carried on the production also becomes a commodity. The contract of sale occupies an important place in a capitalist society. It becomes the legal means for the bourgeoisie to engage in speculation and profiteering, to monopolize the market, and hunt for high profits.

Under the conditions of socialism, there still exist, on an economic foundation of public ownership of the means of production, ownership by the whole people, collective ownership, and other different forms of ownership. This determines that there is, of necessity, commodity production and commodity exchange in the socialist society. The production and exchange of commodities in socialism are different in nature from these [activities] in capitalism. The circulation of commodities in socialism is an indispensably important link in the process of expanded reproduction of socialism. It is the link that binds all the sections of the national economy, especially the workers and peasants, town and country, producer and producer, and producer and consumer together. At the same time, it is a principal form for the exchange among laborers. Consequently, our socialist country must have this legal form of the contract of sale to reflect commodity exchange. Because the nature of contracts of sale in different societies is mainly decided by the nature of the production and exchange of commodities, the contract of sale in China is intrinsically different from those in capitalist countries. The differences are as follows:

(1) The production and exchange of commodities in our country are formed on a basis of socialist state ownership

The state managed enterprises occupy the dominant position. Those [factors] fundamentally determine the socialist nature of the contract of sale in our country.

(2) The production and exchange of commodities in our country are free from participation by capitalists

The scope of exchange of commodities is not, like that in capitalist society, all-embracing. In a capitalist society, all property can be the object of sale. In our country, anything that is not allowed to be circulated cannot be bought or sold. These include mineral resources, flowing water, forests, uncultivated lands, grasslands, and other sea and land resources exclusively owned by the state; as well as state owned banks, railroads, factories, and shops. Our country also prohibits illegal activities like speculation.

(3) The production and exchange of commodities in our country are under adjustment by socialist planning

This makes the contract of sale in our country to be clearly of a planned nature. In regard to important commodities that are related to the planning for the people's livelihood by the state, the plan is one of directives from the state down to lower levels. Contracts are formed according to the plan. At the same time, it is also necessary to make maximum use of adjustment by the market and have contracts of sale formed freely by negotiation between the parties.

(4) The fundamental purpose for the production and exchange of commodities in our country is to meet the ever-increasing material and cultural requirements of the people

This is different from the aim of capitalists in a capitalist society: to seek for high profits. Consequently, the legal form of a contract of sale is an important means to realize the goal of socialist commodity production and exchange. Eight hundred million peasants obtain industrial products through contracts of sale. This assures the production of agricultural sideline products and essentials for daily life. Workers, staff members, and residents in cities uninterruptedly buy consumer goods and daily necessities, which promote their production and work, and enrich the content of their lives.

3. The Scope of Application of the Contract of Sale

In our country, the scope of application of the contract of sale is very broad. Sales relations can arise between citizens, between a citizen and socialist organization, or between socialist organizations. Along with the adjustment of the national economy and reform of the system, socialist commodity relationships are constantly developing and flourishing. Therefore, the scope of application of contracts of sale must inevitably expand accordingly.

In considering contracts of sale according to their forms, there are contracts formed directly and strictly in accordance with the state plan. There are also contracts of sale in the retail trade and in country fairs which [are on the basis] of immediate payment, as well as some other contracts of sale providing for credit or installment payments.

(1) Contracts of sale in the retail trade

[Such contracts] mainly include contracts made between state owned businesses or retail enterprises of the supply and marketing cooperatives and consumers. The buyer in this kind of contract is a citizen, the object is the means of subsistence, and the oral form is used. Through sales for immediate cash payments, the daily needs of citizens are met.

(2) Contracts of sale at country fair markets

This refers to an oral contract of sale to take effect immediately made at rural markets or farmers markets in urban areas. The subjects of the contract are usually the rural collective production unit, peasants, urban residents procuring commodities, and local state-managed commercial bureaux. The objects are, for the most part, the third type of agricultural sideline product that is outside state planned procurement. The form that is used is that of a price negotiated between two parties, but they may not drive up prices nor engage in speculation. This contract is useful for making the circulation of materials in cities and villages more active, for facilitating the livelihood of the masses, and for supplementing the areas where the state managed commercial enterprises are not sufficiently active.

(3) A contract of sale providing for payment in installments

[Such a contract] is also called a credit sale. This refers to a sale by agreement between the parties in which the seller delivers the goods, and the buyer receives them and the buyer pays the price in installments. In capitalist societies, this sort of contract is in fact a device whereby the bourgeoisie dumps goods and realizes surplus value from the masses of working people. The conditions of the contract are often advantageous for the seller and not advantageous for the buyer. For example, raising the sale price, providing that if the buyer delays in making payment of an installment, he must settle the whole price even to the extent of returning the article and losing his right to reclaim the sums already paid. In our socialist country, for a long time socialist enterprises were not permitted to engage in credit sales between themselves. Commercial credit was forbidden. In our country's economic adjustment and reform, credit sales have been permitted for industrial products of which a large amount are accumulated, and in the field of high-grade consumer goods. It is clearly advantageous for enabling enterprises to meet production requirements, for speeding up the circulation of capital, and fulfilling the living requirements of citizens.

(4) Contracts for the sale of buildings

The state protects the ownership rights of citizens to houses and permits individual sales of houses. Since immovable property like houses is an important means of livelihood and affects the use of the land, the rights of citizens to reside [on land], or the rights and interests of third persons, the state has strict rules on the sale of houses. The rules promulgated by the State Council on 17 December 1983, Provisions on the Control of Privately Owned Housing in Urban Areas, state in section 9 that: "In the sale of urban privately-owned housing, the seller must have a certificate of ownership and proof of his personal status. The buyer must have proof of the purchase of the house and proof of personal status and go to the local housing office to handle the procedures."

Among the several sales contracts discussed above, each has its own special characteristics, but essentially they are all sales relationships and make use of the general principles of contracts of sale.

II
THE OBJECT AND PRICE OF THE CONTRACT OF SALE

(1) The object and price are both essential features of a contract of sale

The object and the price must be precisely provided for in the contract of sale. When the contract is formed, if the price can be fixed, it must be fixed. If it cannot be fixed, the manner of setting it must be clearly provided. When the object and the price are not clearly specified, the sales contract cannot be formed.

(2) The object of the contract of sale is property

The object of a contract of sale is usually a thing. The sale of negotiable instruments can only be carried on by a state designated bureau within the scope provided by law.

The results of technology are a sort of property without an owner and are also objects of contracts of sale. There are differences between property with an owner and property without an owner. Consequently, the special transfer of the results of technology is a special sort of sale and requires specialized rules to adjust.

(3) The setting of the price in a contract of sale must be in accordance with the rules of law

Prices of all contracts of sale, which the law declares must be carried out in accordance with the plan, must be set in accordance with the prices decreed by the state price-control agency. In regard to certain commodities whose prices [the law] permits to float up and down within a certain range, the buyer and seller may negotiate and set a price within the range set by the responsible organization. In the case of commodities for which the law permits a negotiated price, the parties may agree upon a price.

The buyer and seller must abide by the rules provided by the state for the administration of prices. If the seller on his own, without authorization, raises the price, or raises it in a disguised way, he must pay double the buyer's loss or assume other liability imposed by law.

III
THE RIGHTS AND DUTIES OF PARTIES TO A CONTRACT OF SALE

The rights and duties of the parties to a contract of sale are reciprocal. The duty of the seller is thus the right of the buyer. Below, the rights and duties of both parties are discussed from the point of view of duties.

1. The Duties of the Seller

(1) The seller must transfer the object of the contract and the ownership of it (or management rights to it) to the buyer

Normally, the seller must be the owner (or in control of the management) in order to assure that the ownership of the object [of the contract] (or its management right) will be transferred to the buyer. At the time the contract is formed, the seller may still not be the owner of the object (or its manager). For example, at the time the contract is formed, the property right to mineral or industrial commodities may not have come into existence, but at the time of the transfer of the commodity, [the seller] must be the owner (manager) of the thing. Under the rules provided by law, it is also possible for the seller not to be the owner (manager) of the object. For example, in a contract made under mandate, the mandatary sells the entrusted object.

The seller has the duty to assure that the property right to the object cannot be traced back to a third person in order to assure the interests of the buyer. If a third person asserts a right against the object, and recovers the object from the buyer, the seller has a duty to prove that the third person has no right. If necessary, he must intervene in the suit and go to the court and present proof.

If a third person has some rights to the object (such as a lessee's right, mortgage right, etc.) at the time of formation of the contract, the seller must explain these rights to the buyer. If he has not explained them, he must assume the appropriate liability.

After the seller has delivered the object, the legal consequences of delivery arise. In order to make clear the parties' responsibilities, the time, place, and manner of transfer must be clearly specified. If they all have not been clearly provided for in the law and contract, the times of the following actions may be regarded as the times of delivery.

(i) If the buyer himself picks up the goods, the time when the seller notifies him to pick up the goods is the time of transfer. The time which the seller notifies the buyer to pick up the goods must include additional time necessary for the buyer [to get there].

(ii) When the seller delivers the goods, the time of delivery is when the seller delivers the goods to the buyer at a place previously agreed on.

(iii) When they are shipped or mailed, delivery occurs when the seller has completed the shipping procedures or mailing procedures.

(iv) When the object is actually possessed by the buyer at the time the contract is formed, delivery takes place when the contract of sale becomes effective.

(v) When the object is one for which the transfer of ownership must be registered, transfer takes place when the transfer registration procedures are completed.

(2) The seller must guarantee that the quality of the object corresponds to what [the standard] provides

The quality of the object transferred by the seller must correspond with the standard of quality provided by the state or agreed to by the parties. Where the contract has no clear provision, standards must be in conformance with normal usage. [The object] may not have any defect that does not correspond with the quality standard. Any defect which can be discovered by the buyer at the time of receipt by the usual kind of inspection is a patent defect. A defect that requires a technical inspection or use (of the object) to be discovered is a latent defect.

When the seller sells a defective item, he must explain this to the buyer. If the seller conceals the defect of the object, he is liable. If the buyer knows of the defect and buys it, the seller is not liable for the defect.

After the buyer receives the object [of the contract], he must immediately examine it. If a time period for inspection has been provided, he must carry out [the inspection] within the time provided. In the case of patent defects, if a patent defect appears, he must immediately notify the seller. The seller is responsible for the defect. If the buyer does not carry out inspection immediately, and subsequently he points out a patent defect, the seller is not liable.

In regard to latent defects and to defects that are intentionally concealed by the seller, after the buyer discovers them, he must immediately notify the seller. The seller must assume liability.

In order to protect the interests of the buyer and seller, and in order to uphold the stability of the sales relationship, it is necessary to provide a time period for the buyer to seek [relief] for defects. When the law or contract has a special provision, that provision will be followed. If the law has no provision, and the parties have not agreed upon one, it must be handled by the general rule of civil law.

2. The Duties of the Buyer

(1) The buyer must pay the price as provided

The buyer must pay the price at the time provided. If the law and the agreement have no provisions, payment of the price must take place at the same time as delivery of the object of the sale.

The buyer must pay the price at the place agreed upon in the contract. If the law and agreement have no provisions, it must be paid at the residence of the seller.

The buyer must pay the price in the manner provided in the contract. In the case of units for which the state provides for cash management, except in cases where the provisions for cash management allow cash to be used, the settlement payment must be handled by means of banks or credit cooperatives. The method of settling accounts must be clearly provided.

(2) The buyer must accept the object as provided [in the law or contract]

The buyer has the right to demand that the seller deliver the object of sale. However, when the seller delivers the object, the acceptance of the object then becomes the duty of the buyer. Under ordinary circumstances, payment of the price is made after acceptance of the object. If the buyer refuses to accept the object, this means he will not pay the price.

The buyer must accept the object according to the time and place, and in the manner, provided in the contract. When the buyer picks up the object, he must go to the prescribed place within the time announced to him by the seller. When it is consigned for shipment to someone acting for the seller, the buyer must complete the preparations for accepting the object within the time and immediately accept. If the buyer delays his acceptance he is liable for the delay.

IV
TRANSFER OF THE OWNERSHIP (OR MANAGEMENT RIGHT) OF THE OBJECT AND LIABILITY FOR UNINTENTIONAL LOSS

1. Transfer of Ownership (or the Management Right) to the Object

After the sales contract is formed, if the thing that is sold is specified, ownership of it (or the management right to it) is transferred to the buyer from the time the contract is formed. The seller then loses ownership (or the management right). He can no longer use or dispose of the object. This is very important for the protection of the lawful interests of the buyer. If, on the other hand, at the time of formation of the contract, ownership (or the management right) to the specified thing still remained in the seller, this would mean that the seller still had the right to use or dispose of the thing sold, and it might be that the seller would sell it [to someone else] for a higher price. This would not be advantageous for protecting the interests of the buyer nor for assuring the stability of the social economic order.

If the object is a generic thing, the ownership (or management) passes at the time when [the thing] is transferred. The essential reasons are: (1) at the time of the formation of the contract, the ownership (or management) right to the thing is frequently not specified. For example, the object has still not come into existence, or it could be that a large number of generic things are grouped together and it still has not been determined which is the buyer's. (2) [This] is advantageous and not injurious to the parties to the sale. The generic thing is something that can be substituted for. After formation of the contract, if the ownership (or management right) is not transferred, the buyer does not have to worry about the question of obtaining the thing. At the same time, if the ownership (or management) right to the object is not transferred, this is beneficial to the seller's right to use or dispose of [the thing] and this speeds up the flow of capital.

2. Responsibility for the Risk of Unintentional Loss of the Object

After the formation of the contract of sale, if there is an unintentional injury or loss that is not the result of an intentional act or negligence of the parties, this is called the risk [of loss]. If the risk is borne by the buyer, then, when the object is lost, he still must pay the price according to the contract. If the risk is borne by the seller, the buyer does not have the duty to pay the price.

In regard to the question of responsibility for the risk, it is normally held that the responsibility for the risk is joined to the transfer of the ownership (or management) right. That is, when the ownership (management) right is transferred to the buyer, the risk is transferred to the buyer along with it. Consequently, there is a difference between specified things and generic things, and using the time of [the physical] transfer of the thing as the time of transfer of the risk is not favored.

To be sure, if, as the result of any party's fault, the transfer is delayed, the responsibility for the risk must be borne by the one who is at fault.

The rule for the transfer of risk in the systems of law for different countries is generally discretionary. If the parties have agreed on it, the agreement is carried out. If not, [the matter] is governed by law.

V

CONTRACTS FOR THE PURCHASE AND SALE OF INDUSTRIAL AND MINERAL PRODUCTS

1. The General Concept and Legal Characteristics of Contracts for the Purchase and Sale of Industrial or Mineral Products

Contracts for industrial and mineral products are agreements between juristic persons for the purchase and sale of industrial and mineral products.

Considered from the point of view of their nature, contracts for the purchase and sale of industrial and mineral products are within the field of contracts of sale. They make use of the general rules of contracts of sale. But contracts of purchase and sale for industrial or mineral products are not the same as ordinary contracts of sale. There are very sharp differences. According to the Provisions on Contracts for the Purchase and Sale of Industrial and Mineral Products promulgated by the State Council on 23d January 1984, (hereafter referred to as The Provisions), contracts for the purchase and sale of industrial and mineral products are a type of independently named contract with the following characteristics:

(1) The object of the contract of purchase and sale of industrial and mineral products is industrial and mineral products

Industrial and mineral products include manufactured products that are the means of production and manufactured products that are the means of daily life. Industrial and mineral products are not the same as agricultural sideline products. The methods of the state for controlling industrial and mineral products and agricultural sideline products are not the same. Reflecting this, the relations of the contracts of purchase and sale are not the same. The special characteristic of the object of a contract of purchase and sale of industrial and mineral products makes it different from purchases and sale contracts for agricultural sideline products, and ordinary contracts of sale.

(2) The subject of the contract of purchase and sale of industrial mineral products subject is a juristic person

Any enterprise that has the status of a juristic person, a rural collective organization, a state organization, an institutional unit, a social group, can be the subject of the contract of purchase and sale of industrial and mineral products.

Section 2.2 of The Provisions states: "Contracts of purchase and sale of industrial and mineral products contracts that are formed between individual management households, agricultural commune members, keypoint households, specialized households, and juristic persons must be carried out according to these provisions." In such circumstances individual management households and agricultural commune members, keypoint households, and specialized households also constitute the subjects of contracts of purchase and sale of industrial and mineral products. Actually contracts between individual management households that manage industrial and mineral products, as well as the agreements they may make with agricultural commune members, keypoint households, and specialized households may be made subject to The Provisions by agreement.

(3) There are planned contracts for industrial and mineral products and also contracts that are not planned

The uses by the state of industrial and mineral products in the state economy are not the same. It carries out differentiated administration. There is a division among planned products that are under direct control, planned products that are subject to state guidance, and products subject to free supply. The object of contracts of purchase and sale of industrial and mineral products include these three kinds. Contracts of purchase and sale for planned products that are subject to state planned control are planned contracts. Their formation, amendment, and termination must be carried out according to a specially designated procedure.

2. The Formation, Amendment, and Termination of Contracts for the Purchase and Sale of Industrial or Mineral Products

(1) The formation of contracts for the purchase and sale of industrial and mineral products

In general, contracts of purchase and sale of industrial and mineral products are long-term futures contracts providing for performance in installments. Contracts [providing for] immediate settlement in cash are few. Contracts of purchase and sale of industrial and mineral products are normally in writing. According to The Provisions, the contract for the purchase and sale of industrial and mineral products, except in the case of immediate sales for cash, must be in writing and be signed (sealed) by the parties' legally authorized representatives or a legally designated representative with proof of authority. Moreover, they should be sealed with the unit's official seal or with a seal specially used for the contract.

A contract of purchase and sale for products that are subject to a directive plan must be executed in accordance with the state plan target and that of the office which has been given authority by the state. If the contract cannot be executed in accordance with the targets of the plan, if there is a dispute between the parties, it must be handled by the higher level office having responsibility for the disputing parties' planned [activities]. If a change comes about because of circumstances, and the planned target that has been sent down is already not in accordance with the facts, there must be a revision in the planned target by means of legally designated procedures. If the parties, proceeding on their own, execute a contract not in accordance with the planned target, the supervisory authority will take appropriate measures to require the parties to execute the contract according to the plan.

(2) The provisions of contracts of purchase and sale of industrial and mineral products

There are many types of industrial and mineral products and the technological standards are rather complicated. Many contracts for the purchase and sale of industrial and mineral products are long-term contracts made between juristic persons for large quantities and high prices. Consequently, the provisions of the contract must be detailed and concrete in order to facilitate the performance and supervision of the allocation of responsibilities. Section 6 of The Provisions sets out more than twelve provisions that are required for contracts of purchase and sale of industrial and mineral products.

The concrete provisions of the contract—that is, the content of the contract—are the specification of the rights, duties, and liabilities of the parties. The parties must decide clearly and concretely on the provisions of the contract.

The Provisions has fairly complete rules on the provisions on liability for breach of contract. Every supervisory ministry in the State Council and the people's governments in every province, city, and self-governing area may, in accordance with The Provisions, promulgate measures for implementation. The Provisions, together with the measures for implementation, are written legal norms and are also the bases of the contract. They implement the requirements of the state's supervisory organizations in regard to the parties' formation of contracts. They also reflect the interests of the parties. The Provisions and the measures for implementation are normative provisions which the parties must respect. The requirements of the parties which they are permitted to agree on must be agreed on by the parties.

(3) The amendment and termination of a contract of purchase and sale of industrial and mineral products

Apart from the general provisions in the Economic Contracts Law, which must be followed, The Provisions has other special requirements for the alteration or termination of a contract of purchase and sale of industrial or mineral products. In the case of products which are subject to a directive state plan, when changes in the plan require changes in or termination of the contract, it is necessary that the contract be amended or terminated according to the directives of the supervisory organization and in accordance with its specialized procedures. When the parties, between themselves, amend or terminate a contract that affects the targets of the directive plan, it is necessary to report the matter to the supervisory office which has sent the plan to the parties and receive its approval.

In order to clarify the responsibilities of the parties among themselves, The Provisions also has rules for the procedure and forms for the amendment and termination of contracts. The Provisions requires that the party who receives the [request for] amendment or termination of the contract must reply within the time set by the parties. If no time has been set, he must reply within the time set in The Provisions. When he does not reply, this is regarded as refusal. The agreement to amend or terminate must be in writing.

The time agreed upon by the parties is the standard for the time to amend or terminate the contract. If it is necessary to report and get permission, the time when the superior level supervisory office gives permission is the standard.

3. The Rights, Duties, and Responsibilities of the Parties to Contracts for the Purchase and Sale of Industrial and Mineral Products

(1) The duties of the supplier

The supplier must deliver the goods according to the contract. Otherwise, he is subject to the appropriate civil law liability.

(i) He must deliver the quantity of goods provided in the contract. The supplier

must deliver the quantity of goods provided in the contract. It may not be either more or less. Because of the nature of the products, the implements for loading, the methods of testing, as well as changes in the weather, etc., it is often very difficult to determine absolutely if the quantity complies with the provisions of the contract. For certain products it is necessary to state clearly in the contract the rules of the supervisory office (if the supervisory office has not made provision, then as negotiated and decided by the parties) for correctly allocating the responsibility for deviations in amount, reasonable deviations in weight, and natural decreases (increases) and methods of measurement. If the actual excess or deficiency of the quantity delivered as compared with the amount provided in the contract does not exceed the scope of the deficiency [allowed] the excess or surplus is not computed. The parties do not take back [the surplus] or supplement [the deficiency].

If the goods are not delivered, or too few are delivered, there is liability for breach of contract. In order strictly to make the parties of the contract perform the contract conscientiously and to assure the realization of the national economic plan, The Provisions states that when a contract is executed according to a state directive plan, and the supplier disposes of his products on his own and does not deliver the goods according to the contract provisions, then, apart from handling it by means of the penalty clause and other related provisions, the Ministry of Industry and Commerce will confiscate the income and receipts from the sale and transmit them to the central treasury.

If the products delivered by the supplier exceed the quantity provided in the contract, and the requiring party does not agree to accept them, the supplier must assume the liability for handling the matter and be liable for the expenses of delivery.

In order to clarify liability the requiring party must immediately carry on inspection and acceptance. The supplying party will arrange a vehicle (or ship) for shipments. If the goods are lost, too few, or injured, the responsibility must be borne by the supplier. The requiring party must notify the supplier within the time provided for in The Provisions or in the contract by the parties. Otherwise, he will be regarded as having inspected and accepted [without a claiming] of variance.

(ii) He must deliver goods that accord with the standard provided by law or that is agreed on. The quality of the goods provided by the supplier must be up to standard. The rules of The Provisions in regard to the technological standard for commodities are that those that have a state standard must meet the state standard. If there is no state standard, but there is a special standard in the trade (ministry) then [they must be] in accordance with the standard of the trade (ministry). If there are no standards of the types discussed above, or if, although there are standards, the requiring party has special needs or requirements, then the goods must be in accord with the technological provisions, a sample, or the requirements for supplemental technology agreed to by the parties.

In connection with the quality of the commodities furnished by the supplier, if when the character, models, specifications, design, and color do not conform to the provisions of the contract, the requiring party agrees to use them, the price must be adjusted according to the quality. If the receiving party cannot make use of them, he must make a report of the actual condition of the commodities. The supplier is liable for the repair, exchange, or return, and is also liable for the expenses of transport connected with repair, exchange, or return. If the supplier cannot repair or exchange, the matter is handled as one where the [obligor] is incapable of delivery.

In handling the problem of the quality of commodities not being in accord with the standard, attention must be paid to protecting the interests of the requiring party and encouraging the supplier to perform the contract while doing so justly and equitably.

In order to clarify liability, the requiring party, after receiving the goods furnished by the supplier, must immediately carry out [the procedures] of inspection and acceptance. If it appears that the quality of the products and the type, model, specifications, design, and color are not in accordance with the contract rules, he must tender a statement of variance within the time provided by law according to the time and procedures set out in the contract. If he has not presented a statement of variance within the time provided [by law] or agreed on, the products that were delivered will be regarded as having been in compliance with the contract.

(iii) He must make delivery according to the provisions and within the time provided in the contract. A supplier must make delivery on time. He may not delay delivery or deliver in advance [of the time set].

If the supplier delivers after the time set, he must pay the contract penalty.

In order to avoid waste and disputes, when the supplier does not deliver on time he must, prior to delivery, negotiate with the requiring party. If the requiring party still needs the goods, the supplier must deliver the quantity [agreed on]. If the requiring party does not still need them, he must, after having received notice from the supplier, notify the supplier within the time limit and take care of the procedures for terminating a contract. If there is no reply [to the notice from the supplier regarding] exceeding the time, this will be regarded as consent to delivery of the goods.

If the supplier delivers in advance, the supplier is liable for the actual expenses of the receiving party incurred in storing and taking care of the goods, as well as for injury [to the goods] not incurred as a result of improper storage by the requiring party.

(iv) Delivery must be made in the manner and the place provided for in the contract. If the state supervisory ministry has provided methods for delivery, these methods must be used. If there are no rules for the delivery, delivery must be in accordance with the agreement of the parties.

Products must in general be delivered or shipped by the supplier. In shipping products, the supplier must fully consider the needs of the requiring party and negotiate and agree on a reasonable route and method of shipment. If the supplier has not obtained the receiver's agreement, and unilaterally changes the route and means of shipment, he is liable for any additional expense thereby incurred.

In order to assure the security of the shipment, the supplier must package in accordance with the standard provided, or in accordance with the standard agreed upon by the parties for packaging in the case of shipment or delivery. Unless the state provides a different rule, the expenses of packing may not obtained from the requiring party. If packing is not in accordance with the rules, the supplier is liable for the expense of repairing it or doing it again. If this causes injury or loss of the goods, the supplier is liable to pay damages.

The supplier must deliver to the places specified in the contract. If the goods go to the wrong place or the wrong recipient, the supplier, apart from being liable to deliver goods to the place of delivery for the goods provided in the contract or to the person who is to receive them, is also liable for any actual increases in delivery expense incurred by the buyer and for the contract penalty for the excessive time of delivery. If the requiring party filled in the wrong place for the delivery or [the wrong] person to receive [the goods], he is liable for the injury [thereby incurred].

(2) The essential duties of the requiring party

The requiring party's principal duties are to accept the goods and pay for them. In addition, there is also the associated duty of storage. [The duties] are divided as follows.

(i) He must accept the quantity of goods provided in the contract. The requiring party who does not accept the goods that are delivered or accepts only a part must pay a contract penalty, and is also liable for any injury this causes and for any fine imposed by the Ministry of Transport.

(ii) He must accept the goods promptly. If the requiring party delays in accepting the goods, or does not pick them up on the day provided in the contract, he must pay the contract penalty and is liable for any expenses incurred by the supplier in storing or caring for them.

(iii) The receiver must make payment on time. The receiver must pay the price provided or agreed upon on time. At the time of payment there can be changes in the price. There may be adjustments in the prices made by the price control organizations. There can also be fluctuations in the market price. In order to make sure that the supplier and the requiring party perform the contract and pay the price promptly, when there is a delay in payment, and there is a change in prices that lowers the price and it is advantageous to one party, it is handled in accordance with the principle of not being advantageous to the party that breaches. The Provisions rule that in enforcing the state-determined prices, when, within the time provided in the contract for the goods to be delivered (or picked up), the state adjusts the price, the price [be] used that was in force at the time of delivery. If the time for delivery is exceeded and if the price is raised, the original price [is] used. If the price is lower, the new price [is] used. If the time for picking up the goods or paying

the price is exceeded, when the price increases, the new price [is] used, and when the price decreases, the original price [is] used.

When the receiver exceeds the time for payment, he must pay the contract penalty for breach.

According to the settlement methods of the People's Bank of China, if the requiring party has a good reason to refuse payment, he has the right to refuse payment. The procedures for refusing payment and the legal consequences are handled according to the rules for settling accounts.

(iv) The requiring party has the duty to store, according to the rules, goods which the supplier has delivered [but] not in accordance with the provisions of the contract. Under some circumstances, the requiring party has no right to refuse to accept the supplier's delivery of goods, but, in order to avoid wasteful loss occasioned by there being no one to take responsibility for them, the requiring party has the duty to store them for [the supplier]. At the same time, he must choose suitable methods of handling them properly. The categories of circumstances [in which this happens] may be categorized as follows:

The products delivered by the supplier exceed the contract amount. If the requiring party does not agree to accept them, and if the supplier and receiver are not in the same place, (but are in different places), the requiring party must receive the goods and is responsible for storing them. Afterwards he will notify the supplier to handle them according to the rules.

If, when the requiring party, in inspecting and accepting, discovers that the quality of the goods is not in accord with the contract provisions as to variety, model, specifications, or design and color, he must, on the one hand, arrange for storage, and, on the other, send a written statement of variance to the supplier.

If, when products are delivered or shipped, they are erroneously given to the requiring party, he must arrange proper storage for the goods that have been shipped and promptly notify the concerned units to investigate and handle the matter.

As to products which he has refused to pay for, the requiring party must accept them, arrange for their storage, and handle the matter according to the procedures that are provided.

VI
CONTRACTS FOR THE PURCHASE AND SALE OF AGRICULTURAL SIDELINE PRODUCTS

1. The General Concept and Legal Characteristics of Contracts for the Purchase and Sale of Agricultural Sideline Products and Supply Contracts

Contracts for the purchase and sale of agricultural sideline products are agreements between juristic persons for the purchase and sale of agricultural sideline products.

Contracts for the purchase and sale of agricultural sideline products are in the category of contracts of sale, but there are differences. According to the Provisions of Contracts for the Purchase and Sale of Agricultural Sideline Products (hereafter The Provisions) promulgated by the State Council on 23d January, 1984, contracts for the purchase and sale of agricultural sideline products are a type of independent named contract that have the following characteristics.

(1) The object of the contract for purchase and sale of agricultural sideline products is an agricultural sideline product

Agricultural sideline products include every kind of product including agricultural, timber, cattle, sideline, and fish products. The production of agricultural sideline products is greatly influenced by natural conditions and seasonal forces. Among them are many fresh and living products. The special characteristics of agricultural sideline products are reflected in the rights-duty relationships of the parties to the contract, which also have their own special characteristics.

(2) The subjects of agricultural sideline product contracts are juristic persons

The Provisions state that the subjects of contracts for the purchase and sale of agricultural sideline products are state farms, agricultural communes, and brigades, units designated by the state to purchase agricultural sideline products, cooperative economic organizations, as well as enterprises and institutional units that have the status of juristic persons. Agricultural sideline products agreements entered into by independently managed households and rural commune members, keypoint households, and specialized households with juristic persons are governed by The Provisions.

The execution of contracts for the purchase and sale of agricultural sideline products, the procedures for their amendment and termination, and the rights and duties of the parties have many similarities with contracts for the purchase and sale of industrial and mineral products. Below, just the differences between contracts for the purchase and sale of agricultural sideline products and contracts for the purchase and sale of industrial and mineral products are briefly discussed.

2. The Execution of Contracts for the Purchase and Sale of Agricultural Sideline Products

The state has chosen different methods of control for different agricultural sideline products. The procedures for the execution of the contracts for the purchase and sale of the different types of agricultural sideline products are also different.

For many years, the state, because of the important position of agricultural sideline products in the national economy, divided agricultural sideline products into three types. The first type of agricultural sideline products consists of the agricultural products which are the most important for the state planning of the people's livelihood—grain, cotton, oils, etc. The state practices unified purchasing in regard to this type of product. Except where, according to the rules, the state practices unified purchasing in regard to this type of agricultural sideline product, and except for the portion left to the agricultural production unit to dispose of according to the rules, they will be purchased by the commercial departments designated by the state according to state unified purchasing orders from superior levels and [at] planned prices.

The second type of agricultural sideline products consists of products whose relationship with the national economy and the people's livelihood is relatively large, such as live hogs, cattle and sheep that are pasturing, tobacco, hemp, silkworm cocoons, tea leaves, etc., for which the state carries out distribution and procurement. The state sends down [directives] for responsibility for sale to the state, and commercial offices are designated by the state to carry out distribution and procurement on the basis of planned prices.

The Provisions state that in the case of agricultural sideline products for purchase and supply contracts that are within the area of unified purchasing and distribution and procurement, contracts must be signed for the unified purchase, and distribution and procurement tasks transmitted from higher to lower levels by the state (the products of cattle that are being pastured are purchased according to a base number determined by the state).

The Ten Point Policy of the Central Committee of the Chinese Communist Party and the State Council Regarding the Advancing and Enlivening of the Agricultural Economy promulgated on 1st January, 1985 (hereafter referred to simply as the Ten Point Policy) provides that except for specific commodities, the state no longer sends down directives to the peasants for the unified purchase or distribution and procurement of agricultural products.

Except for types one and two of the agricultural sideline products, all of the agricultural sideline products are in type three, and are purchased by an agreement of the suppling parties and of commercial departments designated by the state. In regard to the agricultural sideline products which are permitted to go on the market after the completion of the unified purchasing and allocation and distribution responsibility, these are also sold by agreement. The purchasing and selling parties negotiate and execute a contract. The price may be according to the list price of the state. It can also be negotiated by the parties. According to the Ten Point Policy, after procurement by unified purchase and distribution and procurement, agricultural products are no longer subject to the former limits of the division of labor and management, but use many channels to flow in a straight line. The management, processing, and consumption units of agricultural sideline products may all execute purchase and sale contracts with peasants.

3. The Rights, Duties, and Responsibilities of Parties to Contracts for the Purchase and Sale of Agricultural Sideline Products

Apart from the similarities of contracts for the purchase and sale of industrial and mineral products the following are the most important special points.

(1) According to The Provisions, if the agricultural sideline products that are sold are adulterated, making them not what they are supposed to be, or of second rate quality, as opposed to good quality, the requiring party has the right to refuse to accept. A supplier must pay the penalty for breach.

(2) If the time of delivery is prior to that set in the contract and the requiring party has not agreed to this, he may refuse to accept.

(3) In the case of the refusal to accept products that spoil or rot easily or change condition, as well as fresh, living things, the supplier must permit the requiring party to take care of them, after receiving agreement of the concerned ministry to dispose of their property.

4. The Particular Characteristics and Form of a Contract to Purchase Agricultural Sideline Products

(1) Advance purchase contracts

The advance purchase contract is a type of contract for the purchase of agricultural sideline products. According to the advance purchase contract, the requiring party, according to state rules, around the time of sowing, pays a certain amount of money as a deposit to the seller. After the harvest, the seller delivers the agricultural sideline product. The advance purchaser pays the price, deducting the advance payment.

The advance purchase contract is a legal form of the state to develop agricultural production and guarantee the agricultural sideline purchase contract in accordance with the fulfillment of the state plan. The types of products that are involved in carrying out the advance purchase of products according to state procedure are, in general, the important agricultural sideline products such as grain, cotton, tobacco, tea, silk cocoons, etc. According to the actual requirements of the types of products used in carrying out advance purchase agricultural sideline supply contracts, there are different rules at different times.

The deposits made in advance purchase contracts are [measures used] by the state to support agriculture and to assure fulfillment of the work of the purchase contracts. They are actually advance payments and do not serve as deposits to secure the contracts. The advance purchase deposit must be used in the current year's production expenses. It cannot be used to buy tools. It cannot be used for capital construction or other expenses.

The advance purchaser has the right to investigate the carrying out of the advance purchase contract. If, in the investigation of the sowing area and production, problems of administration are discovered, it will supervise and urge and negotiate with the advance seller to settle them.

(2) Combined purchase and sales contracts

The combined purchase and sales contract is called simply a combined contract. It is of active use in strengthening town and country material circulation, promoting the development of rural cooperativization, and increasing accumulation. It not only makes the peasants' production more active, and is a good form for guaranteeing fulfillment of the task of the procurement and sale of agricultural sideline products, but is significant for improving the work of the commercial offices, and strengthening the alliance between workers and peasants.

The important legal characteristics of a combined purchase and sales contract are that the contract at the same time provides for the purchase of agricultural sideline products and the sale of industrial products. It unites purchase and sale. The purchases and sales contained in it are the two aspects of one contract, but are not two contracts, nor things for things. [That is, barter or exchange.]

VII
THE CONTRACT OF EXCHANGE

1. The General Nature and Legal Characteristics of the Contract of Exchange

The contract of exchange is an agreement whereby one side gives one type of property and the other gives another type without the use of money.

To exchange things for things is an early form of the exchange of commodities. From slave society to feudal society, to capitalist society and down to socialist society, this sort of [of contract] has been preserved. At the present time, in international trade, exchange is still used to carry on the exchange of goods. In our country, the contract of exchange is used within a particular area. The rights and duties of parties to an exchange contract [are determined by] the application of the relevant provisions of sales law.

A contract of exchange is a nongratuitous bilateral promissory [as opposed to real] contract. The difference between the contract of exchange and the contract of sale lies in the fact that in the former, the thing is exchanged for a thing, while in the latter, the sale is accomplished by the use of money.

Among contracts of exchange when there is a case in which exchange is of things that are not of equal value, one party needs to give to the other a sum of money as supplementary compensation. This could be called a mixed contract of exchange.

The legal consequence of the contract of exchange is that the property rights (or management rights) of the parties to the things that are exchanged are transferred.

2. The Use and Area of Application of the Contract of Exchange

Citizens, in order to help supply each other's needs and to fulfill their living requirements, may use the materials of daily life that are privately owned as the subjects of exchange. Items that cannot circulate may not be exchanged.

Citizens and social organizations very seldom use the form of exchange. In the case of the exchange of certain types of goods between the supply and marketing cooperatives and citizens, the exchange may be used. For example, citizens exchange eggs for salt with the supply and marketing cooperative. This is advantageous to the masses in simplifying procedures. It is also useful to supply and marketing organizations to obtain more of the minor products of the soil and small miscellaneous products. It can also increase people's income.

Under conditions specified by law, socialist organizations may conclude contracts of exchange among themselves. According to the relevant rules of 1978 and 1979, after they have fulfilled the responsibilities provided by the state plan, provinces, cities, and autonomous regions may carry out organized exchanges among themselves as to products that are allocated locally. As to products which enterprises are permitted to sell on their own, and surplus accumulations of goods and materials, both the enterprises and the production and supervisory organizations may agree to exchange.

The state permits socialist organizations to exchange things for things within a certain defined area in order that each may supply the other's needs and engage in mutual assistance and, thus, promote the state economic plan. But they may not hinder the fulfillment of the state economic plan. The exchange of large quantities of goods and material must be carried on in an organized way as provided by the rules. Contracts, which by rule, must be certified by an economic supervisory organization, must be certified and are only effective upon the receipt of this approval. Exchange is only for the mutual supply of each other's needs and the fulfillment of the requirements of production. It is not permitted to resell, buy back, and carry on unlawful activities.

VIII
THE CONTRACT OF GIFT

A contract of gift is an agreement whereby one party, the donor, voluntarily and gratuitously transfers ownership of his property to another party, the donee.

The contract of gift requires not only that the donor express [his intention] to give his property gratuitously to the other, but also requires that the donee express his agreement to accept this property. Consequently, a gift is a contractual relationship. It is a bilateral juristic act.

The contract of gift is a contract with a single obligation. It is a gratuitous contract. Its special legal characteristics are that the donor assumes a responsibility and the donee acquires rights. The donor reduces his property. The donee increases his property. Moreover, he has not paid a price to the donor.

The contract of gift is a real contract. The gift takes effect after the donor has transferred the object of the gift to the donee. After the agreement between the donor and the donee is completed, but before the gift is delivered, the donor still has the right to cancel the gift. But after the transfer of the gift, unless there are special circumstances, [the gift] may not be revoked at will. If there is a dispute over revocation, the people's court may be asked to decide the matter.

In our country, the principal subject of the contract of gift is the citizen. Citizens may give their property to others. They may also give it to the nation, a collective organization, or a social group.

If there is a provision of law regarding the form of the contract of gift, it must be made in the way provided. If there is no provision, it may be negotiated and agreed on by the parties. For example, the gift of a building must be in written form and the building administrative office must take care of the registration transfer procedures.

In order to uphold the legal effectiveness of proper gifts, and to reduce disputes, the written form may be selected for gifts whose value exceeds a certain amount. Moreover, they may be handled by a notary, etc.

The most important use of the gift is between citizens or between citizens and juristic person. In order to be a donor, a citizen must have the capacity to act (*Handlungsfähigkeit*). A citizen may give his property to another citizen (as in the frequent case where, prior to marriage, one or both parties gives or receives property). They also may give property to a state organization, an enterprise, a social group, or other organizations that are juristic persons (for example, a donation of an individual's collection of cultural objects, the gift of an author's fee, etc.). Gifts between juristic persons are comparatively rare. State property and collective property must all be occupied, used, disposed of according to the plan. Therefore, economic organizations that are carrying on economic economy are not permitted to dispose of property at will without compensation. The objects of contracts of gifts are many. They may be movables or immovables; they may be specified or generic.

In order to encourage citizens to make gifts of property to the state and collectivities, it is necessary to respect the intention of the donor regarding the use to be made of the gift. For example, when the parties have agreed upon a gift of property, cash, rare cultural objects, documentary materials, a book collection, etc., to be used for the benefit of a socially defined purpose, the receiving unit may in accordance with the administrative procedures, give appropriate spiritual or material rewards.

23 Contract of Hire

I
AN INTRODUCTION TO THE CONTRACT OF HIRE

1. The General Concept of the Contract of Hire

A contract of hire is an agreement between a contractor and a contracting party, wherein the contractor is to perform work ordered by the contracting party according to specifications set by the contracting party, and turn over the completed work to the contracting party. The contracting party is to accept the results of the said work, and pay the agreed-upon remuneration to the contractor for the job done. It is a bilateral, nongratuitous, promissory contract.

A contract of hire has the following features:

(1) The object of a contract of hire is not the labor of the contractor itself; rather it is the result of the labor

[This includes,] for example, the prospecting, design, construction, and installation in capital construction, and in contracts for the processing, repairing, renovating, and making of the ordinary articles of daily life of citizens. Some objects are the result of mental labor, some are the result of physical labor, and still others are the result of a combination of both mental and physical labor.

(2) The object of a contract of hire is specified

The contractor is to perform the job according to the specifications laid down by the contracting party. Even though the object does not exist at the time the contract is made, the requirements for it have already been specified. Therefore, it is different from ordinary commodities available in the market.

(3) A contractor performs the job independently with his own equipment, skill, and labor

The provisions of the assignment given by the contracting party determine what production work the contractor is to do, but this does not hamper the independence of the contractor in carrying out the work. The contractor, in order to be responsible for the results of the work, has the right, according to his own conditions of production, independently, on his own, to make his own production plan, allocate his labor resources, and determine the ways in which to perform the work.

In our country's civil law activities, contracts of hire are employed quite widely. The usual needs of people in production and daily life are largely satisfied through contracts of sale, supply, lease, loan, etc., but some particular needs frequently require contracts of hire in order to be fulfilled. For instance, the construction of a library requires that a capital construction contract be signed with an appropriate unit in order to be accomplished. If an individual wants clothing specifically suitable for him, he may obtain it through signing a contract of hire with a tailor shop. Thus, it can be seen that contracts of hire whose purpose is to satisfy the particular needs of persons in production and daily life are not only necessary, but are also widely used in civil law activities.

According to the different content of contracts of hire, they can be divided into two categories. One is the ordinary contract of hire, including contracts for the processing, making to order, repair, renovation, duplication, etc., of articles of daily life. The other is the capital construction contract, including contracts for prospecting, design, construction, installation, etc.

2. Differences Between Contracts of Hire and Other Similar Contracts

A contract of hire is, in some respects, similar to other kinds of contracts. So, in order to understand the nature and special features of a contract of hire, and correctly apply the rules of law, it is important to know the difference between contracts of hire and other similar contracts.

(1) The difference between a contract of hire and a labor contract [employment contract]

Looked at from the point of view of having specified work done, these contracts are similar. However, they are contracts of a different nature and there are major differences between them.

(i) According to a contract of labor, the laborer is bound to carry out the work under the leadership organization of the unit with which he contracts; whereas, in a contract of hire, the contractor is an organization or citizen who carries on his production activity independently.

(ii) In a contract of labor, the laborer should work according to the contract, and from this he gets the agreed-upon stipend. But in a contract of hire, the contractor should turn over the result of his work to the contracting party, and as a result of this, obtain the agreed-upon remuneration.

(2) The difference between a contract of hire and a contract of sale

The act of the contractor in turning over the result of his labor to the contracting party and receiving the agreed-upon remuneration in a contract of hire is very similar to the act of a seller in a sales contract when he delivers the object [of the contract] to the buyer and receives the agreed-upon price. But they are two different kinds of contract.

(i) The object of a sales contract may sometimes be that which exists at the time the contract is made, or it may be something that has not yet been produced when the contract is made, but the objects of all contracts of hire are produced by the contractor by his own labor after the contract is formed.

(ii) In the case of contracts of sale, a buyer cannot ask the seller to perform until the time for performance agreed on in the contract becomes due, and even in supply contracts [i.e., contracts to supply important materials according to the state plan], when the goods contracted for are still in the process of production, the one requiring the goods has no right to ask the supplier how it is organizing its production; whereas, in a contract of hire, the contractor should complete the work according to the assignment and requirements given him by the contracting party, and the contracting party, on the condition that he does not hinder the normal work of the contracting party, has the right to investigate and oversee the course of the work.

(iii) The object of a contract of sale can be specified articles that cannot be replaced by any other things and they can also be fungible things, but the objects of a contract of hire are always specified articles.

(3) The difference between a contract of hire and a contract of mandate

Both the mandatary in the contract of mandate and the contractor in a contract of hire complete tasks according to the requirements laid down by others. The two kinds of contract are similar on this point, but there are obvious differences between them.

(i) The mandatary completes his task in the name, and at the expense of, the mandator; whereas, a contractor [performs his work] in his own name and at his own expense.

(ii) The mandatary, in acting according to the contract, will generally be involved with a third person; whereas, in the contract of hire the contractor is to produce a certain work result according to the contract and, usually, he will not be involved with a third person.

(iii) A contract between the mandator and the mandatary may be gratuitous or nongratuitous; whereas, a contract of hire is always nongratuitous. The contracting party must pay the agreed-upon remuneration when the contractor turns over the result of his labor.

II
THE RIGHTS AND OBLIGATIONS OF THE PARTIES TO A CONTRACT OF HIRE

1. The Major Obligations of the Contractor

(1) A contractor must do the work assigned to him according to the agreed-upon object

This is the essential obligation of the contractor. The object specified in the contract is the particular requirement of the contracting party in production or in daily life. This is the prerequisite and also the essential content of the contract. Once the contract is formed, the contractor should scrupulously keep faith and strictly conform its performance to the contract specifications regarding the object of the contract—its nature, standard, quality, and shape, etc. The contractor may not, on his own, without the consent of the contracting party, make any revision or change; still less may he scrimp work, stint materials, or manufacture in a rough and slipshod way, in order to substitute the second-rate for the good.

In a contract for renovating a building or for mass processing nonstandard products, the contractor should permit, on the condition of its not hampering his normal work, necessary inspection and supervision by the contracting party to ensure that the work result will completely meet the requirements of the contracting party.

After completing the job, the contractor should, on his own initiative, submit to the contracting party's examination and acceptance [of the work]. If the quality or quantity of the objects of the contract do not comply with the requirements of the contract and this is the responsibility of the contractor, the contracting party may ask the contractor to repair or eliminate the defects, or make up the shortage within a specified period, or he may ask for reduction of the remuneration. If the object of the contract is in such a defective condition that it is difficult to correct, the contracting party has the right to refuse to accept and to ask for damages. If the quantity delivered is less than that provided in the contract, and the contracting party still needs them, the specified quantity must be supplied and the missing portion handled as a delayed delivery. If the contracting party no longer needs them, he has the right to cancel the contract and seek damages.

If, within the time provided [by law or contract], the contracting party discovers that the accepted objects of the contract have hidden defects, he must immediately notify the contractor. The contractor should, according to the actual situation, correct the defects at his own expense, or reduce his remuneration, or rescind the contract and pay damages.

(2) A contractor has the obligation to perform the work personally

A contract of hire is executed by the contracting party in reliance on the ability of the contractor to complete the work. This requires the contractor to perform the work personally in order to protect the interest of the contracting party. If the contractor is a juristic person, unless there is a contrary agreement, he should use his own equipment, skills, and labor to perform the assignment given by the contracting party, and, without permission from the contracting party, he may not assign the responsibility he has accepted to a third party. Otherwise the contracting party has the right to terminate the contract. It may be that, because of the nature of the contract, or receipt of the permission of the contracting party, a contractor may assign part of the job or particular work through a subcontract to a third person, but the contractor is responsible to the contracting party for the quality of the work done by the subcontractor.

(3) A contractor has the obligation to examine and take care of the materials [called for in the contract]

The contractor usually has specialized skilled knowledge and practical work experience, and understands the quality and quantity of materials to use in completing the contract given him by the contracting party. Consequently, a contractor should not only be responsible for the quality and quantity of the materials he furnishes, but he must also immediately examine the materials supplied by the contracting party. If he finds the materials do not meet the requirements of the contract, he should notify the contracting party promptly to exchange or to make up [the defect]. Otherwise, the contractor cannot escape his liability with the excuse that the materials supplied by the contracting party are defective or insufficient.

In using the materials supplied by the contracting party, the contractor should carefully calculate, budget, and make reasonable use of these materials. He should also return the leftover materials to the contracting party.

A contractor should not replace the materials supplied by the contracting party with others on his own, nor exchange components of the items the customer handed in for repair. Otherwise, the contracting party has the right to refuse to accept. The contractor is liable in damages for any resulting loss. If the contracting party requires remaking or re-repairing, this must be handled in accordance with the requirements of the contracting party. Moreover, [the contractor] is liable for delayed delivery.

The contractor must provide suitable storage for the raw materials, equipment, packaged things, and other articles. If, owing to the storage being not satisfactory, the above mentioned things are injured or lost, he must compensate the contracting party for the loss.

(4) A contractor has the obligation to complete the work and turn over the result to the contracting party on time

Usually every contract of hire provides the time for the performance. This includes provisions regarding the time for the commencement of performing the obligation—the time limit for the contractor to undertake the job; the intermediate time; the time for completion of certain parts of the job or the time for the partial turning over of the results of the work to the contracting party; the time for ending performance: the completion of the work or the final delivery of the work to the contracting party. In actual contracts of hire, any time limit for the performance of the obligation is provided for by the parties. If, by his fault, the contractor does not begin performance on time, or does not perform according to the rate of performance set in the contract, then when he does not turn over the result to the contracting party at the time required by the contract, he should be responsible for such delay and pay the contract penalty.

(5) The contractor has the duty to maintain secrecy for the contracting party according to the rules or as agreed

Copies, plans, and translations made by the contracting party, as well as tests of the nature and capabilities of articles, and investigations which the contracting party wishes to be kept secret must be kept secret. He [the contractor] may not keep technological materials or copies without permission.

2. Major Obligations of the Contracting Party

(1) The contracting party has the obligation to accept promptly the objects of the contract of hire

The contracting party should examine the objects carefully and accept them at the agreed-upon place and time.

If a contracting party does not accept the work within the time agreed, he must, apart from paying the penalty according to the rules, pay any storage or support expenses actually incurred by the contractor. If the specified period of time for acceptance has passed, the contractor has the right to sell the objects that have been ordered. After he has deducted the fee for the work, the storage fees, and the maintenance fees from the price received, he will return the remainder to the contracting party. To the extent that the amount received is too small to pay for storage, maintenance, and his fee, the contracting party must make up the difference. If the object cannot be sold, he must pay damages to the contractor.

The contracting party is liable for the loss or destruction of the objects of the contract by reason of irresistible force that occurred during the period when the contracting party refused to accept or delays acceptance, and, moreover, he must compensate the contractor for any expenses. When the contracting party changes the place of delivery of the contracted-for item, he is liable for any increased expenses that result.

(2) A contracting party bears the obligation to pay the fee for the work

To get paid is the basic right of the contractor. If the contractor has completed the agreed-upon work and turned over the result, the contracting party must pay the fee as agreed.

The contracting party's payment of the fee to the contractor can be made in a single payment or in installments. Where the contractor is to turn over the result in parts by stages, the contracting party should pay the corresponding fee after the acceptance of each part of the product of the work. If the contract does not call for payment of the fee in installments, payment of the entire fee should be made at the time of carrying out the final delivery and acceptance of the object of the contract.

When the contracting party exceeds the time provided for payment, he must pay the contractor a penalty [computed] according to the rules of the People's Bank of China for short-term payments. On the basis of the [contract] fee, for each day's delay the penalty will be computed as one one-thousandth of the total amount of the fee.

If the contracting party refused or delayed payment of the fee without reason, the contractor has the right to a lien on the object of the contract to protect his obligation right.

(3) If the contract calls for the contracting party to supply materials and data, the contracting party has the obligation to provide the contractor with the materials and data of the stipulated quality and quantity at the time [required by the contract]

In a contract of hire the parties can determine who is to furnish the required materials and data. If the contracting party is to do the furnishing, he should furnish the materials and data that meet the contract standard of agreed quality and quantity specifications. If the contracting party fails to tender the raw materials and data within the time provided and according to requirements, the contractor has the right to cancel the contract. The contracting party is liable to the contractor for any damages that result. If the contractor does not insist on cancellation, then apart from the right to extend the time for delivery, the contractor is liable for any damages suffered in waiting for data.

III
CAPITAL CONSTRUCTION CONTRACTS

1. The General Concept and Special Characteristics of the Capital Construction Project

Capital construction project contracts include contracts for investigation and design contracts, as well as construction and installation construction contracts. According to capital construction project contracts, the contractor (the investigating, designing, constructing, or installing unit) should complete the project that was agreed upon with the contracting unit according [to the requirements of the contract] as to quality, quantity, and time; the contracting party must provide the necessary technical documents, data, and other requirements for the work, and examine and accept the completed project and pay the agreed fee.

Capital construction project contracts are a kind of contract of hire, but they are different from other contracts of hire. Their main legal features are:

(1) The object of capital construction project contracts is a capital construction project

It is not the usual product that is processed or made to order. A capital construction project is the construction of factories, mines, roads, housing, public facilities, etc., that are to be built by using capital, materials, and equipment as resources, and by utilizing science and technology, and through mental and physical labor. It constitutes a construction work to expand "reproductive" capacity and improve the people's material and cultural life. It is work that provides a material and technological basis for every part of the nation's economy, and for the welfare of the people. It is also the basic form of, and an important means for expanding, socialist "reproduction."

(2) Capital construction project contracts are under the strict control of the plan

The capital construction plans issued or approved by the state are the basis of the contracts between the contracting party and the contractor. Consequently, for a party to abide by the contract and perform his obligations is not only an obligation to be fulfilled to the other party, but also an obligation to be fulfilled to the state. This is an important feature of capital construction project contracts.

(3) They are under the supervision of the state

The state not only establishes plans for capital construction, but also supervises, through administrative measures, the signing and performance of capital construction project contracts. The execution of a capital reconstruction contract must have the state capital construction project plan as its basis. The price for such construction must be paid out of the state capital construction funds by means of the bank capital construction account. [The fund] can be expended and used only for that purpose, and the People's Construction Bank of China carries on investigations and supervision of investment in capital construction. In addition, the supervisory state departments directly take part in completing the projects and in the examination and acceptance of some medium and important large-scale construction projects. It carries on checking and acceptance and investigation of the construction unit and the ordering unit in order to ensure the quality and investment and returns. Of course, administrative intervention and supervision of the supervisory organs of the state does not impair the right of the parties to maintain independence and keep the initiative in their own hands, [nor does it impair] the mutual rights and duties of the parties established by their contract.

Capital construction contracts are the basic form, and an important means for the realization of, the state capital construction plans. Through these contracts, the rights and duties of the contracting party and the contractor are established. They divide the work and cooperate, interact with one another, and together assure the completion of the state construction task. Practice has proved that to promote the capital construction contract system helps fully to arouse the construction units, the survey units, design units, and the units in charge of construction, etc. They are also of importance in strengthening the supervision of capital construction, raising the efficiency of capital construction, assuring the quality of capital construction, etc.

2. Execution of Capital Construction Contracts

Capital construction contracts are executed by the construction unit with the surveying, design, construction, and installation units according to state capital construction plans and according to the procedures regarding capital construction approved and set by the state.

(1) Execution of the contracts for surveying and design

The contracts for surveying and design are agreements executed by a mandating [commissioning] unit (the construction unit or a related unit) with the contractor (survey and design units) to complete a certain survey or design project and clearly provide for the mutual rights-duty relationship.

In the case of the survey contract, the contracting unit, the design unit, or related units issue a mandate [commission]. The two parties agree and the contract is formed.

A design contract requires that there be a document from a superior unit authorizing the design project and then it [the design contract] can be established. A small-scale, individual project must have written approval from the superior organization and then it can be entered into.

Bidding is a new legal form which the reform of the economic system has brought forth. Survey and design contracts can use this method to be formed.

A survey and design contract must have the following essential provisions: the name of the construction project, its scale, the amount of the investment, the place of construction, the content of the materials offered by the commissioning party, the technological requirements and the time limit, the scope of the contractor's survey, its schedule and nature, the stages of the design, its schedule, the quantity and number of copies of the design, the basis of the fees for survey and design, the standards for the fees, and the methods of appropriation and responsibility for breach of contract.

Contracts for survey and design must be in written form. If the design responsibility for the construction project is coordinated design by two or more units, if one of them is commissioned to bring it all together, an overall contract can be formed. The overall [contracting] unit will then enter into separate contracts with the individual units. The overall [contracting] unit is responsible to the commissioning unit. The individual units are responsible to the overall [contracting] unit.

(2) Execution of contracts for construction and installation projects

Contracts for construction and installation projects are agreements between the unit ordering the construction and the unit performing the construction for completing the construction and installation project, which clearly specify their mutual rights and duties. Construction and installation projects must respect the law, be in harmony with policy, and be performed in accordance with the capital construction procedures provided by the state and a state authorized investment plan.

The construction and installation contracts for construction and installation should clearly provide: the name and location of the project; the scope and content of the project; the construction period, stages of the intervening work that is to be turned over, and the dates for the beginning and completion of the period of the work; the quality warranty of the project, and the period of the warranty; the cost of the project; the time for handing over the design documents and the general budget and technical materials; the time for supplying and delivering materials and equipment; the settling of the project accounts, the methods for payment delivery, inspection and acceptance; mutual cooperation between the parties; responsibility for breach, etc.

Capital construction and installation projects, with rather a lot of separate projects and comparatively long periods of construction, must have comprehensive contracts that are based on the state long-term plan, approved initial designs, and general budgetary estimates, and carry out the preparations for construction. Afterwards, they must again execute a specific contract based on the approved annual plan, construction plans and budgeting (or technological design and revised estimates), and perform the contract.

The contracting party may commission a construction unit to construct the whole project or commission several units to construct it in part. The contractors may give parts of the work to other construction units and make contracts with them. The construction unit is liable to the contracting party, the unit constructing a part is liable to the unit constructing [the whole]. But the contracting unit may not profit by assigning the project to another unit.

3. Alteration of Capital Construction Contracts

Once the contract is executed, each party should perform its part strictly in accordance with it and may not alter it at its own will. This is not only for the protection of the interests of the parties, but also to ensure the implementation of the capital construction plan of the state.

However, for various reasons, in the course of actual experience, conditions arise that make alteration of contracts difficult to avoid. For instance, the adjustment of national economic plans and the scaling down of capital construction will invariably result in alteration or termination of capital construction contracts. This kind of change is necessary and the parties should take the interests of the whole [community] into consideration, conform to the adjustment, and make necessary changes or terminate their contracts as the situation requires.

If there is a change in the state plan, or one of the parties requires a change, if it is a major change involving the content of the planned project letter, the preliminary design, the construction drawings, etc., the party dealing with the alteration should go through the same procedures through which [the original construction plan] got approved. After the examination and approval by the department that originally approved the plan, it is still necessary to obtain the consent of the original design unit; then the contract can be changed.

A construction contracting unit and a construction contractor can make necessary changes and supplements to their original contract through mutual agreement, provided that such changes do not conflict with the state capital construction plan. The party asking for change has the responsibility to pay damages for the loss resulting from such change. If the change is caused by the serious fault of the surveying unit or designing unit, the surveying or designing unit bears the liability to pay damages.

4. The Rights and Obligations of the Parties to Capital Construction Contracts

(1) The rights and duties of the parties to survey and design contracts

(i) The essential duty of the commissioning party

(a) It must tender to the contractor the essential materials for performing the survey and design work, and [provide] the essential conditions for work and living. It is also liable for the time of tendering, the schedule, and the reliability of the materials. The one commissioning the survey work, prior to beginning the work, must provide the technology required for the work and the working drawings. The one commissioning preliminary designs, prior to the beginning of the designing, must tender the approved design responsibility letter; the announcement of the selection of the factory and the raw materials (or the approved resources announcement); documents on the agreements on fuel, water, electricity, transport, etc., and survey materials sufficient to begin design; and the technological materials for necessary scientific research. The one commissioning the drafting of working drawings, prior to the drafting of the working drawings, must provide the document of approval for beginning the drafting and the necessary survey materials for the drafting of the working drawings, and provide the [proper] conditions for the work, as well as the technological materials and equipment. It will assign the design of responsibility for carrying out the recommended project. It must get the construction unit to participate in inquiring about the price negotiations with outsiders, and every stage of internal and foreign technical investigation up to the beginning of operations. When, owing to a change in the plan, the materials that have been furnished are not accurate, or the survey or the necessary materials for design have not been furnished on time, or the necessary conditions [supplied], and this causes the survey and design to conflict, or the work to stop, or for there to be a holdup in the work, the commissioning party must increase the fee according to the actual amount of work expended by the constructing party. If, because of something that is the responsibility of the commissioning party there is an important reversal to the work or significant repetition of the work, it must again increase the fee.

(b) It must pay the fee for survey and design. How much is to be paid for survey and design, how it is to be paid, and when, are matters that are decided by the parties in the contract in accord with the state rules. If the commissioning party exceeds the time for payment, it must compensate for the excess time.

(c) It will safeguard the survey and design documents of the contractors and may not itself change them and may not give them to a third party to use again.

(ii) The essential duties of the contractor

(a) [It must] deliver the results of the survey and the design document according to the schedule and standards of the contract. This is the basic duty of the contractor. This surveying unit must conduct the survey of the project, survey the location of the project, make a hydrologic survey, etc., according to existing standards, norms, procedures, and technological regulations. Moreover, it must deliver the results of the survey according to the schedule and standard provided in the contract. The design unit must carry out the design [work] on the basis of the approved document of design responsibility or the document approved for higher level design, as well as the related design, technology economic agreements, design standards, technological norms, procedures, quotas, and the survey requirements. It must deliver the design documents (including the budget estimates and the material and equipment inventory) according to the schedule and standards set in the contract. If, owing to the low quality of the survey and design work, the work is hindered, or if the survey and design documents are not delivered on time, delaying the work and causing injury, the survey and design work will continue to be perfected by the contractor. This must be regarded as having caused injury that causes waste and reduces or eliminates the survey and design fee. If serious injury to the project results from errors in the surveys and design, the contractor, apart from not receiving the portion of the fee attributable to the injured portion, must also pay damages equivalent to the part of the survey-design fee that is attributable to the directly injured part [of the project].

(b) In regard to the construction project that has assumed the design responsibility, it must coordinate the construction, explain the design technology, solve the problems of design that arise during the course of construction, be responsible for changes in the design or revisions in the budget, participate in the trial-run test, and the inspection and acceptance of the project. In regard to middle-sized industrial projects, and complicated engineering projects for civil use, it must send representatives to design on the spot, and participate in the inspection and acceptance of hidden engineering projects [e.g., underground projects].

(2) The rights and duties of parties to a capital construction contract

(i) Major obligations of the one hiring (the contracting party)

(a) [The contracting party must] do the preparatory work well prior to construction. Preparations are an important part of the whole capital construction process and the basis for formal construction. Doing the preparatory work well, prior to construction, is important in ensuring that the whole project will be completed in accordance with the requirements regarding time, quality, and quantity. The contracting party is responsible, prior to the construction, for handling the requisition and lease of the land to be used for the formal construction, as well as that for temporary facilities. It is also responsible for applying for the construction license, arranging for permits for occupying roads, and blasting, as well as temporary branch railroad line connections. It must determine the [location of] structures, roads, circuits, stakes for locating the flow of water, bench markers, marks for control points; [it must] connect the construction site with water, electricity, and transport, and clear the site of housing and obstructive materials (or commission the contractor to do this). If the contracting party has not completed the preparatory work described above on time, making it impossible to do the construction work on time, apart from the completion date being extended, he must pay damages to the contractor for any injury suffered in consequence.

(b) [The contracting party must] organize the units concerned to require and approve the work drawings and other technical materials, and deliver them to the contractor according to the time and number of copies agreed on. The work drawings and other technical materials are indispensable for the work, and their conscientious examination and approval and prompt delivery assure that the project will be properly carried out. If the failure to deliver promptly causes the contractor to be unable to begin work on time, then, apart from extending the time for conclusion of the work, he must also compensate the other party for any losses thereby incurred.

(c) Materials and equipment should be supplied according to the scope of the division of work and the requirements agreed to by the parties. Who should supply the materials and equipment for the construction and installation project is determined by the parties in accordance with the spirit of our country's material supply system presently in effect. If the contracting party does not supply the materials or equipment as provided in the contract, and, as a result of this, the construction is delayed or the quality is affected, the contracting party is liable for this. It should pay the contract penalty. Moreover, it should compensate the other party for the resulting losses.

(d) [The contracting party must carry out] the process of timely examination and acceptance of the completed project. The examination and acceptance of the completed capital construction project is the complete examination of the results of the capital construction. It is an important link in the inspection of the design and quality of the project. Doing the work of inspecting the finished project well is important in ensuring that the completed construction can immediately enter into production and be utilized, and bring into play its economic capacity, as well as bringing together experience about construction. This is all very useful. The state pays great attention to the work of examination and acceptance on conclusion of the project, and has laid down rigid procedures for such examination and acceptance. It is the usual practice that the contracting unit organizes the designing, construction, and other hiring units to make a preliminary examination, and to present a report of the examination and acceptance of the completed work to the responsible ministry. The responsible ministry then organizes examination and acceptance on behalf of the state. The contracting unit plays an important role all through the course of the examination and acceptance. Upon receiving notice for the examination and acceptance of the work from the contractor, the contracting unit should immediately report this to the controlling government department and organize the examination and acceptance according to the rules for examination and acceptance of completed capital construction projects. If the examination and acceptance are delayed beyond the time provided, the contracting unit must pay the penalty provided in the contract and make compensation for any loss resulting from such delay. If the completed project meets the required standards, the hiring party is responsible to accept immediately and take care of it. If it appears that the quality of the completed project does not meet the requirements of the contract, the contractor should, at its own expense, repair or redo the work. If as a result of the repair or redoing, there is a delay in the time of turnover, the contractor will pay the penalty for delay. If the contracting party is also at fault, it will be liable for the appropriate share of expenses for the repair or redoing. Upon receiving notice from the contractor for the examination and acceptance of a buried underground completed project, the contracting party should promptly go to the site to examine and accept it. If the contracting party does not go to the site to inspect and accept, the contractor may examine the project himself and make a written record of the buried underground project. The contracting party should acknowledge this record. If the contracting party subsequently conducts an examination and the project conforms to the requirements, then it must bear the expenses for such reexamination.

(e) [The contracting party must] pay the price for the construction on time. Paying the price for the construction at the time specified in the contract is the basic obligation of the contracting party. The contracting party is responsible for organizing the design unit and the construction unit jointly to negotiate and decide on the price for the construction project and the final settlement. It will transfer to the Chinese People's Construction Bank the necessary documents for allocating funds (a project involving loans or self-financing requires assurance of the availability of funds) and makes settlement by means of its handling of the matter. If the funds are not allocated within the time provided in the contract, then the matter will be handled in accordance with the bank's methods for delayed payments or "the methods for settling payments for [construction] projects."

(ii) Major obligations of the contractor

(a) [The contractor must] do the preliminary preparatory work well. The contractor is responsible for levelling the factory site; arranging for water, electricity, roads, and temporary facilities on the site; and working project organization and design (or project plans) and doing well every aspect of the preparatory work for the project. If a contractor does not do the preparatory work well, and this affects the time of construction, the contractor must pay the penalty for delay provided in the contract provisions for breach.

(b) [The contractor must] do well the work of purchasing materials and equipment according to the contract, purchasing, providing, and taking care of the materials and equipment. Whenever, according to the parties' agreement as to the division of work, the contractor is responsible for ordering, purchasing, and providing the materials and equipment, the contractor should do this according to the requirements [of the contract] regarding quality, quantity, and time, and take suitable care of them. If, as a result of its fault, the materials do not conform to the requirements of the contract, or are damaged or lost, and, as a result of this, the construction is delayed or the quality of the project is affected, the contractor must, without compensation, repair or redo the work, and, in addition, pay the contract penalty.

(c) [The contractor must] construct the project strictly according to the working drawings and explanations and ensuring the quality of the project. The working drawings and specifications are the basis of construction. The contractor must follow them strictly and may not make changes on his own. When it is necessary to make a change, the contractor should not do it until he has obtained the approval of the original designing unit. The contractor must immediately give written notice to the contracting party of the beginning of work, a schedule for carrying out the construction plan, notice of examination and acceptance of hidden [underground] projects, notice of inspection and acceptance of completed projects, etc., and reasonably arrange the work to accord strictly with the order of construction. Underground and hidden construction projects, particularly the key parts of the foundation structure, must definitely be examined to see if they meet standards. Moreover, he must do the work of keeping records well. Only then can the next step of construction begin. The construction responsibility must be completely fulfilled by performance, that is strictly in accordance with the requirements of the design and the rules for examining and acceptance, and he must ensure the quality of the project. If it will not hinder normal construction, a contractor must accept investigation and supervision of the contracting party regarding the rate of progress and the quality of the project that is being constructed. Whenever there is any part of the project that does not meet the quality requirements, the contractor should take timely measures to amend it and not leave any hidden problems. A contractor should not turn over [a project] that does not meet standards. If, because the contractor failed to organize the work properly, or did shoddy work and used inferior materials, and the quality of the project is affected, or the construction is delayed, the contractor must, at its own expense, repair or redo the matter, and if the repairing or redoing causes delay, pay the penalty for delay.

(d) [The contractor must] complete and turn over the project at the time required [by the contract]. A contractor should organize its performance according to the plan, in a step-by-step and orderly manner, so as to ensure that the project will be completed as scheduled. After completion of the project, the contractor must follow the rules regarding turning over, inspection, and acceptance. He must do the preparatory work for inspection and acceptance well. He must immediately send a notice of completion, inspection, and acceptance and [prepare for] inspection and acceptance of technological materials after completion of the project. He must take care of a final accounting and participate in the inspection and acceptance. As to hidden [covered] projects, the contractor should notify the customer to come to the site and check before the project is hidden [covered] and inspect [to see if the project meets the requirements]. If a project meets the standards, and the procedures for the turning over and acceptance have been complied with, and the parties have signed and sealed [the necessary documents], the transfer takes effect legally. When a unit completes a construction project, the contractor must, within the period specified, notify the contracting party in writing that it is ready to turn over [the project] for inspection and acceptance to the contracting party. The contracting party, after receiving the notification, should inspect and accept the project within the specified period. If the project meets specifications, the parties will sign the certificate of turning over and examination and acceptance of the project. The contractor has then finished its obligation to turn over the project. If, during the period of the guaranty to keep in repair, there should be a problem of quality for which the contract is responsible, it must repair it without compensation. If the turnover does not take place within the time provided, the contractor must pay the agreed-upon penalty for delay.

24 The Contract of Lease

I
GENERAL DISCUSSION OF CONTRACTS OF LEASE

1. The General Concept of the Contract of Lease

A contract of lease is an agreement for the lessor to deliver his property to the lessee for the latter's use, and the lessee to pay rent for this use to the lessor and return the leased property to the lessor when the lease relationship expires. A contract of lease is a bilateral, nongratuitous, and promissory contract [i.e., it becomes effective upon a meeting of minds]. A contract of lease has the following legal features:

(1) It is an agreement reached between two parties concerning the temporary use of leased property

It is different from a contract of sale because there is no transfer of ownership. In a contract of lease, the lessee only gets the right to use the property and the ownership of the property remains with the lessor.

(2) It is an agreement between the parties concerning the compensated use of leased property

According to this contract, no matter what kind of property the lessee uses, he has to pay rent to the lessor (in money or in kind, usually in money). This shows its compensatory nature and distinguishes it from the gratuitous loan-for-use contract.

(3) In a contract of lease, the parties agree that the original leased property will be returned to the lessor when the contract expires

Therefore, the leased property must be a specified thing or a thing that can be specified and that is not consumed. In this way, some kind of need of the lessee for the use [of the property] is satisfied, and when the lease expires, this causes the lessee to be able to return it to the lessor. In this respect, a contract of lease is distinguished from a contract of loan for consumption where a party obtains some fungible consumable.

(4) Even though it is an obligation relation, it has some property characteristics

According to the contract, the right which the lessee obtains to possess and use the leased property is under the protection of law. Neither third persons nor the lessor (the owner) of the property may violate it. Even where the ownership of the leased property has changed hands, the new owner must respect the lawful rights of the lessee within the effective period of the lease.

A contract of lease has a wide application from the point of view of our country's socialist construction and the daily life of the people. [The lease] is commonly [used] between juristic persons, between citizens, and between juristic persons and citizens. It plays an important role in fulfilling production and work tasks and enriching the material and spiritual life of the people.

2. The Historical Development of the Contract of Lease

The lease relation is a kind of embodiment of commodity relationships, and it is a kind of property circulation relationship that came into independent existence after commodity relationships had gradually developed. Under the feudal system that existed for many thousands of years in our country, land—the basic means of production—whether it belonged to the feudal state or to private person—the landlords—was leased to the peasants, who had no land or had only a little land, for cultivation in a tenancy relationship. Marx pointed out that "possession of rent was the economic form by which the ownership of land was realized." [*Capital*] The feudal landlords and despotic gentry, through leases of land, not only put their tenants in a position of personal dependence, but also by means of the feudal land lease, they obtained the benefits of the ownership rights to the land. They engaged in an extreme degree of economic exploitation. In our country, as early as the Qin Dynasty, there were provisions in the Qin Code about feudal land lease. In the subsequent Tang and Song codes, there were also such provisions. In the Song Dynasty most land tenancy agreements had concrete provisions about the actual amount of exploitation of rent: "The owner of the field gets half, the cultivator gets his half" system of division or "the 4–6 system [the landlord gets four-tenths]." There were other systems for setting the amount of the rent.

In the feudal society of our country there were also leases by which the houses owned by officials, temples, and private individuals were leased. For instance, in the "Bequeathed Records of Yan-Yi" of the Song Dynasty, it is recorded that in the second month of the first year of Zhihe, "There was severe rain and snow, [the emperor] called the high officials of the empire privately to consider carefully public and private house rents and to release three days [of rent?]." In the late Qing Dynasty the development of leases in the large cities along the coast reflected the historical background of the semifeudal and semicolonial society. Taking Shanghai as an example, after the Opium Wars, the imperialists, on the basis of unequal treaties, obtained treaty rights to trade, reside, and to lease land, and construct buildings in particularly designated areas. Under the so-called land charter, they monopolized the lands within the boundaries of the lease under the guise of leases, and not only restricted the original landowners from leasing to Chinese, but also provided that the leases to foreigners could not be terminated nor the rent be raised. After obtaining "eternal lease rights" to the land, the foreign businessmen and adventurers took advantage of the flow of Chinese into the leased territory and their pressing need for housing, and the soaring prices of land; [they] leased land or the buildings they had constructed at high prices and obtained amazingly exploitative income.

In capitalist societies, the French Civil Code divides contracts of lease into two categories: contracts of lease of property and contracts of lease of labor. These two categories can further be divided into leases of houses and leases of furniture, leases of agricultural land, the hire of servants and of laborers, leases of transportation on land or water, contracts of hire for work, contracts of hire for taking care of and feeding domestic animals, and other kinds of contracts of hire. Such extensive scope of the contract of hire [lease], on the one hand, reflects the level of the development of a commodity economy at that time and the situation of the construction of the legal system by encompassing different civil law relations, such as work contracts and contracts for transportation, all within the limits of the contract of hire. On the other hand, recognizing the contract of labor as a contract of hire reflects cap-italism's making everything (including labor) into a commodity.

The German Civil Code of imperialist times, which took effect in 1900, made detailed classifications and rules for the civil law relations in the Obligations part. The contract of work and labor, along with the contract of lease, became separate and independent. The lease relationship contract was confined to the scope of the use by the lessee of the leased property. According to whether the lessee has the right to take the benefits arising from the leased property, contracts of lease are divided into leases for the use of property and leases for taking the benefits of the leased property.

After the Liberation of our country, according to the Land Reform Law of the People's Republic of China promulgated by the Central People's Government, we carried out a land reform of land throughout the entire country, confiscating the land of landlords and condemning the surplus lands of rich peasants, and, thus, eliminating feudal land-lease relations. Since the nationwide agricultural cooperativisation, there have essentially been no lease relations for land. With respect to housing leases, which had commonly existed in cities, on the one hand, there have been contracts of lease regarding state owned housing between the administrative agencies for housing and tenants, and, on the other, contracts of lease executed regarding privately owned houses. After the socialist reform of the capitalist ownership lease relationship of privately owned houses, the lease of private houses that still exist in society is the expression of the relation between citizens of each supplying the other's needs, mutual benefit, and mutual assistance. In addition, there have been leases of production equipment and tools, articles of daily necessity, and recreational facilities. These kinds of relations expand constantly, and they are not of an exploitative nature. They play an active role in advancing the development of production and facilitating the life of the people.

II
CONTRACTS OF LEASE FOR ORDINARY PROPERTY

1. The Definition and Establishment of Contracts of Lease for Ordinary Property

Contracts of lease for ordinary property are agreements entered into by two parties for the lease of property other than houses. Such contracts of lease have a wide application, and the lessor and lessee can agree between themselves for various leases according to the different use value and special characteristics of the leased objects. They are used to meet their temporary needs that come up in the course of production and work, or to meet certain needs that arise in the daily life of individual citizens. Under our country's socialist system, there are numerous leases involving production equipment and tools, the means of transportation, sites, films, books and other objects of culture and recreation, household items, etc. These kinds of leases are increasing in number. The Economic Contracts Law of the People's Republic of China has specific provisions about contracts for the lease of property. In recent years, in response to the demands of economic construction and daily life, there have appeared some juristic persons specifically engaged in the leasing business within the country. There have also been some leasing companies that were Sino-foreign joint ventures. These all show that contracts of lease have great utility.

As to the forms selected for contracts of lease for ordinary property, if the law requires written form, this requirement must be observed. If the law does not have a clear provision, it is better to use written form for important contracts of lease. Other contracts of lease may be oral.

2. The Essential Content of the Contract of Lease of Ordinary Property

A lease contract of ordinary property should include provisions regarding the property to be leased, the rent, and the term of the lease.

The objects of a lease contract may be means of production or means of daily life. They may be movables or immovables. But leased property must be specified and not consumable. Also, leased property must be [property] that is permitted by law to circulate as rentable property. If the property the parties have made the object of their lease contract is that whose circulation is prohibited or limited by law, the parties not only cannot realize their objective, but will have to bear the corresponding legal liability.

Rent (the price of the lease) is an indispensable element of the contract of lease. It is usually calculated in terms of money, and in certain cases in kind. No matter what form it takes, it must be paid and received in the amounts provided by law. Where the law does not set the rent, the parties must reach agreement on the principle of fairness and reasonableness. The rent may not be unreasonably high nor unreasonably low.

The term is also an essential element of a lease contract. The term of the contract includes two types: a lease with an uncertain term and a lease with a fixed term. In the former, the effective term of the contract is the period of use of the leased object. In the latter, the term is a period specified by the parties for the use of the leased object such as years, seasons, months, weeks, ten days, days, hours, etc.

Where the law, regulation, or the agreement of parties requires that there must be security, this security constitutes another essential provision of the contract of lease. That is, the contract becomes effective only when the lessee furnishes the agreed property or an amount of money as security to the lessor.

3. The Rights and Duties of Parties to Lease Contracts for Ordinary Property

(1) The major duties of the lessor

(i) Deliver the leased property to the lessee for the latter's use. This is the most basic requirement of a contract of lease for property. It is the essential duty of the lessor. If, after the making of the contract, the lessor does not perform this duty to transfer, the lessee has the right to request the court to force the lessor to perform or to rescind the contract and be compensated for losses by the lessor.

The property transferred by the lessor must conform to the standard provided [by law] or agreed to (as to quantity, quality, and specifications). Where there is no such standard provided or agreed on in advance, [the leased property] must meet the usual requirements for use as a standard. If the leased property has hidden defects, the lessor should advise the lessee about them in advance. If the property tendered by the lessor violates the above requirements, the lessee has the right to demand a reduction in the rent or rescission of the contract and damages.

(ii) [Bear] responsibility for repairing the leased property. Since the lessor is the owner of the leased property and has the obligation to ensure the lessee's use [of it], he must bear the responsibility of repairing the leased property unless it is otherwise provided by law or agreed upon between the parties. If the quality of the leased property does not correspond with the requirements, and this affects the lessee's normal use [of it], the lessee has the right to demand repair or replacement of the leased object in order to assure its use. If it has caused injury, the lessee has a right to demand damages and payment of the penalty for breach of contract. If the lessor delays in performing his duty to repair or refuses to replace the leased

property, the lessee has the right to repair it, and the expense shall be borne by the lessor. He also has the right to rescind the contract. Injurious consequences are the responsibility of the lessor.

(iii) Return the property put up as security at the termination of the lease. The security given at the time of contracting by the lessee serves as an assurance of performance of the duties under the lease. When the lessee has performed and the contract of the lease has come to an end, the lessor must immediately return the security to the lessee. Only when the lessee has not performed his contractual duty may the lessor exercise his right of lien over the security.

(2) The major obligations of the lessee

(i) [Meet] the requirement of paying rent to the lessor. Payment of the rent is the essential obligation of the lessee. If the lessee did not pay the amount provided [by law], or agreed upon, or pay within the time [set by the contract], the lessor has the right to demand the unpaid rent and to rescind the contract, and damages.

(ii) Use the leased property properly as required by the contract. A lessee has the obligation to use the leased property in the way prescribed by the contract. If the contract does not provide how the property is to be used, the lessee shall not use the leased property [in ways] contrary to its nature and [normal] use. The lessee should also take appropriate care of and check the leased property, including keeping the property in good repair, maintaining it, and not cause it to be damaged. Without the authorization of the lessor, the lessee shall not sublet the leased property. If the lessee violates the above obligations, the lessor has the right, according to the consequences [of the violation], to demand the repairing of the property without compensation or to rescind the contract and obtain damages.

(iii) Return the original leased property at the conclusion of the lease. According to the contract of lease, the leased property which the lessee uses temporarily is a specified item. Consequently, the lessee should perform his duty of returning the leased property on time after the term. If the lessee does not perform his duty to return, the lessor is entitled to demand supplementary rent for the period of delay and the penalty for breach of contract. If the lessee has, on his own, made alterations to the property, the lessor has the right to demand [that the property] be restored to its original condition or to damages. If the leased property has been lost through the lessee's fault so that it cannot be returned, the lessee is liable for damages.

III
THE LEASE OF BUILDINGS

1. General Discussion of Lease of Buildings

Contracts for the lease of buildings are contracts in which leased property is a building (particularly a dwelling). Under this kind of contract, the lessor must tender the leased building to the lessee for his use and the lessee must pay the rent on time. Moreover, he must return the building to the lessor when the lease expires.

The lease of a building is one of the contracts of lease. It has the legal features of other contracts of lease. It is bilateral, nongratuitous, and promissory. During the term, the right of possession of the leased object is transferred by the lessor; the right to use [the property] is given to the lessee, etc. Contracts for the lease of buildings are contracts of lease that occupy a very special position and have great importance. Their application extends to include both the lease of buildings by juristic persons for production and work and the lease of houses for the use of workers and other members of the masses to live in. The civil codes of many countries have special provisions in this area.

The leases of buildings that existed before Liberation in the semicolonial, semifeudal society of our country can be divided into two general categories: one is the lease wherein the feudal bureaucratic-capitalist and feudal despotic gentry are the lessors. By using their reactionary political power, they forced the lessees to accept unequal terms. These [leases] are feudal, bureaucratic-capitalist usurious exploitation. The other kind of lease is that in which the private individual house owner was the lessor. They formed lease agreements with their lessees on the basis of free negotiation. The rents they collected generally represented the social average profits. Therefore, this kind of lease relation reflected a kind of capitalist exploitation relation.

After the founding of the New China, the People's Democratic Government confiscated the building properties owned by the bureaucratic capitalists, enemies and puppet traitors, and other counter-revolutionary elements and returned them to the property of the whole people through revolutionary measures and a whole set of policies, laws, and decrees. Feudal and bureaucratic exploitation were banned. Moreover, the foreign building construction and leasing businesses were outlawed. At the same time, there was the planned construction of a large number of new state owned buildings that were rented to residents. This established socialist lease relationships for housing. As to the capitalistic lease of buildings by private individuals, after the basic reform of individual capitalist industry and commerce was largely completed, the socialist reform of the rental of buildings by private individuals was scheduled. The state carried out socialist reform on the rentals of privately owned buildings that were leased out that reached a certain number and area. Buildings that came within the scope of reform, after the full payment of fixed interest or rent to the owners, became property of the whole people. They were still rented to the original lessees.

2. Leases of State Owned Buildings

(1) The fundamental principles of contracts of lease for state owned buildings

Our country's state owned buildings are socialist property of the whole people. The lease contracts for state owned buildings must implement two basic principles.

(i) Rational allocation and effective use of state owned buildings. The ultimate aim of socialist production is uninterruptedly to meet the ever increasing needs of the people in material and cultural life. Among these, the need for housing is one of the most important. This can be seen from the fact that in our country the staff and workers and most of the residents in urban areas have to make use of the lease of state owned buildings to solve the problem of residence. At the same time, many government organs, social groups, institutions, and enterprises have to use state owned buildings as their places of production and work, through signing of contracts of lease. Thus, to meet the demands of both production and daily life, the lessors of state owned buildings must be reasonable in the allocation and use of the buildings, and ensure that the buildings are fully used. This principle should be carried out in all stages of the leasing contract—its execution, modification, and termination.

(ii) Gradually carry out "use rent to support the building." The state owned buildings in our country will still appear in the form of commodities during the comparatively long period of the establishment of socialism. Theoretically, the total sum of the rent to be collected from leasing a state owned building should equal the selling price of the same state owned building. That is, in speaking of the total rent to be collected for renting state owned buildings, the rent received must include taxes, administrative expenses, repair and renovation expenses, depreciation charges, and the statutory interest on the investment. But the state owned buildings that are furnished by our country to citizens for housing purposes are, at the same time, a kind of welfare. In order to get the rent from the lease of state owned buildings to reach the standard discussed above, and implement the principle of "use rent to support the building," in the process of reforming the management of buildings, there is a plan to adjust the rent gradually.

(2) The execution and modification of contracts for the lease of state owned buildings.

The lease of state owned buildings includes those buildings directly managed by the state agencies of various levels charged with the management of buildings, and those state buildings leased out on their own by enterprises, organizations, institutions, governmental agencies, social groups, and other units of ownership by the whole people. In the former situation, the state agencies that administer state owned buildings at various levels are the lessors. Certain units and individual citizens are the lessees. In the latter, the concerned units are the lessors and the lessees are mostly workers in those units and their family members.

The execution of the contract for the lease of state owned buildings is based on the issuance by the unit that administers the building of a building allocation certificate in accordance with the allocation plan. The lessee then executes a lease with the lessor on the basis of the certificate. The contract then becomes effective. The lessee then obtains the right to use the leased building. Any unit or individual that has not obtained a lease to a building may not forcibly, on the basis of any excuse, occupy a state owned building. The housing administrative agencies or other competent units have the power to order the one occupying forcibly to vacate within a fixed time period, and, upon receiving possession of the building, to impose a fine. If the one occupying forcibly does not move out within the time limit, the agency or units may bring an action in the people's court to have the matter taken care of.

After the lease of a state owned building has been executed, it may be modified when certain circumstances arise. The modifications may be a change of the subject or the object of the lease or both of them. Changes of lessors after the execution of a lease are comparatively rare. Generally, they occur when there is a merger, division, cancellation, or dissolution of a juristic person (the lessor). Changes in the lessee are comparatively more frequent—most often because the lessees of different state owned buildings exchange or transfer buildings they rent. This sort of change must be voluntary and requires the permission of the lessors. Sometimes, for the requirements of work, or because of the increase or decrease of the number of family members, or changes in marital or family relations, or moving [necessitated by] capital construction [which requires] the demolition [of the leased building], etc., there may be modifications in the lease relationship as to the number of rooms to be leased, the area, facilities (utilities), and even revision of the location.

The above modifications are all changes of the original contract for a lease of state owned buildings. After the parties have reached an agreement, the lessor will immediately modify the original contract.

(3) The rights and duties of the parties to a lease contract for state owned buildings

(i) The major obligations of the lessor. The lessor should turn over the leased building to the lessee for the latter's use at the time required by the contract. The lessor should also bear the responsibility of completely maintaining the leased building and its equipment in order to ensure the normal resident's peaceful use [of the building]. The lessor must, according to the standards of maintenance and repairing, examine and repair the building at regular intervals. Where there is some dangerous situation in the leased building, it should be repaired immediately. If the lessor has not performed this obligation, or has performed it improperly through his fault, so that the lessee or third person suffers injury to person or property, the lessor must be liable for damages to the injured party.

(ii) The major duties of the lessee. The lessee must, according to the provision of the contract, pay rent to the lessor. The amount of rent is generally fixed according to the standards for rent set by housing administrative agencies in various cities. [Cf. "Standards for Rents of Public Multi-Story and One Story Buildings of the City of Beijing." 1979.] Rent should normally be paid monthly. No delay is allowed without cause. If the lessee defaults in the payment for a long time, the lessor has the right to demand reimbursement and to be paid the penalty fee or to terminate the lease contract.

The lessee is also obligated to take good care of and protect properly the leased state owned buildings and equipment. He shall not make wrongful use of, or pull down, or make any change [in the building]. Where there is a violation of this obligation by the lessee, and, as a result of that violation, the building or attached equipment is lost or damaged, the lessor has the right to demand that the lessee restore the original condition and pay damages.

3. Contracts for the Lease of Privately Owned Buildings

(1) The nature of the contracts of lease of privately owned buildings and the principles of the state for adjusting them

After the founding of the New China, how to treat the extensive private ownership and lease relations of buildings in cities was a very serious problem. At that time, there were differences in private ownership of buildings in the cities, as compared with the ownership of land in the countryside prior to land reform. The lease of buildings by landlords was also different from the lease of land by landlords because with land it is a natural thing. When a landlord occupied land and then leased it to a peasant, this formed a kind of personal dependency, a feudal exploitative relationship. But a building is a thing produced by labor. It is a constructed object which [results] from investment by the owner of the building. The owner of the building had spent money (through investment) having the land levelled and the building erected. If the owner leases the building, he still has uninterruptedly to pay for maintenance and repair of the building. The rent which the owner collects from the tenant is like the interest or profit from the owner's investment. Basically it is a form of capitalist exploitation. [Cf. Xinhua News Agency Letter Box "Regarding the nature of and policies towards the ownership and lease of privately-owned buildings in the Urban Area," *People's Daily*, August 12, 1949.] It is a special form of loan capital. As Marx pointed out in *Capital*, "A lease is a form of a price for the use of buildings; it is a loan of fixed capital. During the period of the lease, the owner will receive regular interest payments in the form of rent, for the building, and, moreover, part of the price of the fixed capital, that has already been consumed. The unconsumed part of the fixed capital will still come back to the hands of the owner in the form of the actual thing at the end of the term."

Immediately after Liberation, considering the major revolutionary task, the principles which the state used in adjusting the lease relationships of privately owned buildings were: (1) mutual benefit of the landlord and the tenant: causing the owner and the lessee each to receive benefits from the lease relation; (2) to supervise the maintenance and repair of the leased buildings to ensure the security of the residents; (3) gradually to eliminate the intermediate exploitation, that is, to outlaw the sublease by the sublessor and real estate brokers; and (4) according to the Party's policy of utilizing, restricting, and reforming, to create conditions for the elimination of the capitalist leasing relationship.

Although there have continued to be leases of privately owned buildings and houses from the socialist reform of privately owned buildings until now, the leased buildings and houses are no longer capital, and the rents no longer constitute the profits of capitalists. It is thus clear that these lease relationships concerning privately owned buildings are no longer capitalist in nature, but are socialist lease relationships of mutual aid and assistance by which citizens exchange what they have for what they need but do not have.

In December 1983, the State Council promulgated Provisions for Administering Privately Owned Houses in Cities. According to these provisions and the related methods, the principles of the state for adjusting the contracts of lease for privately owned buildings are:

(i) Mutual benefit of the landlord and tenant. That is, the lessee obtains a house to live in and the lessor can obtain some advantage. Therefore, one who resides in the building and does not pay rent, or one who only collects the rent and does not repair the building, are both in violation of this principle.

(ii) Fairness and reasonableness. The rights and duties of the parties should be determined through fair negotiations between the parties on a basis of equality. The rent should normally not exceed the depreciation value of the leased building, the repair and maintenance expense, taxes, and the interest to the bank on the investment. It is prohibited for any lessor to take advantage the dire needs of the lessee to lease the building at an unusually high rent and demand other extra fees.

(iii) Unity and mutual help. The parties to a contract of lease no longer stand opposed to one another so they should carry on the spirit of mutual help in the use and repair of the leased building and solve difficulties by joint negotiations.

(2) The rights and duties of the parties to lease contracts involving privately owned buildings

(i) The payment of rent. It is the major obligation of the lessee to pay rent. The amount of rent should be determined according to the standards for rent set by the state housing administrative agencies. If there are no such standards for rent, the parties can determine their rent through fair negotiation with reference to the actual rent levels in the area on the basis of fairness and reasonableness. The time for the payment of rent should also be fixed according to the relevant regulations or through agreement. Normally rent is paid monthly.

If the lessee, in violation of the contract, delays in paying the rent for a certain period of time or delays in paying it, the lessor has the right to demand that the lessee pay on time. If the lessee does not pay for six months, the lessor, in addition to having the right to demand payment of the amount owed, can terminate the lease and repossess the building.

(ii) Appropriate use of the leased building. Appropriate use of the building includes: (1) [The lessee himself] must use the building. It is a violation of the lessor's rights if the lessee sublets [the premises], or transfers, lends, or permits another person [to use them] without the lessor's consent, and the lessor has the

right [in such a case] to terminate the lease. (2) [The lessee] should use the building according to the rules of law and the terms of the contract. If the lessee uses the building or house in violation of the law or the contract (for example, he carries on illegal activities, injures the public interest, etc.), or does not use the building in accordance with the lease, he shall be liable for the violation of the contract and bear the legal consequences. (3) [The lessee] must take care of the leased building. Any damage caused either intentionally or negligently by the lessee to the building or equipment and any alteration to the building by the lessee without the permission of the lessor constitute improper use of the leased property. When such things happen, the lessor has the right to demand that the lessee repair and restore the original condition and pay damages.

(iii) Timely repair of buildings. Unless the parties have specifically agreed otherwise, it is the duty of the lessor to repair the building (this does not [refer to] repair of the interior of the building). The regulations for adjusting lease relationships and the standard contracts almost all have this sort of provision, and it is the custom of the masses through long usage. Some cities provide that "the lessor is responsible for major repairs and the lessee for minor repairs" and "outside repairs are for the lessor, inside for the lessee." This is the embodiment of the rule discussed above.

If the lessor does not have the strength [resources] to make the repairs, they can be made together with the lessee. If the lessor does not perform the obligation of making repairs on time because he was absent from the place [where the leased building was located] or some such reason, or he refused to perform this duty, the lessee, for his safety of residence, may make the repairs for [the lessor], and the expenses expended on the repair may be deducted from the rent or be repaid by the lessor.

If the lessor has failed promptly and conscientiously to repair, and this causes injury to the person or property of the lessee or a third party, he is liable for damages to the injured party.

(iv) Payment of taxes. Taxes on buildings are imposed on the basis of the ownership of the buildings. Unless the contract provides otherwise, it is the obligation of the owner (the lessor) to pay the tax.

(3) Termination of the contract of lease for privately owned buildings

A lease contract for privately owned buildings can be terminated for the following reasons:

(i) The term of the lease has expired. When the term of a lease with a determined duration expires, the contract originally agreed on should be considered as having come to an end.

(ii) In a contract of lease without a definite term, because of the requirements of his own, the lessor needs to repossess the leased premises and requests termination, or when the lessee gives [a notification of] termination to the lessor.

(iii) When the ownership of a leased building is transferred it is necessary to execute a new contract of lease. Even though the above reasons can result in the termination of the lease, if this involves the lessee vacating the building, [the lessor] must notify the lessee in advance and give the lessee the necessary time until he finds a place to live.

25 Loans for Consumption and Loans for Use

I
GENERAL DISCUSSION OF THE LOAN FOR CONSUMPTION

1. The General Concept of the Loan for Consumption

A loan for consumption is an agreement by which the lender transfers money or other things to the ownership of the borrower, and the borrower, within a certain period of time, returns to the lender the same amount of money or things of the same quantity and quality.

A loan is a type of obligation that is commonly seen. They are very significant as a means in assuring the production needs of the producers of commodities, and in solving various practical problems of the people in their daily life.

A loan for consumption has the following characteristics:

First, a loan contract is a contract for the transfer of the ownership rights (or the right to manage and control) of the property that is lent. By means of the loan contract, the borrower obtains the property that is lent. His purpose is not only to possess and use it, but mainly to dispose of it in order to meet his economic needs.

Second, a loan contract is a real contract. That is, in addition to the two parties reaching an agreement, there still must be delivery of the property that is lent. Only then is the contract effective. Whether or not our country's Economic Contract Law provides that a loan for use is a real contract is a matter over which scholars are not in agreement. We tend to believe that it can be regarded as a promissory contract.

Third, a loan for consumption is a unilateral obligation. Delivery of the property that is lent is a condition for the effectiveness of the loan contract. Consequently, the contract is already formed. There is only an obligation on the part of the borrower to make a repayment. The lender has no reciprocal obligation.

Fourth, the loan contract may be a gratuitous contract and it may also be a nongratuitous contract. Whether a loan is gratuitous or not is determined in some cases by law, in some cases by the agreement of the parties.

Fifth, the property that is lent must be something that can be used and consumed. That is, it must be something that can be replaced. Otherwise the borrower would not be able to fulfill his obligation to repay.

Loan contracts for consumption can be [classified into] different types based on different points of view. The most common [classification] is to divide the loans into loans of money and loans of things, according to the object of the contract.

2. The Historical Evolution of Loans for Consumption

Like contracts of sale and lease, loans for consumption are also the result of a commodity economy. For thousands of years loan relations have been determined by law and have constituted one of the earliest contracts of mankind. The ancient Babylonian Code of Hammurabi presents to us a precious historical record in this regard. The loan also occupied an important position in ancient Roman Law. It not only provided many rules regarding the legal forms, the classification, the rights and duties of the parties, the handling of violations of the contract, etc., but also reflected the historical changes in the loan contract. Moreover, out of them a number of contract theories were drawn. The subsequent Napoleonic Code, which carried on the tradition of Roman law, progressed somewhat in establishing the basic principles of the loan contract. At the same time, in accordance with the demands of the bourgeoisie, it adjusted certain relationships among them, and thus established the general structure for the law of loans in the legal systems of all the continental countries. The loan section of the Japanese, German, and other countries' civil codes were all built on this foundation. They only reflect the special characteristics of the historical background of each country, and of the times, as well as the demands of monopolistic capitalism. The loan law of ancient Chinese law is a mixture of capitalist and feudal loan laws.

From an historical viewpoint, usury is a form of loan. "Usury capital, is a special form of interest-producing capital and was suitable for the economy in which small producers, owner-peasants, and small craftsmen predominated." "Usury knows no limit except the capacity of the one needing money to assume liability or his capacity to resist." [Marx-Engels] The above statement points out the economic conditions from which usury arises. It also outlines the principal features of usury.

In capitalist societies, the circulation of loan capital is mainly conducted through banks. And this creates a new form of loan activity. With the uninterrupted increase in the use of money and banks, capitalist credit became more and more the most important and most frequently seen loan. It occupies the first place among capitalist loans.

Starting with the October Revolution, a new loan relationship, together with a new law of loans, appeared on the world stage. In the more than half century since then, with the advance of human history, this new loan relationship and new kind of law of loans also have been continually perfected. The socialist loan, while keeping the appropriate parts of the traditional forms, has also, in order to meet the requirements of the new economic rules, increased a loan relationship new in human history. The subjects of a socialist loan relationship are juristic persons, citizens, and the state as a special subject, based on a unity of material interests. The main purpose of these loans is to meet the needs of social production and the needs of the people's daily life. The exploiting relationship which had existed in loans for thousands of years was resolutely rejected and the socialist principle of mutual help and cooperation became the fundamental principle of loans. Analyzing socialist loans by looking at their origins, the range of their use, the amount of the loans, and their effect on the national economy, credits issued by the state bank are the most important form for all of them; they are under the unified administration of the state bank and this brings about widespread state involvement in, and supervision over, loan activities. In a certain sense, socialist loans most importantly use the state-credit as the representative loan.

In our country, the state bank acts as an independent subject of civil law and forms equal mutually beneficial loan relations with other subjects of civil law. It also serves as state fiscal control organization. According to law, it has the right to conduct complete credit supervision over juristic persons that obtain payments, on the economic activities of cooperative economic organizations, or citizens. By means of these sorts of supervisory measures, it can assure the reasonable use of capital, prevent the negative use of the law of prices, and further the development of our country's commodity economy.

3. Essential Content of the Contract of Loan

(1) Return of the borrowed thing

The obligation of the borrower to return refers to returning an item of the same kind, quantity, and quality as the borrowed item to the lender. It is not [to return] the original borrowed property. If the borrowed property had some hidden defects at the time of contracting, and the borrower did not, at the time, ask the lender to adjust or replace the defective borrowed property, the borrower may return things with the same kinds of defects. "The same kind of defect" refers either to the actual form of the thing as the standard or to the price of the thing as a standard or both. If, for objective reasons, the borrower has no way to return an actual thing, he may make a substitute return based on the actual price of the thing.

As to the time and place for returning, if there is a contract provision, this should be followed. When there is no provision regarding the time, the borrower has the obligation to return the property at any time [on demand] (however, when it is necessary, there may be an extension); when there is no provision as to the place for return, [the matter] should be handled according to the related general provisions of civil law.

As to the return of a loan of money, because of the special characteristics and function of the money loan, the borrower, in returning the amount of money lent, has to abide by the provisions of the relevant separate legal rules.

(2) The payment of interest

In any loan for consumption, the law or the agreement may provide for interest to be received by the lender from the borrower. Under such circumstances, the payment of interest becomes an essential obligation of the borrower. To maintain a normal order of loans, the law normally clearly sets the upper limit of the interest that is to be paid by borrowers. The parties may adjust the rate of interest within this limit. Any agreement to exceed this upper limit is illegal. When there is a provision regarding the payment of interest in the loan contract, but there is no provision for the interest rate, it must be decided according to the rates set by law.

(3) Responsibility for compensating the borrower for his special damages and expenditures

Special damages refers to those that are caused by the hidden defects of the borrowed property which are capable of harming the borrower, and concerning which the lender negligently or intentionally failed to notify the borrower, thereby injuring the borrower. The special expenditures of the borrower refers to unusual amounts expended by the borrower during the term of the loan that the borrower had to pay to preserve the borrowed property, when, owing to an emergency, the borrower could not notify the lender.

II
THE CONTRACT OF DEBT

1. The General Concept of the Contract of Debt

The contract of debt, also called the contract of credit, is a contract of debt which the bank or credit society acting as the lender makes with the borrower. According to the contract of debt, the lender must lend a certain sum of money to the borrower and the borrower must repay the same sum of money within a specified time with interest (it also may be without interest).

The legal characteristics of the contract of debt are:

(1) The lender who is one of the subjects of the contract of debt can only be a bank or credit society

The other party, that is the borrower, is an enterprise of property of the whole people with the status of a juristic person, or an institution, and also includes urban individually managed households which have management permits, are properly managed and have repayment capability, cooperative economic organizations and peasant contract households. They all may enter into debt contracts with banks and credit societies.

(2) The object of the contract of debt is money

In our country it is usually the means of payment designated by law—the *ren min bi* [the official Chinese currency unit].

(3) The contract of debt must be a promissory contract

It takes effect from the day the parties agree. It is also a bilateral, nongratuitous contract. According to section 5 of the Provisions on Contracts of Debt, "The contract of debt must be in writing." Consequently, it also is a contract with a required form.

2. The Basic Principles of Forming a Contract of Debt

When the bank or credit society enters into a contract of debt with a borrower, it must do so according to the following principles:

(1) The loan is based on the plan

Banks and credit societies, in pursuing the business of lending, must act strictly in accordance with the plan. Section 3 of the Provisions for Contracts of Debt states that the parties to the loan must execute the contract in accordance with the relevant provisions of the state plan. "No unit or individual may compel a bank or credit cooperative society to execute a contract of debt and make the loan." The bank may refuse to execute a contract of debt in the case where there is no planned debt. If, because of the requirements of production, it is necessary to handle the loan outside the plan, the use of the loan must, in accordance with the use prescribed by the plan, be placed in a special fund. The bank making the loan can only sign a contract within the loan target checked and approved by the higher level bank or an already approved existing account.

(2) Emphasizing material assurance

The Provisions on Contracts of Debt provide: "The borrower who seeks a loan must have the ratio of its own capital specified by the People's Bank of China. Moreover, it must have material and property assurance for the proper assumption and use [of the loan]." If the borrower cannot meet these conditions, but there are special conditions that necessitate the loan, it may request [the loan], but it must have a guarantor who meets the requirements of the law and, with the agreement of the lender, after the announcement, of the approval of the lender's superior, it may borrow the money. Therefore, the bank and the credit society may refuse to execute a contract of debt with a borrower who does not have material security.

(3) Insisting on timely repayment

It is only when a money loan is repaid on time that it can maintain the continuity of credit and use to the fullest extent its economic benefits. Insisting on this principle, the borrower improves production and circulation, implements economic accounting, and promotes its utilization [of the law]. It has positive value in stabilizing the state's fiscal order and completely fulfilling the state plan. The essential requirements of this principle are: when the bank or credit society makes a loan there must be clear provision for repayment; the borrower must take the initiative in paying off the loan on time; the bank and credit society must help the borrower to pay back on time by means of the exercise of ordinary business and supervisory functions. When the borrower cannot repay at the appointed time, the bank and credit society will impose sanctions in accordance with the state law and the provisions of the contract.

3. The Formation and Essential Provisions of Contracts for Debt

(1) The essential provisions for forming a contract of debt and the required order for performing it

[The essentials] are: a plan and standards issued by the state for loans; all of the documentary materials required for the borrower to request the loan; the funds to be delivered and copies of the contract; the lender will verify, consider, and go through the required procedure of approval. After the above provisions have been complied with, the parties may then, according to law, execute the contract.

The contract of debt must be signed and sealed by the legally designated representatives of the parties or those with certificates from the legally designated representatives. Moreover, it must be signed and sealed with the official seal of the unit.

(2) The essential provisions of the contract of debt

The contract of debt must be in written form. The provisions which it must normally contain are: the type of loan, the use to which it will be put, the amount of the loan, the interest, the term of the loan, the sources for repayment of the loan and the manner of repayment, responsibility for breach, and other provisions agreed on by the parties.

The type of the loan, the amount, its use, and term [are as follows]. "The type of the loan" refers to what type of fund it belongs to such as agriculture, industry, commerce, capital construction, etc. "The amount" refers to the largest sum the borrower can obtain. According to circumstances, the lender may give the money at one time or on several occasions. The borrower may take less but never more. "The use" refers to the particular area within which the borrower will use the loan. The borrower can only use it for designated purposes. It cannot be transferred to some other use. "The term" is the time within which the borrower must return the loan. It may [be repaid] in advance. It may not be delayed. If there is a proper reason, and the borrower requires a change in the above provisions, in addition to there having to be agreement between the two parties, the procedures for verification and approval must be followed.

In regard to interest and the rate of interest, our country's state loans, unless the law has another provision, must all be interest-bearing. The rate of interest is set by the state uniformly and administered uniformly by the People's Bank of China. The borrower is liable to pay the interest in full and on time.

The sources for repayment and the manner of repayment [are as follows]. The borrower's sources of funds for repaying the loan must be proper. He may not violate the rules of law. The manner of repayment means whether the borrower will repay in one installment or several. If there is a provision of law, he must repay in accordance with that provision.

[The loan may have] provisions on security. If the loan relation has a guarantor participating in it, the guaranty responsibility of the guarantor must be clearly provided in the contract.

Responsibility for breach [may be provided for]. The contract of debt will usually contain a provision for responsibility for breach of contract. But after one party has breached, the responsibility must be investigated and affixed according to the Provisions for Contracts of Debt and other rules of law.

Other provisions [may be] agreed to by the parties. If the parties have other needs, after agreement, they must be clearly provided for in the contract.

4. Types of Contract of Debt

(1) The industrial and commercial contracts of debt

These are executed by the Chinese Industrial and Commercial Bank with enterprises and units of the industrial and commercial system. They are of the following types:

(i) Industrial circulating capital loan contracts, including contracts for loans of fixed amounts or amounts in excess of fixed amounts, loan contracts for winding up accounts, contracts for loans for major repairs, contracts for loans for excess inventory, contracts for loans for goods and material supply and marketing. The term for all of them is one year.

(ii) Contracts for loans for circulating capital for commercial enterprises. This includes loan contracts for the circulation of commodities, loans for purchase and sale contracts for agricultural sideline products, loan contracts for major repairs to commercial enterprises, etc. The term is also one year.

(iii) Fixed capital loans. These are loan contracts that are entered into for the purpose of solving the problem of the unit needing money to develop latent strength for innovations, for reform, and fully to make use of its production capacity. This sort of loan is a type of investment. Previously there were gratuitous allocations by the Ministry of Finance. Beginning in 1979 the plan changed to bank loans. This is an important reform of our economy. At present, the device used by banks is a medium- to short-term loan, including generally two types of loans—the medium- to short-term loan and a special type. The time for repayment is generally limited to from one to three years. It may not exceed five years.

(2) Agricultural credit loans

These are executed by the Chinese Agricultural Bank and credit cooperatives with agricultural production units and peasants. They are divided as follows:

(i) Commune and team agricultural credit contracts. These include loan contracts for production expenses incurred by communes and teams, loans for production equipment, credit union support loans, etc.

(ii) Commune and team agricultural enterprise loans. These include loan contracts for loans for commune and team agricultural enterprise production revolving-fund loans, production equipment loans, special project loans, etc.

(iii) State managed agricultural enterprise loan contracts. These include loan contracts for loans to state managed agricultural enterprises for amounts beyond their fixed capital, temporary loans, loans for winding up, loans for equipment, etc.

(iv) Loan contracts for individual peasants. These include state loans to peasants in disaster areas for grain rations, short-term loans from credit societies to individual peasants. The latter help the peasants solve difficulties in their lives, and also help the peasants solve difficulties in production management, as well as problems in household sideline business and production on individual plots.

The term for the four types of loan contracts listed above is basically the same as in the case of industrial and commercial loans of the same type. The interest rate is lower than in the case of industrial and commercial loans. The interest on the loans of banks to credit societies is sometimes less than the interest that the credit society gets on its revolving amount with the bank.

(3) Contracts for capital construction loans

These are executed between the Chinese People's Construction Bank with capital construction units.

Previously, investment in capital construction in our country was handled by allocation by the Finance Ministry. In August 1979, the State Council decided on the method of bank loans for handling capital construction investment. In November 1980, it decided that, beginning in 1981, all enterprises operated under independent accounting with the capacity to repay would be changed from capital construction allocations to loans.

In carrying out capital construction loans, persistently using lending, paying back, and interest, and using rewards and punishments, are all useful in resisting and changing blind struggles over projects, struggles over investments, struggles over materials and equipment, not to speak of accounting, and drawing out a long battleline over capital construction.

The capital construction loan contract must include [in its terms]: the entire amount of the loan, the use [to which it will be put], the term, the target for when the loan would be used, the repayment plan, etc. The time of repayment is calculated in the light of the time of construction and the time for repayment. The principal and interest run from the time the contract is signed until it is all paid off. The longest period for heavy industry projects is fifteen years. Other projects may not exceed ten years. Small-scale, piecemeal projects may not exceed five years. In capital construction loans the interest is calculated from the day of commencement of payments [of the loan] to according the number of years and the amount [of money] actually used. The rate of interest is, in general, three percent. If the loan has not been settled within the time provided, the interest will be doubled on the portion that is overdue. If capital construction loan funds are diverted, then double interest is added to the diverted portion.

5. The Rights and Duties of the Parties

According to the Provisions for Contracts of Debt the most important rights and duties of the lender (a bank or credit society) are:

(1) After the making of the loan, the lender has the right to receive interest according to the state's uniform rules for interest

If the borrower does not use the loan in accordance with the use specified by law or agreement, the lender has the right to demand to get back in advance all or part of the loan and to cease making payments of the loan.

(2) The lender has the right to investigate the borrower's use of the loan; to acquaint himself with the borrower's carrying out of the plan, his management, and administration; the activity of his property, and the storage of goods and materials, etc.

If he discovers that the borrower's use entails loss or waste, or that he is using the contract of debt to engage in illegal activities, the lender has the right to the return of the loan.

(3) When the borrower does not have the ability to repay the debt, the lender has the right to deal with the borrower as if it were a loan secured by his goods, materials, and property

Moreover, he may get compensation according to the procedure for inventorying property and discharging obligations. If there is a guarantor who has offered security, the lender may dispose of the guarantor's property and be compensated according to law.

(4) The lender must tender the loan on time

If the loan is not tendered on time, through the lender's fault, he must pay the penalty for breach according to the bank's rules for penalty interest. After the contract of debt has been formed, if there is no legally provided rule, he may not change or cancel the contract at will.

The most important rights and duties of the borrower are:

(i) The borrower has the right, according to the use provided in the contract of debt, to use [the loan] on his own. Moreover, [he has the right] to make a profit according to law. But he must use the loan for the use provided by law and contract. He may not divert it to some other use. He may not use the loan to create injurious waste or carry on illegal activities.

(ii) He will repay the loan on time and pay interest according to the contract. If he does not repay on time, he bears legal responsibility. If, because of a legally authorized reason, he is unable to repay on time, he may negotiate changes in the contract or escape liability.

(iii) He will accept the investigation and supervision of the lender. The borrower will, upon the demand of the lender, promptly present plans, statistics, and a financial accounting statement, as well as materials, in order to assure the reasonable use of the loan and its repayment.

Prior to the execution of the contract, upon the proposal of one party or the agreement of both, security may be offered by a guarantor. But the guarantor who offers to guarantee the performance of the debt contract must have sufficient property to take the place of the borrower in repaying the loan. When the borrower does not repay on time, he and the guarantor are jointly liable to repay principle and interest. After the guarantor has paid off the obligation for the borrower, he has the right to be reimbursed by the borrower.

III
THE LEGAL RELATION OF SETTLING ACCOUNTS

1. The General Concept of the Legal Relation of Settling Accounts

Settlement of accounts is a legal relation between a bank and a juristic person, based on the account which the juristic person has in the bank, in which the bank receives payments and settles obligations for juristic persons.

According to our country's law, economic transactions between juristic persons, except for those where the law allows payment in cash, must be carried on by transferring accounts through state banks or credit corporations (hereafter all called banks) in which the juristic persons keep their accounts. Therefore, it is required that all juristic persons must immediately deposit all their capital, except the limited sum which the juristic persons may keep in cash, in a bank. The banks, through settlement, either by transferring accounts or by cash, will, in a timely and accurate way, accept payments from and make payments to the juristic persons, and, in this way, assure the normal needs of production and circulation.

To establish the legal relation of settling accounts, the juristic person applies to the bank according to the rules. After the bank (in the capacity of a state agency) has examined [the application] and the parties agree, the [relationship] is established. After this, the bank opens an account for the juristic person. Then the juristic person can accept or make payments through the account and carry on settlement of accounts. Between the juristic person and the bank (hereafter referred to as the depositor and the settlor), the following rights-duty relationship is created.

The obligations of the depositor. The depositor must deposit all its funds in the bank as material assurance for the settlement of accounts. The customer shall not lend its account [to others]. It is also not permitted for any loan relation with a third person to arise. Any transaction involving a sum above a certain fixed amount must be settled through the bank. Unless there is a state [law] provision, [the juristic person] is not permitted to make payments or to receive payments. It may not pay in advance, sell on credit, or delay payment. It must pay a fee to the bank for the settlement service. The rights of the depositor are to demand that the settlor make and accept payments, and to receive interest according to the statutory interest rate.

The obligations of the bank. The bank shall pay debts on time for the depositor within the balance of the account. Unless there is an express provision of law to the contrary, payments by the bank for the depositor must be agreed to by the depositor. The bank must receive any payments which the depositor obtains under an economic contract which it enters into, and must pay damages for any injury (harm) to the customer resulting from mistakes in the settlement of accounts. The bank must also pay interest to the depositor. The rights of the bank against the depositor include the right to receive a service fee for settlement, the right to settle accounts compulsorily according to law, [and]the right to supervise the financial and economic activities of the customer.

2. The Significance and Principles of Establishing the Legal Relation of Settlement of Accounts

Under socialist economic conditions, the extensive establishment of the legal relation of settlement of accounts is of great importance to the maintenance of the financial and monetary order of the state, to the spread of state credit, and to advancing the development of our economy.

First, it is a legal form by which the state mobilizes society's idle capital, increases socialist accumulation, increases the sources of loan funds for the state, and ensures the fullest use of state credit.

Second, it helps the conscientious performance of contracts by the parties, the strengthening of the economic accounting of enterprises, the saving of unnecessary expenditure. It also helps to save circulation costs and time, and to increase economic benefits.

Third, it is a legal device by which the state regulates the activities of juristic persons, controls the movement of their funds, prevents and corrects their illegal use of funds, and supervises the economic transactions between juristic persons.

Fourth, it ensures that the state can administer the financial and monetary system of the whole country according to state plans, control the purchasing power of society, stabilize the monetary and financial order, and bring about a balance between income and expenditure.

The legal relation of settlement of accounts must be carried on in accordance with the following basic principles.

(i) The principle of actual exchange of money and goods. Banks in settling accounts must see to it that the selling unit receives the contract price on time, prevent the separation of money and goods [i.e., the transfer of either without a return], and ensure that the allocation of goods and money is carried on properly. Carrying out the principle that money and things cancel each other means that in economic contracts entered into by juristic persons, [the parties] must, according to the relevant state laws, select the proper mode of settling accounts and determine a concrete method of paying the price. Moreover, when they enter into an economic contract, the two parties must conscientiously abide [by such payment terms].

(ii) The principle of protecting the lawful rights of the depositor. Banks, in settling accounts, must abide by state laws and uphold financial discipline. That is, on the one hand, they should protect the lawful rights and interests of the depositor. At the same time, they must protect the lawful rights and interests of the obligees and obligors of the depositor.

(iii) The principle that the bank does not advance payment for customers. When a settlor bank accepts a sum for its depositor, it must first place this sum in the depositor's account, then the depositor may request payments. When the settlor makes payments for the depositor it must be limited by the amounts in the depositor's account. It is forbidden to issue a false certificate of payment. Otherwise the circulation of the bank's credit will be greatly expanded, and the normal and orderly flow of money will be affected.

3. The Methods of Settling Accounts

The methods of settling accounts are the procedures and methods of juristic persons carrying out economic transactions themselves and transferring funds among themselves. They are the concrete forms of handling settlement through the transfer of accounts, and indispensable in carrying out the legal relation of settlement of accounts.

According to the rules, the methods of settlement of accounts in our country include settlement between parties located in difference places [areas] and settlement between parties within the same city or county. Settlement between parties located in different areas (different counties within [the same or belonging to different] provinces, municipalities, and autonomous regions) is regulated uniformly by state laws. Settlement [between parties located in] the same city or county is regulated by the respective provinces, cities, or autonomous regions.

(1) Settlements between parties located in different areas

(i) Authorization to receive payment and be responsible for payment. This

[refers to the situation in which] the unit that is to receive payment, after delivering the goods, authorizes its bank to receive payment from the paying unit located in another place. The paying unit, checking the invoices or examining the documents, notifies its bank that it will pay. This is the method of settling accounts by the said bank making payment. This kind of settlement is utilized by units [of property] owned by the whole people, but may also be used by some juristic persons of collective ownership which meet certain requirements. The question of whether this method of arranging receipt and payment in another place is used must be determined by the contract entered into by the parties.

(ii) Letter of credit. This refers to the situation where the unit making payments authorizes its bank to issue a letter of credit within the amount in its account. The bank of deposit of the unit receiving payment in the other place notifies the unit receiving payment. After this unit delivers the goods according to the provisions of the contract and the letter of credit, its bank, acting for the paying unit, makes payment in settlement of the account. This method of settlement, like others, should also be based on the legal relation of settlement of accounts. In our country, it is provided that the transfer of goods and performing of services may use letters of credit to settle accounts, but the payor and payee must enter into a contract that selects the method of settling accounts by letter of credit, and such agreement must be approved by their banks.

(iii) Remittance. This [refers to the] method of settling accounts where the paying unit authorizes its bank to remit the sum due to the unit that is to receive payment in the other place or to an individual. The transfer by juristic persons of allocated funds clearing overdue debts, mutual payments in exchange of credits, [payment in transactions where the buyer] picks up goods [at the seller's place], and transport by its own means of transportation, and occasional purchases, etc., all can use remittance by banks as a method of payment. The depositor who requests a remittance must explain clearly the [intended] use and purpose for it.

(2) Settlement of accounts between parties residing within the same city and county

The most important [methods] are settlement of accounts by check, settlement of accounts by a warrant of payment, settlement of accounts by authorizing collections but not receipt of payments, settlement of accounts for limited amounts [by cash] in rural areas, etc. The selection of all the above methods of settlement cannot be made in the absence of the legal relation of settlement of accounts.

IV
OTHER LOANS FOR CONSUMPTION

Under the conditions of socialism, besides state loan contracts and contracts for the settlement of accounts, there are still the following types of loans that must be discussed.

1. The Loan [for Consumption] of Things [other than Money]

In our country contracts for loans of things [other than money] can be made between citizens, between juristic persons, and between a juristic person and a citizen. Affirming and protecting such loan relations is of great use in helping citizens and juristic persons solve their practical problems and [letting] each supply the other's needs, and adjusting excesses and shortages.

In a loan for a thing where there is a time limit for return, the borrower should return [the kind of things loaned] on time. In a loan where there is no such time requirement, the lender may ask for return at any time, but if the return cannot be made immediately, the borrower may have an extension period determined by law.

Loans of things other than money may be nongratuitous or gratuitous. Only where there is an express agreement between the parties for the payment of interest, does the lender have the right to receive interest.

Contracts for the loan of things may be oral or in writing. However, for the maintenance of a stable order in circulation, the loan of things other than money in a relatively large amount must be in writing. Where there is a rule of law requiring that this kind of loan contract be in writing, the party who does not comply with this rule does not have the right to defend himself with oral evidence against the other party.

Where, in a contract for loan of things, the lender is a juristic person, the scope of the loan shall not exceed the relevant rules of law.

In a contract for a loan [for consumption] of things, the borrower should return the same quantity of things of the same quality [as those borrowed], or other things as agreed to by the parties. When [the borrower] is unable to return the things as lent or agreed, there may be repayment upon agreement by the parties of the price [of the thing] as measured by the local retail market price [of the things lent].

The law prohibits the use of loans to carry on speculation, profiteering, and other illegal activities. Those who violate such law shall be investigated and be made to bear the responsibility fixed by law. Where a contract for the loan of things other than money is formed through an intermediary (or a middleman), such a middleman may not receive a commission.

2. Contracts for Loans of Money Between Citizens

Contracts for loans of money arise between citizens. These contracts possess the general characteristics of every loan, but they are, in several respects, different from state loans. For instance, they are permitted not to have a particular purpose or a definite time for repayment. They may be oral, etc. Moreover, loans of money between citizens in our country do not usually provide for interest. But the law does not prohibit reasonable interest. If there is interest to be paid, the parties must clearly provide it in their contract. The interest rate between citizens may exceed the interest rate of state-bank loans, but may not exceed the upper limit set by law. Loans with compound interest, or usurious interest, or usury in another form, are strictly prohibited.

In our society, sometimes the masses—staff and workers [of the same unit], or residents living in the same street—in order to help each other, set up mutual aid funds. These are based on voluntariness. They take the accumulated savings of the members, and on the principle of repayment of loans and no interest, they lend to members for their needs in daily life or when they encounter temporary difficulty. The law protects and encourages such loans.

3. A Contract for the Loan of Money Created by Savings Accounts

"Savings accounts" refers to the deposit by citizens of their funds in state banks, credit societies, and other credit institutions (hereafter referred to as banks). Moreover, it is a credit activity in which withdrawals can be made at will. This is a kind of monetary loan contract relation in which one party transfers a sum of money, and the other party, after accepting it, pays interest according to law, and has the obligation to repay as fixed by the rules of the contract of deposit. A citizen may decide, according to his own will, whether and when to deposit, how much and for how long a period he will deposit, and he may select the kind of account (deposit) he would like to open and the location in which he would like to open his account. A bank may not refuse to accept a citizen's deposit. Moreover, banks must maintain secrecy regarding their customer's savings.

All the savings [accounts] of citizens are considered to be nongratuitous loans. The banks should pay interest according to the interest rates set by the state.

In recent years, the Chinese People's Bank has increased the kinds of savings account available and has readjusted the interest rate. This has increased the citizens' savings in cities and villages. The increase has great utility in supporting the economic construction of the state, fostering hard work and plain living, and a social spirit of saving through work and thriftiness.

V
LOANS FOR USE

1. The General Concept of the Loan for Use

The contract of the loan for use refers to the agreement by which the lender delivers the borrowed property to the borrower for use without compensation, and the borrower is to return the borrowed property within a certain period. It is different from the contract of loan (the loan for consumption) because:

(1) In a contract of loan for use, the borrower's purpose is to use the borrowed property temporarily. The law requires the borrower to return the borrowed property after such use. In a contract of loan for consumption, the purpose of the borrower is to consume the borrowed property, and the law requires the borrower to return only things of the same quantity and quality as the borrowed thing.

(2) According to the reasons discussed above, the objects of a contract of loan for consumption must be unspecified things, whereas the object of a contract of

loan for use must be a specified thing for which substitution cannot be made.

(3) In a contract of loan for use, the lender, after delivering the borrowed property to the borrower, still retains the ownership, and the borrower obtains only the right to possess and use the borrowed property. In a contract of loan for consumption, the lender loses the ownership rights when he delivers the borrowed property to the borrower. Moreover, he obtains an equivalent obligation right according to the principle of exchange for equal value.

(4) A loan for use is always gratuitous, whereas a loan for consumption may be nongratuitous or gratuitous.

2. The Basic Content of a Loan for Use

(1) During the period of the loan for use, the borrower bears the full responsibility for the protection of the borrowed property, and the law requires that the borrower should take the same care of the borrowed property as he would of his own property of the same type. It is only in this way that [the loan] is consistent with its essential purpose, and only when this obligation is complied with, that the borrower can return the borrowed property to the lender in good condition. If the obligation is violated, and there is resultant damage to or loss of the borrowed property, the borrower is liable to pay damages for the injury or loss. If the borrowed property is damaged accidentally, and if the borrower can prove that even if he had been using his own property he could not have avoided the damage, then he can be relieved from liability for damages. In addition, the borrower is not responsible to pay damages for the normal wear and tear resulting from use.

The normal expenses expended for the use and storage of the borrowed property during the term of the loan should be borne by the borrower.

(2) As to the methods or ways of using the borrowed property, if there are explanations or a specific agreement regarding the ways of using the borrowed thing, the borrower should use the property in a way consistent with the agreement and the explanations. When there are no such explanations or agreements, the borrower should use the property in a scientific way according to the natural attributes of the borrowed property, or use it in a customary way. If the borrower uses the property in a way contrary to the above requirements, and causes injury to the property, he shall be liable for damages.

Unless there is an agreement between the parties to the contrary, the borrower should use the borrowed property himself. Without the permission of the lender, the borrower may not let others use the property. If he does, the lender may terminate the contract in advance.

(3) The borrower must return the original borrowed property. In the usual situation, the returned borrowed property should be in essentially the original condition it was in when it was lent.

As to the time of return, if there is an agreed time, such an agreement may govern. If the parties have not agreed, the borrower should return the borrowed property immediately after its use, and the lender may ask for return of the loaned property on demand, but he must give the borrower a reasonable extension.

Under the following circumstances, the borrower, upon the demand of the lender, has the obligation to return the borrowed property ahead of time: the borrower has used the borrowed property in a way contrary to that which is usual; because of reasons that are subjective to the borrower, the condition of the borrowed property has deteriorated; the borrower, in violation of the contract, has on his own transferred the borrowed property to others; where the loan is for an indefinite time, the ownership of the borrowed property changes, and the new owner, because of his own need [for use of the borrowed property], asks for its return.

A loan for use is gratuitous so the law does not require the lender to bear certain obligations. However, for the protection of the borrower's lawful rights and interests, and to uphold the socialist norms of common life, the lender is required to tell the borrower of the defects of the borrowed property when he hands it over. If the lender has knowledge about the defects, but does not tell the borrower about them, and the defects cause the borrower harm, the lender should be liable for the consequences.

26 Transport Contracts

I
A BRIEF INTRODUCTION TO TRANSPORT CONTRACTS

1. The General Concept of Contracts of Transport

A contract of transport is an agreement by which one party, the carrier, transports the goods, or the passenger and his baggage, to the appointed destination and the consignor or the passenger pays the fee for transportation to the carrier.

There are many types of transport contracts. They may be classified according to what is transported: there are contracts for transporting things and contracts for transporting passengers. They may be classified according to the means of transportation: there are contracts of transportation by rail, by water (on sea and on inland water), by highway, and by air. They may be classified according to the methods of transportation: there are contracts of transportation by a single means of transportation and transport contracts by two or more means of transportation—the latter are called coordinated transport (including domestic coordinated transport contracts and international coordinated transport contracts).

In our country, most carriers in contracts of transport are transportation enterprises of property of the whole people and transportation enterprises of collective property, as well as those verified and registered by supervisory organizations within the scope permitted by law and regulation, specialized management households which are engaged in transportation, and individual workers. The consignor and consignee may be citizens. They may also be juristic persons.

The transportation contract is widely used between socialist organizations, between socialist organizations and citizens, and between citizens. It is the most commonly seen, most widespread, and a very important contract.

Like most other contracts, transportation contracts are bilateral nongratuitous contracts. They also have the following special characteristics:

(1) Transportation contracts are all planned

The socialist transportation plan is a constituent part of the state economic plan. All contracts of transport for large quantities of goods (whether by railway, or highway, by sea or on inland water, air, etc.) are performed according to the state plan. Section 20 of our country's Economic Contracts Law provides that contracts of transport are based on the material allocations plan and are executed on the basis of transport capability and the transport plan. The parties to the contract execute their contract in accordance with the state transportation plan by means of negotiation and, thus, give concrete implementation to the state plan.

(2) Each kind of transportation contract is, in general, adjusted by special transportation laws

The principal content and essential terms of various transport contracts, including the fees, freight, and ticket prices, are determined uniformly by the transportation administrative departments which are authorized to do so by the state. Carriers, consignors, and passengers have to strictly abide [by these provisions] and [no one] may change them at will. Where the carrier is a specialized household, an individual laborer, or a collective organization, the amount of compensation should be determined by the parties through agreement, within the limits set by the competent governmental agencies. The carrier may not obtain from the consignor or passenger extra high freight and other miscellaneous fees that exceed the limit and obtain illegal profits.

(3) A transport contract is a real contract

A transportation contract only comes into being when, in addition to reaching an agreement regarding the necessary terms by the parties, the consignor actually delivers the shipment to the carrier. The contract then becomes effective. But if there is a contrary agreement, the agreement governs.

(4) A transportation contract may involve a third person

Besides the consignor and the carrier who execute a transportation contract for goods, there is usually a third person, that is, the consignee. Of course the consignor himself may also be the consignee. But usually the consignee is a third party. Although the consignee does not participate in the execution of the transportation contract, he may obtain rights against and owe obligations to the carrier.

2. The Function of the Transportation Contract in National Economic Life

Transportation is one of the important components of the national economy. Marx sets it beside the processing industry, agriculture, and mining, and calls it the fourth branch of material production. It is in the domain of material production. Transportation activities make the whole national economy into a tight and unified whole and become the bond which connects the various branches of the national economy, different areas (including cities and rural areas), and enterprises. It is the foundation which ensures the normal progress of the development of the national economy and the activities of social material reproduction. As Lenin pointed out, transportation is an important foundation of our whole economy. Perhaps it is one of the most important foundations.

The transportation contract plays a great role in the activity of the national economy:

(1) It ensures and advances the development of production

Transportation is the lifeblood of our national economy. The performance of the transportation contract effects the movement of goods or persons in space. It changes the locations of goods and men. If the carrier safely, swiftly, uninterruptedly, and economically transports the means of production and commodities, it not only shortens the time of commodity circulation, reduces the storage of raw materials and products, and prevents accumulation, but at the same time it also speeds the circulation of funds, increases the beneficial effects of investment, reduces the cost of products, raises economic efficiency, and the rate of labor production.

(2) It advances and facilitates commodity circulation, and thus helps to meet the needs of the people for consumption

With the continual rise in the people's standard of living, people make still higher demands in regard to consumption of commodities both as to quantity and quality. A transportation contract connects the whole process of the circulation of commodities from the place of production to the place of consumption. In a timely way, it supplies commodities for the market for society, and speedily sends them into the hands of consumers, and continually meets their needs.

(3) It promotes foreign trade and international economic contracts and the development of technology transfer

Carrying on trade with all the countries of the world, and making use of foreign capital and joint commercial activities with foreigners, independent foreign capital enterprises, and compensation trade, etc., all require active cooperation by the Transportation Ministry. Moreover, [transport] offers effective service, attracts foreign investment, makes use of foreign capital, and creates a favorable atmosphere for foreign capital, and is adapted to the struggle to realize the opening to the outside policy and the Four Modernizations.

(4) It protects relations of work and facilitates the life of the people

Our country is one with a large area and population. Regardless of whether it is a matter of work relations between juristic persons, or between juristic persons and citizens, or the indispensable visits of people to relatives and friends, and traveling, all are carried on by means of passenger transportation contracts. The carriers' safe and swift transport of passengers to their destinations ensures that they will complete their business errands on time. It creates conditions for the people to visit each other and to travel.

II
THE MAJOR RIGHTS AND OBLIGATIONS OF THE PARTIES TO A CONTRACT OF TRANSPORTATION INVOLVING GOODS

1. The Principal Obligations and Rights of the Consignor

(1) The major right of the consignor is to demand that the carrier transport the shipment to the destination in the agreed-upon time

A consignor may demand that the carrier cancel the shipment before the carrier sends the goods out, that is, take back the goods from the place of shipment. The consignor may also ask to change the destination or the consignee after the goods have been shipped but before they reach the destination, but the consignor must present an application for such change to the shipment receiving unit and go through the procedures for making changes in shipment. This right to modify the transportation contract does not belong to the consignor only. The consignee also has such a right. The decision of a consignor to cancel and modify the transportation contract is based on his ownership rights and the rights of administration and management of the goods shipped. The carrier has no right to refuse the request of a consignor for cancellation or modification discussed above without sufficient reason. A consignor must pay to the carrier the fixed fee because of the cancellation and modification of the contract. If the other party suffers an economic loss, he is liable for damages.

(2) The major duty of the consignor is to pay the agreed-upon shipping fees, miscellaneous fees, and other required fees on time

Otherwise the carrier has the right to stop transport and, moreover, to demand that the consignor pay the penalty for breach of contract.

The consignor must deliver the goods within the time provided in the contract and of the contract quantity. According to section 41 of the Economic Contracts Law, if the consignor does not deliver the goods on time, he must pay the penalty for breach of contract to the carrier.

If the goods must be packed according to the rules, the consignor must pack them according to the standard set by the state rules. If there are no uniform standards for packing, [the consignor] should pack [the shipped goods] according to their nature, weight, and the distance to be covered by the transport, and similar matters. He must pack the goods according the principle of ensuring safe transport. Otherwise the carrier has the right to refuse to transport [them]. The consignor should also, in accordance with the nature of the goods and state regulations, place labels on the package for shipment.

If the shipped goods are dangerous materials, the consignor must comply with the provisions regarding the transport of dangerous materials. If, because the consignor intentionally conceals or does not correctly explain the dangerous nature of the shipment, or has violated other provisions regarding the transport of dangerous materials, the carrier or a third person is injured, the consignor is liable for damages, and if the violation is serious, the responsible individual shall be punished criminally.

2. The Principal Rights and Obligations of the Carrier

(1) A carrier has the right to demand the fees due for freight, miscellaneous fees, and other required fees from the consignor and the consignee

If the shipper does not pay, the carrier has the right to refuse to transport and, according to the rules, to demand the penalty set for breach of contract. If the consignor or consignee has not paid the freight storage fees, or other required fees, the carrier has a lien on the shipped goods according to law, unless the law provides for the contrary. Moreover, he has the right to notify the shipper or consignee to pay the freight, storage fees, and his other fees that are due within a fixed period. Otherwise, the carrier may sell the detained goods and take the proceeds to deduct from the fees to which he is entitled, or detain all or part of the goods, according to the value of the unpaid fees, to ensure that the carrier receive all the fees provided for in the contract.

(2) After the carrier has transported the shipped goods to the destination, he should immediately notify the consignee to pick up the goods (shipment)

If the address of the consignee is not clear, or, upon notification, he refuses to pick up the shipment, the carrier should notify the consignor to pick it up promptly. Moreover, [the carrier] should take proper measures for storage. If the shipment has not been picked up within the period fixed, the carrier may dispose of the shipment according to the regulations concerning transport. If, owing to the fault of the carrier, the shipment arrives late, and this causes injury to the other party, the carrier is liable according to the provisions [of the contract] for damages for late performance of the contract. He must pay the contract penalty for the breach of contract to the consignor.

(3) The carrier is responsible for transporting and taking suitable care of the shipped goods for the period starting from the acceptance of the shipment delivered for transport to the time of delivery to the consignee

During this period, if the shipment suffers injury, loss, shortage, deterioration, or spoilage, the carrier is liable to the consignor or consignee for damages. Accidents that are the result of the quality of the transport are the responsibility of the Ministry of Transportation. In the case of any direct economic loss that is caused by work that violates the rules, or disorderly loading and unloading, the one who caused the trouble is liable. At the same time, the liability of the vendors should be investigated. In very serious cases, criminal liability should be investigated. The carrier's liability for injury to or loss of the goods, in general, is to compensate for the actual value of the damaged or lost goods. If there is no way to ascertain the actual value of the damaged or lost goods, the carrier should compensate according to the limit set by state regulations for related compensation. If the loss or injury is the result of natural disaster, or the attributes of the shipped goods, or if the fault of consignee or consignor causes loss, injury, spontaneous combustion, internal spoilage, etc., the carrier is not liable to pay damages.

3. The Principal Rights and Duties of the Consignee

(1) A consignee's principal right is, upon presentation of the required document [bill of lading], to pick up the shipment after the carrier has transported it to the destination

A consignee has the right, prior to the arrival of the goods, to have the destination changed or to have someone else designated as consignee.

When a consignee picks up the shipment, he must conduct a joint checking and acceptance of the shipment together with the carrier. If the consignee finds that the shipped goods were damaged, or some part of them was lost, or that there are other inconsistencies with the shipping documents and the bill of lading, he should immediately notify the carrier. Moreover, he has the right to damages from the carrier. If the consignee does not raise objections when he receives the goods, or did not make suggestions for further examination within the period set by the contract, the consignee will be considered to have examined and accepted the shipment.

(2) The principal obligation of the consignee is, upon receiving notification of the arrival of the shipped goods, to pick up the shipment within the specified time and to pay all the required fees

If, for some reason, the consignee does not pick up the shipment within the fixed period, he must bear a certain economic liability. When it is necessary, the carrier has the right to dispose of the shipment.

III
THE CONTRACT FOR THE TRANSPORT OF GOODS BY RAIL

A contract for the transport of goods by rail is the most important and most widely used contract of transport. It will now be discussed from the following three aspects.

1. The Plan for Rail Transport

The transport of goods by rail strictly carries out planned transport. So the plan for rail transport is the basis for the work of the railroad's everyday transport organization. The railroad stations [accept and] transport goods according to approved transport plans. If the consignor needs a whole railroad carriage for its goods, it should submit to the railroad the monthly carriage request plan form. The railroad station will accept and transport goods according to the plan on the basis of the approved request. The monthly goods transport plan is worked out according to the methods provided by the "Regulations for Making Monthly Transport of Goods by Railway." Consequently, the railroad transport plan is a prerequisite for the making of a contract for the transport of goods by rail.

2. The Formation of a Contract for the Transport of Goods by Rail

There are two stages for the formation of a contract for the transport of goods by rail: consigning for shipment and acceptance of shipment. Consigning for shipment refers to the consignor (or shipper), according to the Regulations for the Transport of Goods by Rail promulgated by the Ministry of Railways, requesting the carrier to transport goods. He fills out the shipping documents, indicating clearly the name [type] of the shipped goods, the number of packages, the kind of packing, the names of the places of origination and destination, the names and the addresses of the consignor (shipper) and the consignee, and other matters. And sometimes, when it is necessary, the consignor should submit to the carrier certificates for shipment of the goods [i.e., certificates proving that transport of the goods is not prohibited]. "Acceptance for shipment" refers to the carrier, after making an examination and determining that the goods meet the requirements for shipping, carrying out the procedures for consignment and acceptance, and inspecting and receiving the freight, miscellaneous fees, and other required fees, and executing and issuing the shipping documents—the bill of lading. At this point, the contract is formed. The bill of lading is not only the basic document that the shipper must present to the Transport Ministry when it delivers goods to the carrier for shipment, but also the basic document according to which the carrier collects freight and by which the consignee picks up the goods from the carrier. The shipping bill of lading signed by the railroad and consignor is not only a written contract which defines the rights, obligations, and economic responsibilities of the parties, the consignor and the carrier, and is thus binding upon the parties, the bill of lading also serves as a receipt for the goods and a document of title to the goods.

3. The Transport of Special Goods and the Transport of Dangerous Materials

The transport of special goods refers mainly to the transport of living and fresh goods, including things that are especially susceptible to decay and deterioration and living animals. When a consignor or shipper asks to ship things that are susceptible to decay, or animals, he should indicate this clearly on the shipping documents, and indicate his requirements as to the time to be allowed for the shipment, the preventive measures that are to be taken (refrigeration, ventilation, warmth, or care), the particular kind of cars to be used (heated cars or refrigerated cars), etc. The carrier then, according to such demands of the consignor, assures the provision of suitable facilities and equipment to ensure the performance of the transport contract. If the consignor or consignee must provide a person to escort the shipment, it cannot begin until the escort is provided. The transport of living and fresh things must be handled according to "The Regulations for the Transport of Living and Fresh Things."

"Dangerous things" refers to flammable or explosive things, or things which are very toxic, or radioactive materials. If there is not strict control and the use of preventive measures in connection with the shipment of these things, there may be accidents that may cause injury and damage to persons and property in shipment. So transport of dangerous things and materials should be handled strictly according to "The Regulations for the Transport of Dangerous Things and Materials."

When the consignor or shipper ships dangerous things and materials, it must make this clear on the shipping documents and pack the things and materials according to the regulations. Only after the carrier has established that this has been done, can the shipment begin. After the carrier has transported the dangerous shipment to the destination, it should immediately notify the consignee. It should also closely coordinate its actions with the relevant departments to ensure [that the dangerous shipment] will be unloaded immediately upon its arrival and be speedily removed [to the proper place].

IV
OTHER CONTRACTS FOR THE TRANSPORT OF GOODS

1. Contracts for the Shipment of Goods by Water

Transport of goods by water, like transport of goods by rail, carries out planned transport. The consignor and carrier must execute and perform their transport contract pursuant to the transport plan and the principle of reasonable transport. They must assure priority for the transport of relief materials, materials for relieving emergencies, and materials which the government orders to be transported immediately. The carrier may stop loading or limit the load if there is a natural disaster, or a blockage in the harbor or congestion in the channel, or if the consignee makes a reasonable demand. The stopping of loading or limiting loads are decided separately by the Bureau for the Administration of Transport by Water and the Bureau for the Administration of Harbors—for transport on inland waters or on coastal waters. When the consignor asks to modify the transport plan or asks for transport beyond [the amount approved by] the transport plan, it must submit to the harbor of origin a form for modifying the plan or a form for supplementing the plan. There may be only one modification of a transport plan. In supplementing the plan, the procedures for modification are not used.

When he ships goods, the shipper or consignor has to submit shipping documents to the carrier at the harbor of origin. Every provision of the shipping documents must be written clearly. The content must be accurate and exact. Moreover, the packing of the shipment must be according to the state standards for the shipment of goods. The carrier may ask the shipper to make additional efforts to reinforce or improve the packing or refuse to accept [the goods for shipment] if the packing does not comply with the standards and requirements. The shipper should pay the freight and other miscellaneous fees at the harbor of origin on the day the carrier accepts the shipment. If the shipper delays in payment, it should pay the sum which [the regulations] prescribe for late payment. When the consignor collects the goods and gets them to the harbor according to the prescribed time and place, when the carrier checks and accepts the goods in accordance with the bill of lading, and stamps the date of receipt, the shipment is undertaken.

In the contract for transport of goods by water, there are special provisions for the requirements of special types of transport. A shipper who ships living plants and animals, or things susceptible to decay, must indicate the permissible period of shipment and the requirements of transport. A quarantine certificate should also be furnished. The harbor of origin should carefully verify and examine [the shipment]. If it agrees to the transport, it should assign a suitable ship for loading, and when the ship reaches the destination, the harbor of destination should arrange to unload and deliver at the earliest time possible.

2. Contracts for the Shipment of Goods by Highway

Contracts for the transport of goods by highway are formed in accordance with the transport plan approved by the state. In the case of all goods shipped by highway, the unit which [controls] the goods or materials must, within the prescribed time, submit a transport plan to the highway transportation department which is located in the same area where the goods or materials to be transported are kept. Late submission of the transport plan obliges the transportation department to treat the goods and materials asked to be transported as transport outside the plan; that is, the truck station at the place of origin may make its decision whether to transport according to the concrete situation [the availability of trucks, the needs of the consignor, etc.]. But if there are special circumstances, such as the transport of urgent military materials, as well as materials for natural disasters, emergencies, and for preventing floods, etc., the plan does not apply. According to the contract for the transport of goods by highway, before delivering the goods to the carrier, the consignor must pack the goods according to the standards set by the state and place directions for handling on the package to ensure the safety of the goods. If the goods or materials intended to be transported are dangerous materials or special goods or materials, they are to be handled according to the regulations for transporting such dangerous materials or special goods or materials.

After the carrier has transported the entire shipment to the agreed-on destination, the consignee should sign the bill of lading indicating receipt. Consignees of odd shipments transported by carriers pick up their shipment upon presentation of the shipping document [bill of lading] at the destination truck station.

3. The Contract for the Transport of Goods by Air

The contract for the transport of goods by air is made by carriers (in our country the Civil Aviation Bureau and the local air companies) and consignors according to the state plan for transport by air. Carriers organize the transport of goods on the basis of ensuring the important matters, adjusting [the transport] by taking into consideration what is suitable for a single plane, and reasonable transport, as a principle. In choosing the aviation route, a carrier should use its best efforts to avoid having the goods take a circuitous route and make repeated trips, and it may suspend accepting further shipments according to special circumstances (for instance the decree of the government by law or regulation, natural disaster, suspension of flying, etc.). A carrier should decide the order of priority of transporting the goods according to their nature, their weight, and their urgency. First, materials for relieving disasters and emergency situations, as well as articles which the government orders to be transported by emergency means, materials to meet the urgent needs of agricultural and industrial production, national defense, and scientific research; second, articles that are required at a specified time, valuable shipments, and fragmentary shipments; third, ordinary shipments.

When a shipper sends goods [by air], it should present a letter of introduction from its unit or other documentation. It must take care of the shipping procedures with the carrier, and fill out the goods shipment form correctly according to the rules, item by item. If the goods to be transported are those for whose transport the state imposes some limitations, or those for whose transport certain public security procedures are to be followed, or quarantine certificates, etc., are required, the shipper has to submit effective documents and certificates. In the transport of goods by air, unless there is examination and approval by the relevant bureau of the Civil Aviation Bureau, the loading of weapons, ammunition, explosives, toxic gas, radioactive materials, or other materials or items menacing the safety of flight is strictly prohibited. The packing of the goods that are accepted for shipment must be done in strict compliance with the standards set by the state, so that in the course of the flight they are not scattered or damaged, and do not cause injury or contamination to the aircraft and other shipments. After properly packing the shipment, the consigner also has to place proper directions and labels on the package. If the carrier finds that the packing or the directions and labels do not comply with the state regulations, it may ask the shipper to repack and make improvements on the directions and labels. After careful examination and the final marking of the shipping documents by the carrier, the shipment is accepted.

V
[CONTRACTS FOR] THE CARRIAGE OF PASSENGERS, THEIR BAGGAGE, AND BUNDLES

According to the contract for the carriage of passengers, their baggage, and bundles, the carrier shall carry the passengers, their baggage, and bundles, and deliver them to their destinations at the agreed time. The passengers must pay the specified fee.

A passenger has to have a ticket to take any type of transportation. A passenger ticket is the certificate by which a passenger boards the transport vehicle. It also serves as the evidence of the making of a contract of carriage. A contract for the carriage of passengers, their baggage, and bundles, is made when a carrier sells a ticket to the passenger. A legal relation of rights and duties then comes into being between the carrier and the passenger.

The principal right of a passenger is to have a place on the vehicle agreed upon on the day and on the number indicated on the ticket to get to the specified destination. A passenger has the right, according to the rules for the carriage of passengers, to carry a small child and personal belongings with him and to consign to the carrier his baggage and bundles. He has the right to use the facilities on board provided by the carrier for living and entertainment.

The major obligation of a passenger is to pay the ticket price uniformly fixed by the state, to abide by the relevant regulations, and maintain public order, and to protect state property.

The major right of a carrier is to collect the ticket price from passengers according to state regulations. If a carrier finds that a passenger does not have a ticket, or has used an expired, forged, or altered ticket to board the vehicle, or that a passenger has in his luggage or bundles that he carries, things that are flammable or explosive, or things that are spoiling, or other dangerous and prohibited things, in addition to the carrier being permitted to criticize and educate the passengers, it may collect double the amount of the unpaid ticket price and impose a fine, etc. If the violation is serious, the matter must be turned over to the Justice Ministry for handling according to law.

The major obligation of a carrier is to transport the passenger, his baggage and bundles, safely and on time to the destination. The carrier assumes the responsibility safely to transport the baggage and bundles consigned by passengers for shipment from the time they are delivered to the carrier. If, during shipment, the baggage and bundles are damaged or lost, or if there is a shortage, alteration, or deterioration, etc., the carrier has to pay damages unless it is a case of irresistible force, or because of the nature of the thing itself, or the passenger's fault. During transit, a carrier has the obligation to provide to its passengers the necessary facilities and services, to render special help to pregnant women, the old, sick, and handicapped. If any passenger comes down with a sudden illness or is injured, the carrier should do its best to give assistance. If a passenger dies, the carrier should make a record of the passenger's trip, carefully recording the circumstances of death. It is responsible for handling the matter properly. If death was caused by a traffic accident or is the result of accidental injury, the carrier, should, together with public security officers, look into the scene of the incident, investigate the causes, make a record of it, determine the nature of the fatal injury, and dispose of the incident according to the related regulations and carefully and properly deal with the matter. If a passenger is injured or dies en route and the carrier can prove that this was caused by irresistible force, natural disaster, or because of the passenger's own fault, the carrier is not liable.

VI
THE COORDINATED CONTRACT OF TRANSPORT

"Coordinated transport," also referred to as "mixed transport," refers to the situation where a consignor or passenger makes a contract of transport with the first carrier and makes a single payment of transport expenses, and with the same transport certificate, uses two or more than two connected means of transportation to get the goods to the destination.

Coordinated transport may take many forms. For instance, transport by rail and by water, transport by rail and highway, transport by rail, water, and highway, transport by air, rail, or highway. In transport by water, there is coordinated transport on different rivers and coordinated transport on rivers and the sea, etc. Even in the case of transport by the same means, there can also be coordinated transport on different lines. In addition, there is coordinated transport arranged by transportation departments of different areas between themselves to carry [goods and passengers] for each other, international coordinated transport, etc.

The use of coordinated transport can cause every means of transportation to be fully used, and it effectively connects all phases of transport, [causes] close cooperation, and, thus, makes the best use of transportation capabilities and fully accomplishes the tasks of transport. Therefore, the significance of coordinated transport is not only to simplify transport procedures, but, even more, to make full use of transport capacity, to speed the circulation of shipments, to make travel more convenient for the people, to cut down transport costs, and, finally, to satisfy to the greatest extent possible the needs of industrial and agricultural production and the needs of people in their daily lives.

At the beginning of Liberation, our country managed combined transportation activity in many areas and bureaus. Subsequently, this sort of activity was on the brink of being suspended. At present, owing to the continuing development of socialist construction, particularly following the profound and uninterrupted reform in our country's economic system, coordinated work gradually revived and developed. Recently, owing to the increasing use by all countries in the world of containerization, the international coordinated transport has experienced a great development. Containerization has brought about door-to-door transport, simplified many transport segments, reduced the injuries and shortages of shipments, and has speeded up circulation. It is still in its early stages in our country.

The coordinated transport contract, like other kinds of transport contracts, is formed according to the transport plans made by the state transportation departments. In a contract of coordinated transport by rail and water, if the consignor ships a whole car of goods, he has to submit a planning form for coordinated transport by rail and water. After this form has been examined and balanced [fitted in with other proposals] by the concerned railway and water transportation departments together, a plan for the coordinated transport of goods by land and water will be prepared and jointly checked and approved by the Ministries of Railway and Transportation. All transportation enterprises should give priority to coordinated transport in arranging transport plans.

The special rules and regulations for the different types of coordinated transport all provide for the kinds and quantities allowed in coordinated transport. Goods that fall outside of the designated categories and quantities beyond the designated amounts may be handled by coordinated transport on special routes approved by the office supervising transportation after an agreement between the consignor and carrier is made.

In coordinated transport, the consignor or consignee may request a change in the shipping after the carrier has accepted the shipment, subject to the approval of the carrier, after which it becomes effective. But only one change is allowed. A change as to the place of reloading or as to a portion of the shipment is not permitted. Any change that violates governmental regulations or decrees or other transport restrictions is prohibited. A consignor who wants to cancel the coordinated transport may make its request to the station or harbor of origin.

A transportation supervisory department has the right to use a detour if there are special circumstances, for instance, a natural disaster or a major accident.

As to the transport expenses after a change is made, if the change is requested by the consignor or consignee, they should be determined according to the actual route taken after the change; if the change in the coordinated route is made by the transportation department (as in the case of the detour), the transport expenses should be calculated according to the original route.

Carriers involved in a coordinated transport are jointly liable for the injury, losses, shortages, deterioration, and other injuries suffered by the shipment during the coordinated shipment. The station or harbor of destination will pay the prescribed damages. Afterwards, the carrier of destination will seek compensation from the other carrier. In general, the division of liability for damages among the carriers should be apportioned according the responsibilities which each of them has assumed. If the responsibilities of each carrier cannot be clearly divided, the carriers shall be liable for damages according to the percentage of the freight charge they receive.

The claim for damages for loss of and damage to the coordinated shipments should be made by the injured party to the railway bureau or the harbor bureau at the destination within the prescribed time. If the prescriptive period expires, he loses the right to make such a claim.

27 Contracts of Deposit

I
CONTRACTS OF DEPOSIT

1. The General Concept of Contracts of Deposit

The contract of deposit is an agreement by which the depositor gives things that need to be stored to the depository and the depository returns the things to the depositor at a certain future time.

A contract of deposit has the following special characteristics:

(1) In a contract of deposit, when the depositor gives things that need to be stored to the depository to store, this is only a transfer of possession. He does not lose title. The depository must return things to the depositor within a certain agreed-upon time.

(2) A contract of deposit is a real contract. That is, [in order] to be formed, a contract of deposit requires that, in addition to there being an offer and acceptance by the two parties, there has to be the depositor's act of delivery of the things. Then the contract is formed.

(3) The majority of contracts of deposit are nongratuitous. They may be gratuitous contracts. Whether it is gratuitous or not should be determined by law or the agreement of the parties.

(4) In view of the fact that, in a contract of deposit, both parties bear obligations, it is a bilateral contract.

(5) The objects of a contract of deposit should be specified generic things or specified things in the true sense. They include the means of production and daily necessities of life, public property, and the individual property of citizens. They may be things whose circulation is unrestricted or things whose circulation is restricted. But things whose circulation is prohibited, [as well as] buildings and other things inseparable from the land, cannot be the objects of the contract of deposit.

Contracts of deposit came into being and gradually developed to meet the objective needs of commodity production and circulation. In the earlier contracts of deposit, the rights and obligations of the parties were relatively simple, and the law only recognized gratuitous deposit. Although such historical limitations can still be seen reflected at the time of Roman law, the contract of deposit already had a considerable development and extent in Roman law. It included deposit of things over which there was a dispute, deposit of things for others during a disaster, and the responsibility of a shipowner or innkeeper for the keeping of the things the passengers or guests carried with them. The content of the provisions of the French Civil Code regarding the rights-duties relationship of the parties to a contract of deposit was still more comprehensive. Although the code has been amended or revised nearly a hundred times from 1804 to the present time, the part of the code relating to contracts of deposit has been very little changed.

Beginning at the end of the 19th century, the major capitalist countries adopted monopoly accumulation to meet the demands of social large-scale production. At the same time they maintained the traditional deposit, they gave active support or protection to warehouse storage. They enacted a series of rules that were either in the civil code or in the commercial code. This was an important development in the law of deposit. During this period, the responsibility for storage of those engaged in the business of providing food and drink, etc., greatly exceeded its previous boundaries and this became more and more a characteristic of the capitalist commodity economy.

After the October Revolution, a new form of deposit and the related law of deposits came into being to meet the demands of the economy based on socialist public ownership. The contracts of deposit between socialist organizations almost all serve the national economic plan directly or indirectly. Therefore, special rights-duty relationships developed between the depositors and the depositories. This is a basic point that distinguishes the socialist contract of deposit from capitalist contract of deposit. In the course of the development of socialist construction in our country, deposit relations became very widespread. Among these, the storage of large quantities of materials and commodities is of still greater importance. The "Economic Contract Law of the People's Republic of China" promulgated by the Fourth Plenary Session of the Fifth National People's Congress on 13 December, 1983, provided the basic principles for contracts of deposit.

2. Scope of Application and Types of Contracts of Deposit

Contracts of deposit in our country are used between juristic persons, between juristic persons and citizens, and between citizens among themselves. Those engaged in deposit include the approved and registered juristic persons of either ownership of the whole people or collective ownership, but also include individual citizens who have been granted licenses to engage in storage activities. In recent years, the percentage of storage run by individuals engaged in the storage business has clearly increased because of the correct implementation of the policy of the Party and state towards the individual economy. Juristic persons whose main business is not storage may, however, lawfully engage in the business if the nature of their main businesses requires them to do so. But they are not allowed to make illegal income on this basis.

When citizens and juristic persons deliver their property to train stations, hotels, public baths, and units engaged in the service of providing food and drink, for storage, after these units have accepted [these articles] for storage, a deposit relation arises between them. The storage certificate issued to the depositor is considered to be a contract of deposit.

The temporary deposit relationships that arise in connection with contracts of sale, contracts of lease, and contracts of loan for use, are incidental to the contracts of sale, lease, and loan. In law they are regarded as ancillary. Therefore, they should be distinguished from storage contracts whose only purpose is deposit.

Contracts of deposit can be divided into several types from different points of view, for example, division according to subjects, division according to objects, division according to the length of term of storage, or according to whether contracts are gratuitous or nongratuitous, according to whether they are required by the plan, etc. Here it is important to introduce [some concepts] that bring together the elements and classifications that have been made. One is the warehouse contract and one is the ordinary contract of deposit (contract of storage). The main differences between them are that the subjects of the former are limited to juristic persons but the subjects of the latter are not limited to juristic persons. In the former the objects are large quantities of materials and goods, whereas the objects of the latter are, for the most part, small quantities of daily necessities. The former is not gratuitous, the latter may be gratuitous or nongratuitous. The former is usually connected with national economic plan, the latter is not.

3. The Significance of Contracts of Deposit

With the development of large-scale construction activity the warehousing and storage activity in our country has had to have a relatively great development. Appropriate storage of commodities is an essential condition for maintaining normal social production and consumption. It is the continuance of social production in the area of circulation. Wherever there is commodity production, in order to maintain production in good order, there has to be an appropriate storage of commodities as a circulating reserve. With the development of commodity production, storage must be correspondingly enlarged. At the same time, the usual storage where one or both parties is a citizen has developed to a fairly large extent. For instance, with the development of the individual economy in rural and urban areas, and the development of peasant household sideline production, and with the increase of the number of specialized households and keypoint households, it is necessary for there to be an increase in the related storage. Owing to the rise of the living standard of citizens, and the increase of individual citizens' participation in cultural, athletic, and other leisure activities, there is an increase in storage. With the development of socialist welfare facilities in rural and urban areas, because of visits, touring, and seeing relatives in other places, storage requirements will be increasing steadily. All these are the essential trend of development in the socialist economy of our country.

The different forms of storage (storage for production, commodity storage, and storage for the consumption of individuals) are all continually in a state of transition to commodity storage, and will gradually come together in the form of commodity storage. This is a necessary consequence of the laws of the development of the commodity economy. That is, the greater part of stored commodities have been separated from the domain of production and form specialized commodity storage. They establish new specialized economic agencies, formed as independent accounting units, and promote advanced storage work which will be completely commercialized. In the near future, this trend of development should be encouraged through ongoing economic adjustment and the reform of the economic system.

Establishing and improving the system of storage contracts and using legal means to maintain a good system of storage is important to the development of the production and circulation and exchange of commodities in our country, to the realization of the state plan for storage of materials, and to satisfy the needs of citizens for production and daily life.

II
THE MOST IMPORTANT RIGHTS AND DUTIES OF PARTIES TO A CONTRACT OF DEPOSIT

1. The Major Duties of the Depository

(1) A depository should himself bear the responsibility of keeping the goods, and conscientiously perform well the task of examining and accepting the goods that are to be stored

"Himself bear the responsibility of keeping the goods" means the depository himself must directly fulfill the storage responsibility as to the goods left in his care properly and by means of his own labor. Unless there are no [sic] special circumstances, and the depositor has agreed that he may transfer the goods to a third party, the depositor may not avoid the responsibility of caring for the goods himself.

"Conscientiously perform well the task of examining and accepting the goods that are to be stored" means promptly checking and inspecting the external packing of the goods, the type, specifications, quantity, and quality of the goods according to the provisions of the contract and the materials and inventory furnished by depositor. This is the essential prerequisite for a depository to bear economic liability. If, upon inspection, something inconsistent with the contract appears, the depository must immediately notify the depositor, and if it finds stolen goods or other contraband goods it should report to the departments concerned to handle the matter. If there is an agreement for storage in advance according to a (state) plan, and if, as a result of the depository's fault, the goods cannot go into a warehouse and it is not possible to cancel the contract, the depository is liable to compensate the depositor for any injuries he suffers and to pay the penalty for breach of contract as provided in the storage contract.

(2) [The depository must] take proper care of the things that are stored and keep them in good condition

The meaning of "proper care" includes not injuring the stored goods, not using them (unless there is a contrary agreement in the contract) unless it is necessary, not opening the package on one's own and rummaging through the goods, taking positive measures according to the different kinds of goods and the technical rules for storage or the provisions of the contract, maintaining the goods in good condition, and ensuring the quality and quantity of the goods. The depository shall be liable for damages if, during the period of storage, the goods deposited are injured or lost, reduced in number or altered or contaminated, etc., owing to poor storage. A depository is not liable for damages if the occurrence of the above loss is due to irresistible force, natural loss of the goods, or due to the depositor's fault.

(3) [A depository is obliged] to return the things to the depositor

The obligation of a depository to return refers to returning the original property deposited by the depositor, not that of the same kind, quality, and quantity as the property deposited. The time for return can only be determined according to the contract, and unless the depositor has so requested, the depository may not return the goods before the time for return. The place for return should be the place where the goods are stored, unless the parties provide otherwise by agreement. If the depositor has not picked up the goods at the time set by the contract for return, the depository bears the responsibility of notifying the depositor to pick them up. If he does not give this notification, the depository shall not dispose of the goods for which the term of storage has expired. If the depositor loses the storage certificate (warehouse receipt) issued by the depositor and immediately notifies the depository of the loss, the depository must protect the depositor's rights and interests. If, after the depositor's notice, the goods are picked up by people other than the depositor, the depository shall be liable for this to the depositor.

(4) According to the provisions of the contract, [the depository must] check the circumstances of storage together with the depositor

When important goods are stored, the depository must at a set time, or at a time that is not set, according to the contract, together with the depositor, check the condition of storage of the goods. If some problems appear, the depositor should immediately take proper measures in order to ensure that the goods [remain] in good condition without any loss.

(5) [The depository must] ship the goods according to the contract

Where the contract provides that the depository shall ship the goods at the expiration of the term of storage, the depository must ship them at the time agreed and in the manner provided in the contract. If, because of the depository's fault, shipping does not start on time, or the shipment reaches a wrong destination, or the shipped goods are not sufficient, and, as a result of any of these, the depositor suffers loss, the depository is liable for damages.

(6) [The depository should] take out insurance with an insurance company according to the contract

If the law or the contract provides that a depository should take out insurance on the goods from an insurance company, in getting the property insurance, the depository should immediately take care of the procedures. If the depository does not perform this obligation and injury comes about as a result of an unintended accident, the depository is also liable. If it is because of the depositor's fault that the procedures were not carried out, and, as a result of an unintended act, an injury results, the depository is not liable.

2. The Duties of the Depositor

(1) To furnish relevant information

The depositor should provide the depository with the information necessary for the depository to examine and accept the goods, to understand the properties and characteristics of the goods so that he can elect the proper ways and methods to keep them. The depository is not liable for loss that occurred because the depositor did not provide the information necessary for the proper keeping of the goods.

(2) To ensure proper packing

When the goods are packed, the packing must meet the standards laid down by the state or competent departments. When the packing is not in accordance with these standards, and this causes injury to the goods, the depository is liable. Where it is necessary for the depository to improve, rearrange, or redo the packing because the original packing was not strong enough or because the depositor has to remove some portion of the packed goods, the depositor should furnish the needed packing materials and pay for the packing service.

(3) Special liability for the storage of dangerous materials, or materials that are susceptible to decay

A depositor must comply with the state regulations if it stores dangerous materials that are flammable, explosive, toxic, etc., and materials that are susceptible to decay. A depositor of the above materials must indicate in the contract in detail the properties of the goods and the concrete methods of avoiding the dangers and furnish the necessary information. The depositor is liable for damages if it fails to perform the obligations, and, as a result of this, the depository or other persons suffers injury to property or injury to the person. If the depositor is also involved in the above loss, the depository and the depositor are jointly liable.

(4) To pick up the goods at the agreed-upon time

A depositor should immediately pick up the deposit when the storage period provided in the contract expires or upon proper request of the depository to do so. The depositor should pay the storage fee for the storage period that exceeds the term. He must also pay the penalty provided in the contract. The depositor shall bear the loss or damage or deterioration that occurred after the expiration of the term, and that could not be prevented by the depository's taking necessary measures. The depository may dispose of the goods when the time of storage has expired, according to the time and procedures set by law.

(5) To pay the expenses and storage fees

A depositor is liable to reimburse the depository for expenditures incurred by the depository in performing the storage obligations that exceed the normal scope of storage expenditures and that are necessary for preserving the goods.

Where the storage is to be paid for, the depositor should pay the fee set by state regulations or by contract. If the depositor seeks to terminate the storage relationship before the expiration date set in the contract, the remuneration should still, in principle, be computed according to the originally agreed-upon storage period. The remuneration for storing goods that require special equipment or techniques should be computed according to special rates.

(6) Exercise the right to demand damages within a special period of prescription

Where, according to the contract, the depositor has a claim against the depository for damages, such claim must be made in accordance with the relevant rules of the law of prescription.

28 Partnership Contracts

I
GENERAL DISCUSSION OF PARTNERSHIP CONTRACTS

1. The General Concept and Special Characteristics of Partnership Contracts

Parties may form a contract of partnership to achieve any objective not prohibited by law. But this chapter is concerned only with those partnership contracts that have the carrying out of production management and other economic activities as their objective.

A partnership contract is an agreement between two or more parties wherein they jointly contribute funds and manage the partnership together to achieve their common economic objective. A contract of partnership possesses the following legal features:

(1) The partners contribute capital jointly and manage the partnership together

The joint contribution is a material condition precedent for common management. If there is no joint contribution, there can be no common economic management and no achieving of the common economic objective. Therefore joint contribution is an essential feature of a partnership contract.

According to the partnership contract, each partner's contribution may take the form of money, material, equipment, or a building or land. [A partner] may also provide skill or labor as a contribution. To protect cultivated land, the law prohibits partners from contributing cultivated land as an investment except where the law or regulations specifically permit it. The form the contribution of a partner may take should be determined through agreement of the partners. The proportion of each partner should also be determined through agreement and be recorded in the partnership contract. Where there is no contract provision on this matter, it will be assumed that the contributions of all the partners are the same.

Managing the partnership together means that since each partner has a common economic objective they should all participate in the management and administration of the partnership. If there is only common contribution but some of the contributors do not participate in the management of the partnership, the activity is not a partnership. For instance, if two persons make contributions to buy something, but do not manage it together, then there arises between the two only the relation of common ownership, but not the partnership relation. According to the state policies regarding partnership, all partners have to participate directly in the production and management of the partnership, and the training of apprentices is subject to certain limitations in order to prevent the exploitation of others under the guise of a partnership.

(2) Partners have common objectives and common interests

Partners must have a common economic objective and economic interests. The unity among the concrete objectives and interests of the partners is a legal characteristic that distinguishes [a partnership contract] from other contracts. In other contracts, the concrete economic objectives of the parties are different. For example, in a sales contract, the objective of one party is to get money, whereas the objective of the other party is to obtain the goods. But what the partners do is a joint action. Their rights and duties are equal and stand side-by-side. Therefore their interests are also common.

2. The Significance of Partnership Contracts

A partnership contract is also a product of the commodity economy, and it is one of the earliest contracts. Early in the period of Roman law, there were partnership contracts. These include partnership contracts that were formed to pursue property interests such as two or more persons pooling capital and management to run a workshop, commercial establishments, or transport ventures. [There were also] situations in which several persons formed associations to pursue academic, recreational, or religious objectives. These were also called partnerships that did not have economic objectives. With the development of a commodity economy, particularly with the appearance and development of the capitalist commodity economy, the scale of social production became larger and larger. This demanded large amounts of capital. So partnerships formed by more than one person to establish factories and mining enterprises, and business firms gradually became an important method for capitalists to collect capital and conduct business jointly. Even though the share companies and other business organizations which appeared later are better than partnerships, because the partnership is simple and convenient in organization and may have much or little capital and is flexible in operation, it is still a popular form in the capitalist countries for collecting capital and conducting business. In our country, before Liberation, in the entire country there were about 1,300,000 privately managed industrial and commercial enterprises. Except for about ten thousand companies, all were organized as individual enterprises or partnerships. From this fact, the position occupied by partnerships in the social economic life of the time can be seen.

After Liberation, the state adopted the policy of utilizing, limiting, and reforming privately owned enterprises. In 1956, socialist transformation of the private ownership of the means of production was essentially completed, and partnerships between individuals were gradually replaced by collective enterprises.

Since the Third Plenum of the Eleventh Party Conference in 1978, our country entered the new period of the construction of socialist modernization. To meet the demands of the construction of the Four Modernizations and to stir up the enthusiasm of all elements, the state allows and encourages, on condition that socialist public ownership occupies the predominant position, individual laborers to conduct, within the limits of the law, business in the form of individually owned enterprises under individual management and partnerships. The partnership among individual laborers is a form of joint management of the individual economy. At the present time, there are many forms of partnership in the handicraft industry, in food and drink service, repair and processing enterprises, and other service operations. In consequence of the requirements of the reform of our country's agricultural economic system and the development of the commodity economy, partnership accumulations of capital carried on industrial and agricultural production economy. Joint ventures between agricultural households were especially noteworthy.

During the adjustment and reform of the economy of our country, there also appeared many types of joint ventures between enterprises of property owned by the whole people, between enterprises of collective ownership, and between enterprises of property owned by the whole people and enterprises of collective ownership, and between industrial and commercial enterprises. Among these there were joint ventures between industrial and agricultural entities, joint ventures between an industrial enterprise and a commercial enterprise, joint ventures between an agricultural entity and a commercial enterprise, etc., as well as joint ventures between state managed enterprises, collective enterprises and individual industrial and commercial enterprises, etc. Some of these already form economic entities that are the subject of civil law rights. Some are comparatively loose and rely on mutual joint-management agreements to carry out adjustments. [This] suits the uneven situation of the development of productive forces in our country and the objective demands of the many levels of the economy. Its appearance and development helps socialist enterprises to overcome the limits (restrictions) caused by ownership systems, subordination relations, trades, and areas. It promotes the process of multiplication of economic forms of our country, to mobilize the enthusiasm of all sectors. It develops urban-rural socialist commodity economy. It advances the development of the construction of socialist modernization.

II
THE PRINCIPAL RIGHTS AND DUTIES OF PARTIES TO A PARTNERSHIP CONTRACT

1. The Partner Has a Duty to Make His Contribution of Funds (Things)

After a partnership contract is formed, each partner should contribute his agreed-upon investment on time. These accumulated investments are the property of the partnership. They are owned jointly by the partners and are the essential funds for carrying on the partnership business. If the contributions of a partner consist of some particular equipment or buildings or the right to use land, such property may be used by all the partners in the operation of the partnership, but ownership to this property still belongs to the one who contributed it. So this property is not included in the partnership property.

Partnership property is the common property of all partners. It no longer belongs to the original contributor and cannot be mixed with the property of the partner. Disposition of any partnership property has to be decided on by all the partners together. No individual partner may dispose of any partnership property by his own will. If one partner conveys all or part of his contributed funds to a third person outside the partnership, he must first obtain the permission of the other partners. During the effective period of partnership, no partner may withdraw his contribution. This includes the property he contributed to be used.

If one or several partners has not performed his [their] duty of making the agreed-upon contribution or the contribution does not conform to the agreement, the other partners or the managing partner have the right to demand performance according to the agreement, even to bringing suit in court. If the nonperformance of this duty to contribute injures the other partners [the one who did not contribute] is liable for damages.

2. The Partner Has the Right and Duty to Participate in the Production and Management [Activities] of the Partnership

Joint management by the partners of partnership affairs is an important feature of partnerships. Consequently, participation in the production and management of the partnership operations is a duty of the partners. It is also a right of all partners.

Partnership activities include participatory activities and executive activities. "Participatory activities" means participating in deciding partnership matters such as jointly deciding the partnership plan and other important matters and checking on the execution of partnership matters. In deciding partnership matters, every partner has an equal say. Unless the contract provides otherwise, partners should make decisions according to the principle of coming to a unanimous agreement. Oppression of the few by the many and arbitrary acts by any partner are not allowed. Executive matters are partnership matters that require concrete implementation, and are mainly those that are most important for the daily routines and management of the partnership affairs according to the plan for, and the requirements of, the operation of partnership activities. Executive affairs, such as participation in production and management activities, may be executed by all the partners together. The execution of some of the administrative affairs may also be delegated by the partnership contract or by subsequent agreement of all the partners to one or several partners. For example, the partners can appoint a manager, secretary, accountant, and other officers. The partners who undertake the responsibility for the execution of such affairs are called the managing partners.

3. The Obligation of the Managing Partners to Accept the Supervision and Investigation of the Other Partners

Partnership property is the common property of all partners. Partnership affairs are the affairs of all partners. Thus, the equality of the management of the partnership—good or bad, the profits and losses, have a direct relation with the interests of all partners. Because of this, where there are managing partners, the other partners have the right to supervise and investigate the work of the managing partners, and the managing partners have the obligation to accept such supervision and investigation. Under this obligation, the managing partners should make reports on the execution of partnership affairs and the financial situation of the partnership at the times required by the contract or by other agreements, and make regular reports on the accounts. Partners who are not managing partners may choose to check all the work of the managing partners at any time. To protect the lawful rights and interests of the partners, any agreement by which the right of supervision and investigation is taken away or given up is without effect.

In carrying out the partnership affairs, the managing partner should strictly comply with the relevant state laws and regulations, and conscientiously carry out the contract provisions and the common decisions of all partners. The managing partner is liable for any losses to the partnership property caused by his intentional or negligent act. If the circumstances are very serious, and the decision agreed to by all of the partners, the authority of the managing partner can be withdrawn.

4. The Division of Benefits and Liabilities Among Partners

All of the partners have a right to share in the benefits shared by the partnership. Unless the partnership contract provides otherwise, they share in proportion to their contributions (including contributions of labor).

The partners must be jointly liable for the obligations of the partnership. The obligations of the partnership must first be settled out of the partnership capital. If this is insufficient, what kind of liability each partner must bear as to the deficiency is decided differently in different countries. Some provide that each partner is jointly liable. As in the German Civil Code of 1900—some provide that each partner is liable proportionately to the amount of his contribution. [This is what is provided by the] Japanese Civil Code, the Soviet Russian Civil Codes, etc. At present, the joint venture contracts between socialist organizations in our country, in general, provide that there should be sharing of the benefits and liability for losses proportionately according to the amount of the contribution. Actually, the joint venture obligations choose the principle of proportionate liability. This method is suitable for socialist organizations. It does indeed protect the interests of the obligee and is useful for stabilizing the social economic order. At the same time, it also corresponds with the state's financial and economic discipline in relation to socialist organizations. In the case of partnerships among citizens, unless the contract provides otherwise, there is joint liability among the partners. Since there are limits to the capital of citizens, their property situation is hard to supervise. If the partners are jointly liable for the obligations of the partnership, this results in the partners initially guaranteeing each other. This is advantageous for maintaining the social economic order and protects the interests of third persons.

III
THE FORMATION AND TERMINATION OF A PARTNERSHIP CONTRACT

A partnership contract must be formed by all partners (citizens and juristic persons) according to the principle of voluntary participation and mutual benefit. There must be complete agreement as to the affairs of the partnership. To avoid controversy, parties to a partnership contract must use the written form for their agreement.

The essential contents of a partnership contract include: the scope of activities, the total amount of capital, the amounts to be invested by each partner, remuneration for services, allocation of profits and losses, and the effective period of the partnership contract.

In order that the state can supervise and administer the activities of partnerships, a report of the partnership contract should be made to the local administrative agency for industry and commerce for checking and filing. If, after checking, the agency finds that the contents of the contract are according to law and that the rights and obligations of the parties are clear, the agency should make a file [for it] and issue a business license. Then the partners may begin their activities.

Apart from this, if a third person wants to enter the partnership, he must obtain the permission of all the partners. When a third person enters the partnership he obtains the status of partner and has the legal relation of partnership with the other partners.

A partnership contract may be terminated when one of the following happens: (1) where the partnership contract provides for a term and the term expires; (2) [where] the partners agree to dissolve the partnership relation; (3) where, in a partnership of two people, one of them withdraws; (4) [where] the partnership is ordered to dissolve by the administrative agency for industry and commerce or by the people's court because it has engaged in illegal activities.

When a partnership contract is terminated, for whatever reason, the partners should liquidate the property and the obligation rights and duties of the partnership; allocate, according to state law or the provisions of the contract, the profits or losses; and settle all the economic relations among the partners. In the meantime, partners should apply to the local administrative agency for industry and commerce to close the business. Upon approval of such application the partnership then comes to an end.

29 Mandate, Commission Agency, and Brokerage Contracts

Mandate, commission agency, and brokerage are three different and independent contracts with some similarities among themselves. Each of the three contracts has its own characteristics, but they have one thing in common: in all of them one party, through the other party, forms contractual relations with a third party. In civil law activities, some commission agencies engaged in trade engage in all three of these types of activities. Their relations mutually intersect and are closely related.

Mandate, commission agency, and brokerage are all frequently seen contracts. They play an indispensable role in opening channels for the flow of commodities between urban and rural areas, in adjusting the supply [surplus and deficiency] of goods, and in encouraging material circulation between urban and rural areas and between localities, and in invigorating the economy, and upholding the lawful interests of citizens. They are indispensably useful, and strengthen socialist cooperation, impel economic development, and fulfill and strengthen the results of the flourishing development of the reform of the economic system.

I
THE CONTRACT OF MANDATE

1. The General Concept of Mandate

A contract of mandate is an agreement according to which the mandatary handles matters for the mandator within the limits of the mandate, in the name and at the expense of the mandator. This [contract] is the prerequisite to the establishment of the representation relationship (an intentionally established representation) between the mandator and the mandatary.

The parties to a contract of mandate may be citizens or juristic persons.

The major legal characteristics of a contract of mandate are:

(1) The object of a contract of mandate is a juristic act

Usually, the representative matters handled by a mandatary for a mandator are juristic acts (for instance, representing the mandator in a lawsuit, managing the mandator's property, etc.) not ordinary acts (for instance, giving notification of a meeting, communicating ideas etc.). However, juristic acts that are closely related to the person of a citizen, such as making a will, putting on a show, creating or composing a work of art work, etc., cannot be done by a mandatary.

(2) The formation of the contract of mandate is based on the mutual trust of the parties

When the mandator selects a mandatary, it is always with the desire to select someone he trusts or who has a certain business capacity or specialized knowledge to assume the responsibility. When the mandatary accepts the mandate, he also wishes to be acquainted with the mandator. While the mandatary is carrying out his responsibilities, he must protect the lawful interests of the mandator. Moreover, he must fulfill his responsibilities in the way most advantageous to the mandator.

(3) In a contract of mandate, the mandatary handles the mandated matter in the name and at the expense of the mandator within the limits of the power [delegated in the] mandate

Juristic acts performed by the mandatary have the same legal effect as those performed by the mandator himself.

(4) A contract of mandate may be gratuitous and may also be nongratuitous

Contracts of mandate made in daily life between citizens are usually gratuitous. It is only when the contract or law provides that the mandator must pay a fee that it is nongratuitous. The contract of mandate with a service company of the means of production providing for [the mandatary] to purchase, sell, or engage in processing is nongratuitous because the contract provides that the mandator pay a commission or other fees to the mandatary.

The contract of mandate is also referred to as the contract of authorization. It is widely used between socialist organizations, between citizens, and between socialist organizations and citizens. It helps to solve the problems arising when one is not able to handle the matters personally that are often encountered by citizens and juristic persons because of illness, physical handicaps, being in a different place, overwork, lack of time, unfamiliarity with the business, lack of knowledge, etc.

2. The Major Rights and Duties of Parties to Contracts of Mandates

(1) The major obligations of the mandatary

(i) A mandatary has the obligation to complete the work of the mandate according to the instructions of the mandator. He should, within the scope of the power delegated to him, conscientiously uphold the lawful interests of the mandator and make every effort possible to complete the work of the mandate. He should deal honestly [with the mandator], be conscientious and active in carrying out his responsibilities. He shall not, on his own, change or distort the instructions of the mandator. If he does not respect the mandator's directions and causes injury to the mandator, the mandatary must pay damages.

(ii) Because this contractual relationship results from mutual trust, a mandatary should handle the work of the mandate personally. Only when there is specific authorization by the mandator, or when it is necessary for the protection of the interests of the mandator, can a mandatary transfer the mandate responsibility that has been given to him to another to handle. In civil law this is called "a transfer of the mandate" (or sub-representation). When this happens, the mandatary should immediately notify the mandator about the transfer of the mandate. Moreover, he is responsible to the mandator for the acts of the transferee.

(iii) A mandatary has the obligation to report on the carrying out of the work of the mandate. In the course of handling the work, the mandatary must, from time to time, or at fixed intervals, report his progress on the work of the mandate. After completing the work, a mandatary should make an overall report about the process of the work and results to the mandator and submit related documents.

(iv) A mandatary has the obligation promptly to turn over to the mandator all the property obtained in the course of handling the subject matter of the mandate except the necessary expenses for handling the subject matter of mandate.

(v) A mandatary is responsible for losses of the mandator caused by the mandatary's own fault.

(vi) If there are two or more than two mandataries handling the same subject matter of mandate, they are jointly liable to the mandator for any loss attributable to either one of them unless the contract provides otherwise.

(2) Major obligations of the mandator

(i) He is liable for the legal consequences flowing from the acts of his agent done according to the contract in handling the subject matter of the mandate. But a mandator is not responsible for the consequences of the mandatary's acts that are not within the scope of the power of the mandatary, unless the mandator explicitly or implicitly ratifies those acts afterwards.

(ii) He is liable to pay the mandatary for the expenses incurred in the course of the handling of the subject matter of the mandate (for instance, the storage fees and other necessary fees of trading, and commission agency warehouses which are engaged in the purchase and sale of goods). If the mandatary suffers loss because he acted upon the directions of the mandator, the mandator is liable for such loss.

(iii) After the mandatary has accomplished the subject matter of the mandate, the mandator should pay the remuneration to the mandatary according to law or to the contract (for example, the processing fee, or shipping expenses where the mandatary had the mandator's goods processed or shipped, the attorney's fee for a representation in court). The gratuitous contract of mandate is an exception. If the mandate relationship is terminated before the subject matter of the mandate is accomplished because of reasons attributable to the mandator, or because of the impossibility of accomplishing the object of the mandate, the mandator should pay the mandatary a fee corresponding to the extent to which the subject matter of the mandate has been accomplished.

(iv) A mandator should pay damages to his mandatary for the losses suffered by the mandatary in the course of handling the subject matter of the mandate, either because of the mandator's improper directions or because of other faults of the mandator.

(v) Where two or more mandators engage one mandatary to handle their common matter, they must jointly bear the legal consequences that result from the accomplishment of the work of the mandate by the mandatary.

3. Termination of the Contract of Mandate

The major reason for the termination of a contract of mandate is the accomplishment of the subject matter of the mandate as provided in the contract. If, in a document of mandate, there is an effective period, then the contract of mandate is terminated when the period expires.

In addition to the above, the contract of mandate is terminated in the following situations:

(1) When the mandator withdraws the authorization given to the mandatary, the contract of mandate is terminated

A principal may also withdraw at any time the authorization given by the mandatary to a sub-representative.

(2) When a mandatary resigns as a mandatary, the contract of mandate is terminated

Although a mandatary does not have to get the approval of the mandator to terminate the contract, he should give timely notice to his mandator of his resignation. If he does not resign at a suitable time, and if, as a result of this, the subject of the mandate cannot be transferred to another to replace him, and consequently the mandator suffers injury, the mandatary is liable for damages.

(3) If either the mandator or mandatary dies [the contract is terminated]

When the contract of mandate is terminated because of the mandatary's death, the heirs of the mandatary should notify the mandator in a timely way and take the necessary measures to protect the interests of the mandator.

(4) If either the mandator or the mandatary is declared to be without the capacity to act or to have only limited capacity, or to be missing [the contract is terminated]

(5) Where either the mandator or the mandatary is a juristic person, and such juristic person is dissolved or suspended [the contract is terminated]

If the contract of mandate is terminated because of the dissolution or suspension of the mandatary, the liquidating committee of the juristic person should seasonably notify the mandator and take the necessary measures to safeguard the mandator's interests.

II
THE CONTRACT OF COMMISSION AGENCY

1. Definitions and Importance

A contract of commission agency (also called a contract of entrustment) is an agreement according to which a commission agent under the authorization of an entruster purchases or sells goods for the entruster, or a particular item put by the entruster for sale in the agent's commission shop or given to be sold on consignment, or handles other business for the entruster in his own name and at the entruster's expense.

Both juristic persons and citizens can be entrusters in a contract of entrustment, but only those juristic persons which have been licensed to engage in the commission agency business can be commission agents (also called those entrusted). These juristic persons include state owned and collective owned commission shops, consignment shops, trading warehouses, and others.

The main legal features of a commission agency contract are:

(1) A commission agent conducts its activities in its own name within the limits of the authorization given by the entruster

The common characteristic of a contract of mandate and a commission agency contract is that both the mandatary in a contract of mandate and the commission agent in a contract of entrustment execute juristic acts under the authorization of another person. The difference between them is that in a contract of mandate, the mandatary acts in the name of the mandator.

(2) A commission agent performs the entrusted work at the expense of the entruster (as in the case where a commission shop or secondhand shop or daily-used-articles shop sells things put up for sale by others)

This is very similar to the situation in a contract of mandate where a mandatary handles the subject matter of the mandate at the expense of the mandator.

(3) A commission agency contract is nongratuitous

A commission agent receives a fee for handling entrusted business for the entruster. This is different from a contract of mandate. A contract of mandate is usually considered to be gratuitous. It is only when the law or the contract provides for a fee that it is nongratuitous.

(4) In a commission agency contract the title to the goods purchased by the commission agent for the entruster, or given by the entruster to the commission agent to sell, belongs to the entruster

Commission agency (in our country formerly called *hangji* or *yahang*) is a product of the commodity economy. The commission agency system had its origin in the ancient Roman era to meet the needs of trade movement. Organizations of the nature of commission agents appeared in some cities where business was more developed. These organizations would handle purchases and sales, storage, consigning for shipment, and purchasing insurance for their customers. They accepted trusts, lent money entrusted to them, and engaged in other related activities. The modern system of entrusting is seen in the law of Equity in England, and later found its way to the United States and Japan where it underwent a rapid development. Trust companies of western countries usually handle trust business as well as bank business. In old China, trust companies, copying Europe and the United States, engaged in both bank and trust business. The gradual expansion of the scope of trust business facilitated the development of commodity production and exchange, and at the same time provided more convenient and advantageous means for the capitalists to exploit and extract enormous profits.

In some capitalist countries, contracts of entrustment are governed by the commercial codes. For example, both the French and German Commercial Codes have special and detailed provisions about commission agency contracts. However, in Anglo-American law, contracts of commission [mandate] are placed under agency.

In our country, commercial organizations that had the nature of commission agencies appeared as early as the Han Dynasty. At that time they were called *daidian*. In the Tang Dynasty they were called *didian*, and commission agents were called *yahang*, *yaren*, and *yakuai*. The ancient codes and records of the Tang and Song Dynasties had some provisions about this. In the Ming Dynasty, the *yahang* appeared, and it was provided that the establishment of a *yahang* had to be approved by the government, and that a *hang tie* had to be obtained (*hang tie* was also called a *ya tie*; it was the business license of commission agents). The government then collected contributions and taxes from *yahang* and other commission agents every year. The business of *yahang* and other commission agents expanded from the original purchase and sale of livestock to purchases and sales of other kinds of goods. The main business of these commission agents was bringing possible trading partners together, negotiating purchases and sales, storing and consigning for shipment, and providing accommodations for their customers. From the Qing Dynasty the number of business organizations engaged in commission agency gradually increased. In addition to the traditional *yahang*, *yashang*, and *yadian*, there appeared commission agents' storehouses and warehouses. In old China, trust companies appeared in the early twenties. Later some big banks established trust departments within themselves. Although the names given to the organizations and people who engaged in commission agency business were different—for example, *hangzhan* [broker's warehouse], *huozhan* [commission agent's warehouse], trust company, and other names—they were all exploitative and speculative. Some of them were trust organizations manipulated by the bureaucratic monopoly capitalists, and were the means used by these capitalists and imperialists cruelly to exploit the masses of working people.

After the founding of the New China, the government imposed some restrictions on privately owned broker's storehouses and storage warehouses and other commission agency economic activities, and carried out socialist transformation on these enterprises to make them serve the socialist construction and satisfy the people's needs. At the same time, under the guidance of the principle of "developing the economy and ensuring supplies," the state established and helped to establish state owned and collective owned commission shops, secondhand shops, and trading warehouses in various parts of the country (mainly in cities and towns). These enterprises' main business was to receive commissions from juristic persons, to handle business for them, and to sell what citizens consigned for sale on commission.

Since the main focus of the Party's work was shifted to the construction of socialist modernization at the Third Plenum of the Eleventh Party Congress, a lot of entrustment and other commission agency organizations, like trade and trust companies, companies serving the means of production, trading warehouses, commission shops, and secondhand shops, have been re-established and set up. Therefore, the commission agency business has become an indispensable channel in our economy for the circulation of commodities.

2. The Making and Termination of Commission Agency Contracts

In a commission agency contract, one party is the entruster and the other is the commission agent. When the parties have reached agreement about the commission agency, a commission agency contract is formed. Such contracts should be in writing (for example a written agreement, letter of authorization for sale of goods, etc.). The contract should have clear and definite terms regarding the names of the goods or material, size, quantity, price, packing, rate of commission, mode of delivery, ways and procedures of settlement of accounts, liability for breach of contract, and other matters.

The objects of a commission agency contract should be those whose circulation is not restricted by state laws and regulations. A commission agency contract may not have things whose circulation is restricted by state laws and regulations as its objects. For example, it is not permitted to sell on commission: guns and ammunition, military materials, precious metals, cultural relics with high value, dangerous materials, etc.

The price of the object of a contract of entrustment has to be consistent with the price set by the state, and if there is no uniform price set by the state, the parties may set their price by agreement according to the market price of the same kind of goods. That is, the parties may set their price by agreement according to the principle of fairness with reference to the value of the goods, the market situation, and the other factors. The price of special items may be evaluated by an expert in light of the unique value and quality of the items and set according to the evaluation.

The packing of the goods has to be done in accordance with the standards set by the transportation department. Otherwise the commission agent is not liable for losses that occur during transit, except where the packing was done by the commission agent himself. If the packing does not meet the requirements of transit, and the commission agent repairs and strengthens it, the entruster is liable for his expense.

A commission agency contract should also provide terms regarding the storage of the goods, the place of delivery, the commission fee, and the modes for payment and acceptance, to make clear the rights and obligations of the parties and the scope of their responsibility.

In addition to a commission agency contract being terminated by the full performance of the contract itself, it is terminated when juristic persons serving as entrusters or commission agents are dissolved, or when the entruster dies or is declared to be missing or without the capacity to act, etc. When one of the above situations causes the contract to be terminated, the successor to the rights of the entruster or his representative should give timely notice to the commission agent. Before receiving such notification or other direction, the commission agent should continue his performance of the entrusted matter and the contract is still effective.

3. The Major Rights and Obligations of Parties to a Commission Agency Contract

(1) The major obligations of the entruster.

(i) After receiving notification from the commission agent that the entrusted matter has been completed, the entruster should promptly accept what has been done according to the contract, and if the commission agent was entrusted to buy some kind of goods, the entruster should promptly examine and accept the goods bought. If the entruster discovers that the goods are damaged or are defective, or in other respects do not conform to the contract, the entruster should immediately inform the commission agent. After examination and acceptance by the entruster, the obligations of the commission agent are discharged.

(ii) An entruster should pay to the commission agent the commissions fixed by the contract or by the related competent government department, and this is the most basic obligation of an entruster.

(2) The major obligations of the commission agent.

(i) A commission agent should handle the entrusted matter according to the directions of the entruster. In handling the entrusted matter, the commission agent

must safeguard the lawful rights and interests of the entruster, and should select the terms most favorable to the entruster to complete the entrusted matter.

Only when the circumstances change, and it is necessary to make changes in the original directions, but it is not possible to get the entruster's consent in time, may a commission agent carry out its obligations in a way that does not conform to the directions of the entruster. When the matter is over, the commission agent should also give timely notice to the principal.

(ii) A commission agent should examine both the goods entrusted to him by the entruster to be sold and the goods which the entruster requests him to buy. A commission agent should also take proper care both of the goods to be sold for the entruster and those bought for him. He is liable for losses resulting from injury, loss, alteration, or contamination of the goods because of poor storage. If the loss, injury, or alteration occurred because of the natural attributes of the goods or was caused by irresistible force or other cause not attributable to the commission agent, the entruster has to bear the loss.

(iii) A commission agent should promptly hand over to the entruster all the benefits he received from the performance of the entrusted matter except for the agreed-upon or statutorily fixed commission and other fees. Usually the prices of the goods to be sold or bought are set by the parties, through agreement. In some situations, if the commission agent sold the goods at a higher price or bought goods at a lower price than the prices fixed by the entruster, the benefits resulting therefrom belong to the entruster.

III
THE BROKERAGE CONTRACT

1. Definition and Characteristics

A brokerage contract is an agreement wherein a broker, according to the directions of the principal, finds opportunities for, and makes introductions between, the principal and a third person for them to enter into a contract, and the principal pays the agreed fee to the broker.

In a brokerage contract, one party is called the broker, the other party is called the principal. In our country, brokers, like commission agents, can only be juristic persons who are given permission by supervising organizations to engage in brokerage business, for example, service companies for the means of production, commission shops, etc.

The main legal characteristics of a brokerage contract are:

(1) In a brokerage contract, the broker conducts his brokerage activities according to the directions of the principal, and pursuant to the scope and the requirements of the commissioned actions.

(2) The purpose of the broker in making connections and introductions is to help to create conditions for the principal and a third person to form a contract and

accomplish a result. A broker may participate in the negotiations between the principal and the third person but does not participate in forming the contract. Therefore, a broker is neither a party to the contract between the principal and the third person nor a representative of either of them, but only a middleman who functions as an intermediary—he builds a bridge.

(3) A brokerage contract is usually nongratuitous, but sometimes it may be gratuitous. Only when the broker brings about actual results through his brokerage activities, that is, only when a contract is formed, can the broker obtain his fee.

In capitalist countries and old China, brokerage is a frequent and commonly seen activity. Both natural persons and juristic persons can be brokers. Business organizations engaged in brokerage are numerous and the scope of their brokerage business is extensive. People who engage in brokerage business are called men of business, *jingjiren*, or customarily *jianke*. They are middlemen merchants who are specialized in introducing and providing opportunities between businessmen, and for this they receive commissions. They often take the opportunity as a broker to extract money by cheating, and engage in black market and other illegal or speculative activities.

After the founding of New China, the government took a series of measures by promulgating regulations and decrees to ban illegal brokerage activities. At the same time, it established trust organizations in various parts of the country and laws to protect lawful brokerage business operations.

With the development of socialist construction in recent years, places for the exchange of materials, means of production service companies, trade and trust companies, etc., have been established in various parts of the country and brokerage activities between juristic persons have increased. These organizations have rendered their service on flexible terms, in various forms, and with simple procedures. One of their main functions is to bring potential buyers and sellers together and to help them to accomplish their sale directly. Through market investigation and research, they get to know the names, quantity, quality, sizes, prices of the goods required by the units that are buying and selling; then the needs of both buyers and sellers match. On this basis, they organize planned trade fairs for the buyers and sellers, or arrange meetings for the placing of orders where contracts can be concluded. These all help each supply what the other needs, reduce overstock and speed the circulation of funds, promote economic circulation, enliven the markets, and improve the economy.

2. Major Rights and Obligations of Parties to a Brokerage Contract

(1) Major obligations of the broker

(i) A broker should perform the matter requested by the principal conscientiously and responsibly, and take the initiative in helping the parties to come to an agreement. In making introductions and forming connections for the parties, a broker should act honestly, justly, in good faith, and not in a way contrary to the

notion of fairness. He should not swindle and bluff, or make any false representation for the purpose of cheating, or he is subject to liability for damages or any other legal consequence resulting from his practices.

(ii) A broker must conduct his activities within the limits of the law. The scope of the broker's business, the prices of goods, the commission to be charged, and other matters all have to be consistent with state regulations. The things whose circulation is prohibited cannot be the objects of the brokerage contract. A broker should not act for those who are financially incapable or whose lawful status as a juristic person is not clear.

(2) Major obligations of the principal

(i) He must pay the fee to which the broker is entitled for having accomplished the matter asked to be entrusted to him by the principal. Normally the principal pays according to the commission fixed by the competent government departments.

(ii) He should pay the expenses incurred by the broker in the course of conducting brokerage activities. That is, the principal should pay, according to relevant regulations, necessary expenses incurred by the broker in conducting the brokerage activities.

30 Technology Contracts

I
A GENERAL DISCUSSION OF TECHNOLOGY CONTRACTS

1. The General Concept and Legal Characteristics of Technology Contracts

The [phrase] "technology contract" is a general term for a rights-duty relationship agreement between parties for the development of technology, the assignment of technology, and the use of technology for serving society. The legal rules for adjusting technological relations are a legal device for protecting the normal circulation of technological commodities. They constitute an important part of our country's civil law.

According to the way our country's system of technology contracts is actually used in real life, and the related legislative practice, technology contracts may be of three basic types: technology development contracts, technology transfer contracts, and technology service contracts.

Technology contracts have the following legal characteristics.

(1) The object of the technology contract is not the usual property or labor; rather it is a special kind of commodity

That is, it concentrates on the technological product of the intelligence and the creative labor of mankind. The manner of the appearance of this technological product is usually of many forms and types. That is, it may appear in the form of information, technological material, charts, announcements, films, punch tapes (computer software), etc. It may also be expressed as a certain form of material or intellectual labor such as the prototype for a new product or sample or test product, as well as technological advice, etc.

(2) The technology contract serves as an important component of civil law contracts

It must first of all respect the general rules of obligation law and civil law. But, owing to the fact that technology contract relations arise in the midst of the development and assignment and service of technology, this causes them in many areas, particularly in problems arising from the ownership of the results of technology, to have to observe certain relevant rules of industrial property.

(3) Technology contracts have specified objects for which they are employed

The so-called technology usually refers to knowledge, skill, methods, and procedures whose source is production practice and which are used in production practice. Technology is a sort of invisible property. It may constitute a sort of special commodity that enters circulation as special goods. These are technological goods and are the expression of an important part of the thought and concepts of scientific knowledge. Certain scientific discoveries, particularly those which are the result of basic scientific research, are men's understanding of the rules arising from the phenomena of the natural and social world. Normally they appear in the form of principles, rules, formulas, theories, etc. These sorts of products not only have great value for science, they also have direct economic utility and value. Creativity and circulation must make use of this sort of scientific intellectual activity. In general, it is not advantageous to use contracts.

(4) Technology contract law and patent law are both [bodies of law] for regulating and protecting the property or nonproperty personal relations that arise from the invention and application of technology; but there are differences between the two

The most important matter which is regulated by the technology contract is the obligation relation that arises in the circulation of the products of technology; whereas the most important [object] regulated by patent law is the ownership relation that arises from the products of technology and industrial property rights. The technology contract can also serve as a legal procedure for obtaining and realizing property rights to the products of technology. For example, the parties may sign a contract for the permitted use of a patent or they may sign a contract for the transfer of a patent.

(5) Technology contracts are of many different legal forms

The technology contracts that arise from the development of technology, the transfer of technology, and technology service contracts are all formed differently. In each technology contract there are many different legal forms which contain different rights-duty relations. This is another difference between the general concept of technology contracts and the usual single civil law contract form (such as contracts of sale, hire, lease, etc.).

The concrete types of technology contracts are shown in the chart below:

- **Technology Contracts**
  - Technology Development Contracts
    - Commissioned Technology Development Contracts
    - Cooperative Technology Development Contracts
  - Contracts for the Transfer of Technology
    - Contracts for the Permission to Use Patented Technology
    - Contracts for the Permission to Use Exclusive Technology [Presumably Proprietary Technology such as Trade Secrets]
    - Contracts for the Assignment of Patents
  - Technology Service Contracts
    - Technology Consultation Contracts
    - Technology Assistance Contracts

2. The Formation of a Technology Contract

A technology contract may be executed on the basis of a technology development plan of a state supervisory ministry or other related bureau. It may also be executed on the basis of negotiation between the parties.

The subjects of technology contracts are, for the most part, social organizations with the status of juristic persons. Usually, among the parties to a technology contract, there will be at least one which is able to use its own technology resources in carrying out technological development and technology transfer, or the scientific research for technology service [such as] specialized academic institutions, industrial and mining enterprises, individual citizens, as well as some joint ventures carrying out specialized scientific research.

Except for simple technology service contracts, technology contracts must all be executed in written form.

Prior to executing certain technology contracts that are of high risk or involve very large investment, or are very complicated, the parties must carry out conscientious analysis and research into feasibility. They must execute the contract on the basis of repeated consultations or actual investigations. They must conscientiously draft every clause of the contract.

The principal clauses for technology contracts are specified by the parties according to the actual type and content of the contract. In general, they may include the following: (1) the object, content, scope, and requirements of the contract; (2) the plan for carrying it out, the schedule, and the term [of the contract]; (3) the budget or budgetary estimate for the expenses of the contract; (4) the contract price or fee, as well as the manner of payment; (5) the manner and standards for inspection and acceptance; (6) provisions for maintaining secrecy; (7) the principles for dividing the enjoyment of the products of technology; (8) principles for bearing the risk; (10) [sic: there is no (9)] responsibility for breach; (11) arbitration and legal actions; (12) explanation of special terms; (13) other clauses agreed to by the parties.

Background materials that are related to the contract and proofs of feasibility and reports of evaluations of technology documents itemizing responsibility and planning documents, technology standards, the scale of the technological problem, the original plans, and technological documents, as well as related blueprints, data, computations, and pictures, may, according to the agreement of the parties, serve as supplementary documents to a technology contract.

The parties may, so long as it is not violating state rules, make provision in a technology contract for the preservation of secrecy. When a party reveals a secret he must be liable for breach of contract and damages.

The price and fees of the technology contract may be agreed upon by the parties and specified in the contract according to the economic benefits of the technology, the cost of the research and discovery, the term of use, as well as liability for the risks and the right to the results of the technology, etc.

The manner of paying the price or fee may be either in one lump sum or in installments. There may be payment in advance or some other form of payment agreed to by the parties.

Under certain circumstances the parties may include technological discovery, transfer, and service in one contract. Consequently, the parties may execute one contract or several contracts in regard to the several related contracts discussed above.

II
TECHNOLOGY DEVELOPMENT CONTRACTS

1. The General Concept and Characteristics of Technology Development Contracts

Technology development contracts are those agreements with a specified rights-duty content formed by the parties in order to achieve a certain aim of technological development.

So-called technology development can normally be understood from the broad or narrow point of view. The broad view of technology development is the entire process of discovery and invention based on science and technology developed as social productive forces. It includes basic research connected with scientific and technological development, applied research, and developmental research. Technological development in the narrow sense does not include basic research, but is merely composed of applied research and developmental research. In daily life, when most people speak of technology development they are referring to technological development in the narrow sense.

From the legal point of view, technological development carried on in the contracts for the use of technology only refers to technological development in the narrow sense. It does not include basic research activity that does not have any definite commercial purpose, but is only directed to intellectual, conceptual theories. Consequently, the circulation of technology development contracts as technological commodities must be accomplished with a legal form. The object of the rights-duty relationship is to obtain a certain commercial purpose by carrying on useful research and development activity that creates a technological result. However, scientific knowledge, which is the product of basic research, is usually expressed in a highly abstract theoretical system. Even though these theoretical systems have great academic value in scientific research, and can, moreover, provide theoretical guidance for solving a whole range of practical problems, economically, all in all, they have no direct use value. It is also very difficult for them [i.e., the theoretical systems] to enter monetary circulation as commodities. The products of research for use and research for development are not the same [as the products of basic research]. The fact that they have a greater use value and applicability makes it possible for them to have a direct technological economic relationship with the field of material production. Their value may be realized and supplemented in the process of exchange. Consequently, technology functions as a sort of commodity. It may serve as an object of a contract law relation. For example, the quantum mechanics theory of Heisenberg and Schrodinger (which is basic research) is not a commodity. Anyone may use it "without compensation." But the semiconductor technology produced by the applied research conducted by the Bayer [?] laboratory based on this theory, as well as transistor production formed by intermediate experiments regarding semiconductor technology, the popularization of results, manufacturing trial runs, and other elements, could constitute a sort of special commodity to enter circulation. Consequently, on the basis of what was discussed above, it is only juristic persons and citizens who engage in applied research and development who can be the subjects of a technology development contract. As provided in the Decision of the Central Committee of the Chinese Communist Party Regarding the Reform of the System of Scientific and Technological Research: "Gradually carry out the system of technology contracts in the work of technological development and the work of applied research which is essential to obtain valuable results in the near future."

The work of development referred to in technology development contracts must, most importantly, include the following:

(1) Taking advantage of and being directed towards the achievements of basic research and applied research, developing new technology, new products, new techniques, new equipment, new materials, new standards.

(2) The reform of the enterprise's technology, the recommendation of technology for the enterprise to assimilate, and absorb and bring forth new ideas.

(3) Activities that center on new products and plans for carrying on new engineering, trial manufacture (construction), improving techniques, etc.

(4) Intermediate tests of new technology, new products, new techniques, small-scale trial production, as well as solving technology problems prior to production.

(5) Reasonable utilization and development of natural resources.

(6) Other types of applied research and development for research.

Technology development contracts may be divided into two types according to the differences between the parties' rights and duties, that is to say, the commissioned technology development contract (called simply, the commissioned development contract) and the cooperative technology development contract (called simply, the cooperative development contract). The differences between the two contracts are discussed below.

2. The Commissioned Development Contract

The commissioned development contract is an agreement where one party completes the agreed-upon development work in accordance with the requirements of the other party. The other party must accept the results of the research and pay a fee. The party completing the work is called the research developing party. The party receiving the [research] product is known as the commissioning party.

(1) The legal characteristics of the commissioned development contract

(i) The object of the contract is not the personal labor of the party developing the technology. Rather, it is the technological results produced by research. It is not the same as the usual civil law contract of hire. The objects of the commissioned development contracts are the large-scale products of intellectual labor that may or may not have [tangible] forms (for example, blueprints, materials, punch tapes, intermediate experimental products, prototypes, etc.). These do not include the products of labor in [contracts] of hire such as processing, making goods to order, repairing, and other results of labor included in the contracts of hire.

(ii) The purpose of the joint-commissioned development contract is [the production of] technological products that have creativity. In a commissioned development contract, the development research party, in order to fulfill some special requirement for production or life of the commissioning party, carries out research and development work according to the commissioning party's special economic goal. Consequently, at the time of the execution of the contract, the object of the contract is not some presently existing technology, but the result that is obtained after probing, testing, and research. The special nature of the commissioned development contract causes it to be different from the technology transfer contract which adjusts the transfer of existing technology.

(iii) The commissioning party commissions another party on the basis of assuming the risk to carry on the work of development. Usually, the commissioning party not only has the duty to pay to the one doing the research the agreed-upon fee, but he bears the risk of loss in the research occasioned by irresistible force and other objective reasons that cause the research to fail or the investment to have been in vain. This point clearly differentiates [these contracts] from ordinary civil law contracts of hire [work contracts]. In the contract of hire [work contract] all the risks are borne by the one performing the work.

(iv) In the commissioned development contract the party doing the research and development carries on the work in his own name and with his own technology and labor, although the technological economic requirements of the one commissioning the work determine the essential direction of the work of the one doing the research. It is not possible by means of this to limit the independence of the one doing the research and development. This makes the commissioned development contract different from the ordinary civil law contracts of delegation [commissioning].

(v) According to the contract of commissioned development, the commissioning party must give the party doing the research a specified fee for the research and development. The one doing the research must also, as agreed, give the commissioning party the product of the research. The contract for commissioned development is effective from the time of the agreement. Consequently, the contract for commissioned development is bilateral, nongratuitous, and promissory.

(2) The important rights and duties of the parties to a commissioned development contract

(i) The commissioning party has the duty to pay the technology research fee to the one doing the research in the agreed-upon form and in the agreed-upon time. This is the commissioning party's chief duty. The time for payment of the technology research fee is normally after the execution of the contract and prior to the commencement of the performance of the development and research. But it can also be paid in installments, and in installments of different amounts and at different times, according to the different circumstances, or after the other party has delivered the results of the research. If the commissioning party, without cause, refuses to make payment, or delays in making payment of the research fee, he is liable for failure to perform or delay in performance.

(ii) The furnishing of technological equipment and raw materials, technological materials and basic data by the commissioning party and his completion of the agreed-upon work must be carried out by the commissioning party according to the time, quality, and quantity [of the contract]. If this is not done, and there is a resulting stoppage or delay or loss of the research work, the commissioning party is liable for breach of contract.

(iii) The commissioning party has the duty to accept promptly the results of the research and development. If the refusal of the commissioning party, without cause, to accept the product [of the research], or his delay in accepting, causes a third person to take possession of the results of the research and development in a lawful and good-faith manner, or the product loses the value of its novelty, or the product encounters some unintended harm and is lost, the commissioning party must bear the entire financial responsibility.

(iv) If the commissioning party does not perform a contract, and causes a stoppage or delay in the research and development work, or its failure, then without a contrary provision in the contract, he still has the right to obtain the product of the research and development that was agreed upon, or the results of stages of research and development and the related data and materials. But he must pay the person doing the research the penalty for breach of contract and compensate for loss.

(v) The party carrying out the research and development must complete the research and development work in accordance with the requirements provided by the commissioning party and must promptly turn over the results of this research and development. This is the basic duty of the one carrying out the research and development. The object of the research and development contract is the technological product that is produced in the course of the research and development in accordance with the requirements of the commissioning party. The party engaged in the research and development must complete the research and development work strictly in accordance with the agreed-upon technological and economic standards. He may not, without the consent of the commissioning party, revise or amend the content, scope, and requirements of the object of the contract or the related plans for execution, schedule, or time limit. If, because of the fault of the party doing the research, the results of the research and development do not obtain the required object provided in the contract, or the research and development work is halted or delayed, or fails, he must repay all or part of the research and development fee to the commissioning party. If he causes the commissioning party to suffer property losses he is liable to pay damages. At the same time, this does not excuse the party carrying on the research and development from delivering the research and development (or the results of this stage of the research and development) and the related technology and materials.

(vi) A commissioned development contract is executed on the basis of the faith of the commissioning party that the developing party will accomplish the scientific result. In order to assure the interests of the commissioning party, the research and development party must personally complete the research and development work. Only when he has received the agreement of the commissioning party to transfer all or a part of the scientific research work to a third party [may he do so]. But the party carrying on the development and research must bear responsibility to the commissioning party for the quality of the work done by the third party.

(vii) The one carrying on research has the responsibility, according to the contract, to maintain secrecy in connection with the agreed-upon technological results. Normally, the objects of technology development contracts are the products of research and development that have not obtained protection from patent law (sometimes they are called unpatented technology). Consequently, after the commissioning party has obtained, according to the law or contract, a priority to make use of [the product] for a certain period of time, or "right to monopoly use," the party carrying on research and development has the duty, within the period provided by the contract, not to disclose the technological secret to a third party. In addition, if the commissioning party requires that the technological materials he furnishes be kept secret, the party carrying on the research and development must strictly observe the requirements. He may not, without the consent of the commissioning party, keep copies or disclose [the information] to a third person.

(viii) Generally speaking, the risk of research and development must be borne by the commissioning party. It often happens that there are special circumstances of scientific research which sometimes exist in the process of carrying on research and development—events which in the present state of science and technology cannot be perceived, prevented, or overcome—which cause research and development work to fail. This means that the parties to a research and development contract must bear certain risks while enjoying rights. The commissioning party's research and development fee has, in a different degree, the character of a risk investment. In order to encourage scientific researchers to have the courage to make explorations, and in the spirit of assaulting obstacles, the usual economic interests are protected. Unless the contract provides otherwise, if, in spite of the subjective hard work of a researcher, as a result of causes that arise during the course of the research and development which cannot be foreseen, prevented, or overcome by the other party, which cause the research and development to fail or to fail partially, this is a risk that must be borne by the commissioning party. But when the party engaged in the research discovers these conditions, he must immediately notify the commissioning party and take appropriate measures to minimize injury.

(3) The principle of division of the [right] to enjoy the products of research and development

The problem of the division of the [right] to enjoy the product is the basic problem of technology development contracts. Material commodities are, for the most part, obtained by the producer by the use of relatively simple labor, using equipment, tools, and within the scope of present technology, carrying on processing labor on raw materials. The ownership of these sorts of commodities can belong to the investor who furnishes the production capital (or he may be called the purchaser of the commodity). But the product of technology is obtained by the researcher in a situation where there is no present existing technology and skills to follow. [Rather] they are obtained by using complicated, difficult mental labor and creative activity to bring them forth. This means one cannot necessarily obtain research and development results by investing scientific research funds and using present technological materials and existing apparatus and equipment. Consequently, [to decide on] the ownership of this product one cannot simply apply mechanically the principles of ownership (also called property rights) [that are used for] material production. Based on the special constitution of the value of technological commodities, by reference to the general principles of licensing contracts authorized by the law of industrial production rights, the rights and duties of the parties sharing the results of a commissioned development contract are as follows:

(i) The rights of discovery and invention and the right to get honors and awards. Since these rights are very personal they must not be transferred or divided by the contract or in any other way. But, in accordance with our country's division of the awards for discovery, the above described rights belong to the one who has contributed the creativity in connection with the results of the research.

(ii) Patents and applications for patents that are produced by the results of research and development. According to section 8 of the Patent Law in regard to "two or more units that work together or one unit that received a commission to do research for another unit, as to the invention that results from accomplishing the planned work, unless there is a different agreement, the right to apply for a patent belongs to the unit that obtained the results or jointly obtained them." Where there are no special provisions, the right to apply for the patent must belong to the party doing the research and development, but, according to the principle of equality and mutual assistance, the party engaged in the research and development must tender to the commissioning party which gave him a research fee and assumed the risks in order to arrive at the said invention, the following preferences: (1) the commissioning party, prior to the approval of the application for the patent has the right to use the results of this said invention. But, it has the duty to maintain secrecy. (2) After the patent is awarded, it has the right to ordinary use of the patent without fee. (3) When the research and development party transfers its patent application right, the one commissioning has a preference right to obtain the assignment of the patent application right.

(iii) The right to use and the right to transfer every type of unpatented technological result. This is a complicated question and the one most frequently seen in contracts for the commissioning of research and development. Under our country's present conditions, in order to mobilize the enthusiasm of scientific and research organizations and industrial enterprises, and to forward the close connection of our country's science and technology and economic construction, we can establish the following principles for dividing the rights to the results of [research]: First, we must establish that the two parties both have rights to a share of the results. Particularly, in order to protect the basic rights of the commissioning party which has paid a fee for the research and development work, the party doing the research and development work must assume the basic obligation "not to transfer the results of the research and development to a third party prior to giving them to the commissioning party." Second, the parties may, by reference to the usual principles regarding the rights to the production of industrial enterprises, and according to the different levels of the commissioning party's investment (the research and development fee), make use of the form of a licensing contract to establish the following rights and duties: (a) the commissioning party who pays a *portion of the research and development expense* may have the right to use the results [of the research and development] without a fee. The commissioning party who pays the *entire expense for research and development* to the party doing the research and development may have a preferential right to use the results of the [research and development] without a fee. Within the scope or time limit of the contract, the party doing the research and development may not transfer the said results to a third party, but the party who did the research retains the rights to use the results for himself. The commissioning party which, apart from paying the entire research and development fee to the developing party, also pays the *agreed-upon "fee for exclusive use,"* has the right to insist that the developing party not transfer the results to a third party. In addition, the one doing the research and development does not retain the rights to use the said results.

In general, the parties to the contract, while in the process of specifying the principles for division of the rights to the enjoyment of technological results, must ensure that the party doing the research and development obtain a reasonable fee and also respect the commissioning party's economic interest. The purpose of stimulating the activity of research and production causes the commissioned contract of development to be a new type of contract that mediates between research and production and truly serves as an important tool for advancing technology and economic development.

3. Cooperative Development Contracts

Cooperative development contracts [involve] two or more parties who, in order to accomplish particular research and development work, use each side's personnel together to participate in research and development. It is an agreement [to engage] in joint research and development and to use joint investment to carry out the cooperative work, and enjoy the results together, and share the risks in common.

(1) The legal characteristics of a cooperative development contract

(i) The content of a cooperative contract refers to a rights-duty relationship formed in the joint carrying on of research and development, with two or more persons who are carrying on research and development work as the civil law subjects. It does not include the contractual relations of ordinary economic life in which there is common investment and joint management. This means that a cooperative development contract is not the same as the usual civil law partnership or joint venture.

(ii) The form in which the parties to a cooperative development contract carry on the research and development work is not the same as in the case of a commissioned development contract. The former is a form whereby the parties jointly carry on the research and development work. The latter is a form in which one party carries out the material investment and the other party carries out the research and development work. Consequently, most cooperative development contracts arise between specialized research and development scientific research units (such as research offices, universities, enterprises, etc.). But the commissioned development contracts are mostly between production offices (such as industrial and mineral enterprises) and specialized research and development units.

(iii) The rights-duty relationship between the parties to a cooperative development contract is joint. Each party is basically joined in working together to pursue the common purpose in order to accomplish the work of research and development. The commissioned contract of development is different. Since each party has different economic interests, a mutually opposed rights-duty relationship is formed.

(2) The rights and duties of parties to the cooperative research and development contract [are the following]:

(i) Each party must use his technological strength (or this might be called intellectual labor) to participate in the research and development work. A civil law subject which invests money or other property (movable or immovable) to serve as a contractual investment, but which has not directly participated in research and development work, must not be regarded as a party to a cooperative development contract.

(ii) Each party must work together jointly with the other to establish the plan for research and development to solve jointly the problems that arise in the course of the research and development. Each party must assume liability to perform the responsibilities provided in the contract or decided upon by the subjects of the contract as duties to be performed. Otherwise, if this causes any harm to any of the other parties, he is liable to compensate for injuries.

(iii) The technological results of the joint research and development and their economic benefits are enjoyed jointly by the parties. Each party has the right, within the scope of his own activities, to make full use of the results of the research and development. Unless there is a different provision in the contract, when the results are transferred to someone not a party to the contract, it must be agreed upon by all the parties. Each party shares in the economic benefits that result from the [transfer].

If one party, as the result of deficiencies in his own normal ability to carry on the research, or some other proper reason, requests unilaterally to transfer the research and development results to an extracontractual third party in order to reimburse him for the economic benefits he has lost, the other parties must allow this request. But the assigning party must immediately notify the other parties. If the other parties raise objections, the assigning party then has the right to request the other parties to reimburse him for the economic injuries to his rights.

(iv) With the unanimous consent of the other parties, any party may enjoy a preferential right or monopoly right to the results of research and development. But the said party [should] pay an agreed-upon consideration to the other parties for obtaining the above described rights.

(v) Each party must bear the proportionate or equal share of the risk of research and development failing or partially failing as the result of some cause that was unforeseeable, unavoidable, and that could not be prevented, which occurs during the course of the work. This point causes [this contract] to be different from the usual civil law partnership contract. This principle was decided upon in order to encourage each of the parties to be bold in his research and development contract investments and to avoid the experience of serious losses.

A reasonable formula for the extent of the rights and duties to a cooperative development contract can be agreed upon in the contract according to the extent of the creative work contributed during the course of research and development work, or the actual amount invested, etc. If there is no provision in the contract, then the rights and duties of each party will be regarded as being equal.

When, during the existence of a contract, a party withdraws without cause, he is liable for breach. A party who withdraws during the course of research and development work has the right to demand the return of his investment. If his investment cannot be withdrawn, or the withdrawal of the original property would be disadvantageous to the other parties continuing the research and development work, they may negotiate a new amount to be returned.

If the original investment includes patented or unpatented technology, the other parties may, according to the actual requirements of the research and development work, have the right to demand that the one withdrawing give his permission for the use of the above mentioned technology. Unless there is another provision in the contract, the said permission for use may contain provisions for compensation.

III
CONTRACTS FOR THE TRANSFER OF TECHNOLOGY

1. The Legal Characteristics of Contracts for the Transfer of Technology

A contract for the transfer of technology is one in which the transferor transfers a certain technological product to the assignee, and the assignee must accept this product, and, moreover, pay the agreed-upon fee. The technology transfer contract is an essential legal tool for carrying on the activity of trade in technology.

All technology transfer contracts have the following provisions:

(1) A contract for the transfer of technology is not the same as the usual contract for the sale of goods.

Its object is not solid [material] property. Rather, it is technology that is in the category of the product of intellectual activity. It includes inventions patented by law, new applications, and the transfer of external designs and specialized technological secrets (know-how) that is not patented but can be transferred.

(2) Because of the special characteristics of the transfer of ownership rights to technological commodities, after the transferor has transferred the technology to the recipient he does not lose his ownership of said technology

In most cases, all the transferee obtains is the right to use the technology. Consequently, the transfer of technology normally takes the form of a trade license. This aspect of the contract of transfer is different from the usual contract of sale, lease, or loan.

(3) The contract for the transfer of technology, like the contract for the development of technology, is promissory, bilateral, and nongratuitous

The two are different in that what is reflected in the contract for the transfer of technology is the relationship [arising out of] the transfer of existing technology, while in the technology and research and development contract, what is reflected is a research and development relationship for technology that does not yet exist.

2. The Essential Content of a Transfer of Technology Contract

(1) Patented technology and exclusive technology

There are approximately two types of technology included in technology transfer. One is a patented technology, that is, an invention, application, or design, etc., that is protected by a patent. The other is unpatented technology that does not receive industrial property law protection. The most important is technology that is not public and may be transferred secretly. In practice, the method of license is used to effect the transfer.

So-called patented technology is the product of technology for which the state supervisory agency, in accordance with the petition of the inventor and the provisions of the patent law, issues patent rights to the inventor for a certain period of time. The patentee may transfer his patent to another or he may transfer his rights to use the patent to another to use. In the practice of technology transfer, normally, the contract for the transfer of a patent or the application for a patent is called a contract for the assignment of the patent. The contract for the transfer of the use of the patent is called a contract for use [license for use].

"Exclusive technology" [in the heading of this subsection] comes from the English phrase "know-how." In our country, formerly, there were different translations: "technology secrets," "technology tricks of the trade," and "exclusive technology." Now, the normal translation is "exclusive technology." In regard to the meaning of exclusive technology or know-how, up to the present, both foreign and domestic academic circles have failed to arrive at a generally accepted clear definition. But speaking generally, exclusive technology is technological knowledge or industrial procedures or methods of operation that are essential to production that are not published and that can be transferred by secret means. In particular, it includes certain technological knowledge, technology, methods of operation, and technical knowledge of design and managerial expertise that is required for the production of certain patented goods or for exercising certain patented methods of production.

Both exclusive technology and patented technology are a sort of intangible property. Both have a commercial value that can be transferred, but the important differences are as follows: First, a patent right is a form of industrial property. It is protected by the State Patent Law. But, exclusive technology is technological knowledge that has not received a patent: inventions prior to application for a patent, or in the stage of examination prior to publication, as well as technological inventions which are not patentable under the patent laws, such as biological products, computer software, management techniques, analytical methods, traditional skills, and technological knacks [techniques], etc. Under certain conditions, all are "exclusive technology" [know-how]. Consequently, exclusive technology cannot seek protection under the rules of patent law. Second, patented technology is public, but exclusive technology [know-how] is secret. According to the patent laws of every country, when the inventor applies for a patent, he must place the content of this discovery in the patent application and reveal it, and it is published by the patent office in its official publication and made generally known. Exclusive technology [know-how] is kept strictly secret. It is not published. So far as the owner of the know-how is concerned, maintaining such secrecy is the necessary measure for obtaining its essential commercial value and preventing outsiders from infringing on it. It is also a central condition of the contract for the transfer of exclusive technology. Once the secrecy is lost, it is not possible to get legal protection.

(2) The essential content of a contract for the assignment of a patent

A contract for the assignment of patent rights is one in which there are rights and duties arising from the assignment of the right to apply for a patent or the patent [itself]. It is the central feature of technology transfer contracts.

The assignment of patents refers to the complete transfer of the property rights of patented technology. It is within the range of matters administered by civil law. The general civil law contract provisions are completely applied to patent assignment contracts. To be precise, the assignment of patent rights may use the nongratuitous and gratuitous form of transfer. This causes the rights and duties of the parties to a contract for the assignment of a patent to be largely similar to the basic content of the usual contract of sale or gift.

The contract for the assignment of a patent must be in written form. It can take effect after registration and publication by the supervisory government office. A contract for this transfer of a patent that has not been registered or published by the supervisory organization is legally effective only as to the transferor and transferee of the patent. It is ineffective as to third parties.

In our country, when units of ownership by the whole people transfer patent application rights or patents, they must get the approval of the supervisory organization. Every organization or individual which transfers a patent application right or patent to a foreigner must have the permission of the concerned ministry of the State Council.

When the transferee of the patent has a dispute over the use of or disposition of the said patented technology, unless the law provides otherwise, the transferor is legally liable.

(3) The essential content of a contract for the use of technology

A contract for the use of technology may also be called a "licensing agreement" from the English term. In present-day economic life, it is an essential form for trade in technology. According to the contract for the use of technology, the transferor of technology (or licensor) must permit the transferee of the technology (also called the licensee) to use his patented or exclusive knowledge. The transferee then has the right to use the patent or the exclusive technology and will pay the appropriate fee.

According to the nature and scope of the right to use acquired by the transferee of technology, as provided in the contract, we may divide contracts for the permission to use technology into the following types.

(i) The usual contract for permission to use. The one granting the use permits the grantee the use of the technology under the license for a specified place, but the grantor still retains his rights and still has the right to use within the set area and to transfer these rights to any third party.

(ii) Exclusive contract permitting use. The grantee may exercise the right of use to the technology specified in the contract within a specified area. The grantor retains the right to use the technology in the area, but he may not sell the same license to any third person.

(iii) The contract for monopoly grant of use. The grantee [acquires] the right to use the product of technology designated in the contract within a designated area, and neither the grantor nor any third party may exercise this right in this area.

(4) The essential duties of the transferor

At present, the essential rights and duties of the parties to the contract for the use of technology are as follows.

(i) In accordance with the terms of the contract, to transfer to the transferee the essential technological documents and tender to the essential technological directions.

In some cases, he must also tender to the transferee the necessary materials for the licensing equipment—parts and so forth.

(ii) He has the duty to guarantee that the transferred technology will attain the technological and economic level agreed on in the contract. First of all, he is responsible that the patented or exclusive technology be feasible and economically effective.

(iii) When the transferor has not transferred the technology according to the contract, or the technology he transferred did not meet the economic standard set out in the contract, he must pay the agreed-upon penalty for breach, and return all or part of the fee for the transfer of technology. If this causes injury to the transferee he is liable to pay damages.

(iv) After the transferor has transferred to a transferee a monopoly use permit or exclusive use permit, and he then transfers permission to use the said technology to a third person, or, after having made a transfer of a monopoly permit, he himself makes use of the technology, he must pay the penalty for breach of contract and pay damages to the transferee for any resulting injury.

(v) Unless the contract provides otherwise, the assignor of patented technology must pay the patent fee for the period of his own patent. Otherwise, if, in consequence, the patent becomes ineffective, and this injures the assignee of the patent, the assignor is liable.

(vi) The assignor may not, after a patent has expired, or after the patent has been declared to be ineffective, grant a license to use the patent.

(vii) During the period when, according to the contract, he can use the technology, if his rights are infringed (if a dispute arises over a patent), the assignor must assume the legal and economic liability.

(viii) Unless the contract contains a contrary provision, the transferor may not, on the basis of the following contractual provisions, limit the transferee's usual technological competition and technological development: limiting the transferee from developing and improving the technology it has achieved; requiring the transferee to accept unrelated attached conditions along with the technology, including the purchase of unneeded technology or materials, tools, equipment, commodities, or labor; limiting the transferee from obtaining similar technology from another source, or [from obtaining] supplementary or even better technology; limiting the transferee to being able to buy raw materials or parts only from the commissioning party; without cause demanding that he obtain the rights to the improvements made by the transferee in the technology; and, on his own, without authorization, assigning the improvements in the technology made by the assignee, or demanding that he pay a fee or assume liability for unused or ineffective patented technology.

(5) The essential duties of a transferee

(i) [He must], according to the contract, pay the fee for the transfer of technology. This is the most basic duty of a transferee. If the transferee does not pay the fee for transfer of technology according to the contract, then apart from paying the fee, he must pay the penalty for the breach to the transferor. If he refuses to pay the fee for transfer he must stop using the transferred technology and the technological materials, and compensate the transferor for his injuries.

(ii) The transferee may, within the scope of the country's legal rules, accept the following contractual limiting conditions on the transfer of technology: the time for the exercise of the technology, the place of using the technology, the methods of using the technology. This includes limiting the use [of technology] to one or several forms in creating, using, or selling technology, in regard to the purposes for which the technology may be used, limiting it to one or several purposes and uses, etc.

(iii) If the use by the transferee of the patented technology or exclusive technology exceeds the scope provided in the agreement as to time, place, or manner, or without the consent of the transferee, he transfers it to a third party to use or possess, he must cease this infringement and compensate the transferor for his injuries.

(iv) The transferee has the duty to make prompt use of the transferred technology in accordance with the contractual provisions. If the transferee does not make use of the said transferred technology, or does not make prompt use of it, and this causes the transferor to receive injury, (particularly when there is installment payment of the transfer fee by the transferee) the transferee is liable for damages.

(v) The transferee has the duty to maintain secrecy in regard to transferred exclusive technology. Except where the contract provides otherwise, at the termination of a license for the use of exclusive technology, the transferee is still bound by the provisions on maintaining secrecy.

IV
TECHNOLOGY SERVICE CONTRACTS

1. The Legal Nature of Technology Service Contracts

A technology service contract is a contract by which one party makes use of his existing technological knowledge, experience, and information to accomplish technology service work for another. The other person must accept the said work and pay a service fee. The party furnishing the technological knowledge is the party performing the service. The party receiving the work is the commissioning party.

Technology service work is an essential constituent part of all social service institutions. It is also a special form of technology development and transfer. The special characteristics of the technical service contract can be placed under the following heads:

(1) The technology service contract is a special form of service relationship

According to the technology service contract, the basic rights and duties of the parties are: the party performing the services, on the basis of his own technological knowledge, experience, or information, completes a certain work for the commissioning party, as in carrying out feasibility studies, offering reports of technological calculations, offering engineering plans, drawing construction plans, carrying out engineering designs, making investigations, or training technological staff. The commissioning party will, according to the contract, inspect and check before acceptance, and pay the agreed-upon fee.

(2) The technology service contract and the commissioned research and development contract have points of similarity in their form, but in their nature and content they are very different

Usually, the special characteristic of a technology service contract is that it refers to the present state of knowledge, experience, and information of the parties that are repeatedly used. They are relatively simple technology transfer and assistance [contracts]. The rights-duty relation of the commissioned research and development [contract] lies in the area of investigating technology that is not yet known. Its results are relatively complicated research and development.

(3) The difference between technology service contracts and contracts for the assignment of technology lies in the fact that, normally, technology service contracts do not include patented technology or exclusive use technology [know-how], but refer to ordinary technology other than patented discoveries, new forms of using patents and patented design, and exclusive technology

To be sure, this does not prevent the parties at the same time that they are carrying on technology service [contracts] from assigning patented technology and know-how. Under these circumstances, the parties can execute a technology licensing agreement and, at the same time, execute a technology service agreement.

2. The Essential Content of a Technology Service Contract

(1) A technology service consultation contract

When one party (the commissioning party) engages the other party to be a temporary or long-term technological adviser, or commissions the other party (the party performing the service) in a certain technology project to furnish consulting reports or opinions and pays a technology fee (the service fee), this technology service contract is called a technology service consulting contract.

The most important technology consulting service includes becoming a temporary or long-term technology consultant, making feasibility studies, making technological surveys and economic benefit analyses, furnishing engineering plans, drawing up construction plans, carrying on specialized technological investigations, and submitting detailed reports of appraisals or opinions, etc. The form in which the service is performed is to submit to the commissioning party the relevant technological information and opinions. The technological consulting service project can consist of providing all of the work for an entire engineering project, or it can be a consulting project for a concrete technology project (such as equipment construction, technical processes, etc.).

In a technology consulting service contract, the party performing the service must make use of his own knowledge, experience, and information, and, according to the provisions of the contract, complete the consultative report or solve the technological problems presented by the commissioning party. The party performing the service must guarantee that the tendered consultation report or opinion corresponds with the requirements agreed on by the parties.

If the one performing the service, by his own fault, causes the report of the technology consulting or the opinion not to fulfill the requirements of the contract, he has no right to receive a part or all of the fee.

The commissioning party has the duty to give the one performing the service, or the person engaged by him, the necessary materials and data. If the commissioning party has not, as agreed in the contract, clarified the important points of the problem for consultation, or has not promptly supplied the relevant materials and data, and [has] caused the one performing the service to make mistakes, or has affected the schedule or scale of the work, he must still pay the fee to the one performing the service. The commissioning party must compensate the party for any losses he suffers.

The commissioning party must accept, in a timely way, the products of the work of the one performing the service and pay the agreed-upon consulting fee. Whether or not the commissioning party decides to use the opinion provided by the one performing the service does not affect the requirement that the commissioning party pay the agreed-upon consulting fee. In other words, when the report and opinion supplied by the one performing the service meet the requirements of the contract, even if the commissioning party does not use the consulting report or opinion, he still must pay the agreed-upon fee to the party performing the service. Unless the contract provides otherwise, the party performing the service is not liable for any losses incurred by the commissioning party in using the report or opinions which he submits.

(2) Supplementary service contracts

When one of the parties (the commissioning party) commissions the other party (the party performing the service) to engage in the design of a product, plans, technical drawings, engineering calculations, product and material appraisals, physical and biological analyses, the collection of information, investigating, and arranging, as well as computer services and similar technology service contracts, these are called supplementary service contracts.

Under a supplementary service contract, the party performing the service must, within the time, and according to the manner provided in the contract, complete the service work and guarantee its quality and quantity. He must make appropriate use of, and give an appropriate protection to, the models, raw materials, and technological materials supplied by the commissioning party.

If the party performing the service does not perform the contract, or does not perform it properly, or is not able to complete the work on time and according to the [agreed-upon] quality and quantity, he will not receive part or all of the fee. If the technology service work does not meet the requirements of the contract, or if the care given to the raw materials, models, or technological materials furnished by the commissioning party was not appropriate, thus causing a shortage, alteration, spoilage, and injury, he is liable to pay damages.

According to a supplementary contract, the commissioning party must deliver the model, raw materials, or technological materials according to the provisions of the contract, and accept in a timely way the results of the work of the party performing the service.

If the commissioning party does not perform the contract, or does not perform it properly, causing the technology service work to stagnate, to be delayed, and influences the quality of the work, the agreed-upon fee must still be paid. If the one performing the service suffers a loss, [the commissioning party] is liable to pay damages. If the commissioning party delays in accepting the results of the work, he must pay the specified storage expense.

During the course of performance of the technology service contract, any discoveries or inventions or other technological results obtained by the one performing the service, on the basis of the technological materials, models, etc., furnished by the commissioning party, belong to the one performing the services. But in consideration of the objective conditions provided by the commissioning party while he is obtaining the technological results, regardless of whether or not the reward given by the commissioning party is voluntary, the commissioning party, under normal circumstances, may obtain permission to make ordinary use of the results of the technology, without fee.

31 The Contract of Insurance

I

A GENERAL DISCUSSION OF THE CONTRACT OF INSURANCE

1. The Basic Concept of the Contract of Insurance

A contract of insurance is an agreement between an insurer and an insured regarding insurance. According to a contract of insurance, the insured pays the agreed premium to the insurer, and the insurer is liable, within the amount of the insurance, to reimburse the insured for losses caused by incidents covered by the insurance contract, or to pay the agreed insurance benefits at the time when the agreed-upon term of the insurance contract has come to an end.

The purpose of the insured in making an insurance contract is, by paying the premium as a cost, to obtain the right to demand that the insurer pay compensation when the insured-against incident occurs. Therefore, the insurance relation is different from an obligation for damages for injury. In an insurance contract, the insurer compensates the insured for his loss, not because of the insurer's act that infringes on a right, but because of the contract. An insurance contract is also different from a conditional juristic act. Whether a conditional juristic act becomes legally effective depends on whether the condition occurs, whereas an insurance contract becomes effective when it is made.

2. The Origin and Development of Insurance

The origin of insurance lies in the fact that people cannot guard against the occurrence of all natural disasters and accidents. Once a disaster or accident occurs, it can produce (create) difficulties and setbacks in the production of enterprises and in the lives of the people. Insurance is a procedure by which the insured units or citizens can be reimbursed economically for losses caused by accidents and natural disasters by the use of insurance premiums. For citizens, insurance is a material guaranty for the beneficiary when the insured citizen dies or loses working capacity. Therefore, insurance is an indispensable part of the economic activity of society.

Recognizing the fact that natural disasters or accidents are inevitable in any society, Marx, in his "Criticism of the Gotha Program," points out the necessity in a socialist society that some part of the products of the whole society be set aside as a reserve fund or insurance fund. The reserve fund or insurance fund is mainly intended to be used to prevent possible interruptions of the reproduction process, and to ensure prompt reimbursement for the losses caused by natural disasters and accidents.

Insurance is the product of economic development at a certain stage of human history. It came into being and evolved with the development of the commodity economy. In the Middle Ages, there flourished a kind of marine-risk-loan system in the Mediterranean area. The system worked this way: The ship owner or the owner of the shipment put up the ship or the shipment as security and obtained a loan from the lender. If the ship or the shipment encountered danger and was lost, the lender lost the right to demand the return of the loan, because he [the borrower] could no longer return the security. If the ship or the shipment arrived at the destination, the borrower repaid the loan together with interest, and in return got the ship or goods back. In this arrangement, the borrower was a kind of insured, the lender was the insurer, the interest was a kind of premium, and the loan was the insurance benefit. Later the Lombards, Italian merchants, first wrote transportation insurance. Shortly thereafter, transportation insurance found its way to England. In 1666, the Great Fire of London, England, caused severe losses and fire insurance (insurance against fire) came into being naturally. From then on, the insurance business spread to the various countries of the world, and the kinds of insurance increased and the scope of insurance became even more extended. Since production, science, and technology have developed, and the modernization of industry proceeds uninterruptedly, the economic relations between people become ever more complex. The requirements of insurance are ever more detailed. The new types of insurance increase uninterruptedly. Liability insurance which insures against civil law liability to pay damages and insurance that guarantees credit are an important trend in the insurance business throughout the world. In the present world, almost every country has its own developed insurance business (institution), and many insurance companies have become big financial monopoly organizations. The utility of insurance in every country's national economy is constantly increasing. Particularly, in a number of developed countries it occupies a decisive position.

Before Liberation, the insurance business was operated by the imperialists and bureaucratic capitalists. It was a tool used by them to exploit and plunder the riches of the working people. It is only after the people took hold of political power that the people's insurance business was established.

Shortly after Liberation, the government confiscated the property of those insurance companies that were owned and operated by bureaucratic comprador capitalists, and had other privately run insurance companies undergo socialist transformation. In October of 1949, the Chinese People's Insurance Company was established and it conducted all kinds of insurance business, both domestic and foreign. With the restoration of the national economy and the development of socialist construction, both the scale of insurance organizations and the scope of their business were expanding rapidly. But after 1959, all insurance business except for compulsory passengers' insurance against railroad, ship, and airplane accidents, was suspended, and the development of foreign insurance business was also badly affected.

After the Third Plenum of the Eleventh Party Congress, the insurance business was restored and developed. Throughout the country, large and medium-sized cities and counties with concentrations of business and industry carried on all kinds of insurance activity based on the property of enterprises. Foreign insurance business also developed progressively on its original basis. Recently, with the many types of production responsibility that are being carried on in the countryside, the rural economy has undergone profound changes. The activity of the peasants has been aroused to the utmost; the range of production of agriculture is greatly extended. The peasants have new insurance requirements in order to resolve the losses incurred by the death of livestock and other property losses owing to disasters and accidents. Consequently, more than twenty kinds of insurance are written: rural and urban property insurance, insurance for liability to third persons from automobiles and tractors, etc., peasant household property insurance, cattle insurance, etc. Insurance activity in our country's growing rural areas is appearing step-by-step. It is beginning to open up the new areas of insurance in the rural areas. Enormous vistas of rural insurance are appearing. In the cities, there has been a great development in property insurance, life insurance, and legally required motor vehicle insurance for liability to third persons. Insurance is an indispensable condition for strengthening international trade, foreign economic cooperation, and technology transfer. Since the inception of our country's policy of opening to the outside, insurance has actually served to attract foreign capital. Every kind of insurance has been instituted in order to meet the needs of foreign business. Because of this, section 25 of the Economic Contracts Law of the People's Republic of China enacted by the National People's Congress in November 1981, provided for the property insurance contract. This [provision] was made somewhat more concrete by the Provisions on Property Insurance of the People's Republic of China promulgated by the State Council in September 1983. These laws and regulations are used in principle in maritime insurance contracts and insurance contracts related to foreign property. In 1984, there was a great increase in the income from insurance for every kind of insurance, foreign and domestic. Moreover it exceeded the plan. The objects which are served by domestic insurance activity are increasingly the urban and rural masses. Its capability and economic effectiveness are being utilized even more effectively. Insurance business, as one of the indispensable part of our national economy, will be playing a more and more important role in the course of realizing the Four Modernizations.

3. The Significance of Our Country's System of Socialist Insurance

The insurance system of our country is of a socialist nature and it is of great importance to our socialist economic construction.

The insurance system of our country is one of the means by which the state organizes social forces to fight against natural disasters. Our country's insurance organization is the Chinese People's Insurance Company. The basic insurance fund comes from the payments by enterprises and organizations of premiums to the People's Insurance Company. The insurance company manages the insurance funds. With such funds, they reimburse the insured for their losses caused by natural disasters and accidents. In this way, heavy losses which are difficult to predict are changed into regular payments of small amounts of fixed insurance premiums; the unbearable loss to the individual insured is shared by, and spread over, thousands of other insured units, so that the process of carrying out the national economic plan will not be affected greatly because of unintentional accidents and the material life of the people will be ensured.

Besides accepting insurance premiums and reimbursing losses, the People's Insurance Company also assumes responsibility for taking measures to prevent natural disasters and accidents from happening. For example, they set aside, from the insurance funds, sums of money to do prevention work, giving directions to enterprises and institutions as to how to prevent accidents and disasters, supervising and checking them, etc.

In addition, the state insurance system is also one of the ways to raise funds for state construction. This is so because, besides turning over profits to the state, the state insurance company puts large amounts of insurance funds in the People's Bank and contributes to state construction.

II
THE CLASSIFICATION OF INSURANCE AND THE MEANING OF THE BASIC TERMS OF THE LEGAL RELATIONSHIP OF INSURANCE

Viewing the ever-developing insurance business of different countries of the world, we can see that there are many names for the different types of insurance. Putting them together, we can make the following classifications:

When insurance is divided according to its object, it can be divided into property insurance and life insurance. If the objects of insurance are buildings, production equipment, the means of transportation, goods, etc., the insurance is property insurance. If the object of the insurance is a person's life, health, or working capacity, the insurance is life insurance.

If division is made according to the basis on which the insurance relation arose, both property insurance and life insurance can be divided into voluntary insurance and compulsory insurance. If the law requires that certain property or individuals must be insured in certain circumstances, the insurance is compulsory insurance. It is also called "Insurance Required by Law." In general this is principally social insurance. When this is the case, one party has the obligation to buy insurance, and the insurance company cannot refuse to issue an insurance policy. If the insurance relationship is established through contract negotiations, the insurance is voluntary insurance. When this is the case, the insured may choose to buy or not to buy insurance, and the insurance company also has the right to refuse to issue an insurance policy to those who do not meet the requirements set by the insurance company. But insurance companies cannot refuse an insurance policy to those who meet the requirements.

Further classifications of insurance can be made. For example, property insurance can be further broken down into ship insurance, livestock insurance, water damage insurance, etc. If division is made according to the different kinds of responsibility to be borne by the insurer, there is medical malpractice insurance, traffic accident insurance, etc. In addition, there is letter of credit insurance, political risk insurance, etc. In life insurance, there is death insurance (that is, only when the insured dies does the insurer pay the benefits) and double aspect insurance (the insured gets the benefits regardless of whether he dies during the term of the insurance or is still living after the term of the insurance expires).

Moreover, social insurance must be distinguished from life insurance. The former, including labor insurance and social relief benefits, etc., is the material help our citizens get from society when they are born, get old, become sick, are injured, are handicapped, or die, and the sources of the benefits are the state treasury or the enterprise's administration expenses. Life insurance is a contract entered into between a citizen and the insurance company, and the benefits come from the insurance funds managed by the insurance company. The former is adjusted by labor law and administrative law, whereas life insurance is adjusted by civil law. Therefore they are not the same.

The most important insurance in our country is enterprise property insurance, household property insurance, goods transportation insurance, ship insurance, automobile and other public safety liability insurance, construction all-risks insurance, installation all-risks insurance, as well as live swine insurance, insurance for raising chickens and ducks, cultured pearl insurance, orange and grape insurance, etc. Foreign insurance includes goods transportation insurance, passengers' accidental life [i.e., death] insurance, touring insurance, contract performance insurance, product liability insurance, disaster insurance [against losses caused by disasters], installation risk insurance involving Sino-foreign joint ventures and compensatory trade, etc. With the advance of social production, science, and technology, and with the development of foreign trade and the rise of people's living standards, the scope of both the domestic and foreign business will expand more and more.

Insurance relations have very distinctive features as a kind of civil law relation. To grasp the special features of insurance relation, it is necessary to explain the following basic terms often involved in insurance relations.

(1) The insurer, the policyholder, the insured, the beneficiary

(i) The insurer. The insurer is the party who accepts premiums and pays the benefits according to the insurance contract when the insured-against incident occurs. In our country, the insurer is the Chinese People's Insurance Company. It is a state-run insurance and reinsurance organization, an independent state-owned enterprise that operates throughout the country. The state insurance supervisory organization is the People's Bank of China. The establishment of an insurance business and the carrying on of the insurance business requires the permission of the Bank of China. Moreover, it is necessary to petition the Industrial and Commercial Administrative Control Office for a license. Otherwise, it is not permitted to carry on business. The Chinese People's Insurance Company has established branches throughout the country to carry on business.

(ii) The policyholder. The policyholder is the party who pays premiums to the insurer, and executes a property or life insurance contract with the insurer. Both juristic persons and citizens can be policyholders. In a property insurance contract, the policyholder must be the owner or manager-administrator of the property or some other party who has an insurable interest in the property. Others cannot be policyholders of the insurance contract. In the case of life insurance, the policyholder should be the insured himself, or the spouse of the insured, a direct blood relative of the insured, or a person who has a support relationship with the insured. Whenever one wants to secure life insurance on a third person, he must get the permission of the third person.

(iii) The insured. The insured is the object of the insurance contract. As pointed out above, an insured may be the policyholder himself, and may also be a third person. But the third party, as a party, can only exist in a life insurance contract.

(iv) The beneficiary. A beneficiary is the party who, according to the contract, has the right to receive the insurance benefits. A beneficiary may be the policyholder himself. It may also be a third person. In life insurance contracts, the insured designates the beneficiary. When the insured did not make such a designation, his heirs are the beneficiaries. Where the insured has designated the beneficiary, the insurance benefits after the insured's death should not be counted as belonging to the deceased's estate (that of the insured), but should be received by the beneficiary. In principle, insurance benefits should not be used to pay the obligations incurred by the insured when he was alive.

(2) The object of the insurance, insured interest, insured-against incident, insured-against risk, the risk unit, reinsurance

(i) The object of the insurance. The object of the insurance is the object aimed at by the insurance contract. It may be property, such as a ship, building, etc., and it may also be a person's life, health, and working ability.

(ii) The insured interest. Whether the object of insurance is property or a

person's life, there always exists some insured interest. The insured interest refers to the economic loss resulting from the occurrence of the insured-against accident. Therefore, it is also called the insured loss. An insurance contract that has no insured interest is meaningless and, therefore, cannot come into existence.

(iii) Insured-against incident. Insured-against incidents are those against whose consequences the insurance contracts are entered into. It is also the basis for the insurer's liability to make compensation.

(iv) The insured-against risk. This refers to the situation which the insured-against incident has not yet occurred. The insured-against risk for which insurance is written must be something that can happen, but it cannot be foreseen whether it will happen (this includes the unforeseeability of the time of its occurring).

(v) The insured unit. This refers to the range of the injury that can be caused by the occurrence of the incident which is the object of the insurance. This is the basis on which the insuring enterprise determines the highest insurance liability it can assume.

(vi) Reinsurance. Also called "shared protection." The insurer assigns all or part of his risk [liability] to another insurer to assume. The assignee is also called the "reinsurer." The purpose of reinsurance is to reduce the liability of the assignor to reimburse or pay. If the insured event occurs, according to the provisions of the reinsurance contract, the insurer may receive a certain economic reimbursement.

(3) The insurance premium and insurance benefit

(i) The insurance premium. The premium is the fee paid by the policyholder to the insurer. The premium is fixed according to a certain percentage of the insurance benefits (the insurance premium percentage). Payment of the premium should be made according to the requirements of the contract in a single payment, or in installment payments—annually, quarterly, or monthly.

(ii) The amount of insurance benefits. The amount of insurance benefits is the maximum amount the insurer must pay when the insured-against event occurs. The amount of insurance benefits should not exceed the actual value of the insured property. If the amount of the insurance exceeds the actual value of the insured property, it is called excessive insurance. If excessive insurance is the result of the policyholder's bad faith, the contract of insurance is void and the premiums are not refunded. If the excessive insurance is a result of the policyholder's good faith, then the insurance contract is void only to the extent of the excessive portion of the insurance. To avoid excessive insurance, the parties should evaluate the property for the purpose of insurance when they execute the contract.

In a life insurance contract, there is no need of evaluation, and the insurance benefits are usually fixed by insurance regulations or through agreement between the parties.

(4) The insurance term.

The insurance term refers to the effective term of the contract of insurance. An insurer is responsible to reimburse only when the insured-against event occurs during the insurance term. The insurance term is determined according to the insurance contract or the relevant insurance regulations.

III
THE FORMATION OF INSURANCE CONTRACTS, PRINCIPAL RIGHTS, AND DUTIES OF THE PARTIES

1. The Formation of the Contract of Insurance

The process of forming a contract of insurance begins with the [would be] policyholder requesting insurance, filling out the insurance application form, and coming to an agreement with the insurer over all the terms in the contract. After the parties sign the document, the contract becomes effective.

2. The Major Obligations of the Policyholder

(1) Paying the insurance premiums

A policyholder must, according to the contract, make the single payment or installment payments of insurance premiums. If the policyholder does not pay the premium on time, the insurance contract ceases to be effective.

(2) Doing his best to protect the insured property

A policyholder of a contract of property insurance should accept the insurer's inspection of, supervision over, and reasonable proposals regarding the measures to be adopted by the policyholder to protect the safety of the property.

(3) Salvaging the insured property when the insured-against event occurs

A policyholder should take all effective measures to salvage the insured property and to avoid the spreading of the losses to the extent possible when the insured-against event occurs. After the event, if the policyholder was still able to take salvage measures, but did not actively do so, and let the loss increase, the insurer is not obligated to reimburse the policyholder for the increased loss.

(4) Notifying the insurer of an increase in the degree of the insured-against risk

When the degree of insured-against risk threatening the insured property rises (the risk degree is measured according to the standard of risk in the insurance regulations), the policyholder should give timely notice to the insurer of the circumstances, and the premium rate, according to the rules, should be raised. The insurer has the right to terminate the insurance contract in some circumstances.

(5) Assigning to the insurer the right to compensation

In a property insurance contract, if the insured-against event was caused by a third party's wrongful acts, the policyholder should first ask the third party to pay damages. If, after trying to do so, the policyholder is not able to obtain all or part of the damages due, the insurer must reimburse the policyholder for all his loss or the amount still uncompensated. The policyholder should assign his right for damages against the third person to the insurer after the insurer has reimbursed him to enable him to proceed in his place.

3. The Major Obligations of the Insurer

(1) Paying insurance benefits

An insurer is obligated according to law or the contract, to pay insurance benefits after the insured-against event occurs. The insured-against event is limited to those provided for in the insurance contract. The insurer is not responsible for losses caused by events not provided for in the contract. Further reimburseable loss is limited to the direct loss of the insured property and does not include consequential damages resulting from the loss of the insured property. However, an insurer is responsible for loss suffered by the policyholder in the course of salvaging the insured property.

The amount an insurer should pay in compensation should be determined by the actual value of the insured property, the amount of the insurance, and the actual loss. Where the pro rata responsibility system is adopted by the parties, the method of calculating compensation is: the amount of compensation is equal to the actual loss multiplied by the amount of the insurance divided by the estimated insured price. Some insurance contracts provide that the insurer only pay the actual damages, that is, if the loss is within the insurance amount, if the injury does not exceed the insured amount, the insurer pays the actual damages. At the present time, in domestic insurance contracts, the amount of compensation is calculated according to this latter method.

(2) Conditions required for releasing the insurer from the obligation to compensate

In property insurance contracts an insurer is released from its obligation when one of the following situations occurs:

(i) The insured-against event is the result of the policyholder's intentional act or gross negligence (including refusing to accept the insurer's reasonable proposals regarding safety measures).

(ii) The policyholder fails to notify the insurer of the circumstances within the fixed time after the insured-against event occurred.

(iii) The policyholder releases the third party who caused the damage of the insured property from liability to pay compensation.

In a life insurance contract, an insurer is released from its obligation to compensate in the following situations:

(i) The death or loss of working ability is a result of the criminal act of the insured himself.

(ii) The death of the insured is the result of the intentional act of the insured or that of the beneficiary.

(iii) The death or the loss of working ability is caused by war unless the contract provides otherwise.

It should be noted that, in life insurance, the payment of insurance benefits is not damages for injuries. If the insured-against event is caused by a third party's unlawful act, the injured party, after receiving insurance benefits, still has the right to demand damages from the third person. At the same time, the insurer does not obtain an assignment of the right for reimbursement against the third party after it pays the insurance benefits.

IV
THE PROCEDURE FOR DEMANDING THAT THE INSURER PERFORM HIS OBLIGATIONS

A policyholder or beneficiary must, within the time provided after the insured-against event occurs, request the insurer to pay insurance benefits, and at the same time present to the insurer the following documents: the insurance contract or other insurance documents, proof of payment of premiums, documents proving that the incident causing damage is within the scope of the insurer's responsibility as provided in the contract. In the case of a property insurance contract, a detailed list of the lost property [must be presented]. In the case of life insurance, a valid death certificate or certificate of loss of working ability must be presented. Other certificates must be provided if required by rule.

After receiving the request, the insurer must declare clearly within the time fixed whether to pay compensation and how much it is going to pay. If it has decided to pay, it must make the payment within the fixed period as required by law or the contract.

If the insurer and policyholder have a dispute regarding the insurance compensation, under section 50 of the Economic Contract Law they must first request an arbitration tribunal to arbitrate. If they are not satisfied with the arbitration ruling or award, they can bring a suit in the people's court to decide the matter.

32 Foreign Economic Contracts

I
FOREIGN ECONOMIC CONTRACTS AND OUR COUNTRY'S FOREIGN ECONOMIC CONTRACT LAW

1. General Discussion of Foreign Economic Contracts

A foreign contract is one in which one subject of the contract is a foreign national or juristic person; the object of the contract is foreign; or the execution or performance of the contract takes place abroad, etc.

If foreign economic contracts are compared with domestic contracts the following points [are to be observed]:

(1) Generally speaking, the parties to the contract have a different nationality

Paragraph 2 of our Foreign Economic Contracts Law provides: "The scope of application of this law is contracts entered into between enterprises or other economic organizations of the People's Republic of China and foreign enterprises and economic organizations and individuals." It must be pointed out that [the concept] "foreign economic contract" does not exclude cases in which both parties have the same nationality. For example, in 1980 "The United Nations Treaty for Contracts for International Sales" provided in section 1 for the use of the treaty in connection with contracts for the sale of goods between parties when the place of business was in different countries. Consequently, according to this treaty, if two corporations have the same nationality in the same country but their places of business are in different countries, this is an international contract, and cannot be regarded as an internal contract.

(2) The performance of the contract will inevitably involve property rights, obligation rights, and other rights, or economic interests in different countries

For example, a contract for the formation of a Sino-foreign joint venture may involve foreign capital, including capital funds, technology, machinery, and equipment which enter our country from abroad. The execution of a foreign trade contract can involve the export and import of the goods, international payments, as well as international transport of goods, and many other problems. Consequently, foreign economic contracts have a close connection with the interests of the countries to which the parties belong, and they can have a great influence on the foreign economic relations and the foreign policy of those concerned. In this field, each country's control, supervision, and management regarding the contract are greatly strengthened.

(3) Since in any foreign economic contract, the subject, object, or content have foreign elements, it is inevitable that it will involve different countries' legal systems

The question of what country's law determines the validity of the contract and the rights of the parties depends on the question of the law to be applied regarding the contract. Apart from this, since the contract has a relation with one or more sovereign states, whenever there is a contract dispute, there may also arise a question of court jurisdiction. That is, the contract dispute can be decided in its own country's courts or arbitration tribunals, or it can also be decided in the foreign country's courts or arbitration tribunals.

(4) [Foreign economic controls are frequently influenced by international law]

Following the growth of international economic trade relations, a number of conventions, treaties, and customs have appeared in the international arena to adjust the contract relations between parties from different countries. They all have the character of constituting a body of unified legal rules. Consequently, foreign economic contracts, in addition to receiving the legal influence of the party's own country or that of the other country, also are frequently influenced by international unified law.

After the Third Plenum of the Eleventh Central Committee, and following our country's opening to the outside, the expansion of economic technological joint activities and circulation with the outside, and the monetary value and percentage of foreign economic contracts, have increased greatly. Apart from the sales of goods abroad, such types of contracts as Sino-foreign equity joint ventures, Sino-foreign contract joint ventures, Sino-foreign joint exploration and development of natural resources, international technology transfer, international leasing, international payments, international engineering contracts and distribution, representation, commissioned processing, compensation trade, etc., have appeared. In order to make use of these types of contracts, our country, at the Sixth Session of the Standing Committee of the Tenth National People's Congress, passed the Foreign Economic Contracts Law of the People's Republic of China. Even though this law is designed especially to adjust foreign economic contract relations, its general theme is to protect the lawful interests of parties to foreign economic contracts and to promote the development of our country's foreign economic relations. The objects it adjusts and its basic principles are at one with other countries' economic contract law. Consequently, this is an indivisible part of our country's system of civil law contracts. It has great significance for putting into practice and carrying out our country's policy of opening to the outside, and, building [on a basis] of equality and mutual benefit, promoting our country's foreign economic development, and speeding up the establishment of our country's socialist modernization.

2. The Area of Application of the Foreign Economic Contracts Law

The Foreign Economic Contracts Law is the law that adjusts the relations between our country's companies, enterprises, or other economic organizations with foreign companies, enterprises, and other economic organizations. Not all economic contracts between Chinese and foreigners are adjusted by its provisions. Its area of application is as follows:

(1) Whether or not the contract is governed by our country's law is determined by the law chosen to govern as provided in the contract

Section 5 of the Foreign Economic Contracts Law provides: "The parties may select the law that is to be used to handle disputes that may arise out of the contract. If the parties have not selected [a system of law], the law of the country with the closest connection [with the contract] [will govern]." Consequently, when the governing law is foreign law, the contract must make use of the foreign contract law or civil law. But what must be pointed out is that regardless of what law the contract uses, when there are compulsory or prohibitory rules in the Foreign Economic Contracts Law or other related rules, the parties are not permitted any discretion; the parties must apply [these rules].

(2) [International treaties apply, except to "reserved" areas]

Paragraph 6 of the Foreign Economic Contracts Law provides: "When international treaties which have been adhered to by the People's Republic of China have provisions that differ from the laws of the People's Republic of China the provisions of the said treaty will be used. However, provisions that have been "reserved" by the People's Republic of China are an exception." This is because international treaties or international conventions are agreed upon by sovereign nations. When they are executed they are the effective law. In order to uphold the peace and stability of international society, the signatory countries must strictly honor the related rules, and conscientiously perform and fulfill the international duties which they have assumed.

(3) The Foreign Economic Contracts Law is not used in international transportation contracts

This is most important, because in the field of international transport, there are unified rules generally recognized by every country. The influence of these unified rules or customs is very great. Though we have not formally recognized them in law, in order to develop international economic relations we cannot fail to consider and accept them.

II
FORMATION OF FOREIGN ECONOMIC CONTRACTS

Foreign economic contracts are usually of long duration, for large amounts, and with complicated contents. The parties are from different countries and their legal concepts, customs, and ways of looking at problems are different. Consequently, it is much easier for a dispute or disagreement to arise in the case of foreign economic contracts than in the case of ordinary contracts. In order to reduce the number of disputes and disagreements as much as possible, and fulfill the purpose of the parties who agreed to the contract, it is especially important that the requirements for the formation of a foreign economic contract be more strict than in the case of ordinary contracts. The provisions of the contract must be still clearer and more concrete [than for ordinary contracts].

1. The Required Provisions for the Establishment of a Foreign Economic Contract

(1) The parties to a foreign economic contract

According to economic contract law in our country, the parties who can execute foreign economic contracts are enterprises or other economic organizations. The foreign party, in addition to being an enterprise or economic organization, may also be a natural person.

In regard to the capacity to act of natural persons, each country, in general, believes that [this question] must be governed by its own law of persons, but in order to protect the interests of the parties from its own country, at the same time limits are set to the law [of the country to which] the person belongs. Thus, it is provided in section 7.3 of the law on the application of the German Civil Code quite clearly that "Juristic acts executed in Germany by a foreigner who, by his own law, is without legal capacity, or who has limited legal capacity, but who by German law has legal capacity, will be regarded as having been executed by one having capacity." According to this principle, the capacity of a foreign natural person to conclude contracts in our country must be governed by our country's law.

Our country's law has not yet provided for the capacity of a juristic person. But according to a general principle of private international law, the capacity of the juristic person is governed by the law of the country in which it is formed. Consequently, the capacity of our country's enterprises to conclude agreements must be decided in accordance with our country's law and the capacity of foreign enterprises to conclude agreements must, in general, be determined by the law of the country in which they were formed. But it is most important to note that a juristic person that is formed and that has capacity according to the law of one country does not necessarily acquire the characteristic of having the legal capacity to act in every country. According to our country's law, foreign juristic persons that wish to carry on activities in our country must receive authorization from our country's supervisory authority to have the status of a juristic person. For example, in October 1980, section 2 of the Temporary Rules for the Supervision of the Representative Offices of Foreign Enterprises provided that "a foreign enterprise which has a genuine need to establish a representative office in China must file a petition, and, after approval, take care of the registration procedures. If it has not been approved and registered, it may not begin the activities of its representative office (in our country)." Consequently, when foreign juristic persons are carrying on civil law activities in our country and conclude foreign economic contracts it is not enough merely [to follow] the law of their country. They may only carry on activities within the scope permitted by our country's law.

At the time a foreign economic contract is concluded, because the parties come from different countries, they are not acquainted with each other, and so each must tender to the other documents proving its right to conclude a contract. Section 9 of the Rules for the Shenzhen Special Economic Zone Regarding Overseas Foreign Economic Contracts provides that the parties executing an agreement tender the following documents for the other party to examine: (1) a copy or photocopy of lawful proof of registration from the government of the country or locality of residence, (2) a balance sheet of the company or enterprise verified by a certified public accountant and a certificate of capital credit from a financial organization with which it has business contracts, (3) a notarized guaranty, (4) a written proof of the grant to the representative or mandatary of authority of representation of the corporation or enterprise.

(2) Lawful forms of contracts

The lawful forms of contracts are not only proof that the contract exists, but requirements for the effectiveness of the contract. In order to assure the seriousness of foreign economic contracts, the Foreign Economic Contracts Law provides several compulsory rules on this matter.

First, in order to make it easy to furnish proof and to assign responsibility when disputes arise under a contract, and in order to provide effective protection for the interests of both parties, our country requires that all foreign economic contracts must be in written form signed by both parties. Section 7 of the Foreign Economic Contracts Law provides that "a contract is formed when the provisions of the contract are agreed to in written form by the parties and signed. When an agreement is concluded by letter, telegram, or telex, if one party demands the signing of a confirmatory letter, the contract takes effect when the confirmatory document is signed." According to these rules the following forms have been selected for the formation of the foreign economic contracts according to the types of the contracts and the concrete circumstances. The following forms may be selected: (1) Agreements reached on the basis of a written form which will be signed. This is the parties' formally signed contract in written form. (2) Agreements entered into by letter, telephone, and telex, that is, contracts formed when the parties are in different places—in general these are all foreign trade contracts. (3) Agreements which are reached by means of letter, telegraph, and telex that require one party to sign a written confirmation of the contract.

Second, in order to facilitate the supervision and control of the foreign contract and to insure that the provisions of the contract correspond to this country's policies and law, our country carries out a system of examination and approval for these forms of contracts. The Foreign Economic Contracts Law provides: "When the law and administrative regulations of the People's Republic of China require that a contract be approved by the state, it is only then [that is, when it is approved] that the contract is formed." At present, our country, for the most part, provides for the use of the system of examination and approval of Sino-foreign economic technology cooperation contracts, such as contracts for Sino-foreign [equity] joint ventures, contracts for Sino-foreign cooperative joint ventures, contracts for Sino-foreign cooperative exploration and development of natural resources, joint venture contracts for Sino-foreign processing and equipment, contracts for foreign compensation trade, contracts for introducing technology, and so forth. However, the principle of the usual contract for the purchase and sale of goods does not need to follow this procedure.

(3) Affirming that the contract has been formed

Ascertaining the time and place where the contract was formed is of great significance in confirming the rights and duties of the parties. In the case of a contract concluded by face to face conversation between the parties, unless the parties have agreed otherwise, the day and place when and where the contracts are signed is the date and place of the formation of the contract. Consequently, determining whether or not this contract has been formed is easy.

But in the case of foreign trade, particularly in regard to the purchase and sale of foreign goods, the contract is frequently not formed by the parties within one country but rather between two countries by means of letter, telegraph, or telex. In regard to the question of the time and place of formation for this type of contract formed [by parties] who are separated, there are different legal rules and positions in the international [legal world]. The Anglo-American system adopts the position of the place of sending the letter. That is, the time and place where the promisor makes the promise are the time or place of the formation of the contract. The continental system emphasizes the [time and place of the] receipt of the letter. That is, the time and place of receipt by the promisee are the time and place of the contract. Although our country does not yet have a clear rule on this point, there is a custom that regards the time and place where the promisee receives the promise as the time and place of formation of the contract. Since every country has different rules on the formation of contracts, disputes can arise over this problem. The present international community is, in general, of the opinion that one should suppose that contract is effectively formed and then the question of its formation is to be determined by the law applied by the contract, as section 30 of the 1979 Hungarian Private International Law [Code] provides. But there are also countries whose rules provide that the place of formation of the contract is governed by the law of that country, such as section 565 of the Civil Code of Soviet Russia which provides that "the place where the juristic act is put into effect is determined by Soviet Law."

(4) Legality of contracts

Confirming the effectiveness of a foreign economic contract is like confirming the effectiveness of an ordinary economic contract. It is necessary not only to consider whether the declarations of intention of the two parties are true and identical, but it is also necessary to consider whether its content honors or violates our country's socialist public interest.

Our country has many legal rules that affect foreign economic contracts. For example, our country's constitution provides in section 9 that "minerals, flowing water, forests, prairies, desert areas, sand areas, and other natural resources all belong to the state, that is, to ownership by the whole people except for forests, mountains areas, grasslands, desert areas, sand areas, that by law belong to collective ownership." According to this provision, unless there is permission from the state, no one has the right to execute a contract whereby a foreign business develops state land or manages other natural resources belonging to the state. Again, the rules for application of the Sino-Foreign Joint Venture Law provide, in the general provisions, that in the following situations permission is not given: (1) where there is injury to Chinese sovereignty; (2) where it violates Chinese law; (3) where it does not comply with Chinese national economic requirements; (4) where it creates environmental pollution; (5) where the agreement, contract, or charter is clearly unjust and injures the rights of one party to the joint venture. When the contract offends the provisions of our country's law, the contract is declared to be ineffective. When one of the parties is responsible for the ineffectiveness, then, according to section 11 of the Foreign Economic Contracts Law, he will pay damages to the other party for any losses which were thus occasioned.

2. Essential Provisions for Foreign Economic Contracts

Foreign economic contracts have the general characteristics of the usual economic contract. Consequently, the general provisions of other economic contracts—that is, the object of the contract, the price, and the term—are also the essential provisions of the foreign economic contract. This is all provided for in section 5 of the Provisions for the Administration of Imported Technology promulgated by the State Council in 1985: "The following matters [affecting] both parties must be provided for clearly in the contract: (1) the content of the imported technology, its scope, and its essential explanations, including a detailed list of patents and trademarks that are involved; (2) the plan for attaining the purpose of the said technology and the time and method to be used in attaining this purpose; (3) the fee, the form of the fee, and the manner of payment." However, foreign economic contracts also have a number of differences from domestic economic contracts. That is, the subjects of the contract are in two different countries. The formation or performance of the contract can also be carried on in a foreign country. Under these circumstances, if the formation of a contract is excessively simple, or ambiguous, disputes may arise between the parties in the course of performance. In order to avoid disputes, and to assure the lawful interests of the parties, our country's Foreign Economic Contracts Law and The Rules for Application of the Sino-Foreign Joint Venture Law and The Rules for Foreign Economic Contracts in the Shenzhen economic zone all have clear provisions on the basic content of foreign economic contracts.

According to the relevant provisions of the Foreign Economic Contracts Law, foreign economic contracts in general must have the following provisions:

(1) The portion of the contract [that causes it to be] effective

This portion includes the beginning and the end. It is necessary at the beginning of the contract that the names [of the organization] or [individuals] be written along with the nationality, principal place of business or domicile, and the date and place of the execution of the contract. At the end of the contract, the language to be used in the contract and the effective date must be written, as well as the signatures of the parties. Since these provisions determine the scope and effectiveness of the contract and its conditions for its validity, they are the parts of the contract that make it effective.

(2) The parts dealing with the parties' rights and obligations

This part is the heart of the contract. Its provisions must be completely clear and concrete. Essentially, they include the following: (1) the type of the contract and the type and scope of the object of the contract; (2) the technological conditions of the contract, the quality, standards, specifications, and quantity [of the technology]; (3) the time, place, and manner of performance; (4) the terms of the price, the amount to be paid, the manner of payment, and all the related expenses; (5) the assignability of the contract or the conditions of the assignability of the contract; (6) the damages for breach of the contract and other types of liability. In addition, the contract must also contain agreement on the limits of the parties' risk bearing in performing the contract, and, where necessary, on the scope of the insurance of the object of the contract. The parties must agree on the necessity of relatively continuous performance. The parties must agree on the term of validity of the contract and the conditions for extending the contract, and terminating it in advance. The parties also may agree on a guaranty in the contract, and on the liability of the guarantor and the scope of the guaranty.

(3) The part on resolution of disputes under the contract

This is primarily important because it specifies what methods will be used to resolve disputes when they arise.

III
PERFORMANCE OF THE CONTRACT AND THE GUARANTY OF THE PERFORMANCE OF THE CONTRACT

1. Performance of the Contract

Emphasizing contracts and observing good faith are the basic principles of our country's contract law. These are also the basic principles that are abided by consistently in our country's foreign economic contracts, since it is only when both parties to the contract have the foundation of mutual trust and reliance than they can carry on equal and mutually advantageous economic intercourse. In addition, it is only [in this way] that international economic relations can exist and develop. Consequently, section 16 of the Foreign Economic Contracts Law provides: "Contracts which are formed according to the law are legally binding. The parties must perform the duties agreed upon in the contract. No party may, on his own, without authorization, alter or cancel the contract." In order to eliminate the anxieties of foreign investors that our new laws and regulations can influence the carrying out of contracts, and be injurious to their interests, section 40 provides: "When there is a new rule of law that affects contracts for Sino-foreign joint ventures which have received state approval, contracts for Sino-foreign cooperative joint ventures, and contracts for Sino-foreign exploration and development of natural resources, which are to be performed in China and which have received state approval, they may still be carried out on the basis of the contract provisions." This is legal confirmation of the principle "Emphasize contracts, observe good faith." It is advantageous for protecting the lawful interests of the parties. It is also beneficial for attracting foreign investors to invest in our country.

2. Guaranties and Contract Performance

In foreign economic contracts, since the parties of the contract are from different countries, the trust of each towards the other is not one hundred percent. In order to reduce the risk of forming a contract, a provision of guaranty at the time of formation is essential. Section 17 of the Foreign Economic Contracts Law provides: "When one party has decisive proof that the other party cannot perform a contract, he may temporarily suspend the performance of the contract but he must notify the other. When the other party tenders satisfactory performance he must perform the contract." That is to say, the offering of security must be provided for in the contract. If the contract does not have such a provision, and if, in the course of performance of the contract, one party discovers that the credit of the other has declined to the extent that it has damaged his ability to pay, he may suspend his performance of the contract and demand that the other party send a guaranty. But its condition is that the one party can offer tentative proof that the other party cannot perform. Otherwise this is just an action for breach of contract.

Since foreign economic contracts are contracts, all of the methods of guaranty used for ordinary contracts may be used for them. But, in practice, the most important devices in the law of foreign economic contracts are suretyship and property security interests.

(1) Suretyship

For guaranteeing foreign economic contracts, there are enterprise guaranties and bank guaranties. The enterprise guaranty is a guaranty made by a large enterprise for a small or medium-sized enterprise. For example, the Chinese International Trust Investment Company [C.I.T.I.C.] executes guaranties for our country's domestic enterprises. Foreign mother companies execute guaranties for their subsidiary companies in this country, etc. But, since usually the amount involved in a foreign economic contract is large, and there are limits to the financial resources of the enterprise, and the ability to guarantee is weak, in practice, foreign economic contracts are guaranteed for the most part by banks with high credit and strong ability to pay.

The bank guaranty is a "letter of credit" issued by the bank to the other party. If the party who is guaranteed is unable, during the course of the contract, to perform his own duties, or is unable completely to fulfill the conditions of the letter of credit, the bank will then pay its obligation according to the conditions of the letter of credit to the other party. Although the bank letter of credit is based on the contract between the two parties, its content is based on a concrete transaction. It is a sort of independent written credit guaranty. It is not involved in commercial and technological disputes between the parties. According to the law created by international custom, the beneficiary merely has to give notice in accordance with the requirements sent out with the letter of credit, and the bank must then perform its obligation of payment. Consequently, this bank guaranty is an exceptionally strong guaranty.

(2) The security interest [in things]

In a domestic economic contract, the security interest form of guaranty is very little used. But, in international legal contracts, sometimes the parties do not wish to execute a guaranty on the basis of credit. They want a guaranty based on an actual thing. Consequently, the security interest constitutes an important form of guaranty. In section 12 of The Rules for Foreign Economic Contracts of the Shenzhen Special Economic Zone, it is clearly provided that property security may be selected as the form of guaranty. The Rules for the Administration of House Property in the Shenzhen Special Economic Zone, Chapter 4, specially provide rules for property security contracts. Under these, if the one putting up security does not make payment according to the provisions of the security agreement, the secured party, that is, the Bank of the Shenzhen Special Economic Zone, has the right to sell the collateral forcibly. In practice, when Sino-foreign joint ventures have financial dealings with foreign and Hong Kong banks, structures located within our borders are often used as security.

The security agreement is a sort of ancillary contract. When the performance of the principal contract and that of the security agreement are not in the same country, the contracts are still more likely to use different law. For example, when a Sino-foreign joint venture borrows money from a foreign bank, it may be desired to have the loan contract use foreign law. But, if domestic [Chinese] property is used as collateral for the security agreement, the said security agreement must use our country's law.

IV
LIABILITY FOR BREACH OF CONTRACT

The most important rules of the Foreign Economic Contracts Law regarding breach of contract deal with damages and penalties for breach. These are consistent with the Economic Contracts Law. But their content is still clearer and more concrete.

1. Damages for Injury

Damages for injury, in general, use money to compensate for injury as a principle. Section 18 of the Foreign Economic Contracts Law provides: "When one party does not perform or his performance does not comply with the conditions agreed upon in the contract, this is a breach of contract. The other party has the right to demand payment of compensation for injuries or he may select some other reasonable method of compensation. If, after he has selected some other method of compensation, there is still not enough completely to redress the injury received by the other party the other party has the right to demand damages." Consequently, in foreign economic contracts, money damages are the basic type of liability.

In regard to the scope of the damages, section 19 provides: "It must be equivalent to the injury received by the other, but it must not exceed the loss that the breaching party could have foreseen at the time of forming the contract as being caused by breach of the contract." This rule of our country is consistent with international custom. It upholds the aim of seeking truth from facts. That is, it is in accordance with the actual injury received by the injured party. It also puts into practice the principle of equality and mutual benefit. That is, the interests of the breaching party are considered and limits are placed on damages.

As to the injuries received by the injured party at the time of breach, in general, these include direct injuries and losses. It is the burden of the injured party to produce evidence to prove the direct losses. The determination of the loss of the injured party, in general, refers to the benefit normally obtained under conditions of just dealings. Section 254 of the Czechoslovakian International Trade Code provides: "In order to be compensated for the injuries actually suffered, the innocent party has the right to demand being placed in the same position he would have been in if the breach of contract had not taken place: the benefit normally obtained by the seller when he sends goods in just trade in the said country. In other circumstances, compensate in the amount of the usual gain in that country when a contract is completely performed."

As to the injuries that were foreseeable by the parties at the time they concluded a contract, this is a relatively abstract standard. The key to it lies in the breaching party not being able to escape liability by showing that he did not in fact foresee the injurious consequences. Since this refers to losses the parties must have foreseen, if a party could have foreseen something, but in fact did not do so, the party still must pay damages for the injury. Consequently, this refers to the consequences that could be foreseen by a normal, reasonable person in the position of the one who breached the contract. These circumstances are naturally facts that are already known to the obligee. It is only within this range that the breaching party is liable for damages to the injured party. When a party breaches a contract there may also be circumstances that reduce the liability to pay damages. Section 22 of the Foreign Economic Contracts Law provides: "When one party is injured because of the other party's breach of contract, he must immediately adopt suitable measures to prevent the injury from increasing. If he does not immediately adopt measures to prevent the injury from increasing, he has no right to demand damages for the increased injury." This principle may be used in many situations. For example, in the case of foreign sales contracts, where the buyer does not accept the goods according to the contract, or the seller does not deliver the goods according to the contract, the injured party must, as soon as possible, go into the market and arrange to contract with a third person in order to reduce the injuries received from the breach of contract. If the injured party has not acted in this way, it may be that he has no right to damages for the injury resulting from price fluctuations that occur thereafter.

2. Payment of the Penalty for Breach of Contract

If the contract contains a penalty for breach of contract, the most important liability assumed by the parties is to pay the penalty for breach. Section 20 of the Foreign Economic Contracts Law provides: "A penalty for breach of contract agreed upon in the contract is regarded as damages for breach of contract."

Since payment of the penalty of breach and payment of damages both have the same aim of compensation, if the parties in the contract agree on a penalty for breach, the injured party has no right to demand damages. But, if the penalty does not amount to as much as the actual injury this clearly violates the civil law principle of compensation of equal value, and the injured party still has the right to seek damages for the remaining part [not covered by the penalty clause]. Section 20 of the Foreign Economic Contracts Law provides: "When the penalty agreed on in the contract is much higher or lower than the injury caused by the breach of contract, the parties may demand that an arbitration tribunal or court appropriately increase or diminish it."

3. Payment of Interest

Section 23 of the Foreign Economic Contracts Law provides that "if a party fails to pay on time the amount due under the contract, or some other sum that is due that is related to the contract, the other party is entitled to interest on the amount in arrears. The method for calculating the interest may be provided in the contract." According to this rule, the payment of interest is the only method for the party who has delayed in the performance of his obligation of paying damages. Thus, the interest that is paid is the lowest amount of damages obtained by the injured party. Consequently, he does not have to prove the injury he has received in order to obtain this amount of interest. At the same time, it is also the highest amount of damages that he can receive, because, according to the law, he has no right to other compensation.

In order to encourage the observance of contracts, our country provides for a relatively high legal rate of interest for delays in the payment of funds in commercial trade. For example, section 228 of the German Civil Code sets the interest rate for delay in making payments of money at four percent and section 352 of the German Commercial Code provides that the rate of interest for monetary obligations in trade transactions is five percent. Our Foreign Economic Contracts Law does not have a rule regarding a legally set rate of interest. But the method for computing interest may be provided for in the contract. In order to assure the obligee's interest to supervise and urge the obligor to perform promptly, it is reasonable for the rate set in the contract by the parties to be higher than the legal rate of the country of the obligor's residence or the bank rate. Section 8 of the Temporary Measures of the Bank of China Governing Loans to Sino-Foreign Ventures provides: "When repayment of a loan is not made on time . . . interest shall be charged 20 percent to 50 percent over and above the original interest rate as from the due date."

4. Other Remedial Measures

The types of liability for breach discussed above are not the only legal methods of giving remedies to the injured party. Since the Foreign Economic Contracts Law clearly provides that the injured party has the right to demand that other reasonable remedial steps be taken, here we will talk about the principle of actual [specific] performance. In connection with contracts of our country's socialist economic organizations, actual [specific] performance is an extremely important principle. Since these contracts are often formed under the state plan, it may be that after one party has breached, there is no way to use money to calculate and fully repair the injury received by the other party. But the circumstances of foreign economic contracts are not the same. Since the international market is enormously extended, when one party breaches a contract, it is very easy for the other party to seek a new contracting partner. Consequently, the actual economic significance of adjusting the actual [specific] performance is not very great for the obligee. In addition, since the international economic contract is being performed in another country, it may be difficult for a court to carry out supervision of actual [specific] performance by the breaching party. Consequently, the Foreign Economic Contracts Law principally uses damages to handle liability for breach of contract. To be sure in some circumstances, if the injured party believes that it is necessary to demand that the other party actually [specifically] perform, he still may demand actual [specific] performance. If, after actual [specific] performance, a party believes his injury is not completely remedied, he still has the right to demand that the other party pay damages.

5. The Problem of Unavoidability

Unless the law or contract provides otherwise, the principle of which party is subjectively at fault is a condition for establishing civil law liability. If a party is subjectively not at fault he will escape being legally liable. Foreign economic contracts are often influenced by political and economic conditions in the countries concerned, as well as by natural conditions which make them impossible to perform or impossible to perform fully. Consequently, the problem of irresistible force is an important problem in foreign economic contracts. Usually, foreign economic contracts have special provisions for irresistible force.

In regard to the legal consequences of irresistible force, the Foreign Economic Contracts Law provides for the different consequences presented for performance of the contract by long-term inability to perform and temporary inability to perform: "When a party, as the result of irresistible force, is unable to perform a contract or unable to perform completely, he will avoid all or part of his responsibility." When the circumstances that make performance impossible appear, the party who is unable to perform must immediately notify the other party, and must, within a reasonable period of time, tender proof to the relevant organization in order to facilitate the other party's obtaining information or to take proper measures to reduce losses. If the party does not immediately notify the other party of the appearance of the unavoidable condition, and the other party suffers loss in consequence, the other party has the right to demand damages to cover his portion of the loss.

Although the rules of different countries regarding irresistible force and its legal consequences are largely similar, since custom and legal viewpoints are not the same, different countries often have different understandings of the scope of irresistible force. For example, some countries regard the phenomena of economic depression or soaring prices as irresistible or unavoidable forces. Others believe they are the ordinary risks of business and cannot constitute irresistible force. In order to prevent disputes between the parties when these phenomena appear, it is best if the parties provide for the scope of irresistible force at the time the contract is formed. Section 24 of the Foreign Economic Contracts Law provides: "The scope of irresistible force may be provided for in the contract." In practice, foreign economic contracts generally regard the following conditions as falling within the scope of irresistible force: (1) conditions created by natural causes such as flood, drought, windstorm, blizzard, earthquake, etc., (2) matters arising from social causes, for example, wars, strikes, governmental blockades, import/export licenses, etc. But it must be pointed that everything included within the range of what the parties have agreed to in the contract as being irresistible force is an irresistible force. Deciding whether a certain matter is or is not an irresistible force is something that must be analyzed by the arbitration tribunal or court. Generally speaking, anything that is caused by the parties, such as worsening economic conditions that make performance impossible, or the party who himself is requested to petition for an export license fails to do so causing the contract to be incapable of being performed, or when matters arise after the party is unable to perform, etc., are regarded as not being matters that constitute irresistible force.

V
THE ASSIGNMENT, AMENDMENT, CANCELLATION, AND TERMINATION OF FOREIGN ECONOMIC CONTRACTS

1. The Assignment of Contracts

The assignment of a contract is a change in the subject of the contract. That is, one party transfers all or part of his rights and duties to a third party, but the contract's content and nature do not change. The assignment of a contract may frequently be a question of the credit of the assignee. Consequently, the assignment of the contract must be agreed to by the other party before it can be carried out. Section 26 of the Foreign Economic Contracts Law provides: "When a party intends to assign all or a part of his contractual rights and obligations to a third party, consent should be obtained from the other party." In order to avoid a dispute at the time of the assignment of the contract, it is best to provide clearly at the time of formation of the contract whether or not the contract can be assigned and the conditions for assignment. For example, an assignment may be limited to certain specific persons; [it can be provided that] after the assignment the assignor is liable as a guarantor, etc. In order to ensure the seriousness and stability of a contract and completely to protect the interests of a contracting party, the Foreign Economic Contracts Law provides in section 27: "As for a contract which, as provided by the law or administrative regulations, is formed only after obtaining approval from the competent authority of the state, the assignment of the rights and obligations of such contract should be subject to approval from the original approval authority, but with the exception of already approved contracts in which it is otherwise agreed." In addition, the Rules for the Application of the Sino-Foreign Joint Venture Law provides in section 23: "When one party assigns all or part of his contribution to the capital [of the joint venture] the other parties to the joint venture have a priority right to buy it. The conditions of the assignment to a third party may not be preferential as compared to [those for an assignment to the] other parties to the joint venture. If there is any violation of this provision, the assignment is without effect."

2. The Amendment of Contracts

In order to adjust to changes in the economic conditions that arise after the contract is formed, changes in the provisions of the contract are essential. But these changes must be conditional on unanimous agreement of the parties. Moreover, they are only effective after they have been made in written form. All significant changes in a contract that has been formed with the approval of our government must be approved by the original approving organization. In addition, the Foreign Economic Contracts Law provides in section 24 that changes in the contract do not affect the parties' right to demand damages. Consequently, if the party demanding change causes harm to the other party as a result, he must pay damages.

3. Cancellation of a Contract

According to the provisions of the Foreign Economic Contracts Law, parties may cancel a contract in the following circumstances:

(1) The other party has breached the contract in such a way as seriously to affect the economic advantage hoped for from the contract

That is to say, this sort of contract breach is, in terms of degree, a serious fundamental breach. If the breach is only minor, the injured party has no right to demand cancellation but can only obtain damages.

(2) A period of postponement for the performance of the contract has already been allowed, but it still has not been performed within this period

Even though a party has not performed within the proper time, if performance is still possible, the other party does not have the right to cancel the contract. In this case, the obligee must notify the obligor to perform the contract within a certain reasonable period of time. If, within this specified reasonable time, there is still no performance, the obligee has the right to cancel the contract.

(3) Irresistible forces [have] arisen making it impossible to perform the contract

There are two types of effects of an irresistible force. On the one hand, the contract cannot be performed, and on the other, the contract cannot be performed on time. If the contract merely cannot be performed in time, one party has no right to cancel the contract. It is only when the irresistible force makes it impossible to perform the contract for a long time, or when, after the irresistible force has passed, performance no longer has any economic value for the obligee, that a party has a right to cancel a contract.

(4) The conditions for dissolution of the contract specified in the contract have occurred

This refers to an agreement by both parties to dissolve a contract. It is only necessary that the conditions agreed upon to dissolve a contract have occurred. Regardless of whether or not [the condition] is in one of the three categories above, the parties have the right [in such a case] to cancel a contract.

Internationally there are two ways to exercise the right to cancel. One is an action in court by the party demanding cancellation to have a decision from the court cancelling the contract. The other way is an announcement by one party to the other party. The contract is then cancelled. Our country's Foreign Economic Contracts Law selects the second method. This method is easy to use in international economic trade relations. Cancelling a contract is advantageous for upholding the interests of the injured party. But it also causes the parties to think about the consequences of breaching a contract in advance. Cancelling a contract is an exceptionally serious matter. Hence, the Foreign Economic Contracts Law provides that the announcement cancelling the contract or the agreement of the two parties regarding the cancellation of the contract must be in written from. Moreover, in the case of contracts that are required to have state approval by our country's laws and administrative regulations, cancellation must be reported to the organization that originally gave authorization and a file prepared.

In regard to the relationship between cancellation of the contract and damages, the Foreign Economics Contract Law provides in section 34 that cancellation does not affect a party's right to demand damages. It is a reasonable rule since, when serious breaches occur, merely cancelling the contract cannot cause the injured party to obtain just relief. To be sure, the cancellation of a contract is not necessarily followed by damages, since when there is unavoidable force that makes it impossible to perform the contract, the parties only have the right to cancel. They do not have the right to demand damages.

The Foreign Economics Contract Law provides in section 35 that the provisions in the contract regarding disputes do not become ineffective because of cancellation of the contract. Since the contract provisions on disputes are procedural provisions, they are independent of the substantive provisions of the contract. After cancellation of the contract, these provisions continue to be effective. Section 21.2 of the Arbitration Rules of the United Nations Committee on International Trade provides: "The arbitral tribunal shall have the power to determine the existence or the validity of the contract of which an arbitration clause forms a part. An arbitration clause which forms part of a contract and which provides for arbitration under these Rules shall be treated as an agreement independent of the other terms of the contract. A decision by the arbitral tribunal that the contract is null and void shall not entail *ipso jure* the invalidity of the arbitration clause." Moreover, the Foreign Economic Contracts Law provides in section 36 that the provisions on settling and clearing accounts do not become ineffective after cancellation of the contract. Since the purpose of settling and clearing accounts includes the resolution of the property relations of the parties after the conclusion of the contract, if a cancellation of the contract caused these provisions to be ineffective, they would lose their basic significance.

4. Termination of the Contract

The Foreign Economic Contracts Law provides in section 31 that under the following circumstances a contract is declared to be terminated:

(1) The contract has been performed as agreed

This is the principal basis for the termination of the contract and is also the most common.

(2) An arbitration tribunal decides that a contract is terminated

This usually occurs when there is a very serious breach or an irresistible force and, upon the demand of a party, an arbitration tribunal or court declares the contract dissolved. Or, after the contract has been formed, one party is declared to be bankrupt. After the bankruptcy proceeding is completed, the court announces the dissolution of the contract.

(3) The parties agree to the termination of the contract

This may occur after the passage of many years. For example, one party, with the other party's consent, transfers all of his contract rights and duties to a third party. When the contract is completely assigned, the contract relationship between the original parties is dissolved. The parties to the contract may also use a new contract in place of the old and this causes the rights and duties created by the old contract to be dissolved. In addition, after the occurrence of a condition which the parties have agreed would dissolve a contract, the contract is dissolved.

Like the cancellation of a contract, the termination of the contract does not affect the parties' right to demand damages. Likewise, the provisions of the contract for settling disputes and settling and clearing accounts do not become ineffective because the contract is terminated.

VI
THE SETTLEMENT OF DISPUTES

In general, the content of foreign economic contracts is complicated. The performance of a contract is influenced to a certain degree by political, economic, and natural conditions and other elements of the related countries. Consequently, in the course of the performance of the contract, it is impossible to avoid having the parties develop all sorts of disputes. Since, in our country, the execution of foreign economic contracts is constantly increasing, contract disputes are also increasing. Accordingly, in order to increase the development of our country's foreign economic relations, the Foreign Economic Contracts Law provides many ways of deciding contract disputes in order to facilitate selecting the appropriate method and satisfactorily settle these disputes.

(1) Negotiation and adjustment

Section 37 of the Foreign Economic Law provides: "Any disputes arising from a contract ought to be settled by the parties, if possible, through consultations or mediation of a third party." The good point of negotiation and adjustment is that the atmosphere is friendly, and flexibility is great. It is advantageous to the parties to continue to carry on the economic and technological work together on the basis of mutual understanding and consideration. In addition, negotiation and adjustment do not have to go through the process of an arbitration tribunal or a suit in court. The parties save a lot of trouble and expense. In practice, a number of long-term contracts, such as those for the Sino-foreign joint ventures and Sino-foreign cooperative joint ventures, chiefly select this method of settling disputes. Most of the disputes in our country that arise in connection with foreign contracts are settled in this way.

(2) Arbitration

To speak only of foreign economic contracts, when a dispute arises between the parties that cannot be solved by negotiation or adjustment, the general custom is to seek arbitration and not to seek to settle it by way of the courts. The reasons for this are as follows:

(i) Arbitration is considerably more flexible than [adjudication in a] court. Since an arbitration organization is a sort of organization among the people, the

arbitrators are selected by the parties themselves. Because of this, arbitrators do not have to arbitrate strictly in accordance with the law, but, most of all, they must consider the relevant international customs.

(ii) The arbitrators, in general, understand the business. They are well known persons with practical experience and specialized background. They decide questions speedily. Moreover, arbitration procedure is simple. The expenses of the parties are relatively low.

(iii) The decisions of courts can be published in official publications. But arbitration decisions cannot be published without the consent of the parties. Consequently, it is easy for the parties to maintain secrecy. This is useful for maintaining the parties' economic trade relations.

The power of the arbitration tribunal to decide the contract dispute comes from the arbitration agreement of the parties. The arbitration agreement, in general, includes four parts. The place of arbitration, the arbitration tribunal, the arbitration procedure, and the effectiveness of the arbitration.

In forming an agreement to arbitrate a foreign economic contract, the most sensitive question for the parties is the selection of the place of the arbitration. Since the place of the arbitration is related to who does the arbitrating and what substantive law will be applied, it has a direct relation to the result of the arbitration. Each party helps select a place of arbitration that will be advantageous to him. The Foreign Economic Contracts Law provides that the parties may refer the dispute to [a] Chinese arbitration tribunal or to some other arbitration tribunal. In practice, the following three methods are the principal ones used:

(i) Arbitration in our country. This is commonly used. It is also the most advantageous to our side. Our arbitrators in the field of foreign trade have thirty years of practice, and have already amassed a rich experience in resolving international economic disputes. Moreover, they have acquired a high reputation internationally. In addition, the great majority of foreign economic contracts are formed and performed within our borders. Not only is conducting arbitration within our country convenient, saving time and expense, but it is also just and reasonable. For reasons of tradition and custom, the Arbitration Committee for Foreign Trade in our country selects the method of combining conciliation and arbitration. That is, usually it first selects [the method of] conciliation and adjustment [of the dispute], and only when conciliation is ineffective, does it adjudge the matter in an arbitration proceeding. In recent years our country has also adopted the method of combined conciliation. That is, the arbitration tribunals of the countries of the two parties each selects an equal number of conciliators who negotiate together. If negotiations fail, then arbitration is carried on in accordance with the contract.

(ii) Arbitration in the country of the defendant. This method realizes the principle of reciprocity. In general, it is easy for the parties to accept. Particularly in the case of our country and Japan, whose arbitration organizations have reached an agreement recommending that parties from the two countries select this method

of arbitration. Generally, Sino-Japanese economic trade contracts provide for arbitration in the country of the defendant.

(iii) Arbitration in a third country. This is usually the result of each party wishing to select a place of arbitration advantageous to itself. This is a matter as to which, as yet, they cannot come to an agreement, since they cannot make any concessions that are not mutual. At present, there are foreign economic contracts that provide for arbitration in third countries. In selecting a third country we must consider the arbitration tribunals of neutral countries that are friendly to our country, relatively just in handling cases, and which have a relatively high international reputation.

(3) Suit in the people's court

When a contract dispute cannot be settled or conciliated, and the contract either does not have an arbitration provision, or when it has a special arbitration agreement, The Foreign Economic Contracts Law provides that the parties may bring suit in the people's court. This includes bringing suit in a foreign court that has jurisdiction. The party to a contract exercising civil procedural rights and duties in our country must make use of section 5 of our country's [draft] Code of Civil Procedure: "Special rules for the procedure for foreign civil law actions" and its related provisions. According to section 23, if the place of performance or formation is in our country, our country's people's court has jurisdiction over the contract dispute. According to section 17, the intermediate people's court has the right to decide foreign economic contract disputes at first instance.

VII
THE QUESTION OF THE APPLICABLE LAW OF THE CONTRACT

1. The Use of the Applicable Law of the Contract

The question of the applicable law of a contract is a special problem of foreign economic contracts. It refers to the law that will govern the rights and duties of the parties when a contract has foreign elements. This law is also called the law governing the contract. The most important use of the contract's governing law is when the parties cannot negotiate a settlement to a contract dispute, and it also cannot be settled by provisions of the contract or other governing international customs or treaties entered into between the countries of the parties or international agreements or conventions adhered to by the countries of the parties. Then it has to be decided by the governing law of the contract. According to every country's private international law, decisions, and relevant international treaties, the governing law of the contract essentially decides: (1) the interpretation of a contract; (2) the performance of a contract; (3) relief from breach of contract; (4) cancellation of the contract; (5) the consequences of ineffective contracts.

Determining the governing law of the contract is exceptionally important in foreign economic contracts. This is not only because the application of different laws affects the interests of the parties, but also because it can stabilize contract relations and cause disputes to be settled speedily. Consequently, our country's Foreign Economic Contracts Law, in principle, provides in connection with the principle of the applicable law of the contract that "the parties to a contract may choose the law to be applied to the settlement of the disputes arising from the contract. In the absence of such a choice by the parties, the law of the country which has the closest connection with the contract applies." [Section 5] This rule of our country is reasonable and feasible. It corresponds to the usual international practice and upholds the sovereignty and interests of the state.

2. The Contract Employs the Applicable Law Selected by the Parties

At the present time, every country, in connection with the problem of the law that is applicable to the contract, permits the parties to choose the applicable law. Our country's Foreign Economic Contracts Law also permits the parties to select the law that will govern disputes arising under the contract. This is because this [rule] includes the following reasonable elements.

First, the selection of the law by the parties is advantageous for the clarity and stability of the contract. It enables the parties to predict the results of disputes. Moreover, in connection with a particular dispute, regardless of what country the lawsuit or arbitration procedure is brought in, in general, there will be the same results. Since foreign economic contracts are, in general, long-term, and the amounts involved are large and the contents are complicated, it is especially important for the parties to have the contract relations stable, foreseeable, and integrated.

Second, the contract is, of course, an agreement of the parties. This applicable law should also be considered and agreed to by the parties. Permitting them to select the applicable law causes them to be able, within a certain range, to select the law to govern the contract that is regarded by them as appropriate. So it is very important for encouraging the development of economic relations among different nations.

Finally, selection by the parties of the applicable law does not harm the sovereignty of the state, since the selection of the applicable law by the parties is a right granted by the state by law, and, moreover, the parties can only exercise this selection within the range allowed by law. The Foreign Economic Contracts Law provides that when the parties select a law it must be subject to the following limitations: (1) according to section 4, in forming a contract, it is necessary to abide by our country's law and it is not permitted to injure our country's public social rights. Consequently, if the foreign law selected by the parties violates our country's law or injures our country's social public interest, the said foreign law may not be used. Rather, our country's law must be used. (2) Moreover, according to section 5, in the case of any contract that affects our country's sovereignty, or that is related to an important interest of our country's society and economy, such as Sino-foreign equity joint ventures, Sino-foreign cooperative joint ventures, as well as Sino-foreign contracts for cooperative exploration and development of natural resources, the parties cannot select the law. They can use only our country's law.

3. The Applicable Law of the Contract Is the Law of the Country With the Closest Connection With It

Generally, the parties designate the applicable law for foreign economic contracts in the contract. But in practice, because each party wishes to select his own law, they are often unable to reach agreement on this point. Consequently, many contracts do not have a provision for the applicable law. When disputes arise under the contract, and must be settled by law, the arbitration tribunal or the court must decide on the applicable law and The Foreign Economic Contracts Law provides for this: "The law of the country with the closest connection with the contract will be used." [Section 5] When the parties have made no selection, the principle that the law of the country having the closest connection with the contract is to be used. At present, this is an extremely important principle for determining the applicable law of a contract. In the majority of the countries of both the Anglo-American system and the continental system this principle is used.

4. Several Limitations on the Selection by the Parties of the Applicable Law

The Foreign Economic Contracts Law provides that Sino-foreign joint venture contracts, Sino-foreign cooperative joint venture contracts, and Sino-foreign joint contracts for joint exploration and development of natural resources must apply our country's law. This principle upholds our country's sovereignty, [and] is in harmony with the basic principles of international private law. Consequently, it is completely reasonable.

(1) These contracts all involve foreign capital directly entering our country's production or commerce. They all have a basic and very close relation with our country. This is expressed in [the following ways]: (i) According to the relevant law of our country, the formation of these contracts must be approved by a government department. The content must also be registered in the relevant government department of our country. Consequently, these contracts are all found in our country. (ii) In order to perform a contract, both parties' management capital, management activity, and the results of their management activities are all inside our country. Thus, the contract has the closest connection with our country. (iii) Regardless of whether it is in accordance with the principle of determining the nationality of a juristic person by reference to the place of its formation, or the principle [of reference to] the principal [place of] business, enterprises and juristic persons which are formed according to these contracts are all enterprises or juristic

persons of our country. (iv) These contracts are all formed within the area permitted by our country's economic development plan. Whether or not the contract can be performed will naturally affect our country's economic development. According to what has been discussed above, these contracts have the closest connection with our country. Thus, they must apply our country's law.

(2) According to section 2 of the Charter of Economic Rights and Duties of Every Country promulgated by the 24th General Assembly of the United Nations in 1974, the host country has the sovereign right to control, supervise, and, in a necessary case, confiscate and nationalize foreign investment. Consequently, these contracts can only be adjusted by our law. Our country's law is the governing law of these contracts. When there are contractual disputes, in fact, there is no dispute over the law. There can be no question of choosing the applicable law.

(3) These contracts not only affect the economic activity of foreign investment in our country, they also frequently affect our country's natural resources or other immovable property. According to the principle of international private law, immovable property contracts must apply the law of the place where the immovable property is located. These contracts also use our country's law.